THE ROYAL SCOTS

H.R.H. PRINCESS MARY (VISCOUNTESS LASCELLES).
Colonel-in-Chief, The Royal Scots (The Royal Regiment).

Frontispiece.

THE ROYAL SCOTS
1914-1919

BY

Major JOHN EWING, M.C.

WITH A FOREWORD BY
THE RIGHT HON. LORD SALVESEN

EDINBURGH
Published for the Association of Lowland Scots by
OLIVER AND BOYD, TWEEDDALE COURT
LONDON: 33 PATERNOSTER ROW, E.C.
1925

To
H. R. H. PRINCESS MARY
(VISCOUNTESS LASCELLES)
COLONEL-IN-CHIEF, THE ROYAL SCOTS (THE ROYAL REGIMENT)
THIS BOOK, BY PERMISSION, IS DEDICATED

PREFACE

THIS story, compiled from battalion war diaries, supplemented by the narratives sent by individual officers and men, has been, as far as possible, treated chronologically. The difficulties experienced in the preparation of the narrative are those incidental to all regimental histories of the Great War, namely, the variation as regards both the quality and the quantity of the material contributed by the several units, and the fact that the tactical unit during the war was not the battalion, but the division; the war diaries, also, vary considerably in value, and the failure of some units to comply with *King's Regulations* as regards the recording of casualties has rendered it impossible to give a complete list of the losses sustained by the Regiment during the war.

Colonel A. C. H. MacLean, C.B.E., kindly collected the battalion photographs showing original groups of officers, and the list is complete except for the omission of the 12th Battalion, of which no photograph could be procured.

To all those—and they are too numerous to mention individually—who have helped me by suggestions, criticisms, the loan of documents and maps, and the correction of proofs, I gladly take this opportunity of expressing my sincere thanks. In particular, I owe a debt of gratitude to Mr C. Maitland Smith, C.A., Hon. Secretary of the Lowland Scots Association, and to Captain W. Clark, M.C., Secretary of The Royal Scots Club, for their unfailing and courteous assistance; to Lieut.-Colonel A. E. Everingham, D.S.O., for the great trouble which he has taken to supply me with material; to Lieut. Gordon Hislop, for the shrewd criticism and advice which he placed at my service in the correction of the final proofs; and to the late Lieut.-Colonel M. Henderson, D.S.O., whose sudden death, in 1923, was deeply mourned throughout the Regiment, for the loan of his valuable collection of diaries and maps. To my wife I am indebted for assistance at all stages in the preparation of these two volumes.

J. EWING.

December 1925.

CONTENTS

CHAPTER I

MOBILISATION OF THE ROYAL SCOTS

Outbreak of War. 1st and 2nd The Royal Scots. 3rd The Royal Scots. Territorial Battalions. Lord Kitchener's Appeal. The New Armies. Formation of First-line Territorial Units. Raising of 15th, 16th, and 17th The Royal Scots. 18th and 19th The Royal Scots and 1st and 2nd Garrison Battalions. . . **3**

CHAPTER II

MONS AND LE CATEAU

August to September 1914

2nd Battalion in France. Plans of the French and Germans. Task of the B.E.F. March of 2nd Royal Scots. The position at Mons. Action of 23rd August. Retreat of Royal Scots to Audencourt. Situation on evening of 25th August. Stand at Le Cateau, 26th August. Continuation of the Retreat. Route of the Royal Scots. End of Retreat, 5th September . . **12**

CHAPTER III

THE MARNE AND THE AISNE

September 1914

Counter-attack of the Allies. Advance of 2nd Royal Scots. Action at Orly, 8th September. The Marne crossed, 9th September. Situation on night of 9th September. The Aisne reached. Action of 13th September. The Struggle on the 14th. Trench Warfare , ... **40**

CONTENTS

CHAPTER IV

EVENTS IN THE WEST

October 1914 to March 1915

PAGE

"The Race to the Sea." Task of II. Corps. 2nd Royal Scots in French "Black Country." Progress of the Advance, 12th and 13th October. Events on the 15th. German Raid at Fauquissart. Trench Tours. Condition of Trenches in 1914. 2nd Royal Scots near Kemmel. Action of 14th December . . . 57

CHAPTER V

THE 8TH, 1ST, AND 9TH BATTALIONS IN FRANCE AND FLANDERS

November 1914 to March 1915

Situation at close of 1914. The Probability of Deadlock. Origin of Dardanelles Campaign. Arrival of 8th, 1st, and 9th Royal Scots in the West 77

CHAPTER VI

THE SECOND BATTLE OF YPRES

March to July 1915

8th Royal Scots at Neuve Chapelle. Opening of Second Battle of Ypres. Adventures of 9th Royal Scots near St Jean. The 9th at Sanctuary Wood. Readjustment of British Line, 3rd to 4th May. 1st Royal Scots in Action. 1st and 9th Royal Scots at Armentières and the Somme. 8th Royal Scots at Festubert. Death of Lieut.-Colonel Brook. A V.C. Feat . . . 88

CHAPTER VII

THE APPRENTICESHIP OF THE 11TH, 12TH, AND 13TH BATTALIONS

May to August 1915

The New Armies proceed to France. Benefits and Disadvantages of Trench Warfare 107

CONTENTS   xiii

CHAPTER VIII

GALLIPOLI

February to June 1915

PAGE

The Dardanelles Campaign. 5th Royal Scots proceed to the East. Description of Gallipoli. Plans of Sir Ian Hamilton. The Landing, 25th April. The Struggle for Achi Baba. Action of 28th April. Failure of the Attack. Trench Warfare sets in. Discomforts of Gallipoli. Events on night of 1st May. Action of 6th May. Attack of the 5th Royal Scots, 7th and 8th May. Situation after the Action. Attack of 4th June . . . 116

CHAPTER IX

GALLIPOLI

May to August 1915

The Fifty-second Division. Railway Disaster at Gretna. 4th Royal Scots in a collision at sea. Successful counter-attack by 5th Royal Scots on 19th June. Arrangements for 28th June. Action of 4th Royal Scots. Action of 7th Royal Scots. Effect of the success of 4th and 7th Royal Scots. Action of 5th Royal Scots. Share of 4th and 7th Royal Scots in operation of 12th July. The Suvla Bay project 143

CHAPTER X

THE 2ND BATTALION AT HOOGE

April to October 1915

Lull on the British front in the West. 2nd Royal Scots at Railway Wood and at Hooge. German successes in the East. Reasons for the Battle of Loos. Attack of 2nd Royal Scots, 25th September. German counter-attack. Attack of "C" Company, 30th September 171

CHAPTER XI

THE BATTLE OF LOOS

25th to 28th September 1915

Objectives for 25th September. Nature of the Terrain. Rôles of the Ninth and Fifteenth Divisions. Action of 11th and 12th Royal Scots, 25th September. The Attack on Haisnes. German counter-attack. Position at close of 25th. Events on 26th. Fosse 8 lost, 27th September. Fifteenth Division at Loos. Action of 13th Royal Scots, 25th September. Situation at nightfall. Attack on Hill 70, 26th September German counter-attacks. Gallantry of Private Dunsire. Evacuation of Hill 70. Results of the Battle 183

CHAPTER XII

THE EVACUATION OF GALLIPOLI

September 1915 to January 1916

Deadlock in Gallipoli. Trench life at Cape Helles. Attack on West Krithia Nullah by Royal Scots, 15th November. Turkish counter-attacks defeated. 5th Royal Scots at Suvla Bay. Winter conditions at Cape Helles. Decision to abandon Gallipoli. Difficulties with regard to Evacuation. Measures taken at Cape Helles. Incidents during the Evacuation, 8th January 1916 . 207

CHAPTER XIII

THE BALKANS AND EGYPT

September 1915 to June 1916

Importance of Mediterranean Littoral. Reasons for Intervention in the Balkans. 1st Royal Scots at Salonika. Defences of the Allies. The Position in Egypt. 6th Royal Scots at Cairo. Expedition against the Senussi. 6th Royal Scots at Matruh. Action of 13th December. Action of 23rd January. Advance on Sollum. 6th Royal Scots at Sollum. The Battalion embarks for France. Eastern Defences of Egypt. 5th Royal Scots embark for France. 4th and 7th Royal Scots in Egypt. Turkish Attack on Dueidar. Routes across the Sinai Desert. Defensive Arrangements of Sir Archibald Murray 227

CHAPTER XIV

EVENTS IN THE WEST

October 1915 to June 1916

German Offensive against Verdun. 2nd Royal Scots in the Salient. Tribute to Major A. E. Everingham. 11th and 12th Royal Scots in the Salient. "Plugstreet." 11th Royal Scots raided, 13th May. 13th Royal Scots in Loos Salient. Death of Lieut.-Colonel MacLear. The Battalion raided, 11th May. 8th Royal Scots at the Somme and Arras. 9th Royal Scots at Vaux and Arras. First Experiences of 15th, 16th, and 17th Royal Scots. The 15th and 16th at the Somme. 5th and 6th Royal Scots formed into one Battalion. Plans of Sir Douglas Haig for 1916. Significance of Battle of the Somme 247

CHAPTER XV

THE BATTLE OF THE SOMME—LA BOISSELLE, DELVILLE WOOD, AND LONGUEVAL

July 1916

Description of Terrain. The German defences between the Somme and the Ancre. Three phases of the Battle. Sector of Thirty-fourth Division. Objectives of 15th and 16th Royal Scots. Attack of 15th and 16th Royal Scots. Importance of La Boisselle. Wood Alley. Situation at nightfall, 1st July. Sir George McCrae at Wood Alley, 2nd July. Capture of Scots Redoubt. Events on 3rd July. Achievements of Thirty-fourth Division. Relief of 15th and 16th Royal Scots. 11th and 12th Royal Scots at Montauban. The 12th at Bernafay Wood, 3rd July. 2nd Royal Scots. Longueval. Arrangements for Attack on 14th July. The Assembly. Action of 11th Royal Scots. Attack on Longueval by 12th Royal Scots. 2nd Royal Scots in Action, 14th July. Gains of the Battle. Continuation of Attack on Longueval, 15th July. 11th Royal Scots attack Longueval, 16th July. Heroism of 2nd Lieut. Turner and Sergeant Allwright. Longueval, 17th July. Relief of 11th and 12th Royal Scots. German counter-attack. 2nd Royal Scots . . . 265

CHAPTER XVI

BATTLE OF THE SOMME—GUILLEMONT, HIGH WOOD, MARTINPUICH, AND THE BUTTE DE WARLENCOURT

July to October 1916

Third Division at Guillemont. Assaults of 2nd Royal Scots, 22nd and 23rd July. Battalion relieved. 17th Royal Scots at the Somme. Fifty-first Division at the Somme. Happy Valley and High Wood. Attack of 9th Royal Scots, 23rd July. Adventures of Major Moncrieff. Relief of Fifty-first Division. 15th and 16th Royal Scots near High Wood. Attacks on Intermediate Trench, August. 17th Royal Scots. Fifteenth Division arrives at the Somme. Situation at beginning of September. Arrangements for attack on 15th September. Effect of wet weather. 11th and 12th Royal Scots at Vimy Ridge. The Butte de Warlencourt. A difficult relief. Incidents at Snag Trench 299

CHAPTER XVII

THE BATTLE OF THE ANCRE—BEAUMONT HAMEL AND SERRE

October 1916 *to February* 1917

13th Royal Scots near Martinpuich. 17th, 11th, and 12th Royal Scots at Arras. 8th and 9th Royal Scots near Armentières. 15th and 16th Royal Scots at Bois Grenier. 2nd Royal Scots in the Hulluch Sector. 5/6th Royal Scots. Beaumont Hamel and Serre. Situation at the Ancre and preparations for Attack. Raids by 9th and 2nd Royal Scots. Work of 8th Royal Scots. Attack on Beaumont Hamel, 13th November. Attack of 2nd Royal Scots at Serre, 13th November. 5/6th Royal Scots near Beaumont Hamel. 8th and 9th Royal Scots at Courcelette. Successful enterprise by 2nd Royal Scots at Serre, 5th January 325

CHAPTER XVIII

EVENTS IN THE EAST

June to December 1916

Events in the Balkans, 1916. 1st Royal Scots at the Struma. Operations against Bala and Zir, 30th September. Attack on Homondos, October. British preparations in Egypt. The Position at Romani. Turkish Attack on Romani. Part played by the 7th Royal Scots, 4th August. Defeat of the Turks. March across Sinai begins, 11th October. El Arish reached, December 343

CHAPTER XIX

THE SECOND BATTLE OF GAZA

December 1916 *to April* 1917

Gaza. Entry into Palestine. Preparations of 156th Brigade for Attack on Gaza. Dispositions of 4th and 7th Royal Scots. The Attack, 19th April. Failure of the Attack . . . 364

CONTENTS

CHAPTER XX

THE GERMAN RETREAT AND PREPARATIONS FOR THE BATTLE OF ARRAS

February to April 1917

Situation at beginning of 1917. Plans of Sir Douglas Haig. German Retreat to Hindenburg Line. Advance of 5/6th Royal Scots. Advance of 17th Royal Scots. Situation at Arras. Royal Scots Battalions at Arras. Raid by 16th Royal Scots, 7th April. Daylight raid by 13th Royal Scots, 5th April. Reconnaissance by 11th Royal Scots, 21st March. Gallantry of 2nd Lieut. Storey. The struggle for air supremacy. Arras. Arrangements for the Battle. Objectives 374

CHAPTER XXI

THE BATTLE OF ARRAS

9th to 13th April 1917

Action of 12th and 11th Royal Scots. Action of 16th and 15th Royal Scots. Action of 9th Royal Scots. Blangy captured by 13th Royal Scots. Action of 2nd Royal Scots. Gains of the 9th April. The struggle south of the Scarpe, 10th to 13th April. Events north of the Scarpe. Abortive attack by 11th and 12th Royal Scots, 12th April. Work of 15th, 16th, 9th, and 8th Royal Scots 389

CHAPTER XXII

THE BATTLE OF ARRAS

Actions of the 23rd April, 28th April, 3rd May, and 5th June 1917

Reasons for continuation of Arras Offensive. 9th Royal Scots near Mount Pleasant Wood. 13th and 9th Royal Scots in action of 23rd April. Result of attack on 23rd April. Work of 8th Royal Scots. 15th and 16th Royal Scots at Rœux and Chemical Works, 28th April. Attack of 2nd and 12th Royal Scots, 3rd May. Attack of 11th and 12th Royal Scots, 5th June . . 413

CHAPTER XXIII

THE EVE OF THE PASSCHENDAELE CAMPAIGN

May to July 1917

Divisions at Rest. Location of Royal Scots Battalions. Pelmanism. Development of offensive methods in the Air. Object of Passchendaele Campaign. How the situation on the Western Front was affected by events in other theatres. Capture of Messines Ridge, June 1917. The German plan of defence in Flanders. Difficulties of the British. Work of 8th Royal Scots   435

CHAPTER XXIV

PASSCHENDAELE

Actions of 31*st July and* 22*nd August* 1917

British Offensive begins, 31st July. 13th Royal Scots at Frezenberg. German counter-attack. 13th Royal Scots at Beck House and Square Farm, 1st August. 9th Royal Scots near the Steenbeek. Work of 8th Royal Scots. Campaign interrupted by rain. Fruitless attack by 13th Royal Scots, 22nd August   447

CHAPTER XXV

THE 15TH AND 16TH ROYAL SCOTS AT HARGICOURT

July to September 1917

Thirty-fourth Division at Hargicourt. Action of 26th August. Attack of 15th and 16th Royal Scots   460

CHAPTER XXVI

PASSCHENDAELE

September and October 1917

Action of 20th September. 11th and 12th Royal Scots at Frezenberg. Gallantry of Captain Reynolds. 9th Royal Scots at the Stroombeek. Counter-attack against Fifty-first Division. Attack of 2nd Royal Scots, 26th September. Action of 11th and 12th Royal Scots, 12th October. Action of 15th and 16th Royal Scots, 22nd October. Close of the Passchendaele Offensive   470

CHAPTER XXVII

CAMBRAI

November to December 1917

British preparations for attack at Cambrai. Work of 8th Royal Scots. The German defences. Task of Fifty-first Division. Result of the attack, 20th and 21st November. German counter-attack, 22nd November. Operations of 23rd November. German counter-thrust near Gouzeaucourt and Gonnelieu. 9th Royal Scots at Mœuvres 491

CHAPTER XXVIII

THE STRUMA VALLEY, 1917

Events in the East. The 1st Royal Scots at the Struma. Raid on Homondos by 1st Royal Scots, 22nd July. Operation against Homondos, October. Training and Sport . . . 502

CHAPTER XXIX

THE FALL OF GAZA

November 1917

Preparations for Attack on Gaza. Patrol adventures. The Turkish positions. The Terrain. Sir Edmund Allenby's plan. Attack on Umbrella Hill. 4th Royal Scots at El Arish Redoubt. Turks evacuate Gaza. Beginning of the pursuit, 8th November 1917 508

CHAPTER XXX

THE 4TH AND 7TH ROYAL SCOTS IN PALESTINE

November 1917 *to April* 1918

Burkah and Brown Hill. Advance into the Judean Mountains. Nebi Samwil. Turkish counter-attack, 27th November. Fifty-second Division at the Auja. Preparations for Attack. The crossing of the Auja, 20th/21st December. Advance continued, 22nd December. Fifty-second Division transferred to France, April 1918 520

CONTENTS

CHAPTER XXXI

EVE OF THE GREAT GERMAN OFFENSIVE

September 1917 *to March* 1918

Situation on the Western Front. British Brigades reduced to three Battalions. Defensive arrangements of Sir Douglas Haig, 5/6th Battalion at Nieuport and Houthulst Forest. Movements of 2nd, 8th, 9th, 11th, 12th, 13th, 15th, 16th, and 17th Battalions. German plan of attack 545

CHAPTER XXXII

THE GREAT GERMAN OFFENSIVE (PART I.)

March 1918

Opening of great German Offensive, 21st March. Retreat of Fifth and Third Armies. Failure of Germans to achieve their objective. 9th Battalion near St Quentin. Its movements from 21st March to 3rd April. 11th and 12th Battalions near Gouzeaucourt. Their movements from the 21st to the 27th March. Arrival of 17th Battalion in the Battle Area. Its movements from 24th to the 29th March 559

CHAPTER XXXIII

THE GREAT GERMAN OFFENSIVE (PART II.)

March 1918

Position of Fifty-first Division. Action of 8th Battalion, 21st to 26th March. Death of Lieut.-Colonel Gemmill, 25th March. Position of Thirty-fourth Division. Action of 15th and 16th Battalions, 21st to 23rd March. Third and Fifteenth Divisions near Arras. Readjustment of Line, 22nd/23rd March. Great German attack, 28th March. Action of 2nd and 13th Battalions. 5/6th Battalion at Ayette 582

CHAPTER XXXIV

THE GERMAN OFFENSIVE ON THE LYS

April 1918

German Break-through at Lys, 9th April. Attack on Givenchy repulsed. German advance on Merville and Béthune. Action of the 8th, 2nd, and 9th Battalions. German advance on

CONTENTS

Bailleul and Hazebrouck. Action of 15th and 16th Battalions. Armentières abandoned, 10th April. Loss of Bailleul, 15th April. 11th and 12th Battalions near Hollebeke; German Attack on Kemmel, 25th April. Action of 11th and 12th Battalions. Hostile advance checked 604

CHAPTER XXXV

THE TURN OF THE TIDE

May to August 1918

Situation at end of April. 15th and 16th Royal Scots disbanded. German Attack on Chemin des Dames. Location of Royal Scots Battalions. Operations by 2nd Royal Scots near Locon. German gas attack near Locon, 20th May. 4th and 7th Royal Scots in France. Beginning of Allied counter-attack, July 1918. 8th Royal Scots at the Bois de Coutron. 9th and 13th Royal Scots near Buzancy. Action of 1st August 635

CHAPTER XXXVI

THE ADVANCE TO VICTORY

August and September 1918

Opening of British Attack, 8th August. Action of 5/6th Royal Scots. 11th and 12th Royal Scots at Meteren. Attack of 2nd Royal Scots, 21st August. General British Attack, 23rd August. Action of 5/6th Royal Scots. Action of 2nd Royal Scots. Gallantry of Private H. McIver. 2nd Royal Scots at Noreuil. Action of 4th and 7th Royal Scots. Storming of Drocourt-Quéant Switch. Work of 8th Royal Scots. Result of Operations from 23rd August to 2nd September. Development of the Offensive. Advance of 5/6th Royal Scots. 2nd Royal Scots at the Canal du Nord. 4th and 7th Royal Scots at Mœuvres. Task of 9th and 13th Royal Scots. Situation near end of September. Arrangements for Renewal of Offensive . . 656

CHAPTER XXXVII

THE COLLAPSE OF BULGARIA

1st Battalion The Royal Scots, 1918

Position in the Balkans. 1st Royal Scots transferred to the Vardar. Plan of General Franchet d'Esperey. Task of 1st Royal Scots. Collapse of Bulgaria. Advance of 1st Royal Scots. Capitulation of Turkey 691

CHAPTER XXXVIII

THE FINAL BLOW

September to November 1918

Attack of the British Fourth, Third, and First Armies, 27th and 29th September. 5/6th Royal Scots at Sequehart, 1st to 5th October. Action of 2nd Royal Scots, 27th September. Further operations of 2nd Battalion. Attack of 4th Royal Scots, 27th September. The Flanders offensive. Action of 17th Battalion, 28th to 30th September. Action of 11th and 12th Battalions, 28th September to 1st October. Continued success of Allied offensive. Operations of 17th Battalion, 14th to 31st October. Operations of 11th and 12th Battalions, 14th to 24th October. Advance of 9th and 13th Battalions. Battle of the Sambre, 1st to 11th November. Work of the 8th Royal Scots. 2nd Royal Scots at Vertain, 23rd October. 5/6th Royal Scots at the Battle of the Sambre. Last operations of the 4th and 7th Royal Scots . 699

CHAPTER XXXIX

THE 2/10TH ROYAL SCOTS IN NORTHERN RUSSIA

August 1918 *to May* 1919

Reasons for expedition to Northern Russia. History of 2/10th Royal Scots. Importance of the Dwina. Operations between the Dwina and the Vaga. Adventures of Major Skeil's Company. Limit of Royal Scots' advance, September. Operations from October 1918 to May 1919. Winter conditions. Return of 2/10th Royal Scots 738

CHAPTER XL

THE ROYAL SCOTS MEMORIAL

Movements of battalions after the Armistice. Demobilisation. Battle Honours. Reorganisation of Territorial Battalions. The Royal Regiment. Activities of The Royal Scots Association. Suggestion of a Club as the Regimental Memorial. Dedication of the Memorial and formal opening of the Club, 12th August 1922, by H.R.H. Princess Mary 759

APPENDICES

	PAGE
I.—Divisional and Battalion Histories of the Great War concerning The Royal Scots	771
II.—A Brief Account of the Home-Service Units	772
III.—19th Battalion The Royal Scots, and 1st Garrison Battalion The Royal Scots	782
IV.—Victoria Cross Awards	786
V.—The Royal Scots Association	789
INDEX	793

LIST OF ILLUSTRATIONS

FULL PAGE

H.R.H. Princess Mary (Viscountess Lascelles)	*Frontispiece*
	FACE PAGE
Lieut.-General Sir E. A. Altham, K.C.B., K.C.I.E., C.M.G.	1
Private H. H. Robson, V.C.	74
Lieut.-Colonel A. Brook, V.D.	102
Lance-Corporal W. Angus, V.C., and Lieutenant J. Martin, M.C.	104
W Beach, Cape Helles	122
Lieut.-Colonel S. R. Dunn	158
Officers of the 8th Royal Scots at Bouzincourt	172
Lieut.-Colonel R. C. Dundas	192
Private R. Dunsire, V.C.	202
Lieut.-Colonel H. MacLear, D.S.O.	252
Lieut.-Colonel H. L. Budge	284
Breastworks at Armentières	328
Cologne Ridge	462
Captain H. Reynolds, V.C., M.C.	474
Nebi Samwil	528
Judean Hills	528
Lieut.-Colonel W. Gemmill, D.S.O.	588
Brig.-General A. F. Lumsden, D.S.O.	640
Lieut.-Colonel J. A. Turner, D.S.O., M.C.	652
Lieut.-Colonel A. G. Scougal, M.C.	712
Memorial Tablet	766
Lieutenant D. S. M'Gregor, V.C.	788
Officers of 1st Battalion The Royal Scots	*End of Vol. II.*
Officers of 2nd Battalion The Royal Scots	,, ,,
Officers of 1/4th Battalion The Royal Scots	,, ,,
Officers of 5th Battalion The Royal Scots	,, ,,
Officers of 6th Battalion The Royal Scots	,, ,,
Officers of 1/7th Battalion The Royal Scots (April 1915)	,, ,,

xxvi LIST OF ILLUSTRATIONS

Officers of 8th Battalion The Royal Scots . . *End of Vol. II.*
Officers of 1/9th Battalion The Royal Scots (July 1914) „ „
Officers of 11th Battalion The Royal Scots . . „ „
Officers of 13th Battalion The Royal Scots . . „ „
Officers of 15th Battalion The Royal Scots . . „ „
Officers of 16th Battalion The Royal Scots . . „ „
Officers of 17th Battalion The Royal Scots (February 1916) „ „

TEXT MAPS.

MAP		PAGE
I.	General Map of Western Front	*face* 4
II.	Route of the 2nd Royal Scots (20th August-13th October 1914)	„ 16
III.	Fauquissart (1914), Neuve Chapelle, and Festubert (1915)	63
IV.	The Salient, 1914 and 1915	79
V.	Gallipoli	117
VI.	Cape Helles, showing British Trench System	145
VII.	Action of the 28th June 1915	153
VIII.	Action of the 12th July 1915	167
IX.	The Battle of Loos, 25th to 28th September 1915	185
X.	Action of the 15th November 1915	214
XI.	The Senussi Campaign, 1915-1916	237
XII.	The Battle of the Somme, 1916	267
XIII.	The Battle of the Ancre, 1916	335
XIV.	The Struma Valley	345
XV.	The Sinai Desert	355
XVI.	Gaza	365
XVII.	The Battle of Arras, 1917	391
XVIII.	Passchendaele, 1917, and the Offensive in Flanders, 1918	449
XIX.	Hargicourt, August 1917	461
XX.	Battle of Cambrai, 1917	493
XXI.	Palestine	521
XXII.	German Offensive against the Fifth Army, March 1918, and Advance of Fourth Army, August-October 1918	561
XXIII.	German Offensive against the Third Army (March), and Advance of Third and First Armies, August-November 1918	583
XXIV.	The German Offensive at the Lys, April 1918	605

LIST OF ILLUSTRATIONS

MAP		PAGE
XXV.	Coutron Wood, July 1918	649
XXVI.	Buzancy, August 1918	653
XXVII.	The Vardar Valley	693
XXVIII.	The Final Advance (9th, 13th, 4th, and 7th Battalions), September-November 1918	701
XXIX.	Battle of the Sambre, 4th November 1918	735
XXX.	The Dwina and Vaga	743
XXXI.	Archangel-Vologda Railway	753

FOLDING MAPS.

At End of Vol. I.

The Salient, 1914 and 1915.
Gallipoli.
Cape Helles, showing Trench Systems.
The Battle of the Somme, 1916.
The Sinai Desert.

At End of Vol. II.

Passchendaele, 1917, and the Offensive in Flanders, 1918.
Palestine.
German Offensive against the Fifth Army, March 1918, and Advance of Fourth Army, August-October 1918.
German Offensive against the Third Army (March 1918), and Advance of Third and First Armies, August-November 1918.
The German Offensive at the Lys, April 1918.
The Final Advance (9th, 13th, 4th, and 7th Battalions), September-November 1918.

FOREWORD

By THE RIGHT HON. LORD SALVESEN

THE part played by The Royal Scots Regiment (The Royal Regiment and the First Regiment of the Line) as told by Major Ewing in this book is one that must thrill the heart of every Scotsman, and of many Englishmen whom the exigencies of recruiting absorbed into its ranks. From the first moment that the war commenced until its victorious close some unit of the Regiment was engaged in the great struggle for our existence as a free, self-governing State. Of its fifteen front-line battalions (with Labour and Garrison Battalions bringing the number up to seventeen) only two belonged to the Regular Army—all the rest were originally formed of volunteers, some who had already joined the Territorial Army, and the remainder recruited from erstwhile civilian elements who had never handled a military rifle. In all the fighting on the vastly extended front in Europe, Asia, and Africa the Regiment took its full share, and not one of its units failed to cover itself with glory. On the devastated plains of Flanders and Northern France there are thousands of graves which testify to the stupendous losses which the Regiment sustained in stemming the tide of German invasion, and eventually in driving the enemy from his entrenchments behind the Hindenburg Line in the great push that commenced in 1918. Against the fortified rocks of Gallipoli wave upon wave of Royal Scots beat in vain and died. In Egypt and Palestine the Regiment gave splendid service in breaking the power of the Turks and clearing the Holy Land of its oppressors. In Macedonia and in the White Sea campaigns Royal Scots nobly helped to maintain the prestige of the British Army, with its long record of courage, high endurance, and chivalry. Few regiments, if indeed any, fought on so many and so diverse fronts as the First Regiment of the Line, and none earned more imperishable fame.

During the period of the war more than 100,000 officers and men passed through the ranks of the Regiment: of these, 11,162 were killed and over 40,000 wounded. At its conclusion all the battalions that had been temporarily enlisted were disbanded, and the Regiment now numbers only two Territorial Battalions, or less than one-third before the declaration of war.

The publication of a history of seventeen battalions was a task so large and costly as to make it highly improbable that it would be undertaken on commercial lines. Some of the units that remain might, no doubt, have seen to it that the part that their particular battalion played should not be forgotten—four Territorial Battalions have already done so more or less adequately —but the disbanded units whose surviving constituents have been scattered all over the Empire possess no organisation which could attempt a similar undertaking. The Association of Lowland Scots (of which I have the honour to be Chairman), which was founded in 1917 to promote the interests of the Lowland Regiments, accordingly resolved to shoulder the burden and to discharge what they conceived to be a pious duty. They deemed it right that the gallant deeds of the whole Regiment should be gathered into one complete history, which would form a memorial, not merely to the heroic dead, but to the equally heroic survivors. The Volunteer Battalions have at least as convincing a claim on the gratitude of their country as the Regulars, and yet it was almost certain that their share in saving the Empire from unthinkable calamity would pass into oblivion. No doubt in the archives of the War Office there are preserved the diaries of each battalion, but these are but the dry bones of history without flesh to clothe them or spirit to animate them. This history is a living record. Of other memorials in stone or bronze there are already several, but these again are but records of a single fact with at most lists of names of those who perished. The best Memorial of a regiment is in our view a well-told and reliable history of its achievements and of the spirit which prompted them and made them possible. Such a Memorial the Association thinks Major Ewing, himself a Royal Scot, has successfully produced in the two volumes in which this history is contained. Future generations of Scotsmen will glean little from the monuments that are consecrated to the dead, but so long as libraries exist this history will be accessible to every Scot who yearns to know how his ancestors demeaned themselves in the fiercest struggle that the world has ever seen.

EDW. T. SALVESEN,
Chairman, Association of Lowland Scots.

NOTE.

The sketches included in this History were drawn by Royal Scots during the war.

The official designation of a battalion, for example, 2nd Battalion The Royal Scots, is given only in first references to units; thereafter the definite article has been omitted in order to avoid an appearance of clumsiness.

Except when otherwise stated, all battles are described from right to left.

For the convenience of readers the more important maps are reproduced on a larger scale at the end of each volume.

Lieut.-General Sir E. A. ALTHAM, K.C.B., K.C.I.E., C.M.G.
Colonel, The Royal Scots (The Royal Regiment).

THE ROYAL SCOTS

THE ROYAL SCOTS

CHAPTER I

MOBILISATION OF THE ROYAL SCOTS

Outbreak of War. 1st and 2nd The Royal Scots. 3rd The Royal Scots. Territorial Battalions. Lord Kitchener's Appeal. The New Armies. Formation of First-line Territorial Units. Raising of 15th, 16th, and 17th The Royal Scots. 18th and 19th The Royal Scots and 1st and 2nd Garrison Battalions.

FROM the beginning of the twentieth century crisis after crisis in international affairs kept Europe rippling with excitement. The passion for war within Europe itself, it was thought, might be satisfied by the struggle in the Balkans in which first Turkey, then Bulgaria was the victim, but the murder of the Archduke Francis Ferdinand at Serajevo on the 28th June 1914 showed how fragile were the foundations of this hope. Germany, by her conduct and temper, suggested that she was bent on inflaming rather than extinguishing the national and racial passions aroused by the crime and that her aim was similar to that of Mark Antony:

> "Now let it work—mischief, thou art afoot,
> Take thou what course thou wilt!"

In face of the European crisis internal dissensions within Britain ceased as if by magic, and the nation showed an extraordinary degree of unanimity as to its proper course of action. It was instinctively felt that both existence and honour were at stake, and that the country would be justly execrated by all decent-minded people if, through timidity or through the base design of profiting from the misfortunes of others, it refused to plunge into the fateful struggle. The decision to assist France, however, was made in no lighthearted mood, for deep in the national mind was the conviction that war with Germany would prove the most searching test to which the British Empire had ever been subjected.

In some respects Britain was well prepared for war. The machinery of imperial co-operation had been devised several years before 1914, and when the crisis came, it was swung into action with such smoothness that the great majority of people failed to appreciate the immense amount of labour and planning that had been entailed. The British naval and military services, as regards quality of personnel, training, and experience were unsurpassed in the world. The Army, though small, was a magnificent and highly-trained fighting force and was available for immediate service overseas, since the defence of Britain itself could be undertaken by the Territorial battalions.

Of The Royal Scots there were two regular battalions. The 1st, commanded by Lieut.-Colonel D. A. Callender, C.M.G., being in India at the outbreak of hostilities, could not be included in the B.E.F. which was earmarked for service on the Continent. The 2nd Battalion, under Lieut.-Colonel H. McMicking, D.S.O., was engaged in firing field practices at Willsworthy Camp when it received instructions on the 29th July 1914 to return to its station at Plymouth. It had followed with the keenest interest the course of events in Europe since the Serajevo murder and it interpreted this sudden move as the herald of war. Any doubts that the crisis would blow over were set at rest when the order to mobilise arrived on the 4th August, and measures were

MAP I

GENERAL MAP OF WESTERN FRONT

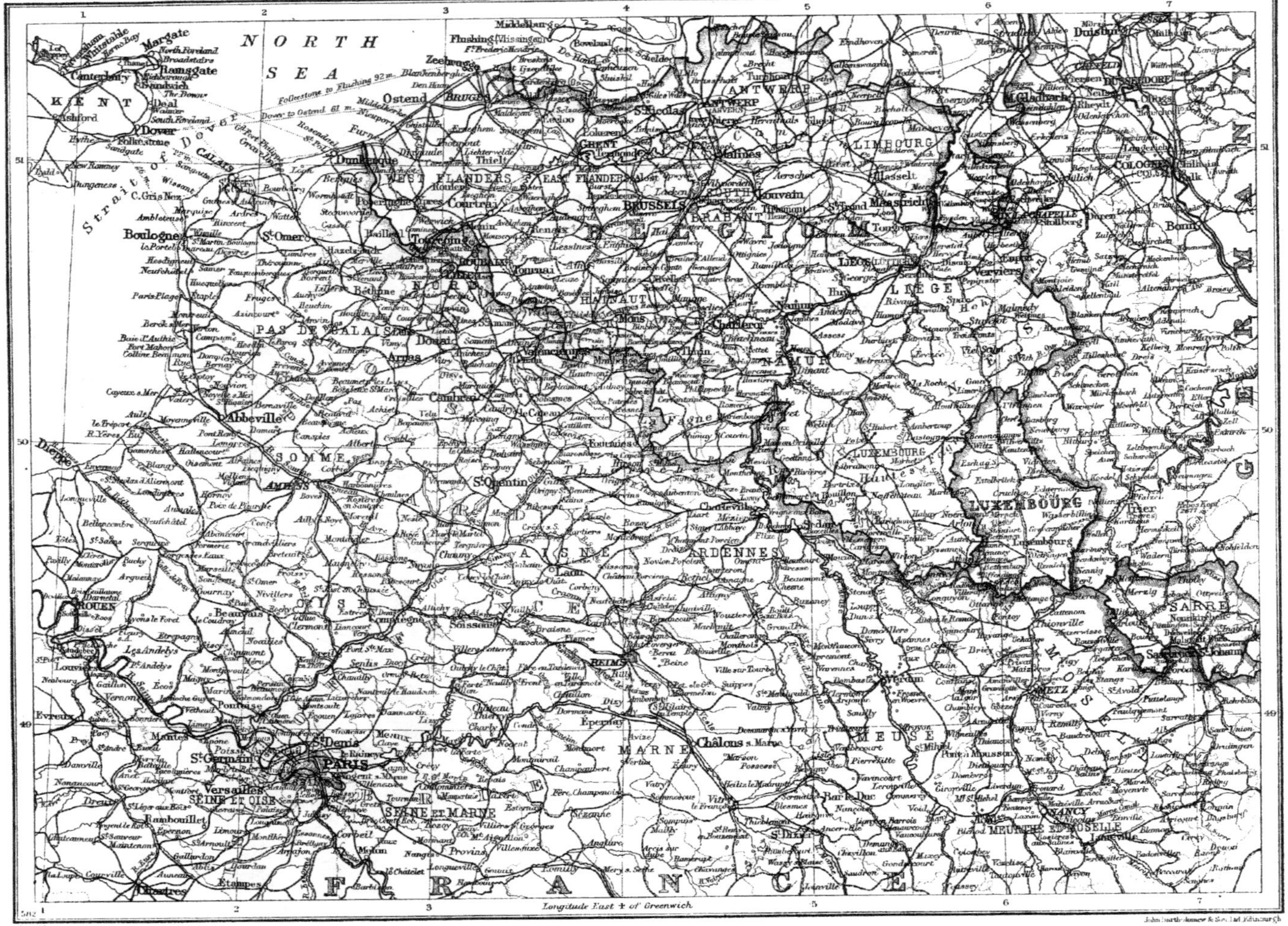

Scale 1:2,000,000

English Miles 0 10 20 30 40 50 60

Kilometres 0 10 20 30 40 50 60 70 80 90 100

John Bartholomew & Son, Ltd. Edinburgh

at once taken to bring the battalion up to its war establishment.

In 1914 the war establishment of an infantry battalion, as laid down in the manual of *Infantry Training*, 1914, consisted of 30 officers and 972 other ranks organised on the basis of Battalion H.Q., a machine-gun section,[1] and four companies, each composed of four platoons, these in turn consisting of four sections.

In peace time a battalion was normally about half this strength, so that much had to be done after the order for mobilisation was issued. The duty of filling up the gaps caused by casualties and disease in the line battalions was performed by Militia (known after 1907 as Special Reserve) units, and the 3rd (Reserve) Battalion[2] The Royal Scots, commanded by Lieut.-Colonel The Earl of Ellesmere, M.V.O., acted as the feeder to the 1st and the 2nd Battalions. Mobilisation entailed a tremendous amount of work for the staffs of the reserve units and the recruiting depots of all regiments, but the organisation of the Army splendidly vindicated itself by the efficiency and rapidity with which it satisfied every demand created by the emergency.

War was the business, always hazardous and frequently unpleasant, for which the professional soldier had been trained, and he consequently looked upon the outbreak of hostilities from a different point of view than that of the civilian; to the latter war was a catastrophe, to the former it was the supreme test to the preparation for which he had devoted his career. Thus during the bustling days that followed the orders for mobilisation, when batches of reservists were

[1] With two Vickers guns.
[2] See Appendix II. A.

thronging to Plymouth, the sensations of the 2nd Royal Scots were akin to those of a trained mountaineer about to essay the ascent of a difficult peak.

For the purpose of home defence there were no fewer than seven Territorial battalions of The Royal Scots, of which the 4th and 5th (Queen's Edinburgh Rifles), the 6th and the 9th had their H.Q. in Edinburgh, the 7th in Leith, the 8th in Haddington, and the 10th, a cyclist battalion, in Linlithgow. All these units had completed their annual training at summer camps about the end of July, and officers and men being, therefore, fit and keen when war was declared, the order to mobilise was responded to with immense enthusiasm. The stations to be occupied by the several units had all been arranged and to these they now proceeded.

No one knew precisely what would be the effect of a general European war, but most people took it for granted that the fighting on land would be carried out by professional soldiers, assisted perhaps by volunteers, as had been the case in the South African War, and that the worst that could happen to a civilian would be that he would probably be called upon to dig more deeply into his pockets to meet the expenses of the contest. Fortunately there was a national leader to show what required to be done. Lord Kitchener, brushing aside the airy optimism that predicted a short sharp struggle, solemnly warned the nation that it was on the threshold of a long and doubtful conflict and that the numbers of the fighting forces must be augmented beyond precedent without delay.

His call received an immediate and heartening answer. The heady wine of youth scorns sober caution and young men in thousands flocked to the Colours. To them the war was mainly an adventure, and they were inspired by the age-long motives that have served to lure men into the uncharted seas of peril :

> " Que toute joies et toute honnours
> Viennent et d'armes et d'amours."

There were many, too, of more mature age who, stirred by a profound sense of duty, offered themselves for service. Their sacrifice was great; for they were detaching themselves from the anchorage of what had promised to be a settled and contented life, to drift deliberately into unknown and turbulent waters. To such the war was an ordeal rather than an adventure. The call of duty smothered every personal and selfish consideration and the flower of British manhood was soon decked in the trappings of war.

Edinburgh, as the capital of Scotland, took a keen interest in every Scottish Regiment, but it was peculiarly and intimately concerned with that Regiment so honourably associated with Royal service, The Royal Scots. With one or other of its battalions the largest proportion of the citizens of Edinburgh and Midlothian who fought in the Great War spent their service.

Four additional units, the 11th, 12th, 13th, and 14th Battalions, were formed within a few weeks, and at their origin were commanded respectively by Lieut.-Colonels H. B. Dyson, D.S.O., G. G. Loch, H. E. P. Nash, and A. H. Battye. Britain was fortunate to possess a goodly sprinkling of men who had at one time in their careers held commissions in the Army, and N.C.Os., whose service with the Colours had expired, volunteered in hundreds for military duty. These in tutoring the uninitiated in the stratagems of war rendered invaluable assistance. The new units were concentrated in the south of England for purposes of training, the 11th and 12th Battalions being included in the 27th Brigade of the Ninth (Scottish) Division, and the 13th in the 45th Brigade of the Fifteenth (Scottish) Division. The 14th Battalion[1] was raised as a service unit, but the wastage caused by the war was so vast that it was transformed into a reserve battalion.

The institution of the New Armies created much stir among Territorial troops, many of whom were not content with the passive rôle assigned to them under the regulations of 1908. Application was therefore made to the War Office for permission to raise first-line or active service units, and the ready granting of this request had a most beneficial effect upon Territorial recruiting. Many of the former pupils of George Watson's College, including several of the most celebrated Scottish Rugby players, joined the 9th Royal Scots, the only kilted unit of the Regiment, and Herioters similarly enlisted in the 5th.

In spite of the keenness of the populace, some time elapsed before all the Territorial battalions of The Royal Scots were able to form two lines. The 5th and the 9th were among the first to be completed. In 1914 all Territorial units were on an eight-company basis, and the first-line of the 4th Royal Scots was only brought up to strength by a reinforcement of two companies from the 6th. Similarly, the 7th Royal Scots were reinforced by two companies (afterwards "B" Company) of the 8th Highland Light Infantry, and the 8th Royal Scots were completed by the addition of one company from the 6th Royal Scots and one company from the 8th Highland Light Infantry. At the beginning of 1915 all battalions were reorganised on a four-company basis.

Before the expiration of 1914 all the Territorial

[1] See Appendix II. c.

battalions had formed first-lines under the following C.Os. :—

4th Royal Scots	(Q.E.R.)		.	Lieut.-Colonel	S. R. Dunn.	
5th	,,	(Q.E.R.)	.	,,	J. T. R. Wilson.	
6th	,,	.	.	.	,,	T. E. Turnbull, VD.
7th	,,	.	.	.	,,	W. C. Peebles, TD.
8th	,,	.	.	.	,,	A. Brook.
9th	,,	.	.	.	,,	A. S. Blair.
10th	,,	.	.	.	,,	A. P. Simpson.

As the war went on, third-line units were formed, but since, with one exception, the first-line were the only units that were on active service, these are referred to in the narrative as 4th instead of 1/4th Royal Scots, and so on. The one exception was in the case of the 10th Royal Scots, of which only the second-line went overseas. It is to be remembered that in the later stages of the war the vast majority of the officers and men in the second and third-line units[1] consisted of soldiers who were recovering from the effects of wounds received while on service with the first-line units. The service rendered to the country by the training and draft-producing Territorial battalions was of incalculable value; without any previous experience and usually with very inadequate staffs they were required to instruct, fit out and dispatch for duty overseas, drafts adequate and sufficient in all details of training and equipment.

In October 1914 two additional New Army battalions of The Royal Scots, both closely connected with Edinburgh, were raised. The 15th The Royal Scots, with which the name of Colonel Sir Robert Cranston will ever be honourably associated, consisted of citizens of the capital with a strong leaven of Scots from Manchester; they were known as "Cranston's Battalion." The eloquent zeal and abounding energy of Sir George McCrae led to the establishment of the 16th The Royal

[1] See Appendix II. B.

Scots. After a recruiting campaign of only thirteen days a force of 1350 men was formed; it was appropriately called "McCrae's Battalion," since its first commander was the one whose enterprise had brought it into being. It comprised men from all classes, students from the training colleges and the universities, artisans, clerks, and a phalanx of footballers; in this connection the patriotic lead given by the Heart of Midlothian Football Club will always be remembered with gratitude and satisfaction by the people of Edinburgh.

Before the close of the year still another Royal Scots battalion, the 17th, consisting of Bantams, was instituted under the command of Lieut.-Colonel R. D. Cheales. It was named after Lord Rosebery, a tribute to the important part taken by that nobleman as a recruiting officer.

The wastage caused by modern war proved to be so enormous that the system of voluntary enlistment soon became totally inadequate to meet the needs of the fighting services. The recruits who volunteered during the early months of 1915 barely sufficed to balance the normal drain of casualties. Conscription was temporarily staved off by Lord Derby's scheme, which came into operation in October 1915, but even this failed to secure the number required, and in May 1916 a general system of conscription was introduced.

A few more Royal Scots battalions were formed in the course of the war, the 18th, 19th and the 1st and 2nd Garrison Battalions. The 18th[1] consisted of the surplus troops left behind by the 15th, 16th, and 17th, when these proceeded to France, and served first as a local reserve for these units and later as a general reserve. The 19th[2] was a Labour Battalion, composed of men either

---

[1] See Appendix II. c.
[2] See Appendix III.

unfit or incapacitated by wounds or illness for active service. The 1st Garrison Battalion,[1] also consisting of unfit men, was sent to garrison Mudros, thus performing a duty that might otherwise have had to be carried out by service troops. The 2nd Garrison Battalion was never required to leave the country.

Altogether in the course of the war thirty-five battalions of The Royal Scots were at one time in existence: the two line battalions and their reserve (three), twenty-one Territorial units, eight New Army units, and three special units, the 19th (Labour) and the 1st and 2nd Garrison Battalions. Of this number fifteen were on active service, and The Royal Scots were represented in every theatre of the war except Mesopotamia and East and West Africa.

[1] See Appendix III.

CHAPTER II

MONS AND LE CATEAU

August to September 1914

2nd Battalion in France. Plans of the French and Germans. Task of the B.E.F. March of 2nd Royal Scots. The position at Mons. Action of 23rd August. Retreat of Royal Scots to Audencourt. Situation on evening of 25th August. Stand at Le Cateau, 26th August. Continuation of the Retreat. Route of the Royal Scots. End of Retreat, 5th September.

AFTER the orders for mobilisation were received, there was not an idle officer or man in the 2nd Royal Scots, and under the capable direction of the C.O., Lieut.-Colonel H. McMicking, D.S.O., assisted by his Adjutant, Captain C. L. Price, D.S.O., and his Quartermaster, Captain A. E. Everingham, the battalion was soon brought up to its full war establishment. On the 7th August about 500 reservists joined the unit and two days later all arrangements were complete. Orders to move did not arrive till the 12th August, but the interval was profitably employed in assimilating the reservists, who formed nearly fifty per cent. of the battalion. These in their service with the Colours had been trained with the long Lee-Enfield rifle, but they quickly mastered the new weapon, the short service rifle (S.M.L.E.), with which they were now issued, while their muscles, softened by a period of civilian life, were hardened by route marches and physical exercises.

The 2nd Royal Scots were included in the 8th Infantry Brigade, commanded by Brig.-General B. J. C.

Doran, C.B., the other three battalions being the 2nd Royal Irish Regiment, the 4th Middlesex Regiment, and the 1st Gordon Highlanders. This Brigade, along with the 7th and 9th, formed the main part of the Third Division, which was commanded by Major-General Sir Hubert Hamilton, C.V.O., C.B., D.S.O., who had already singled himself out as one of the most promising of the younger generals in the British Army.

On the 13th August two trains carried the 2nd Royal Scots from Plymouth to Southampton, where the unit embarked on the s.s. *Mombassa*. Leaving the port at 8 P.M. the vessel, after a leisurely voyage, early in the afternoon of the 14th, entered the harbour of Boulogne, the wharves of which were densely packed with French people, who gave the troops a tumultuous and rousing welcome. The glengarries of the Scots at once took the eye of the enthusiastic Boulognese and the battalion, having formed up with difficulty, moved off surrounded by throngs of volatile Frenchmen brandishing flags and shouting out hearty greetings, which few were able to comprehend. The warmth and exuberance of the welcome thrilled even the most phlegmatic of the Scots, and as the battalion marched slowly up the long hill to a rest camp at St Martins the pipers struck up the Marseillaise. One night was spent at Boulogne and next day the Royal Scots marched down to the station to entrain for their concentration area. The British and French had previously arranged that the whole of the B.E.F., which then consisted of only four divisions, should assemble in the district between Maubeuge and Le Cateau. Of this area the portion assigned to the Third Division comprised the villages of Marbaix, Noyelles, and Taisnières, and it was in the last of these that the Royal Scots, after detraining at Landrecies, were billeted.

The plan, in accordance with which the movement of the B.E.F. was directed, had been drawn up by the French, who were at this time obsessed with the idea of an offensive *à outrance*. By the 16th August General Joffre was convinced that the Germans were attempting to outflank the Allies by a thrust through Belgium, and he proposed to upset their schemes by a daring counter-offensive. Two armies marching through Luxembourg were to strike at the flank and the communications of such German forces as had crossed the Meuse river between Namur and the Dutch frontier and if possible to attack them, before they had time to deploy for battle by wheeling southwards. The remaining German armies were to be pinned by a series of containing attacks carried out between the Vosges mountains and the fortress of Metz, while the left wing of the Allied forces, consisting of the French Fifth Army and the B.E.F., was to move up and engage such of the hostile forces as might advance from the Meuse, and so gain time to allow the main attack through Luxembourg to be effective. The scheme was clear and straightforward; the Allies were to smash the enemy's centre and then to throw every available force against the German western or right wing.

The French commander made no error in his forecast of the enemy's intentions. The general plan of the Germans was to outflank the left wing of the Allied forces by a drive through Belgium and to pile up the French troops against the Swiss frontier. In order to accomplish this, the armies on the left and centre would have to contain those of the French opposed to them, while the right wing advanced rapidly until, having passed Paris, it should wheel to the south-east and drive the Allied forces against the Swiss mountains. The pivoting point for the German armies was Thionville.

The scheme was vast and ambitious in scope and, though simple in design, required enormous forces, and in 1914, as it turned out, even the Germans had not sufficient numbers available to make it feasible.

The flaw in the plan of General Joffre was that through an under-estimation of the strength of the German right wing, he had based his measures on the assumption that the outer flank of the army of General Von Kluck, who commanded the foe on the right, would not extend west of Mons. Furthermore, the enemy had anticipated the strategy of the French commander and had taken measures to meet it.

None of the Royal Scots had any authentic knowledge of the general situation; that was a matter for the High Command. No one knew definitely how strong the Germans were or where they would be met. Meantime the proper thing to do was to keep the battalion at concert pitch, and much time was devoted to route marches and training to fortify the men for whatever ordeal was in store for them. Glorious summer weather, excellent billets, and the friendliness of the French peasants contributed to make the sojourn at Taisnières an agreeable memory, and the numerous streamlets which graced the country-side afforded welcome opportunities for bathing, of which all ranks took full advantage. The period of preparation did not last long. By the 20th August the concentration of the B.E.F. was complete, and on the same day the 2nd Royal Scots marched from Taisnières to Dourlers, where they were accommodated in billets.

The B.E.F., it became known, was to take part in the great counter-offensive planned by the French. On the 20th August General Joffre issued orders for the advance, but the French commander was now uneasily aware that the menace of the hostile enveloping movement was more formidable than he had originally supposed. For on the same day as General Joffre gave this order, German troops forced an entry into Brussels and compelled the Belgian Army to fall back on Antwerp. The task of the B.E.F. was to advance on the left of the French Fifth Army, and in accordance with this arrangement Sir John French issued his instructions.

The destination of the 2nd Royal Scots on the first day of the advance was the village of Gognies, just over the Belgian frontier. Acting as advanced guard to the division they left Dourlers at 5 A.M., their route taking them through the fortified town of Maubeuge, where French civilians and Territorial troops were diligently felling trees and demolishing buildings which obscured the view from the ramparts; it was all too evident that the defences had been sadly neglected. The heat was of almost tropical intensity, and all the men, especially the reservists, suffered severely. The irregular, cobbled surfaces of the village streets through which the battalion threaded its way were a punishing test for the feet, and many were limping before Gognies came into sight. The officers had an arduous time and a thankless task in attempting to protect their men from the exuberant hospitality of the French country-folk, whose offerings of luscious fruit, water and wines seemed to promise immediate and material relief to men who were suffering from the heat of an oppressive sun. It is never easy to be cruel in order to be kind, but the first consideration of the officers was the fitness of their men, and hardening their hearts, they did their utmost to prevent the troops from accepting the seductive gifts. It was impossible to stop the traffic entirely. A staunch teetotaler, who had been presented with a bottle of red wine, silenced an officer, who warned him that the water of which it was composed was probably bad, by replying: "It's all right, sir, it has got plenty of condy in it." The frontier of Belgium was marked by a barricade across the road guarded by a few Belgian soldiers, who contented themselves with making a formal protest when the Royal Scots passed into their country. On arrival at Gognies the battalion was accommodated in billets, outposts being furnished by detachments from each unit of the 8th Brigade. On that evening the battalion received its first definite news of the enemy's movements. The stationmaster at Quévy explained that trains could not proceed the whole way to Brussels, because parties of hostile cavalry had cut the line to the south of that city, and later in the day Lieut.-Colonel McMicking learned that a party of British cavalry had encountered a force of Germans about 15 kilometres to the north-east of Gognies.

The certainty that another day's advance would bring them close to the enemy created much stir among the Royal Scots, and the mental excitement helped them to make light of the dusty and sun-scorched march, which on the afternoon of the 22nd August took them to the village of Petit Spiennes. Every precaution was taken against surprise, and "C" Company under Major G. S. Tweedie formed the inlying picquet and established outposts on the Mons-Harmignies Road. The remainder of the battalion had a less anxious time and many of the men gathered at the village mill-pool and bathed their feet in its cool water. Lieut.-Colonel McMicking had now no doubt that the enemy was close at hand; he was informed that squadrons of British cavalry were in touch with German cavalry at Binche and that four German Corps were marching westwards to the north of Mons.

The B.E.F. had now reached the outskirts of Mons in the very heart of industrial Belgium. Every coal district presents well-marked characteristics; it offends the eye with ugly mounds of debris and rubbish, which mask the softer hues of nature and irresistibly remind one of a kitchen kept by an untidy maid; it seems in dire need of being cleaned up. Such was the nature of the country where the B.E.F. was to fight its first battle. It was a landscape profusely sprinkled with hamlets, enclosures, dykes, and slag-heaps. The most natural defensive line was that formed by the Mons Canal and along this the B.E.F. took up its position. This canal runs round the north side of Mons, forming a salient, from the base of which the ground rises gradually from north to south for about a mile, till it culminates in three prominent features—a round tumulus immediately south of the town called Mount Erebus; a whale-backed ridge rising abruptly from the plain on every side except the east, and flanked at its northern and southern edges by two heights, Mont Panisel on the north and Bois la Haut on the south; and a slight eminence known as Hill 93, separated from Bois la Haut by a shallow valley. It was with the last of these features that the 2nd Royal Scots were concerned. All these points, especially the last two, furnished excellent observation posts. From Hill 93 there was a splendid field of fire towards St Symphorien, but Bois la Haut, being thickly wooded in parts and crowned with buildings, offered less scope for the free use of the rifle. Immediately west of the canal the ground is dissected by a series of artificial dykes and water-courses, overgrown in patches with rushes and osier beds. The ground is really a marsh, but its instability is disguised by the accumulations of rubbish which a coal-field always produces. The whole of the country occupied by the II. Corps, in which the Third Division was included, has been described as forming one huge unsightly village; certainly a more unromantic setting for a great battle could scarcely be imagined.

Early on the morning of the 23rd August Lieut.-Colonel McMicking received orders to post his battalion along the Mons-Harmignies Road on a front of 2½ kilometres and the men at once began to dig entrenchments. A frontage of 2½ kilometres was greater than that prescribed by the military text-books for a battalion, so that Lieut.-Colonel McMicking had to content himself with a smaller reserve than he would have wished. Fortunately the road was lined by a ditch and bank, so that the position could be quickly strengthened without making it unduly conspicuous. Three and a half companies occupied the fire trench, the other two platoons being kept as a local reserve. "B" Company, under Major Duncan, was on the left; "A" Company, under Captain Leggatt, held trenches slightly in advance of the road, with the machine-gun section under Lieut. Laidlay on its left flank; the larger portion of "C" Company was posted on Hill 93, which formed approximately the right boundary of the battalion. Two platoons of "D" Company, commanded by Captain Shafto, lay immediately on the right of "B" Company, the other two platoons lining the road to the left rear of "C" Company. The C.O. established his H.Q. near the junction formed by the Mons-Harmignies and Spiennes - St Symphorien Roads; on his left were the 1st Gordons, who extended the line to the north-east corner of Bois la Haut.

On the 23rd August a wet and misty dawn was speedily conquered by the sun, which by 9 A.M. diffused a sultry heat from a hard blue sky. The expected collision with the enemy took place at an early hour, and the units of the 8th Brigade that were guarding the canal salient experienced the full weight of the German onslaught. The Royal Scots, however, favoured by the fact that their road was practically invisible to the enemy, were free during the greater part of the forenoon to devote themselves to the improvement of their position, although in other sections of the front a critical battle was already in progress. Gradually the area of strife expanded, and about 11 A.M. a cyclist of the Third Division exchanged shots with German cyclists near St Symphorien; the foe was at last feeling his way towards the line held by the Royal Scots.

It was confidently expected that the Germans would make for Hill 93, but no sustained attack developed against the Royal Scots until the afternoon. Then took place the first of the enemy's onsets, but Major Tweedie's men by accurate rifle fire broke it up. The German infantry issuing from a cluster of woods south-east of St Symphorien in their attack on the hill moved diagonally across the front of "A" and "D" Companies and Lieut. Laidlay's machine-gun section. They formed an ideal target for the trained riflemen and machine gunners of the Royal Scots, and after suffering very severe losses they were brought to a stop about 300 yards from the hill. Happily the German gunners, unable to locate the position of the Royal Scots, could not adequately support their infantry and most of their shrapnel burst either well to the rear or too high to do much damage.

In spite of this eminently satisfactory start the position of the Royal Scots and the Gordons had been seriously affected by the events that had taken place in the salient. There the close conformation of the country had enabled the Germans to outflank the defenders, and a hostile thrust against the right of the salient threatened the left flank of the Gordons. There was in fact a possibility of the Royal Scots being overwhelmed and isolated, but Major-General Hamilton, who had foreseen this danger, about 4 P.M. reinforced them by two companies of the Irish Rifles from the 7th Brigade, which were placed in position between "B" and "D" Companies. Following up his success in the salient, the enemy between 7 and 8 P.M. delivered a violent assault against the line of the Royal Scots and the Gordons, but the attack melted away before the deadly rapid fire of the defenders. This check was decisive, for the enemy made no further effort to drive them from their position, but was content to wait till the increasing pressure on the flank forced a retirement.

As the day wore on the position of the 8th Brigade became most precarious. Germans were in force on its front and in its rear; parties of the enemy had bored their way through Mons as far as Hyon. Towards dusk a battalion of the Irish Guards arrived and took up a station to the right of the Royal Scots on the Harmignies Road, but it withdrew about 9 P.M. to join its own brigade. At the same time Lieut.-Colonel McMicking was warned by Major-General Hamilton to be ready to retire about 10.30 P.M. Cloaked by the gathering darkness groups of the enemy crept closer and closer to the road, till it was possible for our men to hear them talking, and in order to prevent Hill 93 from being rushed the defenders at intervals discharged bursts of rapid fire from rifles and machine-guns. During the night there was at least one false alarm; a message was passed along the line to the effect that a horseman was crossing our front, but he turned out to be a hare which, scared by the unwonted noise of battle, rushed madly along the front. There was a hum of noise from the enemy's lines; German bugles sounded the assembly, and ambulance men, carrying lanterns, were seen searching the ground for wounded.

The B.E.F. extricated itself from the clutches of the

foe with greater ease than might have been expected. On the evening of the 22nd August Sir John French was aware that General Joffre's plan had miscarried, but in order to relieve the pressure of the Germans against the French Fifth Army he had pledged himself to maintain his position on the Mons Canal for twenty-four hours. Having now redeemed that promise he had to save his own force from being overwhelmed by the enemy's enveloping movement. Fortunately the fighting on the 23rd August inspired the Germans with so much respect for their British adversaries that they almost seemed happy to allow them to slip away unmolested.

The 2nd Royal Scots were the last unit of the Third Division to retire. They covered the withdrawal of the Gordons, who moved off about midnight, and while the retreat was in progress the men fired at frequent intervals in order to drown the tramp of their comrades and the grinding of wagons on the cobbled roads. When all the Gordons were clear, the Royal Scots, company by company, commencing from the right, stealthily left their battle positions. In this, the first engagement of the battalion, the casualties were trifling; Major Tweedie and one man were wounded and four men were missing, but the enemy opposed to it had sustained losses out of all proportion to these. A gentle rain came as a soothing relief to men who had endured much from the heat and dust of the day, and in inky darkness the battalion quietly marched through Spiennes to Nouvelles, where having formed up in a field near the village the men piled arms and lay down to sleep. Their rest was soon disturbed and they were called to arms again at daybreak, when breakfasts were prepared. Snatching a hurried meal the men packed up and began to dig trenches. Though tired from want of sleep they toiled most industriously, but the trenches that they excavated represented wasted energy, for the retreat had to be continued.

The French Staff, it seemed, had concentrated on the offensive and had prepared no definite scheme for the defence of the country; at any rate no particular line had been fixed on for a stand to be made. After the collapse of his aggressive plans General Joffre at first was fully occupied in averting a shattering disaster, and it was not till the first pressure of the enemy's pursuit had been shaken off that he found opportunity to excogitate plans for a counter-defensive.

In the long line of the Allies no part was exposed to more immediate peril than the B.E.F., which was face to face with the army of Von Kluck, who had been entrusted with the duty of carrying out the wide turning movement upon which the German command depended for a decisive success. The first aim of the German commander was to shepherd the B.E.F. into the fortress of Maubeuge, where it would be accounted for without difficulty by the forces that were following in the wake of the main hostile armies. But the trap was so evident that only obtuseness or despair could have taken the British Army into Maubeuge. Sir John French saw the snare and determined to avoid it by carrying out a longer retreat than he had at first contemplated.

It was owing to this decision that the Royal Scots ceased digging and withdrew through Nouvelles, which was being vigorously shelled. On reaching Bommeteau at 11 A.M. the battalion was ordered to take up a position to the north of the village and remain there until 3 P.M. when it was to be relieved by the Irish Guards. This was done, but later on instructions were received from Major-General Hamilton to resume the retreat and after a long and arduous march the bulk of the battalion ultimately halted near Bavai, while H.Q. and the transport went on to Amfroipret. In several ways the 24th was a more trying day than the 23rd, though the enemy kept at a respectful distance and the battalion was not required to fire a single shot. The roads and the heat caused greater distress than the enemy; for the ground was iron, the soft rain of the early morning had vanished and the sun shone with frizzling power. The country was thickly dotted with hedges and lines of trees, which seemed to capture and hold the rays of the sun so that the troops had the sensation of passing through a series of hot ovens. Their faces, brown as their rifles, were crinkled with strain and they were so parched with thirst that their throats swelled till swallowing was a pain. The most severe test of discipline came when it was seen that some units had discarded their greatcoats and in some cases even their packs, but Lieut.-Colonel McMicking sternly refused to allow his men to copy this example. To carry greatcoats in the broiling heat seemed a farce, but the C.O. was an experienced campaigner, and none knew better than he that the cold raw nights were not far distant when the men would be thankful that they had clung to their coats. The long march came to a welcome end about 9 p.m., when the battalion bivouacked in a gully on the outskirts of Bavai; so exhausted were the troops that they practically dropped asleep in their tracks.

Early on the 25th August Sir John French resolved to continue the retirement to the neighbourhood of Le Cateau. This would take his army past the tempting shelter of Maubeuge, but the movement was bound to be exceptionally difficult, because during the march the two wings of his army would be separated by the extensive Mormal Forest. Moreover, General Sordet's Cavalry Corps passed right across the British line of retreat, blocking the roads for a considerable time, so that our infantry were an hour later in setting out than the British Commander had intended.

Nevertheless the Royal Scots had to make a very early start. Leaving their bivouacs at 3 A.M. they began to enter Bavai, where the streets were already thronged with the transport and guns of the artillery. Thanks to the foresight of Lieut.-Colonel McMicking and Captain Everingham the men found an excellent breakfast waiting for them in an orchard at Amfroipret. Only half an hour could be spared for the enjoyment of this meal, then the battalion continued its march through Le Quesnoy, where a train was waiting to transport to Maubeuge those who were unfit to walk any farther. As on the previous day there was no trouble from the enemy, but the torture caused by the roads and the sun seemed if anything to become more intense. A few minor excitements diverted the minds of the men from the rigours of the march. A hostile aeroplane was shot down and Lieut.-Colonel McMicking sent Lieut. Graham Watson with his platoon to capture the pilot, but the 9th Lancers reached the wrecked machine first. After a halt for dinner the march was resumed, sounds of firing to the right rear indicating that some part of the army was in contact with the Germans. Going down a stiff decline the cooker of "D" Company was capsized and the men of No. 16 platoon remained to put it right. Wearily trudging through the narrow alleys of Solesmes the battalion reached the hamlet of Béthencourt, where it halted for two hours. For some time, but with astonishing rapidity, hordes of black and grey clouds had been mustering densely in the sky, and suddenly overmastering the sun, they now crushed the earth under heavy torrents of rain. The baked ground rattled under the shock, and the people of the village offered umbrellas to the soldiers, who scornfully rejected them. The shadows were deepening when the men once more moved off, to halt ultimately at the village of Audencourt, where after some confusion, since the whole brigade was to be concentrated there, they were accommodated in billets.

There can be little doubt that the B.E.F. owed its salvation to sheer military skill and to the magnificent tenacity of the troops. The pursuit was vigorous enough to transform into a rout the retreat of any force that was deficient in training or lacking in resolution. Every day witnessed the arrival of fresh German troops, the same men never fighting two days in succession, and the German marches were really wonderful as regards the distance covered. But our rear-guards discharged their duties in model fashion, making the hostile forces deploy as soon as they came within range, and never allowing them to rush headlong on to the retiring columns.[1] The most critical moment in the retreat came on the night of the 25th August. Throughout that evening the villages round Le Cateau were so crammed with men and vehicles that for long intervals no forward movement could be made. The transport of the B.E.F. had not cleared Solesmes when the Germans commenced to close in, and for some time the villages of Le Cateau and Viesly were almost completely blocked. Even a few shells would have caused widespread havoc, but the enemy fortunately was unaware of what was happening. Since the pressure exerted by the foe was obviously increasing, Sir John French reluctantly abandoned his plan of making a stand at Le Cateau; he felt that the only safe way to

---

[1] On the 28th August a German officer remarked to Lieut.-Colonel McMicking as they were lying together wounded in a barn :—"When we deploy and advance against your positions, you don't move away, but shoot us down at close range. The Belgians never did that. Our casualties have been terrible." This was not intended as a compliment but as a complaint, for the speaker seemed to consider it quite wrong that anyone should dare to prevent the German Army from going where it chose and doing what it wished.

thwart the enveloping tactics of the enemy was to continue the retirement and at 7.30 P.M. he issued orders to this effect. The instructions of the Commander of the II. Corps, General Sir H. L. Smith-Dorrien, G.C.B., D.S.O., issued about three hours later, were to the effect that the transport was to start at 4 A.M. on the 26th and the main bodies at 7 A.M. Previous to this he had ordered the 8th Brigade to take up a position in front of the village of Audencourt.

Circumstances however made it difficult for the II. Corps to retreat in accordance with the intentions of the British Commander-in-Chief. North of Viesly the ground swells to a height, which enables those occupying it to overlook the village of Solesmes, and unless this rise were in the possession of friendly troops, the retirement from Le Cateau would have to be begun before daylight. If this could not be managed, the only course was to stand and fight. Such was General Smith-Dorrien's estimate of the situation. At the time that he issued his orders for the retreat to be continued, several of his units had not yet arrived. By 2 A.M., on the 26th August, some of the units of the Third Division were just struggling in, and Major-General Hamilton informed his Corps commander that his men could not be ready to move before 9 A.M. General Smith-Dorrien was satisfied that many of his troops were too exhausted to make the early start that would be necessary for a secure retreat, and he reluctantly decided that his Corps would have to give battle in its present position. He undertook a tremendous responsibility, for he was committing himself to accept a battle under circumstances that were universally believed to invite disaster. Both his flanks would be in the air and for their defence he had only the tired-out and overworked Cavalry Division, commanded by Major-General E. H. H. Allenby, C.B. To stand and fight was, therefore, a desperate measure, but General Smith-Dorrien was convinced that nothing else could save him.

The village of Le Cateau, which has given its name to the battle that was fought on the anniversary of Crécy, lies in the deep and narrow valley drained by the River Selle. From both east and west it is dominated by open undulating country, mostly cultivated but interspersed with patches of moorland. The landscape is not raddled with enclosures; few fields are marked off by fences and the only conspicuous trees were those that bordered the main roads. The ground on the east, occupied by the Germans, is higher than that on the west, so that the enemy enjoyed the advantage in observation during the battle. The river was to some extent a protection since, though comparatively narrow, it could not be crossed except by bridges. Le Cateau lies practically at the junction of a T-shaped spur, the cross-bar of which to the east of the Selle runs north and south, while the stalk extends from the village westwards to Crêvecœur. On the southern side this stalk descends abruptly to a tiny brook called the Warnelle, beyond which the land, richly garnished with villages and copses, spreads out in undulations, the whole forming a terrain that could be turned to account by brave and skilful troops carrying out a retirement in face of a more numerous foe. Much of the ground was then covered with beetroot and clover, but the other crops had been mostly cut and to some extent harvested; in many of the fields browsed herds of cattle, picketed in forage patches. Coming from a country where the rights of property have always been most scrupulously respected, the British troops at first felt that they were committing a heinous crime when they trampled the crops underfoot.

It was probably well that the men as a whole were ignorant of the extremely critical situation in which the II. Corps was placed. When the instructions to continue the retreat were cancelled, Lieut.-Colonel McMicking was informed that 40,000 French soldiers were marching from Cambrai to our assistance and that further retirement would not be necessary. It was not generally known that the I. Corps under General Sir Douglas Haig was already in retreat, and the intimation that French help was expected inspired the hope that our retrograde movement was at an end and that the Allies would now adopt the offensive. Hence the Royal Scots were in high spirits when they received the order to stand and fight.

The right of the Corps position was held by the Fifth Division under Major-General Sir Charles Fergusson, C.B., M.V.O., D.S.O., and the left by the Fourth Division, which had recently arrived from England; the Third Division was in the centre. The 9th Brigade held the section from Troisvilles west to Audencourt, the line being continued thence by the 8th Brigade to Caudry, which was occupied by the 7th Brigade. Long before dawn on the 26th the Royal Scots were improving some shallow trenches which had been dug by the French villagers, and halted only when the instructions to retire reached the battalion; but when these in turn were cancelled, the troops continued to deepen the trenches and stored them with supplies of water and ammunition. While this work was going on Lieut.-Colonel McMicking despatched Lieut. Saward with his platoon to man the high ground between Inchy and Béthencourt in order to assist the retirement of the British cavalry; this platoon returned when its task was accomplished. From the garden fences of Audencourt the Royal Scots stripped sections of barbed wire, using this to fringe their trenches which, situated east of the hamlet, directly fronted the twin villages of Beaumont and Inchy. From right to left the Companies were "A," "B," "C," "D."

The position of the Royal Scots, though not ideal, presented a good field of fire, while the trenches were so sited that the enemy would find it difficult to distinguish them provided our men kept their heads down. Lieut.-Colonel McMicking established his H.Q. in rear of "D" Company, and by means of the private field telephone, which the battalion had maintained for two years, was able to keep in touch with his companies during the battle until the apparatus was destroyed by shell fire. The Royal Scots formed the right battalion of the 8th Brigade; on their left were the 1st Gordons. The brigade on the right of the 8th had not sufficient men to cover the whole of its front, and accordingly asked the 8th to extend its line for a quarter of a mile; this extra space was occupied by a platoon from "D" Company under Lieut. Henderson which took up a position on the right of "A" Company. The 4th Middlesex Regiment, which had sustained heavy casualties in the fighting at Mons, was in support about 400 yards to the rear of "B" Company.

The men looked forward to the battle with some zest; the prospect of holding the foe in check while 40,000 Frenchmen struck at the German flanks promised a new and pleasing phase of the operations. But there were no such illusions to comfort General Smith-Dorrien and, as he feared, the most dangerous onslaughts of the Germans were directed against the flanks of his force. The centre was the last part of the Corps to be involved in the action. At 9 A.M. the engagement of the 8th Brigade began, when the machine-guns of the Middlesex Regiment and of the Royal Scots, advantageously sited on a country track just north of Audencourt, opened fire on parties of Germans who exposed themselves to view while slipping down the hill towards the Cambrai road. The front of the 8th Brigade consisted of an extensive tract of land, bare and flattish, upon which the Germans, aware that it was commanded by the rifle fire of the best shooting army in the world, were slow to venture. They prudently preferred to delay their attack until the effects of the flank assaults made themselves felt. Consequently in this section of our line the fighting during the forenoon of the 26th was only of a desultory character.

But from 6 A.M. till noon a desperate fight was waged on both wings, where the stonewall resistance of the Fifth and Fourth Divisions foiled every attempt of the enemy to turn our flanks. Only west of Le Cateau had there been any penetration of the British line, but with the passing of the day the situation grew in gravity, for each hour added new strength to the foe. In the afternoon the pressure on the right flank became so menacing that General Smith-Dorrien instructed Major-General Sir Charles Fergusson to withdraw his men as soon as he thought fit. After the Fifth retired, the Third and Fourth Divisions were to withdraw in succession, and the route which the former was to follow was the road leading through Montigny to Jeancourt.

The hostile assaults developed in fury during the afternoon, and between 2.30 and 2.45 the Germans swooped down on the right flank with overwhelming force. Shortly before this the enemy's pressure had extended to the centre of the line and about 2 P.M. large infantry forces attacked the village of Caudry and the junction of the Royal Scots and the Gordons. The latter kept back their assailants by rifle and machine-gun fire without great difficulty, but the Germans managed to force an entry into Caudry, thus driving an ominous wedge into the position of the Third Division. Meantime a destructive bombardment fell on the village of Audencourt, and reduced to splinters and fragments practically the whole of the transport of the 8th Brigade. The dreadful power of modern artillery was convincingly shown. Nothing could be done to avert the mischief, and from the shelter of a ruined house Captain Everingham, in angry silence, watched the holocaust which swallowed up the pipes and drums as well as the transport of the Royal Scots.

Till 4.30 P.M. the Royal Scots held their ground in front of Audencourt, when in accordance with orders they withdrew along with the Middlesex Regiment. The instructions were sent out from battalion H.Q., but in addition the Brigade-Major of the 8th Brigade rode behind the line shouting the command to retreat. The battalion thereupon retired by alternate companies from the right, in full view of the enemy, and sustained its heaviest losses while carrying out this movement. Two platoons of "D" Company remained with the Gordons who, it seems, received no orders. The Highlanders along with the detachment of the Royal Scots and two companies of the Royal Irish maintained their position with undaunted confidence till dusk, and about 5 P.M. shattered a vigorous German attack by the accuracy of their fire.

This splendid resistance was of signal service to the rest of the Corps. Though the Gordons and their comrades were unable to extricate themselves, they made it a simpler matter for Major-General Hamilton to withdraw the centre of the British line from under the very eyes of the enemy with surprising ease and without disproportionate losses. The bulk of the Royal Scots, following the rapidly westering sun, were reorganised by Captain Price outside Audencourt and marched to Elincourt, reaching there about midnight. Owing to the withdrawal in full view of the enemy their casualties could not have been light. Captain Shafto of "D" Company had been killed, while Lieut.-Colonel McMicking, Captain Hill-Whitson and Lieut. Laidlay were known to be wounded. Several other officers[1] were missing, but nothing definite was known then about their fate. Two of these, however, Major Duncan and Captain Leggatt, had moved off with small parties and next day they rejoined the battalion. The losses in other ranks were numerous, and at the time could not be estimated precisely; "D" Company was hardest hit, and at the end of the day mustered only seventeen men under Lieut. Henderson. Unfortunately the battalion was unable to bring back Lieut.-Colonel McMicking who, severely wounded, fell into the hands of the Germans. During the brief but critical period when he led it, the battalion stood out as one of the most efficient in the whole army. It amply justified his complete confidence which he expressed thus: "There was no weak link in the battalion: exceptionally efficient at manœuvre and as easy to handle as a well-trained pack of foxhounds; when once 'laid on' the line, the C.O. had nothing more to do until the action was over."

Whatever be the estimate of the generalship shown by the British Commander at the battle of Le Cateau, there can be no doubt that the chief result of the engagement was to allow the B.E.F. to continue its retirement without serious molestation by the enemy, and this may be accepted as a sufficient vindication for the

[1] Lieuts. G. C. C. Strange, C. G. Graves, A. F. Graham Watson, C. E. Scarisbrick, 2nd Lieuts. E. P. Combe, A. J. L. Donaldson, R. C. Ross.

battle. The German Commander, Von Kluck, conducted the battle throughout as if he suspected that the whole of the B.E.F. was opposed to him. This in all probability had been counted on by General Smith-Dorrien, and most people will be satisfied with the summing-up of Brig.-General J. E. Edmonds: "The whole of Smith-Dorrien's troops had done what was thought to be impossible. With both flanks more or less in the air, they had turned upon an enemy of at least twice their strength, had struck him hard, and had withdrawn, except on the right of the Fifth Division, practically without interference, with neither flank enveloped, having suffered losses certainly severe, but considering the circumstances by no means extravagant."[1]

The 26th August closed despondently in a dreary drizzle of rain, and the men were mainly kept together by the compelling influence of discipline. Their eyes were dull through lack of sleep and their shoulders ached under the gall of their equipment; at every halt they dropped asleep, for they had reached the stage when compared with slumber nothing mattered. The battalion moved off again in the small hours of the morning. It started in chilly darkness, but as the sun rose above the horizon its rays dispersed the morning mists and the road was seen to be lined with men in clusters, some asleep, others "fallen out." The groups embraced men of so many different units and even different corps that a casual onlooker, viewing the variety of badges, on a first impression would have concluded that the whole organisation of the army had collapsed, but if he had watched the troops for some time he would have reached the decision that what he witnessed was an organised disorganisation. The whole peace-time training of the British Army had been directed to teach the men to

[1] *Military Operations* (*France and Belgium*, 1914), vol. i., p. 181.

organise themselves, when there was no officer to do so, and the immense value of this training was never better exemplified than during the retreat from Mons, which was almost entirely free from the disorder and confusion that sullied the famous retreat of Sir John Moore to Corunna.

After marching for seven hours the battalion halted at 9 A.M. for a rest of three hours, when the men were refreshed with a meal of bully, marmalade and biscuits, after which they lay down and slept. It was during this halt that Major Duncan and Captain Leggatt rejoined the battalion; Lieut. Laidlay and Captain Hill-Whitsun, it was learned, though wounded, had been safely evacuated. After this welcome respite the march was resumed, a shower of rain spangling the grass and pleasantly cooling the air. A general sense of insecurity brooded over all ranks, for the rear-guard was but a short distance behind and the German guns were drawing perceptibly nearer. Vermand, through which the battalion had to pass, was thronged with transport and guns, and the infantry fretfully waited until the streets were clear. The Royal Scots were then detailed to act as escort to the guns, but they were not called upon to go into action, and after a brief rest they again set off at 8 P.M. The events of the 26th and 27th August had imposed a most exacting strain on the soldiers of the II. Corps, but when night fell on the 27th their worst troubles were over, for the German pursuit had been shaken off. Since the 23rd August the men of this Corps had covered at least 75 miles and had fought in two general engagements.

With limbs like lead the Royal Scots plodded doggedly throughout the long hours of the night, and so bemused were they with the want of sleep that the men in front of them seemed to be floating visions rather than beings of flesh and blood. At the hourly halts they lay down in their fours on the road and immediately dropped off to sleep. The route took the battalion through the village of Ham, on the eastern side of which a halt was called, and during this interval Major Duncan and Captain Price effected a notable capture, in the form of some tea and a supply of fresh meat sufficient to feed the whole battalion; no other unit fared so well that day. Unfortunately the men had to march again before they had time to cook the meat, but they carried it with them. The rays of the scorching sun seemed to exert a diabolical vertical pressure and soon reduced to silence the few individuals who sought to start a contrapuntal accompaniment. The men trudged along almost mechanically for hours and the evening shadows were lengthening when they entered the village of Genvry, where they were put into billets.

On the night of the 28th/29th August the men enjoyed their longest rest since the 23rd August, and they became quite buoyant when in the morning the first mail from England was delivered. The opportunity was used for inspecting rifles and the feet of the troops. Some men were suffering from monstrous blisters, and Lieut. Saward's feet were so badly affected that he had to wear French shoes; the worst cases had to be sent ahead in vehicles. The rest of the battalion commenced its march at 3 P.M., and about three hours later passed through the almost deserted streets of Noyon. The march dragged on till nearly midnight, when the men were allowed to fall out and sleep for three hours. Then came another long spell of marching under a pitiless sun, against which the glengarry furnished no adequate protection, but a few of the troops managed to secure the broad-brimmed straw hats usually worn by French peasants. In spite of the dust and the heat most of the men were in high spirits; they knew that the Germans were not pressing the pursuit, and they had learned that day the good news of Admiral Beatty's victory off Heligoland. So in comparatively cheerful mood, they toiled on through the villages of Autrêches and Vic-sur-Aisne till Courtieux was reached, where they were billeted for the night.

The 31st was yet another day of frizzling heat, and those who were not lucky enough to possess a straw hat put cabbage or mangold leaves under their glengarries. There was scarcely a breath of air, and the open, treeless expanse which the battalion had to cross appeared more like the parched and arid plains of India than the lush meadows of France. The arrears of sleep had to some extent been made up, but all were suffering now from scarcity of water. In the afternoon, however, the route brought the Royal Scots to a more pleasing landscape, and the men marched through a spacious beech forest which provided a most refreshing shade. In going through the village of Villers Cottérêts the battalion passed Major-General Hamilton, who was standing outside an *estaminet*. He stopped Major Duncan and informed him that he was to command the battalion, while Major Dundas, who had acted as C.O. since the loss of Lieut.-Colonel McMicking, was to go to the staff of the Third Division.

On the 31st August the German right flank commenced the fateful wheeling movement which was intended to sweep into its net the French and British forces, and on the 1st September several rear-guard actions, in which the Fifth Division and the I. Corps were involved, indicated that the enemy was closing in once more on the B.E.F. At this time the Third Division was untroubled by the Germans, but still suffered from the continued heat wave. The Royal Scots were marching practically all day, tired of the monotony of the rows of trees that lined the long, white, straight roads to the horizon. In the village of Lévignen they passed General Smith-Dorrien who was overheard to remark, "There is not much wrong with that lot." After reaching the hamlet of Villers St Genest, the men had to march back about 3 miles and take up an outpost position on the Betz-Fresnoy Road. The pickets were withdrawn at 2.30 A.M. on the 2nd September, and the Royal Scots followed in rear of the brigade, eventually halting about noon at Monthyon and being there billeted. The prolonged spell of well nigh tropical heat that marked the summer of 1914 was making itself felt, and several men were admitted to hospital suffering from heat-stroke.

The Royal Scots departed from Monthyon about 6 A.M. on the 3rd, accompanied by the Maire who took with him only a bundle of rugs and his dog. In some respects this was the most trying day of the retirement. Uninterrupted marching under a fiery sun which spread over the earth like a rich amber sheet had brought many of the men almost to the limit of their powers of endurance. Apart from the stewy heat and the rough cobbled streets, movement on this day was tiresomely hampered by the clumsy wains and carts, packed with refugees and their belongings, which congested the roads. But if the day was one of physical distress for our men, it was more notably distinguished for the collapse of the German plans. Von Kluck's stroke had missed its mark. His wheeling movement, though executed with energy and rapidity, had failed to catch in its orbit the French Fifth Army and the B.E.F. The former was now safely across the River Marne and in line with the latter, though there was a gap of 10 miles between them. The failure of the enemy now presented General

Joffre with a glorious opportunity for a deadly counter-stroke. There was a distinct chance of smashing the German right wing by a swift attack from the west, and already an army was being secretly mustered in Paris to come in on the left flank of the B.E.F.

The 4th September was an easy day for the Royal Scots; they were not required to form up till 6 P.M., when they paraded for a night march. This was a slow process, interrupted by many checks. The Grand Morin river was crossed and the battalion passed through Crécy Forest; about daybreak Châtres was reached. All the roads were packed with artillery, which had been the cause of many imprecations from the infantry during the dark watches of the night. Eventually, about 10 A.M., the Royal Scots entered Rétal, where they met their first reinforcements under the command of Captain Hewat. In a vague way the men felt that matters were "on the mend," and this optimistic turn of mind was thoroughly justified, for the ordeal of the retreat was over. Throughout the thirteen days when the withdrawal was in progress, the 2nd Royal Scots had magnificently responded to all the calls made on them. Their organisation and discipline had triumphed over every strain, and on the two occasions when they had been in conflict with the enemy, no Germans had succeeded in breaking through their defence.

CHAPTER III

THE MARNE AND THE AISNE

September 1914

Counter-attack of the Allies. Advance of 2nd Royal Scots. Action at Orly, 8th September. The Marne crossed, 9th September. Situation on night of 9th September. The Aisne reached. Action of 13th September. The Struggle on the 14th. Trench Warfare.

THE opportunity for the Allies' counter-attack was rendered possible by the modifications which the Germans were compelled to make in their original plan. Von Kluck had intended to press forward to the west of Paris before commencing his wheel, but, in 1914, even the Germans had not the numbers that were necessary to make the scheme practicable, and on the 3rd September the enemy's right wing began to wheel before Paris was reached. This movement could be justified only on the assumption that the left flank of the Allies, consisting of the B.E.F. and the French Fifth Army, was impotent to interfere, for Von Kluck's Army had now to march across the front of these forces. But the assumption had no basis in fact; the left wing of the Allies had not been driven out of action, and in anticipation of the enemy's tactics a new French Army had been gathered under the shelter of Paris. Thus the Allies had three armies available to hurl against Von Kluck's flank, and provided the Allied line in the centre and south held firm, the attack had a reasonable prospect of scoring a substantial success. The new French Army, the Sixth, came up on the extreme left and next it was the B.E.F.

The terrain over which the British troops were now required to advance was mainly the extensive plateau to the east and north-east of Paris, which, standing nearly 500 feet above the plains of Champagne, is fringed on the east by the towns of Craonne, Rheims, Epernay, Nogent sur Seine. The whole district, though highly cultivated, spreads out in a panorama of spacious meadows straddled by clusters of trees and hamlets. To the south of Coulommiers the plateau is darkened by the extensive forests of Crécy, Armainvillers, and Malvoisine.

From south to north it is cut by a succession of deep ravines (running east and west) which form the beds of the Grand Morin, the Petit Morin, the Marne, the upper waters of the Ourcq, the Vesle, the Aisne, and the Ailette, not one of which is fordable. These rivers marked the only definite positions where the enemy might be expected to stand.

As a preliminary to its attack the B.E.F. was to wheel to the east, pivoting on its right flank, until it came up on a line extending from La Chapelle Iger to Bailly, roughly parallel to the Grand Morin and about 7 miles from it. This manœuvre was to be completed by 10 A.M. on the 6th September, after which the whole force was to move forward in an easterly direction.

The first day of the advance entailed no fighting for the 2nd Royal Scots, who left their billets at Rétal at 6 A.M. In spite of the windless heat of the day the men marched with great zest, for they realised that they were now moving in the proper direction. To his intense disgust Lieut. Saward had to report sick, his feet being so badly blistered that he could hardly put them to the ground; it was in fact a marvel that he had been able to hold out so long. After stopping for some hours at the

Château du Chemin the battalion continued its route through La Houssaye, where there had been a cavalry skirmish, to Crêvecœur where the men piled arms in a sheltering orchard. As they were resting Major-General Hamilton suddenly appeared, and complimented them highly on their excellent conduct during the retreat and reminded them that they still had much to do before they settled their score with the enemy. This little word of praise from the General cheered the troops immensely, and with renewed vigour they pressed on through Crécy Forest to Courtoisoupe near which the battalion bivouacked.

Next morning, at 8 A.M., marching was resumed, "A" and "B" Companies forming the advanced guard. An occasional dead horse by the roadside was for a time the only indication of war. Then our guns were heard firing from the high ground above Coulommiers, but the troops could not see what was their target. The leading men of "B" Company soon became aware that the foe could not be very far ahead; village streets were strewn with rubbish and empty bottles, while the cottage doors were disfigured with German billeting marks. The battalion halted for the night at Chauffry, where reinforcements, consisting of Lieut. Perry and 93 men, were cordially welcomed.

The route had taken the battalion across the first river obstacle, the Grand Morin, which the enemy had made no attempt to defend. Everyone was full of confidence, and there were even optimists who declared that the foe had been utterly routed and was now completely demoralised. The track of the enemy's retreat could be easily followed by the trail of broken bottles, and numerous tales were told of German soldiers who had imbibed too freely. Our men readily believed that this drunkenness was a clear sign of demoralisation; but those who had been most galled by the heat asserted with some reason that the empty bottles were due more to thirst than to panic, and that if the weather continued to be sweltering they would be glad to be demoralised in the same fashion.

So far there had been no fighting with the retreating foe, but there was a strong possibility that on the 8th September the Germans, with a view to preventing congestion at the Marne, would stand and fight, since the lie of the ground gave them considerable advantages for defensive action. The narrow gorge of the Petit Morin, with its steep slopes thickly covered with trees and shrubs, could be approached only through close country broken with clusters of groves, villages, and hamlets, while the river itself was spanned by only six bridges in the sector of the B.E.F.; and after the Petit Morin was crossed an obstacle of similar difficulty was presented by the Marne.

Moving off at 5 A.M. the 2nd Royal Scots were confident that they would soon be engaged with the Germans, a column of whom, estimated at 2000 strong, was reported to be just ahead, but five hours elapsed before the battalion came under fire. At 10 A.M. shrapnel bursts exploded over the men when they entered the expanse of wide and open ground lying to the west of the village of Orly, and the companies immediately spread out into artillery formation. The Royal Scots were the rear battalion of the brigade, the whole of which was the target of the hostile shells. The Germans had dug in on the slopes of the Petit Morin. An advance towards the river bank was promptly carried out and the men, quickly crossing some coverless ground, reached the shelter of a wood on the slope of a ridge immediately opposite the enemy's position. But the eastern margin of the wood was commanded by the

German machine-guns, so skilfully ensconced that the guns of our field artillery could not get at them, and every attempt of our men to issue from the wood was frustrated by the accurate fire of the enemy machine gunners. 2nd Lieut. G. H. Hay of "C" Company, unsurpassed by any in hardihood, crept from the wood and made some ground, but the vigilant foe observed him as he endeavoured to conceal himself behind a bush, and a whole belt of machine-gun bullets was directed on the shrub, literally combing the gallant officer without killing him.

The whole of the 8th Brigade was pinned to its position until the attack of the other two brigades of the division compelled the Germans to retire. Then the general advance was resumed. On the north side of the Petit Morin the enemy had built a dummy trench in a field near a bridge and left along the parapet a row of Bavarian helmets, which were seized by the men as souvenirs. Some of the enemy were not given time to escape. Lieuts. Hall and Henderson surprised a small party hiding in a patch of Indian corn and forced it to surrender, and in a silo, which had been used as a supporting trench, other 9 prisoners were taken. The enemy, it appeared, was endeavouring to make war as luxurious as possible, for few carried bottles containing water only; most had filled them with choice wines or a mixture of liqueurs and each man was well supplied with stolen cigars. In the vicinity of Orly the Royal Scots encountered 150 unhappy Germans whom they disarmed and took prisoners. Near the main road the battalion suddenly came under fire apparently directed from a patch of Indian corn 1400 yards away. This target was at once signalled to the gunners, who had fired a few shells at it when a khaki figure hurriedly emerged from the corn and frantically waved a white handkerchief. A body of Cameronians, it seemed, belonging to another division, had surprised and captured a large force of the enemy; they had then perceived the Royal Scots and had mistaken them for Germans.

Orly was reached and occupied about 5 P.M. and the battalion billeted in the village for the night. The men were exuberantly confident, for their losses had been slight, and the foe seemed to be "on the run." "We are getting our own back with interest," was the phrase on all lips. Two officers had been lost; in addition to 2nd Lieut. Hay who was wounded, Captain Hewat was killed while directing the fire of "D" Company. There was only a score of other casualties. Lieuts. Strange and Combe, who had been with other units since Le Cateau, rejoined the battalion on this day. An hour after the Royal Scots entered Orly a terrific thunderstorm, which had been heralded by a day of stifling heat, suddenly broke and the rain descended in such torrents that it was difficult to move and practically impossible to see.

On the 8th September the B.E.F. had devoted its energies to forcing the passage of the Petit Morin, and the tenacity with which this had been disputed by the defenders seemed to presage an even more turbulent struggle at the Marne. On this day it became clear to the commanders of the Allies that the right wing of the German Army had been split into two groups, which were only linked together by means of cavalry divisions. The obvious aim of the Allies was to smash the extreme right group under Von Kluck before the gap could be filled with fresh forces set free by the fall of the fortress of Maubeuge. This was the immediate task of the French Sixth Army and the B.E.F., and the latter was now to direct its advance northwards in order to assist the right wing of the former.

To the general surprise the Germans made no effort to dispute the passage of the Marne on the 9th September. The 2nd Royal Scots, leaving Orly at 7 A.M., reached Citry on the south bank of the Marne and found that the guns of the divisional artillery had already crossed the river and were shelling the enemy. A few German shells were bursting on the Marne ridge, but were insufficient to be really troublesome, so some of the officers and men took advantage of the long halt to enjoy a bathe in the river. In the evening, when the light was failing, the battalion crossed the Marne and went into billets at Crouttes.

On the 9th September the Allies did not secure the advantages that they had expected. The most considerable progress had been made by the Third Division, and its leading brigade, the 9th, reached the point of farthest advance made by the British that day: if the I. and III. Corps could have kept pace with it, Von Kluck's army might have been utterly overwhelmed. But the advance, though it did not come up to expectation, had been more fruitful than was at the time realised. Von Kluck was thoroughly scared by the progress of the British, and to prevent himself being outflanked he determined to withdraw. Thus the battle of the Marne, the series of operations which came to an end on the 9th September, was undoubtedly a victory for the Allies. The Germans had been unable to realise their scheme of crushing France at a blow and the initiative for the moment passed to the Allies. The first concern of the former was to close the gap between the forces of Von Kluck and Von Buelow before it could be penetrated by the French and British. Retirement was a necessity for Von Kluck, and it was a difficult and delicate operation, since his line of retreat would take him right across the front of the B.E.F. Sir John French was naturally anxious to lose no chance of punishing his adversary, and resolving to maintain a relentless pressure against the German right wing, he issued instructions that the entire British Army should carry on the pursuit at an early hour.

At daybreak on the 10th, the sky was troubled with low clouds and dense mists which prevented our flying men from following the movements of the enemy. In the Third Division the advanced guard was again furnished by the 9th Brigade. The march of the Royal Scots, who left their billets at 5 A.M., was broken by frequent stops, for the dismal soggy roads were littered with vehicles and carts which the enemy, in his hurried flight, had been compelled to abandon. About 4 P.M. the noise of battle swelled in front, and on passing through Vinly the battalion saw the traces of what had been a sharp rear-guard action. Our leading troops experienced some lively and successful fighting, and several batches of forlorn Germans were marched under escort past the Royal Scots, who did not come into contact with the enemy on this day. The grilling summer heat which had scorched France since the opening of the campaign had given place to a soaking autumn, and the roads, now spread with mud and churned by wagons, rendered a speedy advance out of the question. Though suffering from cold and damp the Royal Scots spent the night at Chézy in comparative comfort, for by a stroke of luck they had been able to procure greatcoats, piles of which had been left behind by the decamping enemy.

As the Germans after Mons believed that they were chasing a vanquished foe, so the British after the Marne regarded themselves as carrying on a pursuit. But the enemy had not been broken. The swiftness of his retreat was caused by his desperate anxiety to get nearer to his reinforcements, which had been released by the capture of Maubeuge on the 7th September. If these were able to come up and fill the fissure between Von Kluck and Von Buelow, then the thrust of the Allies against the German right flank would be adequately parried. The rank and file of the British, with no knowledge of the general situation, naturally attributed the rapidity of the German retirement more to fear than to intention. So quickly did the enemy carry out his movements that on the 11th the B.E.F. never came into contact with him, and the worst trouble experienced by our troops was the congestion of the roads, which seriously impeded the advance. Torrential rain fell in the afternoon, drenching the men to the skin, but about 3 P.M. Oulchy-la-Ville was reached, and there the march of the 2nd Royal Scots came to an end for the day.

The weather conditions on the 12th were still unsatisfactory, and dark threatening clouds filled the sky when the Royal Scots paraded at 6 A.M. for the resumption of the pursuit. The next great river barrier was the Aisne, and the B.E.F. set out with the object of seizing the crossing places and occupying the high ground north of the river. No glint of sunshine graced the day, and the lowering clouds dissolved into sheets of rain which beat the roads into seas of mud, so that marching was irksome and observation well nigh impossible, but the advance was carried on steadily. Although once again the 8th Brigade was not engaged, throughout the day the Royal Scots could hear the sound of firing on both flanks. About 5 P.M. their march ended at the village of Braisne, six miles from the south bank of the Aisne. The 12th was another day of disappointment to the B.E.F., for at nightfall not a single bridge on the Aisne was in British hands.

The high ground on the north bank of the river presented an awkward obstacle. The valley of the Aisne is banked on both sides by fairly steep hills, and on the far side the enemy was established on the ridge along which runs the now famous Chemin des Dames. This ridge, rising out of the plain of Champagne near Craonne, twists along for some 25 miles between the valleys of the Aisne and the Ailette in a westerly direction to the vicinity of Soissons, and from it numerous underfeatures and spurs slope down to the Aisne valley. On this commanding ground the Germans took post, and thus protected by a bastion fashioned by nature were in a position to put up a most desperate resistance. Their main line, on the average, stood 2 miles from the river.

Their intentions were put to the test on the 13th September. In the Third Division the 8th Brigade relieved the 9th as advanced guard. Starting from Braisne the Royal Scots were passing through the village of Chassemy when they were shelled by guns cunningly posted on the bold spur of Chivres which descends to the Aisne valley from the Chemin des Dames. Promptly breaking into artillery formation the men pushed on to a wooded ridge above the village. On the right flank of the Royal Scots was the 9th Brigade and on their left the Royal Irish Regiment. Screened from view by the greenery of the trees, the battalion advanced to a position in front of the canal at the Aisne, reaching it about 10 A.M. The outlook at this stage was most unpromising. There was every indication that the enemy was bent on a stern resistance, and there appeared no easy means of crossing the river. The railway bridge had been demolished and a road bridge near the village of Vailly had also been destroyed. But at the latter place a narrow plank with ropes attached to it stretched across the river, the Germans in their haste having omitted to pull the plank away when they retired.

This precarious means provided the only chance of gaining the other side, and by this rickety and perilous route Lieut.-Colonel Duncan despatched his battalion. By 3 P.M. "A" and "C" Companies and the Royal Irish were on the other bank of the Aisne and, though they were shelled by the German guns, reached the village of Vailly where some of the houses had already been battered by shell fire. North of the village the ground ascends sharply to an irregular ridge and along this slope a picquet line was formed by these troops. A few hours later "B" and "D" Companies succeeded in crossing, and by 6 P.M. all the Royal Scots were on the same side of the river as the Germans. On the 8th Brigade being ordered to occupy the high ground commanding Vailly the Royal Scots held the left of the picquet line. Their left flank was in the air, the disposition of the companies from left to right being "D," "B," "A," and "C." An uneasy night was spent. The sound of voices and the grinding of wheels on roads never ceased, and from the direction of Soissons boomed the noise of heavy gun fire. During the hours of darkness the 9th Brigade crossed the river and relieved "A" and "C" Companies of the Royal Scots, which then went into support of the other two companies. The greatest vigilance was observed, for the Germans were dangerously close to our lines, and after dusk Lieut. Combe of "A" Company captured a prowling Boche patrol of one N.C.O. and fifteen men.

On the 13th September the B.E.F. made little headway. The Aisne had been crossed, but in no part had British troops succeeded in mounting the main ridge; they had only won a precarious footing on some of the smaller spurs leading down from the ridge to the river valley. Even this, considering the stubborn resistance of the enemy, was a noteworthy gain, but the commanders of the Allies had set their minds on breaking through the opening between Von Kluck and Von Buelow. No effort was to be relaxed until this was accomplished, and accordingly, on the 14th Sir John French determined to attack along his whole front. But unknown to him the situation had completely changed. On the previous day the German VII. Reserve Corps had arrived and had come into line between Von Kluck and Von Buelow. The gap had been closed, and the German position on the Aisne being absolutely secure, Von Buelow was encouraged to begin a counter-attack with the object of sweeping the Allies back over the river.

A thick mist hugged the earth on the 14th, causing shrubs and undergrowth to drip with moisture, and owing to this and to the nature of the terrain, split into numerous pockets, the fighting that ensued resembled rather a series of local combats, as between individual gladiators, than a sustained contest between two large armies. Once the battle was joined, control passed entirely to the local officers. Shivering with cold the Royal Scots stood to arms at 3 A.M. It was almost impossible for the eye to discern any object more than a few yards away, but their patrols reported all clear in front. A little later, however, a patrol of "D" Company came back with the news that Germans were occupying rifle pits on the edge of a beet field about 300 yards in front of the company's position. Lieut. Henderson, who commanded the company, then went forward with Lieut. Hall of "B" Company, and having verified the report resolved to attack the enemy without delay. This advance, it so happened, forestalled a hostile attack and "D" Company, being met by superior numbers, had to fight hard to maintain its ground. While the cool, steady shooting of Lieut. Henderson's men sufficed to take the sting out of the enemy's attack, the urgent nature of the situation was reported to Lieut.-Colonel Duncan and he sent up reinforcements. "B" and "C" Companies, advancing under heavy rifle fire, pressed on almost to the crest of the ridge. The German fire by this time was positively murderous, yet Captain Morrison of "C" Company crawled out and gallantly brought back a wounded man who was lying in the open.

Early in the fray Lieut.-Colonel Duncan was wounded, his horse being shot under him, but Captain Price, the Adjutant, directed the operation with admirable coolness. The Royal Irish were on the right of the Royal Scots and to some extent mixed up with them. At this moment the tender spot was the left, where the Germans were already beginning to work round our men. Fortunately the Middlesex came up on this flank, but these in turn were menaced by the enemy's enveloping movement. The Divisional Artillery, with no convenient positions to site their guns, could not adequately support the infantry, and having to fire at long range and without satisfactory observation at first dropped several shells among our own men, but later got the range of the German trenches.

The Royal Irish ran out of ammunition and were given some by the Royal Scots, although they were seriously concerned about their own supplies, but in spite of every disadvantage our men held on grimly, each frontal attack by the enemy being completely repulsed. On this occasion at any rate the Germans failed to display the dash which alone would have enabled them to profit by the difficulties of their opponents. Possibly they were misled by the vigour with which they had been assailed by a force weaker than their own and in consequence exaggerated our numbers. While the 8th Brigade was pinned to its ground, the 9th on its right, though blinded by a driving mist, commenced a courageous attack against the enemy.

The accumulation of advantages possessed by the Germans eventually caused our troops to retire for some distance. About 9 A.M. the enemy attempted to rush the 8th Brigade from its position round Vailly, supporting the attack by a fierce machine-gun fire which enfiladed the whole line of the brigade from the left. With ammunition running short our men could not hope to stand their ground and about 10 A.M. they reluctantly began to withdraw. They were not a moment too soon, for the Germans were now rapidly working round the left flank. About the same time the attack of the 9th Brigade was thoroughly checked, and if the enemy had seized his chances he should have been able to press the whole division into the Aisne. Much more was at stake than a reverse to the Third Division. An alarming gap had developed between the I. and II. Corps, and if the Germans had passed through it they could have rolled up Sir Douglas Haig's force from the north. Luckily the foe appeared to be unaware of his advantage and continued to display the timidity that marked his conduct throughout the battle. Major-General Hamilton had time to send his 7th Brigade to the succour of the 9th, and after some confused fighting, the 2nd Royal Scots and the remainder of the 8th Brigade were able to take up and hold a line on a low ridge just above the village of Vailly. When darkness brought to an end a day of desperate and critical struggle, the 9th Brigade lay in front of Vailly with the 2nd Royal Scots on the left. During the lull the companies were reorganised and the men dug themselves in.

The British had good reason to congratulate themselves on the result of the fighting on the 14th September. They had escaped from an extremely nasty situation and during the night they had time to consolidate their position. At the best, however, our line on the Aisne was not a satisfactory one. Nearly every point of vantage was held by the enemy and practically the whole of the river valley was under his direct observation. Noting the scarcity of bridges our men thought uneasily of what would happen if the Germans should bring off a successful attack. The sappers laboured assiduously to put up new crossings, but owing to the observation commanded by the enemy, the only considerable traffic across them took place after dark.

When the clash on the Aisne failed to bring a decisive advantage to either side, a period of trench warfare set in and contests partook more of the nature of operations against fortifications than of struggles between forces of trained men. The line could hardly yet be said to be stabilised, and the first few weeks of the new warfare were far from apathetic. On the 15th a series of attacks was essayed by the Germans, but all those directed against the Third Division were easily beaten off by rifle and machine-gun fire. The position of the British at the end of the day was in fact stronger than at the beginning. During the intervals between the attacks the trenches were repaired and deepened and the bridges across the river were strengthened. Though constantly shelled by the enemy our lines were held with tolerable security. But there was no improvement in the weather, and cabined between two ramparts of earth less than a yard apart the Royal Scots, with their feet embedded in the muddy floors of the trenches, suffered severely from damp and cold. These hardships were mitigated greatly by the excellent rations which the Quartermaster, Captain Everingham, never failed to send up, no matter how appalling the weather was or how heavy the shelling.

At this early period our trenches were rarely continuous and consisted as a rule of a succession of rifle pits capable of holding a few men; they were never more than 2 feet wide and the traverses were tiny. As a protection against bullets they were admirable but they did not offer secure shelter against a heavy bombardment. The new conditions caused us to recast our notions as to what constituted a field of fire. The South African campaign had demonstrated the deadliness of the modern rifle over a wide field of fire, but at the Aisne, where the combatants took shelter in trenches, it became obvious that a short field of fire, flanked by machine-guns, formed the most effective position. The rifle was still the chief weapon of the infantry, but for the army as a whole the artillery now assumed an importance it had never previously obtained.

The B.E.F. remained at the Aisne for upwards of a week, during which period discomfort increased owing to the continuance of the drenching rains and the intermittent bombardments of the enemy. At first the greater initiative was shown by the Germans, who advanced their trenches to closer quarters with their foes. It was they who attacked, and making the most of their superior gun positions they inflicted considerable casualties on the British. The H.Q. of the Royal Scots, situated in a shallow dug-out covered with a scrap of corrugated iron, were so flimsy as to be hardly proof even against bullets, and on the 16th the popular and energetic Adjutant, Captain Price, was killed by a shrapnel bullet. The defences had to be improved in order to give protection against shell fire. The strain on the men gradually relaxed as reinforcements from home arrived, but the sloppy trenches and the piercing chilliness of the evenings played havoc with the men's health and several had to be sent to hospital. On the 16th Captain Tanner and Captain Croker joined the battalion and three nights later Lieut. Trotter brought 100 reinforcements. On the 20th there was a series of German attacks, but all were beaten off and the Royal Scots were not required to fire a single shot.

After this date there was comparative quietness. On the 22nd September Sergeant Whaley, with a small patrol, surprised and exterminated a German patrol of one officer and three men. Then, on the 25th, the 2nd Royal Scots were relieved by the Lincolns of the 9th Brigade and proceeded to Courcelles, about 2 miles on the other side of Braisne; there the whole of the 8th Brigade was concentrated. After a long spell of inactive warfare the men's feet were very soft and the next few days were devoted to bringing the troops back to the spick-and-span condition which it was the pride of the battalion to maintain. On the 29th the Royal Scots were inspected by General Smith-Dorrien, who complimented them on their fine appearance and congratulated them on the excellent work that they had done.

CHAPTER IV

EVENTS IN THE WEST

October 1914 *to March* 1915

"The Race to the Sea." Task of II. Corps. 2nd Royal Scots in French "Black Country." Progress of the Advance, 12th and 13th October. Events on the 15th. German Raid at Fauquissart. Trench Tours. Condition of Trenches in 1914. 2nd Royal Scots near Kemmel. Action of 14th December.

AT the end of September the B.E.F. bade farewell to the Aisne and proceeded to a quarter where it was destined to win unfading glory. When fighting reached a deadlock at the Aisne, the only direction offering scope for manœuvre was towards the sea or western flank. General Joffre still believed that he had a chance of enveloping the right wing of the Germans, and he threw in a new army under General Maud'huy to do what the French Sixth Army had done at the Marne. Even if the enveloping manœuvre failed, the Allies would certainly strengthen their position by joining their line on to Antwerp, and in response to this movement the Germans were obviously bound to extend their line to the sea. Considerations of defence also urged the Allies towards the Channel. Britain at any rate was vitally interested in the security of the Channel ports, for Calais in the hands of the Germans might well be regarded as a cannon pointed at the heart of England. In their spirited dash on Paris the Germans had neglected the Channel ports, because their immediate object was to destroy the French field armies, and they had not sufficient armies for the two purposes. But having failed in their first object it was fairly probable that they would now attempt to seize the ports. The considerations that caused the Allies to extend for defence impelled their opponents to extend for attack. Thus both sides had substantial motives for expanding to the shores of the Channel. The "race to the sea" was the inevitable outcome of the deadlock on the Aisne. Consequently, as the opposing groups began to extend westwards, each inspired by the hope of enveloping the other, a succession of shocks ensued till the coast was reached. The success of General Joffre's plan depended upon the ability of the Belgian Army at Antwerp to stand its ground, for if that fortress should pass into the hands of the Germans, there could be no assurance of the war being brought to a speedy and favourable conclusion.

With these important developments in progress it was natural that the B.E.F. should be brought into a position that would enable it more easily to maintain its communications with England; it was therefore transferred to the left of the Allied line. Britain, in her anxiety for the safety of the Channel ports, would be happier about their defence if that task were entrusted to her own soldiers. Moreover, the change held out the possibility of the navy and the army being employed in a combined operation.

In accordance with this programme the first part of the B.E.F. to move was General Smith-Dorrien's II. Corps. During the fighting at the Marne and the Aisne it had been the left of the B.E.F.; it was now to form the right wing, with the III. Corps in the centre and the I. Corps on the left. The object of General Smith-Dorrien was to seize the high ground near La Bassée and Aubers commanding the approaches to Lille, and to occupy that town.

The 2nd Royal Scots under Captain Croker left Courcelles in the Aisne sector on the 1st October. Marching proved a severe test to the men after their long spell of trench work, and during the first few days an exceptionally large number of them fell out. Eventually, partly by route march and partly by train or bus, the battalion arrived at Perthes on the 10th October. Leaving this village on the following day the Royal Scots passed through the hamlets of Auchel and Lozinghem, crossed the La Bassée Canal in the afternoon and halted at a ramshackle village called Le Cornet Malo. A body of French cavalry was holding the ground across the canal, but withdrew on the arrival of the Royal Scots. Two platoons from each of "B" and "C" Companies were sent forward as outpost, while the rest of the battalion went into billets with the warning to be ready to turn out at a moment's notice.

The II. Corps was now operating in the Black Country of France. This district with its smoky factories, kilns, and spoil heaps, has never attracted tourists, and the dismal landscape aroused no enthusiasm among our soldiers. From the strictly military point of view it had many disadvantages. The land is flat and soggy, almost destitute of cover, and intersected by broad, deep dykes where a heavily laden man might easily be drowned, while the numerous mining structures and cottages furnished natural resistance points from which a determined foe could be ejected only at a great cost in life. The outstanding feature of the whole area is the ridge that looks down on Lille from the west; this is a low yet clearly marked rise that splits towards the west into two spurs, one mounted by the village of Aubers, the other by Illies. If he could only secure this ridge, General Smith-Dorrien had a good prospect of saving Lille.

Since it expected to be opposed by merely a few cavalry divisions, the II. Corps anticipated small difficulty in effecting its purpose. But the Germans were pressing towards the sea as rapidly as the Allies, and after fighting for a few days the Corps realised that instead of attacking it would have to strain every nerve to stem the advance of the foe. The October battles that raged in France between Arras and the Channel were in reality one battle, brought to a head by the efforts of the combatants to turn each other's flank, and it is impossible to say that the struggle at one part was more critical than at another. The strenuous fighting experienced by the soldiers of the II. Corps in one of the most sombre districts of France attracted little attention at home as compared with the conflict round Ypres. In the French Black Country there existed no spot like the picturesque Flemish town to touch the imagination of men; the ugly, grimy buildings of La Bassée were a nightmare compared with the beautiful edifices of Ypres. Yet the men who closed the way to Ypres had no harder or more important task to perform than those who fought amidst the slag heaps and dykes near La Bassée. And without doubt the soldiers of the II. Corps rendered a service to their country no less valuable than that which they had performed at Le Cateau; for though in spite of all their valiant efforts they were unable to save Lille, they shattered every attempt of the Germans to cut through between the French and the British forces. Had the enemy penetrated between General Smith-Dorrien and General Maud'huy, he would have reaped an advantage in comparison with which the loss of the Channel ports, from the point of view of the general interests of the Allies, would have been of small account.

In the first days of October both the Germans and

the British were groping for each other, neither being sure where, or by what force, they would be opposed. Contact with the enemy was established by the Third Division on the 12th October. Leaving Le Cornet Malo at 7 A.M. the Royal Scots reached Les Lobes, where they remained in a field till 3 P.M., when in conjunction with a force of French cavalry they were ordered to make for Croix and Pont du Hem. But the enemy was in strength on the front, and the Royal Scots moving with difficulty over the open water-logged country suffered many casualties from hostile rifle fire. "A" and "B" Companies led, followed by "C" and "D." A few shells proved that the German infantry were being supported by guns, but the Royal Scots pressed on steadfastly. Still it was plainly beyond mortal power for them to reach Pont du Hem against the enemy's resistance, and a nearer objective, the bridge that spanned the Lawe Canal near Vieille Chapelle, was assigned to them. The C.O., Captain A. E. Croker, was badly wounded just as he reached the bridge and the command was then taken over by Captain E. L. Strutt, who had joined the battalion on the 10th. Near the objective many of our men, about seventy in all, fell victims to the enemy's fire, among them being Lieut. Trotter who was wounded, and Captain Heathcote of "B" Company who was shot through the leg. Lieut. Henderson, leading up "D" Company, saw about thirty dead or wounded. The enemy, however, was clearly fighting a rear-guard action; he always drew off when the Royal Scots closed in on his positions. Just before dark the canal was crossed and the battalion took up a position on the Fosse Vieille road, with "A" and "D" Companies in front and "B" and "C" in support. The Middlesex were on the right and the Gordons on the left, but in that troublesome boggy country it was almost midnight before the Royal Scots succeeded in gaining touch with them. A burning farm in the rear cast a fitful radiance through the pitch blackness of the night, and some of the men went back to rescue the wretched animals shut up in the outhouses.

The fighting on the 12th October had been carried on under conditions wholly repugnant to the Royal Scots. They had been operating against an enemy whom they could not see and who, well supplied with motor-cars, moved off to a fresh post whenever the Royal Scots came within striking distance. In close touch with a foe of whose strength they were uncertain our troops spent a cold and watchful night. The advance was to have been resumed at dawn on the 13th, but a raw, chilly mist, which muffled the ground, caused the start to be delayed till 7 A.M. In artillery formation the Royal Scots set off, with "C" and "D" Companies leading, and "A" and "B" in support. Sinking to the ankle in the black loam and soaked by the water in the ditches that bounded every field the men had covered a toilsome mile, when a German gun opened on them and a small cottage in front suddenly burst into flames. The hostile guns were so skilfully hidden that though they were firing at comparatively close range they could not be located, and their shells inflicted several casualties on the leading companies. Then the enemy's infantry from concealed positions plied our ranks with machine-gun and rifle fire and our advance, owing to lack of weight, could not be pushed any farther. "C" Company, led by Captain Morrison, reached the cross roads near Croix Barbée, but being isolated could not maintain its position and fell back to a tiny hamlet about one and a half miles from the Croix Barbée Road. Lieut. Henderson with "D" Company was constantly troubled by the lack of support on his left flank, but eventually

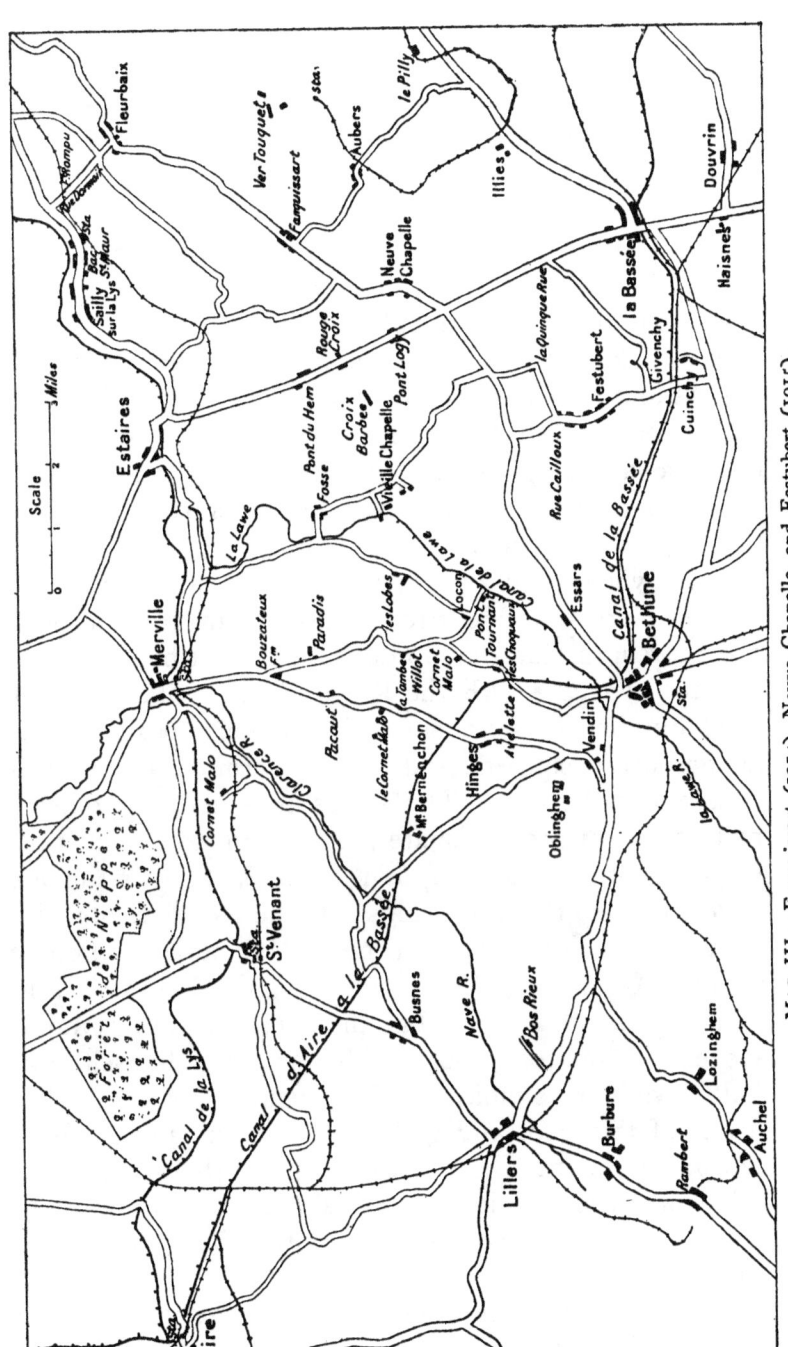

MAP III.—Fauquissart (1914), Neuve Chapelle, and Festubert (1915).

the Gordons arrived and "D" Company came into line with Captain Morrison's men. Both the leading companies suffered heavily during the advance, many officers being hit; Lieut. Hewitt and Lieut. Ker were killed and Captain Morrison, Lieuts. Henderson, Perry, Crockatt, McBraine, and Wilkinson were wounded. The day was unrelieved by any glint of sunshine and a steady drizzle soaked the earth. At one time several wounded officers and men were cooped up in a small tumble-down barn, upon which the rain rattled dismally while the door was alarmingly often punctured by bullets.

During the night the battalion was reformed and the supporting companies reinforced "C" and "D" near the village. No progress was possible on the 14th, for the Germans were strongly posted and obviously in great strength, and the Gordons on the left had not been able to keep pace with the Royal Scots. Standing out from our line in a salient the battalion's position was dangerously exposed and was intermittently shelled throughout the day. The losses in experienced officers had been disproportionately high, and on the 14th Captain Strutt and Captain Tanner, both wounded, were added to the list. This left the Royal Scots with none but subalterns, and on the 15th Captain G. Thorpe of the Argyll and Sutherland Highlanders was sent to take command. The battalion was visited by Major-General Hamilton who, rashly exposing himself, was killed while reconnoitring the enemy's position. The death of this cool and gallant officer was a great blow not merely to the Third Division but to the whole army. The only cheerful item on this unlucky day was the arrival of 2nd Lieut. Cowan with about 100 reinforcements.

General Smith-Dorrien still hoped that the advance could be carried on and he gave orders that it should be resumed on the 15th. The Royal Scots however had to wait until the Gordons came up on the left, and the latter succeeded in doing this before dawn, when the whole position was entrenched. Then Captain Thorpe, after conferring with the Gordons, thrust forward his left company covered by the fire of the Highlanders. When this movement was completed, our guns for forty-five minutes shelled various positions where parties of the enemy were suspected to be concealed, and at 2.15 P.M. the whole line moved forward. The attack was conducted with great skill, the men baffling the German marksmen by proceeding cautiously along the floors of the ditches, and with trifling losses the Royal Scots came to a row of cottages about 500 yards west of Rouge Croix. But at the far end of the houses the advance was swept by the enemy's machine-gun fire, which fell with deadly accuracy on the Gordons, and all progress was stopped. Darkness was creeping on apace and it was very doubtful if the Pont du Hem-Neuve Chapelle Road, the objective of the brigade, could be gained that day, though instructions had been received that it had to be reached. This meant that in difficult country the men would have to undertake a night operation, "A," "B," and "C" Companies carrying it through, with "D" in reserve. The objective was achieved with amazing ease. On a verbal order delivered by some unknown person, "A" and "B" Companies set off and arrived at the main road without encountering any opposition. Thus successfully ended the operation for the 15th October, "A" and "B" Companies manning the road with the remainder of the battalion in support.

General Smith-Dorrien's principal aim had been frustrated on the 13th October, when the wealthy city of Lille was captured by the Germans, but he had still the prospect of establishing a strong position if he could expel the enemy from La Bassée. His frontal assault against that point on the 12th had been defeated and he now essayed to win it by a flanking attack from the north. This was the movement in which the Third Division was engaged. The 8th Brigade, which had hitherto borne the brunt of the fighting, was relieved on the 16th and went into reserve. For a few more days the division drove the Boches from village to village and even obtained a footing on the important Aubers Spur, but this marked the full tide of the advance, for the foe was attacking in his turn. On the 17th the 2nd Royal Scots, now under the command of Major H. B. Dyson, marched into the town of Aubers, which was so vigorously shelled on the 18th that the battalion withdrew to a neighbouring field. On the following day the menacing sound of heavy firing continued all day and seemed to presage a hostile attack, which indeed was delivered on the 21st, but not against the Royal Scots. The Germans on the right, after nightfall, crept stealthily up to the position held by the Royal Irish Regiment at Le Pilly and practically annihilated that battalion, nothing remaining of it except the transport. This catastrophe necessitated a rearrangement of the line. The advanced positions were difficult to defend, and on the night of the 22nd/23rd October the Third Division took up a new line west of Aubers, the retirement being covered by the Royal Scots. The new position, which lay approximately 200 yards in front of the Fauquissart-Neuve Chapelle Road, had been marked by wisps of straw placed by the sappers of the Third Division, and on this line the Royal Scots dug in, with "C" and "B" Companies in the front line and the others in support; on their left were the 1st Gordons.

The withdrawal was effected just in time, for on

the night of the 24th/25th the Germans attempted a repetition of the tactics that had been successful at Le Pilly. A strong hostile patrol tapped our line in front of "C" Company, but the Royal Scots were alert and dispersed it by rifle fire. About two hours later another patrol, which must have been about 300 strong, silently crawled up to the trenches occupied by the Gordons and took the Highlanders by surprise. On this occasion at least cold steel was the only weapon employed. The Royal Scots awoke to what was happening through the babel of tongues that suddenly broke the stillness of the night, and at first thought that the Meerut (Indian) Division, on the left of the Gordons, was making a raid. Then came a message from the Highlanders that Boches were in their trenches, and the Royal Scots promptly brought up "A" and "D" Companies to form a flank towards the north; in addition Lieut. Robson-Scott brought the battalion's machine-guns and trained them along the road towards Fauquissart.

Then patrols of the Royal Scots, investigating in the direction of Fauquissart, came upon knots of Boches and Gordons attempting to take each other prisoner. Telephonic communication with the brigade was impossible, the wires having been cut by the enemy's artillery fire, so Major Dyson sent an orderly to report the situation to the 9th Brigade on the right. The Germans now endeavoured, in a somewhat faint-hearted fashion, to storm the trenches of the Royal Scots, but were kept back by the fire of "A" and "D" Companies, assisted by Lieut. Robson-Scott's machine-guns. The enemy made no other attack and returned to his lines. Strong patrols were immediately sent out to clear up the situation, and the Adjutant, Captain Combe, with Captain Strange of "A" Company, reconnoitred the trenches of the Gordons and found them unoccupied except by dead and wounded Highlanders and Germans. Meantime the 5th Northumberland Fusiliers had been sent up by the 9th Brigade, but the danger was over and no help was required. The 4th Middlesex then arrived from the 8th Brigade to take over the trenches of the Gordons and they occupied them without meeting any opposition. The soldierly conduct of the Royal Scots had in fact prevented the situation from ever becoming really critical and, while suffering few casualties themselves, they had inflicted severe punishment on the enemy.

Next day there was an aftermath of turbulence in the form of incessant rifle and gun fire. 2nd Lieut. R. C. Cowan was killed, 2nd Lieut. Robertson wounded, and several men killed and wounded. The alarms continued into the night, which was disturbed by gusts of rapid fire, a sign of taut nerves, and splashing rain added to the general discomfort. The soft earth, dissolving into mud, crept into the bolts of the rifles and prevented them from being fired. At this time four officers, Captains Royle, Sewell, Crackenthorpe, and Horne, from the Border Regiment joined the battalion. After the 25th the tension relaxed, and in the small hours of the 27th the Royal Scots were relieved by the Suffolks, but the relief did not connote rest. A determined German onset in the neighbourhood of Neuve Chapelle was rewarded by the capture of the village, which, since its position was of considerable tactical importance, General Smith-Dorrien was anxious to win back. The operation, which was to take place on the night of the 27th/28th, was to be undertaken by the Sikhs, who were to be supported by the 2nd Royal Scots. The latter accordingly marched towards Neuve Chapelle in the evening, but on the attack being postponed, they took shelter in a farm for the night. On the morning of the 28th, Major Dyson was summoned to H.Q. and given verbal orders to lead the Royal Scots against Neuve Chapelle, and at 1 P.M. he deployed his battalion for the assault. The church, the only prominent building in the village, was given as the objective. The operation was a difficult one, since before the Royal Scots could come to grips with the enemy, they had to pass through trenches occupied by the Northumberland Fusiliers. When the advance started, vicious rifle and machine-gun fire enfiladed the battalion from the left and the air was vibrant with the bursting of shrapnel, but the men held on with fine steadiness. One officer, Lieut. R. M. Snead-Cox, was killed during the advance. After passing the trenches of the Lincolns and the 5th Northumberland Fusiliers the Royal Scots received orders to stand fast, so they took refuge in some disused trenches. Some time later, instructions arrived for the battalion to withdraw to a position covering Neuve Chapelle at Pont Logy. This new position was particularly uncomfortable, as Pont Logy seemed to be a favourite target of the German gunners. The battalion H.Q. were established in a trench under a haystack which was frequently and accurately shelled; eventually the stack toppled over into the trench, but fortunately the H.Q. Staff had vacated it less than a minute before. Thrice during the night of the 29th/30th the enemy threatened an attack, but his infantry never moved out to the assault. Early on the 30th the Royal Scots were relieved by an Indian battalion, and under severe indirect fire marched to Baquerot Farm. Next day they returned to their old position near Fauquissart, where they relieved the Middlesex in the Gordons' old trenches.

During the latter part of October the fierce onslaught

against the II. Corps began to die down. The enemy had failed in his attempt to sever the French and the British Armies and the fury of battle had rolled northwards to Ypres. Yet till the close of the year the line of the II. Corps was constantly tested by the Germans, and the conditions under which our men existed beggared description. So inadequate were our reserves at the end of 1914 that a battalion seldom enjoyed more than a two days' rest at a stretch from the trenches. During November the 2nd Royal Scots held trenches at Fauquissart, Neuve Chapelle, Messines, and Wulverghem, and their longest respite occurred when they were out of the line from the 27th November till the 3rd December. The occasions when the battalion was out of the line in the early part of the month meant additional worry, for on the 11th November half of the unit was in support of the Seaforths and the remainder in support of the 19th Indian Brigade, and on the 13th the battalion was again in support of the Gharwal Rifles during an abortive attack by that battalion on a German trench. In November the troops rejoiced in the return of two of their original officers, Lieut.-Colonel Duncan and Captain Saward.

In such trenches as existed in 1914 it was impossible to stay with any degree of comfort, and the weather conditions were abominable. Trench warfare during the first winter of the war was more unpleasant and dangerous than it was in later years. The trenches were only taking shape, and once a man was dumped in them, there he had to remain until he was relieved. With practically no communication trenches in existence, the men were like prisoners, for normally there could be no daylight journeyings between the support and the front trenches, and a man had little more to do than sit in mud and water gazing at the sloppy breastwork in front of him. With movement so greatly restricted, it is not surprising that men sometimes fell into moods of profound despondency; they had no water except for drinking, they were limited to a diet of bully beef and bread or biscuits, and their chief companions were their own thoughts. Only at night, under showers of bullets and shells, was exercise with any freedom possible. On the conclusion of a spell of trench duty a man resembled a scarecrow, every furrow of his face filled with mud and a stubbly beard upon his chin.

In the low-lying country between La Bassée and the sea, the trenches were always seeping with water and floor-boards had not yet been introduced to ease the footing of the troops; a trench in which the water did not rise above the ankle was exceptional. Snow, sleet, drenching rains, and driving winds constantly assailed the tired frames of the men and made the winter of 1914 a nightmare even to recall. The route to the trenches lay usually through a sea of mud, and on the 16th November the 2nd Royal Scots on their way to Messines had to wade knee-deep through a morass under galling shell fire. The trenches, when reached, turned out to be, as the writer of the battalion diary bitterly remarked, "an impossible line of water-filled trenches with no communication"; but into these the troops had to go, since there was no other place to put them. Possibly the worst ordeal of this description was that experienced by the men of "D" Company, when, owing to the bursting of a field drain on the 6th December near their trenches at Kemmel, they had to stand for some hours waist-deep in filthy, slimy water. Everyone suffered acutely from cold; it was impossible to keep warm, and an attempt to alleviate the excessive chilliness by installing charcoal braziers was not wholly satisfactory, a man being asphyxiated on one occasion. Near the end of November there was keen frost; the thermometer fell well below freezing-point and the trenches were fringed with icicles. The severity of the conditions told so heavily on the men that the surprising thing was that the whole battalion had not to be sent *en masse* to hospital. The soldiers who in France and Flanders upheld their country's cause throughout the awful first winter of the war, showed a hardihood and stoic endurance that served to remind an age, which exulted in the triumph of the pen, that the glory of man is his strength.

The hardships occasioned by water, mud, and frost were augmented by the systematic shelling to which the Germans from their commanding positions subjected our lines. It was at this period that our supply of munitions caused some real misgiving and the number of shells to be fired by our guns was strictly limited. "The Germans have all the fun," was the bitter remark of an officer, when he noticed how puny was our artillery support compared with that of the enemy, and so far as regards shelling, the Boches for many weary months continued to have all the fun.

The hard-earned rest towards the close of November was greatly appreciated by the 2nd Royal Scots, and at Westoutre they seized the chance to have a thorough clean up. On the 30th November they were inspected by Major-General Haldane, who had succeeded Major-General Hamilton; he complimented them on the courage and endurance that they had shown throughout the campaign. Later in the day the battalion moved to Locre, where, on the 1st December, it was visited by the Corps Commander who cheered the troops considerably by telling them that the worst part of the war was probably over. On the 3rd December, the day fixed for the return of the battalion to the trenches, H.M. the King and H.R.H. the Prince of Wales passed through Locre, the Royal Scots lining the streets outside their billets. Fifty men under Major Dyson along with similar contingents from each of the battalions in the 8th Brigade were drawn up in a field, where they were inspected by His Majesty. Both the King and the Prince of Wales conversed for a short time with Lieut.-Colonel Duncan.

After this inspiring visit the Royal Scots moved up and took over in the neighbourhood of Kemmel such water-logged trenches that it was impossible for a man to remain dry. The battalion had been brought to this sector to take part in an operation of some importance, which was eventually carried out on the 14th December. It has the interest of being one of the first in which particular and detailed arrangements were made for a trench to trench attack; the preliminary bombardment and the allotment of limited objectives, the principal features of the "set" battle, were all in evidence on the 14th. On the previous evening the 2nd Royal Scots were at Kemmel, where the packs of the men were stored. "C" and "D" Companies were to lead the attack, which was to be launched at 7.45 A.M., with "B" in support and "A" in reserve; French troops were on the left and the 1st Gordons on the right.

At 3 A.M., on the 14th December, the Royal Scots marched through the Château grounds at Kemmel and entered the front-line trenches. The German lines at the Petit Bois were the objective. Owing to the scarcity of ammunition, the preliminary intensive bombardment was of short duration, only fifteen minutes, and at 7.45 our infantry left the trenches. The bombardment had not been heavy enough to shake the defenders, who met their assailants with a storm of rifle and machine-gun fire. "D" Company at the start sustained numerous casualties, for on account of a thick hedge, which lay immediately in front of the fire trenches, the only line of advance was by means of a gate, through which the men filed as rapidly as possible. In two lines "C" and "D" Companies charged with the bayonet with such impetuosity that they broke down the German defences, took prisoners one officer and 60 men and seized two machine-guns; "B" Company in support occupied the fire trenches vacated by "D" Company. The two lines of captured trenches were quickly consolidated, while a patrol from "D" Company exploring the wood discovered another line of hostile trenches unoccupied except by water. "C" Company's plucky attempt to make further progress was disastrous. Led by their intrepid young commander, Lieut. Robson-Scott, the men valiantly tried to move over the bullet-swept zone separating them from the enemy. Lieut. Robson-Scott, three times hit, nobly held on until he dropped, mortally wounded, just outside a German trench, and every effort to rescue him was baulked by the enemy's murderous fire.

The gallant charge cost the battalion many good officers and men. The commander of "D" Company, the Hon. H. L. Bruce, was shot dead while leading his men. Captain Crackenthorpe and 2nd Lieuts. Harrison-Wallace, Maltby, and Pecker were wounded and 2nd Lieut. E. F. Mackenzie[1] was missing. The casualties among other ranks amounted to nearly one hundred, "C" and "D" Companies suffering grievously. Unfortunately, the units on the flanks having been checked at the beginning of the attack, the Germans were able to concentrate on the heroic Lowlanders. Men faced death over and over again in noble efforts to succour wounded comrades, and Private H. H.

[1] He was killed.

Private H. H. ROBSON, V.C., 2nd Battalion, The Royal Scots.

[*To face p.* 74.

Robson particularly distinguished himself by crawling through the mud under heavy fire and bringing back a wounded N.C.O. In a second sally he was struck by a bullet on leaving his trench, but continued to crawl forward until a second wound rendered him completely helpless; it is pleasant to record that Private Robson was rescued later in the day and recovered from his injuries.

The magnificent feat performed by the battalion in capturing two lines of hostile trenches under unfavourable circumstances evoked the plaudits of the High Command. The German shelling during the day was stoically endured by the Royal Scots, who were extremely gratified when our own guns for fifteen minutes indulged in a bombardment sufficiently heavy to earn the description of "stupendous." In the early evening a battalion of the Suffolks came up and amid a hiss of bullets relieved the Royal Scots, who marched back by companies to Kemmel, where they remained in reserve during the night. Till the end of the year the battalion was in the Kemmel sector, and on the whole enjoyed a quieter time than any it had yet experienced.

Mount Kemmel was destined to be a familiar landmark to the 2nd Royal Scots for many weary weeks. On the 10th February 1915 the battalion took over trenches near Vierstraat, but the new neighbourhood was even more unpleasant than the one which it had left; the village was a heap of mouldering ruins and the surrounding area was littered with the decomposing corpses of French soldiers and of animals. Much hard work had to be done before the place was tolerable, but for many days a nauseating atmosphere of pollution seemed to linger about the district. From January till April there was more strenuous manual labour than fighting. The trenches, constantly dissolving into liquid mud, always required strengthening, and despite ceaseless bailing the floors could not be kept dry. Some protection against water was given to the men by the issue of gumboots on the 19th January, and a modicum of comfort was added when towards the end of February wooden floor-boards were brought up and fixed in the trenches. As regards shelling, the enemy had the advantage owing to his greater stores, but as far as sniping and patrolling were concerned, the 2nd Royal Scots were confident that they more than held their own. On the night of the 9th/10th March a patrol from "C" Company slipped along the Wytschæte road and shot a German sniper as he was making for his advanced post, and on the same evening four men of "D" Company crawled up to the Boche lines and threw hand grenades into them. On more than one occasion troubled nights were passed owing to the expectation of German attacks, but none were directed against the 2nd Royal Scots. Both in and out of the trenches the battalion maintained its high standard of discipline and continued to be cheerful in spite of a steady drain in casualties. Two officers, Captain H. D. Saward and Lieut. C. G. Hedderwick, were killed during this period of trench warfare.

CHAPTER V

THE 8TH, 1ST, AND 9TH BATTALIONS IN FRANCE
AND FLANDERS

November 1914 *to March* 1915

Situation at close of 1914. The Probability of Deadlock. Origin of Dardanelles Campaign. Arrival of 8th, 1st, and 9th Royal Scots in the West.

WHILE the B.E.F. was taking the first shock of the war, the youth of Great Britain was keenly striving to learn the soldier's craft. At the end of the first year, British opinion was not dissatisfied with the results of the fighting and even predicted extensive gains from the campaign of 1915. In spite of Lord Kitchener's solemn warning, people inclined to the belief that the struggle would soon be over. With the opposing armies already in close contact the issue could not be long deferred; the enemy having had his innings, it was now the turn of the Allies. The sudden check to the advance of the Allies at the Aisne and the fierce contest that ensued between Arras and the sea did give rise to some uneasiness, but on the whole people consoled themselves with the suggestion that our forward movement had been halted less by the power of the foe than by the lateness of the season. With the coming of spring, and the consequent hardening of the ground, our men would be able to drive the Germans back into their own country.

All this was illusion. Few realised that a situation unparalleled in the annals of war had arisen. By the end of 1914 two systems of garrisoned field fortifications faced each other from the Alps to the English Channel, and for the first time within the memory of man war had taken a course in which there were no flanks to be turned. The scope for strategy on the Western front was limited, hence those who were responsible for the prosecution of the war were greatly perplexed as to the best measures to be taken.

But the illusion served to keep the country in good humour. The young men in the Territorial and Kitchener battalions applied themselves to their military training with tremendous eagerness, and were desperately anxious that they should be given a chance of proving their mettle before the struggle came to an end. The whole country became a vast training camp, and military jargon formed the stock phrases of conversation. Scares of invasion were not infrequent, and in the early days of the war the performance of guard duties on the East coast was by no means perfunctory, but when the principles of military drill were grasped, as they quickly were by the intelligent men who now composed the army, those in uniform became restive and lived only for the day when they should be sent on active service. Their destination, it was taken for granted, should be France or Flanders.

But those responsible for the conduct of the war had other possibilities to consider. Before 1914 reached its stormy end, it was clear that in Western Europe matters were drifting towards a deadlock, and that neither side could expect to force a rapid decision in its favour without acquiring an irresistible preponderance in munitions and men. There was no magic wand to produce such superiority in a moment. Unlimited resources, unflagging industry, ceaseless training, and careful organisation, which were the only means by

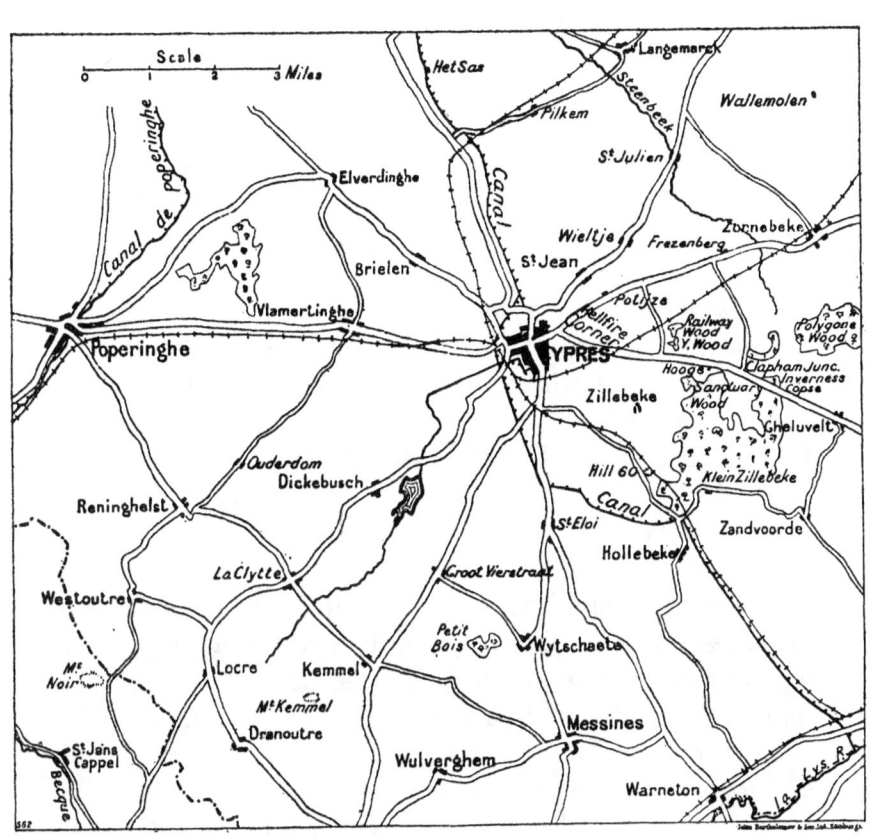

MAP IV.—The Salient, 1914 and 1915.
(*See also* large scale Map at end of volume.)

which the desired result could be obtained, required months if not years for their harvesting. Hence even before 1915 the British leaders began to turn their minds towards other theatres, where, while a force of sufficient strength to hold the Germans at bay was maintained in France, an operation might be undertaken that would yield fruitful results. The safety of the Western front remained the keystone of successful defence, but the difficulty was to determine the minimum of strength necessary to secure it. Once this was fixed, it remained to be settled how we should make use of our surplus men and resources.

Should they be sent to France and kept there in reserve in the hope that an opportunity would present itself for a break through, or should they be despatched to another theatre where the enemy's strength was less formidable? The British Commander in France, Sir John French, was of opinion that a speedy decision could not be looked for in the West, and this tended to direct the thoughts of men towards the East. In previous continental wars Great Britain had worn down her adversaries by blows shrewdly planted at the points where they were weakest. In these campaigns the navy had played a decisive part, and the happiest results had come through the co-operation of the British land and sea forces. Thus in the Seven Years' War had the French been expelled from America, and in the great war at the close of the eighteenth century, the power of Napoleon was sapped by the inability of his lieutenants to hold Spain against Wellington's army, co-operating with the navy which guarded its northern flank. In the present struggle an operation against the northern flank of the Germans along the coast of Flanders suggested itself as a possibility for naval and military co-operation, but though Sir John French was disposed to favour such a scheme, the French were opposed to it.

Outside the boundaries of France the Near East formed a tempting field of operations. One of the factors generally reckoned as favourable to the ultimate prospects of the Allies was the man power of Russia, but she was deplorably deficient in the war material necessary to equip her huge numbers for the field, and this deficiency had to be made good by the Allies. But every approach by land was cut off by Germany and Austria, and even the approaches by sea were limited. The only direct marine connection between Britain and Russia was through the port of Archangel on the White Sea, and this was barred by ice during the greater part of the year. Then, too, the land-locked Baltic was completely controlled by Germany. There remained the Mediterranean, but the only access of Russia to this great inland sea was through the narrow stretch of the Dardanelles, which, commanded by the forts and guns of Turkey, had been neutralised by an arrangement among the great powers. In short, there existed no satisfactory line of communication between Russia and the Western Allies, and the most obvious approach, by means of the Mediterranean, was controlled by Turkey.

Turkey however was induced by the ingenuity of German diplomacy to range itself among our foes, and the neutralisation agreement was rendered nugatory by the very fact of the war. The fertile brain of Mr Churchill at once grasped the importance of the Dardanelles, and he was convinced that if the Allies could secure command of this vital sea-route, our enemies would in a short time be compelled to sue for peace. As, during the Seven Years' War, France had been conquered in America, so Germany was now to be conquered in Gallipoli. The harvest of success certainly promised to be bountiful. The Russian Colossus would remain anæmic until, through the opening of a direct sea-route between East and West, it received an uninterrupted flow of arms and munitions under the shield of British sea power. If only to secure this end, an expedition would be worth while, but other results of at least equal importance would spring from success. Turkey would probably be driven from the war and the wavering Balkans would be won over to our side. Such triumphs would give an overwhelming advantage to the Allies and portend a speedy and favourable termination to hostilities. From these general considerations the Gallipoli campaign was evolved.

Unfortunately no definite unanimous agreement was reached as to the manner in which the 1915 campaign should be conducted. The lack of unity of command among the Western Allies left the field open for differences and finally led to compromise. With much of their country already under the heel of invaders, the French were not in the mood to acquiesce in plans that would entail large forces being despatched to other corners of Europe. No one was prepared to state the minimum of strength necessary to maintain the stability of the Western front. Sir John French across the Channel, and Lord Kitchener in London, were still nervous about the safety of France, and were inclined to regard with disquiet the diversion of any large body of troops from that country to any other area. In fact our commanders in France and Flanders believed that the security of the Western front could only be assured by sending to it the vast proportion of our trained men and resources. Thus the Gallipoli project was handicapped from the outset by the inability of the British as well as the French military leaders to decide what size of force was essential for the safety of the Western front.

During the first months of the war all reinforcements were of course sent to France. The next battalion of the Royal Scots to proceed overseas was the 8th, which had the distinction of being the first of the Scottish Territorial units to be employed on active service. The battalion, under Colonel Brook, left Haddington on the evening of the 2nd November and arrived at Southampton next morning. On the following day it embarked on the s.s. *Tintorette* and was taken to Havre, which was reached on the 5th. After a night's rest at a camp near the French port it marched down to the station and experienced its first railway journey in France. The train appeared to crawl along, and it was nearly 9 A.M. on the 7th when the battalion detrained at St Omer, whence it marched to billets at a small straggling village called Heuringhem. All the Territorial units sent out at this time were concentrated near St Omer for training, but so fit were the 8th Royal Scots that they were in the firing-line soon after their arrival. They earned the favourable notice of Sir John French. "The Queen's Westminsters and the 8th Royal Scots only embarked on the 1st and 4th of November respectively, yet their condition was so good that they were able to be sent to the front immediately after the H. A. C."[1]

After being inspected by General Chichester the battalion proceeded on the 10th to Wallon Cappel and thence on the 11th to Merris, where it was attached to Brig.-General Lawford's 22nd Brigade of the famous Seventh Division, commanded by Major-General Capper. Like all units that now came to France, the 8th Royal Scots were required to handle their picks and shovels

---

[1] See "1914," by Viscount French, p. 297.

before they used their rifles, and on the 15th November they were hard at work digging communication trenches. On the night of the 20th/21st November the battalion had its first experience of front-line duty. Henceforward the misery of that dreadful winter was its close companion, and this grim contact with the realities of war brought the overwhelming conviction to officers and men that the struggle would be both long and painful. But physical fitness and a firm belief in the righteousness of their country's cause enabled the will to exert its lordship over the flesh, and the 8th Royal Scots allowed no hardships to blunt the keen edge of their purpose.

Their first experience of action was on the 18th December, when the battalion covered with its fire an attack by the Royal Warwick Regiment on some German trenches near Touquet. The battalion bombers and a number of men of "A" Company, under Lieut. A. Burt, participated with the Warwicks in the attack, which took place at 4.30 P.M. But the enemy's defence was impregnable; Lieut. Burt was killed, while two of his men were wounded and missing. Private Cordery of the Royal Scots was absolutely reckless in his gallantry. Though the Germans continued to rain bullets across the corpse-strewn No-Man's-Land, he went out and brought in four wounded men, but on a fifth sally he was hit when near the hostile trenches and was taken prisoner. During the action the Boche gunners vigorously shelled the positions of the Royal Scots, ultimately setting fire to the farm at Touquet, where the battalion H.Q. and dressing station were established, but the damage done was happily limited to breastworks and trenches. Long and weary were the weeks spent by the 8th Royal Scots in the neighbourhood of Touquet, and the change that took place in March 1915, when the unit was moved south to Neuve Chapelle, was regarded with favour by all ranks.

The despatch of the 8th to France was closely followed by that of the 1st Battalion. Leaving India on the outbreak of war it arrived at Devonport on 16th November. Disembarkation was completed on the 19th, and the battalion proceeded to Winchester, where it joined the 81st Brigade of the Twenty-seventh Division, the other units in the brigade being the 2nd Gloucestershire Regiment, the 1st Argyll and Sutherland Highlanders, and the 2nd Cameron Highlanders. The brigade was commanded by Brig.-General Macfarlane and the division by Major-General T. D'O. Snow, C.B. Mobilisation was immediately commenced, and by the 16th December the Royal Scots were up to their war establishment.

On the 19th December the battalion, under Lieut.-Colonel D. A. Callender, C.M.G., marched from Winchester to Southampton where it embarked and sailed the same night in the *City of Dunkirk*, reaching Havre on the morning of the 20th, when it proceeded to a rest camp near the city. From Havre it was taken by train to Aire, where it was billeted in French barracks on the 22nd, and here the men enjoyed a rest and put in some useful training. On the 6th January they left their comfortable quarters and two days later arrived at Dickebusch, normally a pleasant rural district but now one of the dreariest spots in Flanders. The weather was miserable beyond description, and many of the men, fresh from the constant heat of India, suffered intensely from the cold. In the neighbourhood of this mud swamp, the battalion from January to March went through the monotonous and depressing routine of trench life—relieving, holding, being relieved, and resting

—with the attendant casualties,[1] sickness and working parties.

It was the misfortune of the unit, composed of first-rate professional soldiers, to have reached France at a date too late for it to demonstrate its skill in open warfare. Its arrival, however, allowed it to exchange civilities with the 2nd Battalion. The first meeting was on the 7th January, when the 1st marched past the billets of the 2nd at La Clytte on the way to Dickebusch. In the annals of the Regiment the occasion was notable, for this was only the second time since the Crimea that the two battalions had met. Afterwards, whenever chance favoured, there was an interchange of visits, and one day, the 3rd April, they were able to arrange a football match at Reninghelst which, after a good keen struggle, ended in a narrow victory for the 1st Royal Scots.

Early in the year the 81st Brigade was joined by the 9th Battalion, which for several months had been impatiently awaiting orders to proceed on active service; it was the first Edinburgh Territorial battalion to go to the front. As early as November 1914 it was under orders to join the B.E.F., but these had been cancelled, since it could not be spared from coast defence duties. At last, on the 23rd February, the unit left Edinburgh and sailing from Southampton in the *Inventor*, arrived at Havre on the 26th. The following morning it was sent "up the line" and attached to the 81st Brigade. Soon after its arrival the battalion was introduced to all the discomforts of trench warfare, and on the 14th March, when the Germans launched an attack against our line in the neighbourhood of St Eloi, "C" Company had

---

[1] Five officers, Captain A. F. Lumsden and Lieuts. G. M. V. Bidie, D. R. Currie, G. W. T. Chree, and H. M. W. Wilmer were wounded during this period.

the responsibility of holding the front-line trenches on the southern flank of the enemy's onslaught. The first company to suffer considerable losses was "D." On the 7th April it was in billets at Ypres when, at 8 A.M., a salvo of shells crashed into the building. The men had no chance to protect themselves, and in a short time the company had sustained more than fifty casualties. For a brief spell there was a harrowing scene of confusion, but above the pitiful groans of the wounded rose the commands of the N.C.Os., under whom those who had not been hit quickly rallied. The wounded were taken out and carried to safety. Though shaken by the suddenness of the shock, the unwavering fortitude of the men was worthy of the reputation of the battalion, which had already shown itself capable of sharing all the duties and vicissitudes of active service with the regular units with which it was now associated.

CHAPTER VI

THE SECOND BATTLE OF YPRES

March to July 1915

8th Royal Scots at Neuve Chapelle. Opening of Second Battle of Ypres. Adventures of 9th Royal Scots near St Jean. The 9th at Sanctuary Wood. Readjustment of British Line, 3rd to 4th May. 1st Royal Scots in Action. 1st and 9th Royal Scots at Armentières and the Somme. 8th Royal Scots at Festubert. Death of Lieut.-Colonel Brook. A V.C. Feat. (See Maps III. and IV.)

WITH the advent of spring in 1915 British hopes rose to soaring heights, when the news was published that on the 10th March our troops had won a great victory near Neuve Chapelle. But subsequent tidings stilled the shouts of triumph and spread uneasiness throughout the country. The British objective was the Aubers Spur, where the 2nd Royal Scots had been engaged in October 1914, and Sir John French hoped that if Lille could not be carried, our advance would at least be sufficient to cut off La Bassée. As in the case of the assault on the 14th December, the infantry attack was preceded by an intense artillery bombardment which was intended to rip the wire and flatten the defences of the Germans. On the right, where this purpose was fulfilled, the attack was successful and the troops in this sector even reached the slopes of the Aubers Spur, but on the left, where the German defences escaped serious damage, the assailants, in spite of the utmost gallantry, could not make progress. After fighting for two more days the British were forced to abandon their project.

The Seventh Division had the misfortune to be thrown into that part of the battle where a lengthy casualty list was the melancholy result of true heroism. The 8th Royal Scots, forming the left pivot of the division, were not called upon to advance, and their participation in the conflict was confined to standing fast in the trenches, which were intermittently bombarded by the enemy. Few things in war are more nerve-racking than the garrisoning of trenches in a battle area. For seventeen days at a stretch the Royal Scots were kept in the trenches, pounded daily by heavy shell fire, and during all that period were forced to use their meagre supplies of water for drinking purposes only. One officer only, 2nd Lieut. J. B. Greenshields, was wounded, but the casualties in other ranks were considerable.

The affair of Neuve Chapelle was followed in April by the furious fighting which left us in possession of Hill 60, and on the 22nd the Germans retaliated with an attack on Ypres, which remains one of the most memorable episodes of the war. On a fresh spring afternoon clouds of sea-green vapour, wafted by a favouring wind, drifted towards our lines and rolled over trenches, which were held by French Territorial soldiers. In a moment the garrison was gasping for breath and, completely unnerved by the unexpectedness of the attack, fled before a devilry more terrifying than the ordinary rough usages of war. Against the full blast of this gas attack men without any chemical protection were helpless, and the Germans advancing in the track of the poison wave found none but dead or dying in their path. The road to Ypres seemed open, but the enemy fortunately must have been unaware of the deadly potency of his experiment, and came forward with a hesitancy that allowed the Allies to send up fresh soldiers and save the town of Ypres. The immediate effect of the disaster was to uncover the left flank of the Canadians who held our line from Langemarck to Grafenstafel. The situation was saved by the devoted heroism of the troops of the Dominion, but succour had to be sent without delay if the line was to be held.

The 1st and 9th Royal Scots were involved in the battle, and the turn of fortune threw the more arduous task on the Territorials. About the beginning of April the 81st Brigade had taken over a section of trenches lying about 4 miles due east of Ypres. Under the relief arrangements in vogue in the Twenty-seventh Division, one battalion from each brigade remained in rest while the others garrisoned the line. The 1st Royal Scots from the 16th April occupied trenches that cut the Menin Road east of a wood known as Inverness Copse, and there they were fated to remain till the 4th May.

When the trouble was brewing the 9th Royal Scots were quartered in huts at Vlamertinghe, where they expected to have a four days' rest. There was no anticipation of anything untoward. Ypres, though bruised and torn, still held a goodly proportion of her citizens who chose to take the risks of the occasional shells that dropped into the streets. But on the morning of the 22nd shells were poured like a cascade into the doomed city, and in fear and panic the Belgian civilians streamed down the road leading to Poperinghe. At Vlamertinghe the Royal Scots watched the pall of smoke that lay over the town, and presently the eastern sky was bright with the flames of burning buildings. The pavé in the middle of the road clattered under the heels of the refugees, old men, women, and children, who, half-crazed with terror and despair, were staggering towards Poperinghe taking with them only such of their household goods as they could carry or wheel on hand-carts. Our men were struck silent by the sheer pitifulness of the spectacle. Then behind the civilians tramped unarmed groups of Turco soldiers with eyes wild with fright and the strain of suffering in their faces. These were the first victims of the poison gas that the Royal Scots saw.

Some terrible calamity had obviously happened, but no one knew precisely what it was. The wildest rumours were afloat; it was even whispered that the Boches were already in Ypres, and the men looked anxiously eastwards half expecting swarms of Germans to follow on the trail of the Turcos. The inactivity to which the battalion was condemned was depressing, but in the evening at 7 o'clock orders were received for the 9th to move forward and the men marched off in the direction of Ypres. To proceed along the road, which was an indescribable confusion of weeping refugees, ambulances, and vehicles of every kind, was all but impossible, and the battalion left the highway and progressed painfully along the railway line. After resting for some hours in a field it set off again, and about midnight reached the mass of smoke and flame that had been Ypres. Sinister crashes betokened that the town was still being shelled, and in Indian file, with 50 yards between platoons, the Royal Scots hurried through the inferno. Hugging the sides of the ruined houses, the troops by some miracle passed rapidly through the town and out by the Menin Gate without a casualty. All were too anxious to get out of the place to do more than glance at what was happening, and the impression that remained with the men was a baroque vision of leaping flame and inky blackness. On leaving the Menin Gate the 9th turned to the left and moved up to Potijze where, at 3 A.M. on the 23rd, they sheltered in a wood. Tired and weary, the men had as yet no idea of what they would be called on to accomplish; sleep was the one relief they craved, and thankfully they tucked themselves into some "one-man" scrapings that were popularly referred to as "graves."

Potijze Wood was intermittently shelled by the enemy, but the Royal Scots remained there unscathed until midday, when they were ordered to advance with the 2nd Duke of Cornwall's Light Infantry (of the 82nd Brigade), under the command of the C.O. of that battalion. Their function, though neither officers nor men were at the time aware of it, was to assist in filling up the gap on the left of the Canadians, which had been created by the retirement of the French Territorials. For this purpose the resting battalions of the Twenty-seventh Division were hurriedly formed into a brigade under the command of Colonel Turner of the Duke of Cornwall's Light Infantry. From Potijze Wood the Royal Scots, setting off in a north-easterly direction, struck the Ypres-St Julien Road near Wieltje, where the battalion split into two parts. Orders had been received by Lieut.-Colonel Blair at 12.30 P.M. for "A" and "B" Companies to proceed to St Julien and support the Canadians, while the remainder advanced under Colonel Turner. Accordingly, at Wieltje Lieut.-Colonel Blair with "A" and "B" Companies turned to the right and marched towards St Julien, while "C" and "D" Companies, under Major Taylor Cameron, went to the left and halted in the village of St Jean.

The chief adventures befell Major Cameron's party. It was noticed that the Duke of Cornwall's Light Infantry had commenced to deploy on the left front of the Royal Scots, and Major Cameron was not surprised when he was asked to send a company to extend the line on the left. "D" Company under Captain Green was given this task and Major Cameron accompanied the party. "C" Company under Captain Moncreiff was for a short time left on its own, but soon afterwards it was instructed to advance on the right of the Cornwalls and to conform to their movements. Accordingly the company moved forward in two waves of two platoons each. From the St Julien Road the direction of the advance was approximately north-westwards towards the Pilkem Ridge, to which from the road the ground, after a slight rise and a shallow valley, ascended. The ridges were really inconsiderable elevations, but in the low, flat country of Flanders they were of supreme tactical importance.

The advance was taken to the top of the rise, when the men looking across the slight dip towards Pilkem at last saw the Germans, evidently in force, on the farther ridge. Hearts quickened, for now it seemed matters were hastening towards a clash, since as soon as the Royal Scots topped the ridge they came under long range rifle and machine-gun fire and a number of them were hit. The men pluckily descended the slope until the whole line came to a halt near a road. Meantime "A" and "B" Companies under Lieut.-Colonel Blair had been recalled, and having been ordered to support the attack now made an opportune appearance, while Colonel Turner's brigade was halted. "A" Company moved up and reinforced Captain Moncreiff's company, while "B" extended the line to the right. Thus at this stage the disposition of the 9th Royal Scots from right to left was "B," "C," "A," the Cornwalls, and then "D" Company.

Knowing that the advance was about to be resumed,

all ranks began to make ready for it. "C" Company had come to a halt behind a hedge which was so thickly girt with barbed wire that men could not break through without great labour. Noticing this, Lieut. Lyon very coolly stood up and taking out his wire-cutters, began to make gaps. Machine-guns played on him, but without any sign of haste he proceeded with his task, never stopping until he had rendered the hedge penetrable. He had just finished when the Cornwalls rose up. This was the signal for the whole line to advance, and amid bullets throwing up clouds of dust from the soil the Royal Scots moved forward, until they found themselves in dead ground, where the German rifle and machine-gun fire could not touch them. There the men reformed, and in the gathering dusk the whole line swarmed up the far slope in the expectation of rounding off the day's work with a bayonet charge. But when they reached the ridge the enemy had vanished, and patrols despatched immediately could find no trace of him.

Colonel Turner's brigade had fulfilled its purpose. The mere sight of our men had scared the enemy, who was cautious and prudent to a fault. He failed to realise how wide was the gap prepared for him by the poison gas and allowed himself to be frightened away by a few troops, hastily formed together and sent to the post of danger. "It would appear," so ran the report of the Twenty-seventh Division with regard to this section of the line, "that only a small detachment, composed of men of various regiments, stood between the Germans and Ypres in this locality." Possibly the unlooked-for appearance of kilted soldiers in this part of the battlefield caused the enemy to believe that reinforcements from Britain had arrived; at any rate the fact remains that the opportune advance of a weak British brigade, by the moral effect it produced on the enemy, disposed him to caution, when audacity would have been his wisest course of action.

It was out of the question for our small force to push on indefinitely with no support on either flank. Burdened by their packs, in sore need of rest and food, the men had already done far more than normally they could have been expected to do. Accordingly, after consultations among the officers, the various units withdrew to the first ridge, where a line was formed. In the pitch-black night the retirement was carried out with some difficulty. Unprovided with guides, "B" and "C" Companies after reporting at Divisional H.Q. were ordered to return to their "graves" in Potijze Wood, and no sooner was this done than they had to leave them again and rejoin the rest of the battalion, the H.Q. of which were now at St Jean. "A" Company held the ridge, "C" and "D" were in support, and "B" in reserve. The worst trials of the battalion in this action were at an end. For nearly forty-eight hours many of the officers and men, galled with their packs, had not tasted food, but about midday on the 24th April they had full opportunity of appeasing their hunger. The one drawback in the position of the brigade was the gap between its right and the Canadians, but in the afternoon this was partly filled by "C" Company, and between it and the Canadians there was only a space of about 100 yards uncovered.

On the 25th April the battalion held the same line, which it had rendered much more secure by unflagging and skilful use of entrenching tools. Vigorous counter-attacks near St Julien by British troops at least prevented the enemy from pursuing his advance, and throughout the day a constant stream of ammunition wagons was wending its way towards St Julien. There was a good deal of heavy shelling to endure, and on the

24th the 9th Royal Scots had witnessed an impressive demonstration of the deadly effect of concentrated shell fire, when a Canadian battery of field-guns was wiped out in less than two minutes. The Medical Officer, Captain Bowie, and his staff displayed fine grit and bravery. Three times their dressing-station was fiercely shelled, but the work of succouring the wounded was carried on without interruption until Captain Bowie and Sergeant Milligan were both severely wounded. The 9th's most critical part in the battle came to an end early on the morning of the 27th April, when they were relieved by an English battalion and returned to Potijze Wood, where they remained in support during the rest of the day. At night the battalion, with the exception of "C" Company, proceeded to the more peaceful vicinity of Sanctuary Wood, while Captain Moncreiff and his men went to Polygon Wood in support of the 80th Brigade. Two days later "C" Company was restored to the battalion, and on the 29th the 9th Royal Scots at last rejoined the 81st Brigade in Sanctuary Wood. During the period from the 22nd April five officers, Captains Taylor, Bell, Green, Lieut. D. A. Ross Haddon, and 2nd Lieut. Richard had been hit—all wounded—while there were over one hundred casualties in other ranks.

Meantime the 1st Battalion had not met with any experiences beyond those generally associated with holding the line, save that its trenches were more violently and continuously shelled than usual, for the 81st Brigade happened to be holding a part of the front against which the enemy at first made no infantry attacks. The shelling was particularly severe on the 23rd, and enfilade fire from the left caused numerous losses among the 1st Royal Scots. This constant subjection to pitiless shell fire imposed an enormous strain on the men, but the discipline on which the battalion had just reason to pride itself was proof against any tendency to panic.

Our line in the north had been so dented that those trenches which we held throughout the first part of the battle now protruded in a narrow shell-exposed salient towards the German positions. It was both perilous and stupid to hold on to them, so every man that could be spared was set to dig a new line of trenches. The 9th Royal Scots plied their spades most industriously in Sanctuary Wood, but twice their work was interrupted by two excursions which they had to make across the Salient owing to the furious Boche attacks farther north. On the 2nd May they marched to Potijze but, not being required, returned in the evening to Sanctuary Wood; again on the following evening, according to instructions, they went to Railway Wood and, after occupying some trenches in that vicinity, marched to Frezenberg, but shortly after their arrival they were sent back to Sanctuary Wood, the stamina of the men having been severely taxed by what appeared to be a purposeless errand.[1]

The new line of trenches had been sufficiently prepared to allow the general withdrawal to be carried out on the night of the 3rd/4th May. South of the Menin Road the 1st Argyll and Sutherland Highlanders fell back through the 9th Royal Scots, who now found themselves in the front line, holding the trenches they had dug in Sanctuary Wood. The 1st Royal Scots were required to go back to a position astride the Menin Road, about 200 yards east of Hooge. At 10.30 P.M. half of the garrisons of each trench retired

[1] The march to Frezenberg was in the nature of a precaution. The evacuation of the nose of the Salient by the Twenty-eighth Division was in progress, and the 9th Royal Scots were sent up to support the line in the event of the enemy making an attack.

G

and at midnight the rest withdrew, while a few bold scouts under 2nd Lieut. Campbell remained to fire their rifles and send up Very Lights so that the enemy might not suspect what was taking place. "D" Company, which had been in battalion reserve, took over the front line, with "A" in support and the others in reserve. The scouts who were out all night returned at 4.30 A.M. with the news that the Germans had made their way to that point on the Menin Road known as Clapham Junction. On that same day the 1st Royal Scots were relieved by the 2nd Camerons and moved back to the neighbourhood of Vlamertinghe.

The alterations which we had been compelled to make brought our cordon round Ypres uncomfortably close to the city; at no point was it more than 3 miles away, and we had just sufficient elbow space to keep hold of the town. The Germans lost little time in following up our withdrawal, and the new line was soon tested by their shells. For some days, however, no assault by the enemy's infantry was attempted, and when the 7th May passed comparatively quietly it was felt that the crisis was over and that the new line was firmly established. But the peaceful interlude was due to the fact that the Germans were consolidating their gains and completing their preparations for a new drive.

On the 8th May the storm broke out anew. Our trenches north of the Menin Road were subjected to a terrific and fiendishly accurate bombardment, which smashed in the parapets and obliterated entire sections of the defenders. South of the Menin Road the shelling was not so continuous or relentless as it was farther north, but it caused several casualties among the 9th Royal Scots. Lieut. W. S. S. Lyon, who had distinguished himself by his cool daring on the 23rd April, was among the victims. The trenches were unstable and the parapets, as fast as the men built them up, simply crumbled away again beneath the enemy's fire, while the 9th Royal Scots were denied the satisfaction of beating back the Boche infantry, who never attacked the front of the battalion.

Violent blows however were directed against its neighbours, especially those on the left, but even the prodigal gallantry with which the German attacks were conducted could not overcome the stonewall resistance of the defence. The assault gathered fury on the 9th May, and the enemy in the afternoon succeeded in entering the churned-up ditch south of the Menin Road, which was all that remained of the trenches manned by the Gloucestershire Regiment. That battalion pluckily tried to win back the lost ground by a counter-attack, but the wood through which it had to advance had been transformed into an almost impenetrable abatis by the trees brought to earth by German shells; the spreading branches interlaced almost the entire area of the forest and the men were helpless in face of the murderous gusts of bullets, which scurried like storm-driven leaves along the few rides where alone easy progress was possible. Happily the lost trenches were not of vital importance, and the position of the 9th Royal Scots, on the right of the Gloucesters, was not seriously affected.

The enemy's assault on the cluster of woods lying south of the Menin Road was so menacing that the 1st Royal Scots on the 9th/10th May were again brought up to the line. The position of the 81st Brigade, forming a salient, inevitably exposed it to fierce attacks, especially on the left, and a message received by the 1st Royal Scots indicated that the line to the north of the battalion was sagging. Lieut.-Colonel Callender therefore ordered Captain Farquharson with "B" Company to proceed there and clear up the situation. He found that the unit on the left of the 1st Royal Scots had been literally blown from its trenches, and the Germans were on the point of occupying them when the Lowlanders appeared on the scene. Captain Farquharson with admirable decision ordered his men to charge, and the enemy flinching before the gleaming bayonets of the Royal Scots fled in disorder and confusion. The 1st Royal Scots were now neighbours of their Territorial comrades and together they stuck to their trenches without losing even a sap, till they were relieved on the night of the 22nd/23rd May. During this period the hostile shelling seldom slackened and both battalions sustained several losses[1]; they were the last units of the 81st Brigade to be relieved. They were not involved in the fighting caused by the last furious endeavour of the enemy to blast a path into Ypres on the 24th May. From this date the battle gradually ebbed away, but the fluttering set up by the Second Battle of Ypres never entirely subsided throughout 1915, and the Salient was till almost the end of the war the most nerve-racking region where men were required to soldier.

Pericles once remarked that the highest praise to be given to the women of Athens was to say nothing about them. The same might be said of the Quarter-

---

[1] Of the 1st Royal Scots, five officers (Captains L. S. Farquharson and E. J. F. Johnston, Lieuts. H. C. Pecker and N. M. Young, 2nd Lieut. W. A. Copeland) were killed, and four (Captain K. S. Robertson, Lieuts. G. M. V. Bidie and H. F. M. W. Wilmer, and 2nd Lieut. W. G. Cochrane) were wounded, while the casualties in other ranks totalled 332. In the 9th Royal Scots Lieut. W. S. S. Lyon and 2nd Lieut. A. H. Macfarlane were killed, and the losses in other ranks amounted to 93. Among the latter was Private James Pearson, one of the most skilful and lion-hearted threequarters who ever played for Watsonians and Scotland, and his death was mourned far beyond Edinburgh.

masters and the Transport Officers of the 1st and the 9th Royal Scots. The absence of references to them in the diaries is due to the fact that they continued to discharge their daily or rather nightly duties quietly and well. Seldom however has the ordinary routine been so beset by peril as at Ypres which, being the sole route available for our transport, was savagely shelled by the enemy every night. Officers and men openly made light of their adventures in running the gauntlet, but there was not one that did not harbour in his mind some personally dramatic moments.

The Second Battle of Ypres was the only engagement of note in which the Twenty-seventh Division took part in France. After a short rest it was sent to a less dangerous sector in our line near Armentières, which, compared with the Salient, seemed a veritable haven of peace. Casualties were few, but the victims of hostile shelling included 2nd Lieuts. J. Hobbs and R. T. M'Ivor of the 1st Royal Scots who were both killed. The only untoward incident that blemished the sojourn in the vicinity of Armentières happened to the 9th Royal Scots. At 11 P.M. on the night of the 10th June Captain Macdonald with Private Ross and Private Mathieson, having been instructed to place newspapers "tending to discourage the enemy" in the German wire, crawled across No-Man's-Land to do so. Unfortunately after the party had discharged its mission and inspected the hostile wire, a stray bullet hit Private Ross, who involuntarily gave a shout, and the Germans turning on a search-light observed and opened fire on the three Royal Scots. Private Mathieson managed to crawl into safety, but Captain Macdonald, unwilling to leave Private Ross whose leg was broken, bandaged the knee, then tried to hoist him on to his back. His self-sacrifice was ill-rewarded, for a patrol moved out and captured both officer and private. Apart from this episode life for both the Royal Scots battalions was uneventful. In September the division left the peaceful surroundings of Armentières and on taking over the sector near Fontaine Les Cappy earned the distinction of being the first British formation to campaign south of the Somme since the Battle of the Aisne. Here in October the 1st Battalion again entered the trenches, but the 9th was now to sever its connection with the Twenty-seventh Division; on the 26th November it was transferred to the 14th Brigade of the Fifth Division.

Generally, as far as the British were concerned, the spring and summer of 1915 were, with the exception of the fighting at Ypres, lacking in interest. The forces at the disposal of Sir John French were still inadequate for bold and ambitious enterprises. The Germans were firmly established in their defences in front of Lens and Lille, and it was largely the desire to win these two industrial centres that spurred the Allies to activity in May 1915. Attacks by the British and French were opened on the 9th May, and on the whole the latter met with the greater success, for they secured Carency and Souchez after herculean efforts and carried their line to the western slopes of the Vimy Ridge. The first British onset near Neuve Chapelle on the 9th May was a failure, and the second attempt on the 16th near Festubert, though it gained some ground, did not appreciably affect the enemy's position.

The Festubert offensive brought the 8th Royal Scots into action, though their participation was limited to suffering all the evils without experiencing any of the pleasures of war. Since the attack in March the battalion had been enjoying the pleasant side of campaigning; from the 14th to the 27th April it was

Lieut.-Colonel A. BROOK, V.D., 8th Battalion, The Royal Scots.

[*To face p.* 102.

out of the zone of bullets and shells at Estaires, where it won the warm friendship of the French peasants, who ever afterwards cherished a sincere attachment for our Scottish troops. Then followed a period of sore trial in the neighbourhood of Festubert. The German positions near Fromelles were to be assaulted by the Eighth Division supported by the Seventh. Accordingly on the night of the 8th/9th May, the 8th Royal Scots marched up to assembly trenches in reserve behind Rue Petillon. The operation failed, and the 8th Royal Scots with the 22nd Brigade moved back to bivouacs in the rear and on the 10th the battalion marched to Essars.

It was the second phase of the battle, begun on the 16th May, that brought hardships to the battalion. On the 15th, when arrangements were made for an attack by the Seventh Division to be delivered on the following day, the 22nd Brigade occupied a section of trenches astride the Rue Cailloux; the 8th Royal Scots were put into trenches in reserve. After a heavy cannonade the battle opened early on the 16th and our troops broke through the German first-line on a front of about 3000 yards, but the gain was hardly commensurate with our losses, and in the early afternoon the 8th Royal Scots were brought up to hold a section of the captured trenches. From this time until the night of the 18th shells rained almost incessantly on the battalion's position, but the men stuck unflinchingly to their posts and never gave ground. The losses were appallingly severe, over one hundred and eighty being killed or wounded. The most murderous experience was on the 18th, when shells dropped in the trenches like a storm of hailstones. The C.O., Lieut.-Colonel Brook, was mortally wounded, and the command of the battalion was assumed by Major Gemmill. For nearly thirty years Lieut.-

Colonel Brook had served with the Royal Scots, and no more gallant leader ever set foot in France; at his funeral the Brigade-General remarked about him: "I think Brook was the bravest man I ever knew"![1] But no troops in the world surpass the Scottish Lowlander in sheer endurance, and by steadfastly holding their trenches through a prolonged and critical part of the battle, the 8th Royal Scots provided an opportunity for fresh troops to continue the attack. In the late afternoon the 4th Guards Brigade passed across the left front of the battle, while nearly an hour later Canadian soldiers went through the Royal Scots and helped to carry forward the line to the cross roads at La Quinque Rue. Having finely accomplished its task the battalion was relieved after darkness and, greatly depleted in strength,[2] withdrew to Béthune.

Another quiet spell was the reward of the battalion for its part in the battle. After sampling billets at Béthune, Lillers, and Essars, it returned to the line on the 9th June, when it took over trenches at Givenchy. The ordinary routine of trench life was broken by a raid on the same night. Captain T. W. Watson with 20 men of "A" Company and Lieut. Martin with 15 bombers tried unsuccessfully to rush a crater in the enemy's lines. The attempt was repeated on the night of the 10th/11th, and when the raid was in progress the Germans suddenly exploded a mine. This caused the raiders to dash back to their trenches and it was discovered that Lieut. Martin was missing. Early next morning his body was seen lying on the German parapet, but a slight movement of the limbs indicated that he was still alive. Lance-

---

[1] See Weaver's *The Story of the Royal Scots*, page 222.

[2] The C.O. was the only officer killed, but ten (Major Todd, Captain Rowbotham, Lieuts. Kerr, Nicol, Wallace, and 2nd Lieuts. Blair, Bremner, Jamieson, Weir and Lindsay) were wounded, as was also the Medical Officer, Lieut. Smith.

Lance-Corporal W. ANGUS, V.C., and Lieutenant J. MARTIN, M.C.
8th Battalion, The Royal Scots.

[*To face p.* 104.

Corporal W. Angus,[1] who like Lieut. Martin belonged to the company of H.L.I. that had joined the battalion when it proceeded overseas, immediately volunteered to bring him in and paid no heed to the warning: "It's certain death, lad." One might indeed have thought it a lesser ordeal to make a 50 yards' dash across red-hot ploughshares than to traverse, as Lance-Corporal Angus had set himself to do, the 50 yards and more of earth under a rain of fire from German riflemen and machine-gunners. With a rope tied to his waist, he used the folds of the ground so cleverly that he reached Lieut. Martin without being spotted by the enemy. Seizing the officer by the shoulders, he raised him a little, but by this time the Germans must have seen or heard him, and from a range of less than 6 feet opened fire. Fortunately the parapet was high, forming a clear mark for the Royal Scots, who disturbed the enemy's aim by keeping up an accurate fire. A shower of bombs burst round the officer and his rescuer, and when the smoke cleared Lieut. Martin was seen to stagger to his feet and, directed by Lance-Corporal Angus, make a rush for our lines; he covered about 20 yards and then collapsed, but managed to crawl the rest of the distance. Lance-Corporal Angus, taking a slightly different route in order to distract the Boches, had at least a dozen bombs thrown at him, and he sustained about forty wounds before he succeeded in reaching safety. "No braver deed," wrote Lieut.-Colonel Gemmill, "was ever done in the history of the British Army."

Relieved on the 13th June the battalion returned to the trenches behind Festubert on the 20th, where it remained for ten days, when it was relieved by

[1] Lieut. Martin and Lance-Corporal Angus were fellow-citizens; they hailed from Carluke.

another battalion of the Royal Scots, the 11th, which had come to France with the Ninth (Scottish) Division. After this rest and another spell of holding trenches near Neuve Chapelle the unit, on the 27th, was selected as a pioneer battalion. Composed principally of miners, its work with pick and shovel had always been remarkably good, and for this reason it was now put through special training for the rôle in which it was destined to add lustre to a reputation that had already been solidly established.

CHAPTER VII

THE APPRENTICESHIP OF THE 11TH, 12TH, AND 13TH BATTALIONS

May to August 1915

The New Armies proceed to France. Benefits and Disadvantages of Trench Warfare.

DURING the opening half of 1915 the New Armies remained at home undergoing a course of intensive training. The vast majority of the soldiers composing these forces comprised the pick of the country's manhood; young men in the prime of their glorious physique, of whom many had already won a name in the world of sport, literature, and even politics, to whom honour meant more than a phrase and who in the pursuit of it scorned to count the cost. They were the chivalry of democracy. Most of them were too intelligent ever to become mere machines, and having grasped after a few months' training the principles of soldiering, they tended to grow stale, when week succeeded week in the performance of a routine that had become wearisome. But when orders to proceed overseas were received, dullness dropped from them like a discarded cloak, and they set out on their adventure with the confidence and enthusiasm of Crusaders.

So adaptable is human nature that the citizen soldiers accepted the abnormal as normal; soldiering which had been looked on as an interlude in 1914 was now regarded as a career. Over the mind the war exercised a sovereignty that tolerated no rival, and all pre-war conceptions of existence appeared fantastic and unreal images. The visions of quiet peace that occasionally visited a man rose in his mind like a succession of vignettes, which had no relation to actuality and simply represented an idyll that might be realised in the dim future. The human mind all over Europe was attuned to violence and destruction, and thought was despised as valueless unless it contributed to immediate action.

The first New Army battalions, having enjoyed the enormous advantage of being trained under the supervision of regular officers, in appearance and smartness challenged comparison with the best units of any army. In the vanguard of these citizen forces came three more battalions of the Royal Scots; the 11th and the 12th commanded respectively by Lieut.-Colonel R. C. Dundas and Lieut.-Colonel G. G. Loch, in the 27th Brigade of the Ninth (Scottish) Division; and the 13th, now commanded by Lieut.-Colonel H. MacLear, D.S.O., in the 45th Brigade of the Fifteenth (Scottish) Division. The Ninth Division, crossing the Channel at the beginning of May, was concentrated by the 15th round the town of St Omer, while the Fifteenth Division landed in France at the beginning of July.

It is a matter of doubt as to whether the Kitchener battalions were favoured or handicapped by the nature of the conditions that prevailed on their arrival at the Western front. The art of soldiery, which finds its greatest opportunities in open warfare, demands a high degree of discipline and training, and in these respects the first units of the New Armies, led by regular officers, had attained a standard so high that they might confidently have been trusted to sustain with credit under any circumstances the reputation of their regiments and the cause of their country. Yet there is always the risk of troops who have never been under fire being thrown into confusion when they enter their first battle, thus failing to do themselves justice, and one great advantage of trench warfare was that it furnished a ready means for breaking in raw troops.

This was the case even in 1915, when bursts of liveliness were not infrequent in the different parts of the British line, but it was not till the opening of the Battle of the Somme that it was realised that a division, which was garrisoning trenches outside the area of the offensive, was for the time "out of the war." The front trenches were, or came to be, not so much the firing line of a battle actually in progress as the outer ramparts of a gigantic fortification, where a man was exposed to hostile fire, the experience of which gradually gave him confidence in himself, until he gained mastery over his nerves and an assurance that in the din of battle he would acquit himself in a manner worthy of his battalion. And in other respects troops derived benefit from trench warfare. With a battalion in a definite sector the task of the Quartermaster in arranging for the regular delivery of rations was rendered easy, and in consequence the troops never lacked a plentiful supply of nourishing food. The periodic fixation of a unit in any place also facilitated the operation of other services, so that the sick and the wounded could always depend upon receiving prompt attention, while during a spell in the hinterland, baths, changes of clothing, and entertainments formed pleasant interludes in the ordinary round of training. Moreover, with the development of the trenches, it became possible to supply regularly to the men hot meals instead of bully beef and to introduce remedial measures for the prevention of frost-bite, which was widely prevalent throughout the first winter of the war.

It would, however, be a mistake to imagine that trenches were at any time a haven of rest or comfort. Cold, especially at night, hard toil, rats and vermin were the constant companions of the men, while salvos of shells and other obnoxious projectiles frequently brought danger to life and limb. The unwary or the careless, who exposed themselves too openly, were liable to be picked off by snipers. Existence was troglodytic and vision became myopic; all that a man could see was the twisting riband of sky that followed him round the snaking lines of trenches. In 1915 his view of the enemy's country was usually through a periscope and, never seeing a human antagonist, he identified the Germans with the sinuous parapet that concealed them from his eyes. In keeping with the distortion of life caused by the war, the landscape of No-Man's-Land, stark and desolate, mocked the soldier's dreams of peaceful, unviolated haunts, while the Germans' nightly pyrotechnic displays evoked more admiration than a sunrise or sunset. Gas scares were all too common, and a raucous carillonage at night frequently roused men from slumber to don hastily their chemicalised masks.

After a very brief experience of active service most soldiers could distinguish without difficulty the various projectiles used by the enemy: the trench mortar, the "whizzbang," the "woolly bear," the 4.2 and the 5.9 became all too familiar. The 4.2 was regarded as the most innocuous, though in a general bombardment it was very effective. Veterans professed to scoff at the trench mortar as a mere "wind up" weapon, for most of the types used, especially the enormous "rum jar," could be easily detected in their flight through the air. Sentries kept a look out for them and the blast of a whistle was a signal to their comrades, whose safety depended upon their ability to judge where the missile was likely to fall. A trench mortar exploded like the crack of doom; no dug-out was safe against it and as a weapon for the obliteration of trenches it had no superior. A smaller type of mortar than the "rum jar" was also used—the aerial torpedo, called usually "pine-apple" or "fish-tail"—which, though exploding with a less terrifying noise, probably secured more victims than the larger variety. The 5.9 however was the most feared of all the Boche weapons; even the hardiest soldier could never quite overcome a jelly-fish feeling in the stomach when he heard its sinister crash. It was, as a rule, fiendishly accurate and was equally destructive to life and entrenchments.

The most horrible of all trench ordeals was the violent bombardment, the precursor of a hostile raid, that broke with the suddenness of a thunderstorm upon a sector. At such times a trench was more a trap than a protection, and amid the rising and falling earth, when parapets collapsed under the impact of exploding projectiles, men were as impotent as puny wriggling insects. Those who felt intensely lived through æons of torture even during the briefest bombardment, and within a man a host of emotions waged tumultuous war, until consciousness was blurred by the savage din and he was only dimly aware of shrieks of human pain and the shrill screams of terrified rats. It was not surprising that when the inferno suddenly ceased, the survivors as a rule were too bemused to be capable of offering any resistance.

Mining, too, was not regarded with favour by the ordinary infantryman. The dread of being suddenly blown into the air kept men on edge, and a nervous sentry was always certain to hear sounds, which he would report to the officer on duty as "subterranean noises, probably German sappers mining." The craters formed by explosions were invariably centres of local activity and allowed little rest to the sentry groups stationed near them.

Of these general conditions the officers and men of the 11th, 12th, and 13th Royal Scots had gathered some knowledge from lectures before they set foot in France, and experience showed them that if the daily round was less full of peril it contained more discomfort and hard work than they had imagined. Sectors varied in danger and in importance. The Salient was in a class by itself; everything that could contribute to the misery of man was marshalled there in an unholy alliance—mud, gloom, shells, snipers, mines, and poison gas. The very name "Ypres" came to signify something evil; it was personified as a malevolent demon with an insatiable passion for human sacrifices. Till the end of 1917 the sector retained its sinister pre-eminence, and many who underwent the ordeal of its horrors averred that they would rather face the most murderous battle than hold the line in the Salient, of which no unit had a more comprehensive knowledge than the 2nd Royal Scots, who practically till the opening of the Battle of the Somme in 1916 were never away from it. The line at Festubert and Neuve Chapelle was also generally recognised as an unpleasant one to hold. In 1915 few places enjoyed a greater esteem for comparative safety than Armentières.

The social centres then were few and on that account were widely celebrated. Poperinghe was the natural rendezvous for the troops in the Salient, while Béthune and Bailleul were the centres of attraction for the more southerly parts of the line.

At the beginning of July 1915 the 11th and the 12th Royal Scots had their first experience of trench duty when they occupied the line near Festubert. The 13th

Royal Scots, a month later, took over a sector of trenches in front of Philosophe. The numerous returns that had to be rendered added new clichés to the military vocabulary of the men, for uniformity of phrase was as much a feature of army life as khaki tunics. This was due partly to the fact that the unusual physical exertion occasioned by war sought compensation in economy of speech and description, and partly to the advantage accruing from the general use of expressions with which everyone was familiar.

During their apprenticeship all battalions suffered casualties, the 11th being the most unfortunate as regards officers. In July Captain Bell and 2nd Lieuts. J. W. Brown and Winchester were wounded, and on the 14th August a farm occupied by "C" Company was savagely shelled, Major W. H. Evans and Lieut. J. A. H. Smith being killed and Lieut. Lemmey wounded. Near the end of the month two more officers, Captain Drysdale and 2nd Lieut. Cabon, were wounded. The 12th Royal Scots were more kindly treated by fortune, two officers only, Major Ritchie and Captain Mackenzie, being hit, the former of whom was able to remain on duty. In the 13th Royal Scots Lieut. A. E. Considine was wounded and Captain M. Halcrow was also slightly injured during August.

During this period of warfare the principal interest was bombing, fostered by the underground type of fighting that had developed in France, for it became the object of a man to kill his adversary without exposing himself. Many kinds of bombs were at first manufactured and numerous catapult appliances were employed in the trenches. In the early stages none were very effective, being frequently more dangerous to the person that used them than to the enemy against whom they were directed, but later both bombs and mortars were standardised,

H

instruction becoming uniform and results more certain. According to experts a bomb had an extensive danger area, and since it might put out of action quite a number of the enemy, while a bullet could account for only one, it was regarded at first with a feeling of considerable awe. But the effectiveness of the grenade was grossly exaggerated; in the so-called danger zone a man might stand for hours and never be hit by a fragment, and a bomb has even been known to explode in a shell-hole where half a dozen men were sheltering without inflicting a scratch on one. At the best it was only a siege weapon, undeniably very useful in trench-to-trench fighting and for clearing dug-outs, but for all-round purposes much inferior to the rifle and bayonet. This was not fully realised till 1916, when it became alarmingly apparent that the skill of British troops in handling the rifle had sensibly declined. For repelling an attack across the open the bomb was useless.

In 1915, however, this missile was at the height of its fame, and in every battalion bombing and trench-mortar officers with specially trained men were appointed. The bomb was the favourite weapon for patrol work, which gave the widest scope for individual initiative, and in this type of enterprise the New Army units showed much enthusiasm. The actual danger was less than the mental strain; the most terrifying foes of men, lying out in No-Man's-Land, were born of their own imagination:

> "Or in the night imagining some fear
> How easy is a bush supposed a bear!"

Fancy was most misleading when a man was serving his apprenticeship at the game; the dry rustle of wind through long grass heralded a German patrol, and when the darkness was cut by a flare of light a man felt as helpless and conspicuous as a broken-down motor-car at the West End of Princes Street, when the traffic is at its busiest. After a little experience, however, most men were inclined to be rather too careless than the reverse, but patrol encounters were rare. The 11th, 12th, and 13th Battalions never failed to send out patrols when they were in the line, and though no Germans were eliminated, the Royal Scots maintained a general supremacy in No-Man's-Land.

While these battalions were engaged in settling down in France, it was Gallipoli that chained the attention of the British people.

CHAPTER VIII

GALLIPOLI

February to June 1915

The Dardanelles Campaign. 5th Royal Scots proceed to the East. Description of Gallipoli. Plans of Sir Ian Hamilton. The Landing, 25th April. The Struggle for Achi Baba. Action of 28th April. Failure of the Attack. Trench Warfare sets in. Discomforts of Gallipoli. Events on night of 1st May. Action of 6th May. Attack of the 5th Royal Scots, 7th and 8th May. Situation after the Action. Attack of 4th June.

IT has been seen that in anticipation of the deadlock in France the British had considered the advisability of carrying out a subsidiary operation in the Dardanelles, but fears for the safety of the Western front might have led to the abandonment of the project, had it not been for the determination of Mr Churchill. He was convinced that success in this quarter would be the shortest and least costly road to a victorious peace, and his reasoning sufficed to win the consent of his colleagues for an operation to be undertaken by the navy. Lord Kitchener's assent was given under the impression that in the event of failure the enterprise could be abandoned by Britain without discredit; it might be regarded as a feint which, if it came off, would yield a rich harvest and if unsuccessful, would not result in serious loss. Between the 18th February and the 18th March 1915 the navy made several futile attempts to force a passage through the narrow straits that divide Europe from Asia, and the conviction was driven home that a purely naval expedition could not hope to be

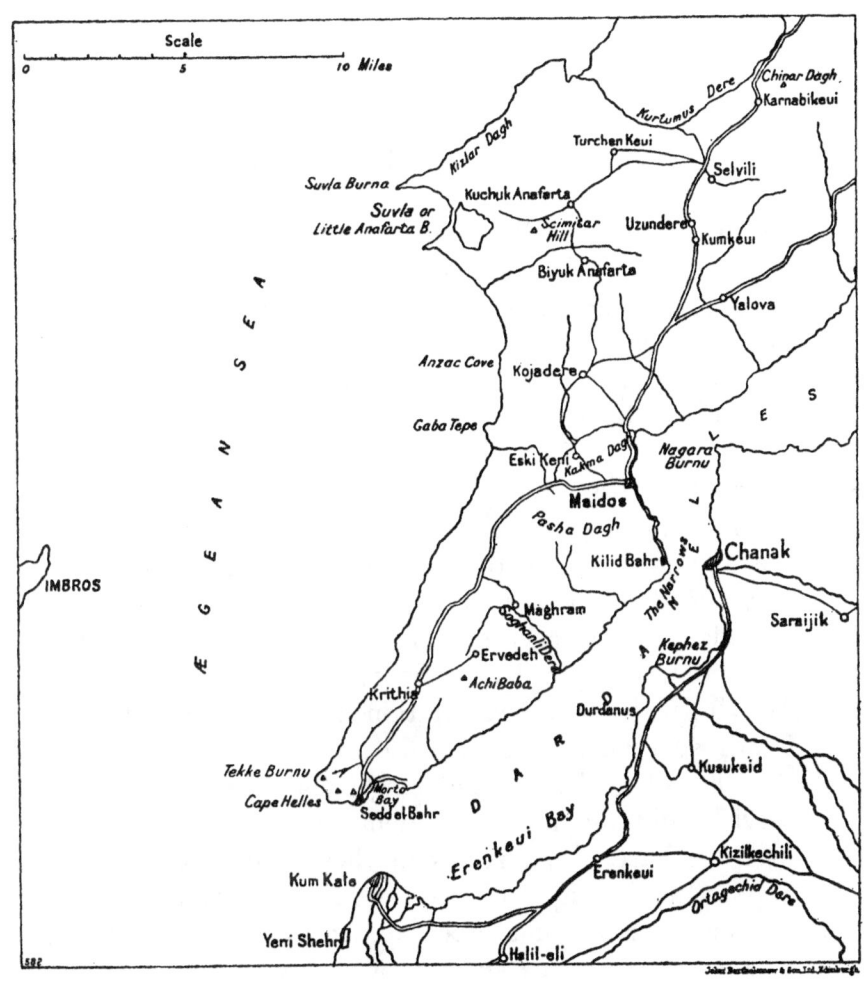

MAP V.—Gallipoli.
(*See also* large scale Map at end of volume.)

successful, unless the high ground on the European side of the Dardanelles was picketed by a military force.

There was no thought now of withdrawing from the enterprise. Lord Kitchener, with his intimate knowledge of the East, knew infinitely better than most men how profoundly success or failure influences the Oriental mind, and now he realised that submission to defeat at the Dardanelles would gravely prejudice the prestige of Britain in Asia. We were now in the critical position of being tied to a task that could not be abandoned without disaster, and we were therefore compelled to back up the navy with an army, which was to facilitate the forcing of the strait by occupying the southern portion of the Gallipoli peninsula. Hence in the summer of 1915 events in France were dwarfed by our operations in the Near East.

The military force, 70,000 strong, was placed under the command of General Sir Ian Hamilton. It included only one division of first-line troops, the Twenty-ninth, to which was attached one of the Edinburgh Territorial battalions, the 5th Royal Scots. At the beginning of March this battalion was stationed at Portobello, whence it was sent on the 10th to Leamington where it joined the 88th Brigade. It had long been waiting for active service, and the men, impatient and keen as all were in those early days, regarded these orders to proceed abroad as a high favour. After a short stay at Leamington, the unit proceeded to Avonmouth, where, on the 20th, it embarked on two vessels, the *Caledonia* and the *Melville*. In their billets at Edinburgh the men with the roominess of civilian life in their minds had often complained of being crowded; but all their previous experiences faded into insignificance compared with the restrictions on a troopship. The interior of the boat was fitted for hammocks, so closely strung together that a man had barely the space in which he stood for dressing. During the day the hammocks were fastened in bundles on hooks in order that as much space as possible should be available for exercise.

The first few days of the voyage were none too pleasant for any one, but brought unmitigated misery to those afflicted by sea-sickness. The daily routine seldom varied. Every morning at 10 o'clock there was a strict inspection of the ship, after which some time was devoted to physical training. The real pleasure of the voyage began when the Mediterranean was reached, and the men, few of whom had previously left the shores of the United Kingdom, showed the liveliest interest in the strange scenery. The staple of conversation was naturally the ship's destination, of which no one had been informed, but after a stop at Malta, where those of the men who had the opportunity vastly enjoyed stretching their legs on shore, it became known that the ship was bound for Alexandria, and there the Royal Scots arrived on 2nd April. A few days on land were spent in training to harden the men after their long voyage, and on the 6th April the battalion re-embarked on seven small vessels, reaching on the 13th the spacious Bay of Mudros. The sky was a forest of masts, for at Lemnos was mustered the expedition with which we were to attempt the capture of Gallipoli. There followed a week of hard training for the Royal Scots; daily the men, in full kit, had practice in descending and ascending rope ladders leading from the ships into lighters. As far as the troops were concerned this training was necessary and devoid of danger, but the officers were always uneasy lest a rifle should become disengaged and drop to the bottom of the Mediterranean. The reproof which such a mishap earned caused the unfortunate officer to recall with a feeling of painful guilt the story of the nail that led to the loss of a kingdom. There was no doubt now as to where the 5th Royal Scots were to be employed, for it was an open secret that Gallipoli was their goal.

Gallipoli is the narrow peninsula which forms the northern shore of the Dardanelles and stretches out from the mainland mass of Europe in a south-westerly direction. The most southerly portion, with which we were principally concerned, presents on the map the shape of a roughly-made shoe with the toe at Cape Helles, the heel at Kilid Bahr, and the ankle at Maidos. We had to capture the heel to enable the navy to force the passage of the Dardanelles, for at this point where Kilid Bahr is fronted by Chanak on the Asiatic shore, the straits are at their narrowest. The whole of the shoe is naturally severed from the remainder of the peninsula by a valley, the Kilid plain, which runs from sea to sea between two ridges; thus the portion which we hoped to capture had the advantage of being a self-contained block of land. The position at Kilid Bahr is immensely strong, having on the north the rampart of the Kakma Dagh Ridge and on the south the Kilid Bahr Plateau, a natural bastion extending from Kilid Bahr to the Soghanli Dere. The plateau even extends south from this point in another ridge, which, crowned by Achi Baba and stretching right across the peninsula, forms the obvious outpost for the main plateau. Near this ridge the peninsula is about 5 miles broad but shrinks to a mile and a half near the toe.

Rugged and scrub-covered, running out like a wedge between the Ægean and the Dardanelles, Gallipoli viewed from the deck of a troopship gracefully breaks and sets off the blue of sky and sea. It has none of the stark plainness of Aden, nor does it strike the spectator as a natural fortress like Gibraltar. In itself it has no particular attraction, for it is not a land flowing with milk and honey and is peopled by rough and illiterate peasants who, herded together in squalid hovels, scrape a bare subsistence from niggardly soil. In the southern portion there is not a decent road and the ridges are clothed with thick scrub similar to our native gorse, which afforded ideal cover for the Turkish machine-gunners and riflemen. Though from the sea one has no impression of any towering height, the ground nevertheless rises abruptly from the water, leaving here and there a few patches of narrow foreshore.

The British plan was to capture the Kilid Bahr Plateau by a *coup de main*, and with a view to this possibility, landing places had to be selected within easy striking distance of the plateau. It was obviously important to carry Achi Baba as soon as possible, because it provided the best observation post for artillery fire in the southern part of the peninsula, and with observers posted on its summit the fire from our big warships could be efficiently directed and controlled. The landing places had, therefore, to be close to Achi Baba. The Turks, warned by our abortive naval attack in the spring, had been industriously fortifying their chief positions and had posted guards to watch the most tempting landing places, but they did not know precisely where we intended to effect a landing. Consequently we hoped to deceive the enemy by feints at various points, while the main landings were being carried out near the toe of the peninsula.

Unfortunately a less satisfactory spot for achieving a landing could hardly be imagined, but this very fact gave us the chance of taking the Turks by surprise. The very few places where there was comparatively easy access from the narrow foreshore to the escarpment of the crumbling cliff had already been thickly wired by the enemy, who had even dug entrenchments across the very tip of the toe from the Old Castle above the village known as Sedd El Bahr. Achi Baba Ridge, near the sea, runs down from three heights, Hills 114, 138, and 141, to the capes of Tekke Burnu, Helles, and Sedd El Bahr. It was clearly prudent for the British to select for landing a point that would enable them to outflank the Turkish fortifications near Sedd El Bahr. Morto Bay on the south, and Gully Beach on the north seemed admirably suited for this purpose, but their very obviousness was a drawback; the latter was so strongly guarded as to be virtually impregnable, while the former, in addition to being open to gun fire from the Turkish batteries on the Asiatic coast, was so encumbered with reefs that the naval authorities considered it unfavourable for the disembarkation of a big force. It was therefore decided to leave Gully Beach alone and make a subsidiary landing at Morto Bay in order to protect the flank of the chief attack. Similar subsidiary landings were arranged for the northern shore of the toe, one at X Beach south of Gully Beach, and another at Y Beach more than a mile north of Gully Beach. Another diversion was to be provided by the Australian and New Zealand Army Corps (Anzac) which was to force a landing still farther north near Gaba Tepe.

Our main forces were to land at the beaches known as V and W, right on the toe of the peninsula. It was with the latter, the more northerly one, that the 5th Royal Scots were concerned. At this point a belt of soft powdery sand, varying in breadth from 15 to 40 feet and covering an expanse of nearly 350 yards, stands in a natural amphitheatre flanked at each extremity by inaccessible cliffs, but between these natural walls the ground ascends

W. BEACH, CAPE HELLES.
(Sketch by the late 2nd Lieut. W. B. Hislop, 5th Battalion, The Royal Scots.)

gradually from a series of sand-dunes to the lower terraces of the Achi Baba Ridge. It could not be expected that this tempting foreshore would be neglected by the enemy, and it was in fact freely strewn with barbed wire, some of which was washed by the sea, while, hidden in the sand-dunes, Turkish riflemen could pick off our men as they scrambled through the obstacles on the sand. In addition trenches had been dug on the higher ground above the sand-hills, and the crest was further protected by redoubts in the rear of the beach. These had to be captured if the crest of the cliffs was to be held, and no force could have any sense of security until Hill 114, which frowned down on the northern portion of the toe, had been seized. V beach, to the south, was even more formidable in character, and it was here that an old collier, the *River Clyde*, was used for running a bridge to the shore. The whole enterprise was of a desperate nature, and without the assistance of the heavy bombardment to be delivered by the fleet could not have had any prospect of success.

As was to be expected from the composition of the Twenty-ninth Division, the Royal Scots were kept in reserve; the best chance of overcoming the manifold difficulties of the landing lay in using the experienced soldiers of the line battalions. Thus the 5th Royal Scots, to their chagrin, were compelled to accept the rôle of spectators during the first phase of the memorable enterprise which opened on the 25th April. They left Mudros Bay on the 24th and arrived near Cape Helles before dawn broke. Two companies, "W" and "X," were with Lieut.-Colonel Wilson and his staff on the s.s. *Dongola;* the other two companies, "Y" under Captain MacIntosh and "Z" under Captain Mure, were deputed to help with the loading of stores and ammunition after the landing had been effected.

At the break of day on the 25th the guns from every ship opened a terrific bombardment on Gallipoli. From the decks of the *Dongola* which lay close to the gigantic *Queen Elizabeth* the Royal Scots witnessed its effects. The morning broke in one of those beautiful pearl-misty dawns with which the East delights the eye of man, but none on the *Dongola* had any thoughts to spare for the charms of nature. Every discharge of the warships' guns made the transport reel, while officers and men gazed with fixed eyes on the clouds of thick dust thrown up by the explosion of the shells on the crumbling cliffs. It was impossible to detect clearly what was taking place, but soon the satisfactory tidings came that the 1st Lancashire Fusiliers had forced a landing at W beach without undue trouble. Shortly after 9 A.M., under Lieut.-Colonel Wilson, "W" and "X" Companies were transferred from the *Dongola* to a lighter, which approached as close to the shore as it could.

Over the remaining stretch of water the men were taken in rowing-boats almost on to the shore. The 5th Royal Scots now experienced their baptism of fire. The beach, though in our hands, was under full view from Achi Baba whence the Turks straddled the shore with artillery and rifle fire. Gouts of water and sand rose skywards, but without a casualty the 5th crossed the sand and found cover in the natural folds of the ground. From a hard blue sky the sun was shining with intense heat, but the men ignoring discomfort worked assiduously during the afternoon, scraping trenches which they occupied during the evening of the 25th.

But though all who took part in the Battle of the Landings acquitted themselves like paladins, our position on the evening of the 25th was less satisfactory than we had hoped. The diversionary landing of the Anzacs at Gaba Tepe had been a brilliant success, and our troops had also secured a footing on the peninsula at all the beaches except V, between Sedd El Bahr and Cape Helles. But this last, where blood had been shed freely and fruitlessly to form a bridge from the *River Clyde* to the shore, was the most important of all, and our failure to secure a lodgment at this point frustrated the scheme of carrying Achi Baba by a rush. The night was noisy with the sound of continuous firing and no man was able to snatch more than a few moments of sleep. During the brief interlude when dusk was merging into darkness, rendered more intense by rain, parties of Turkish infantry tested our lines, but each counter-attack was foiled with the help of accurate fire from our warships. On the next day the different landings were firmly consolidated except that at Y, which we abandoned, and the troops gloriously defying death earned the admiration of the Turks by forcing the landing at V Beach and carrying the ruins of Sedd El Bahr and Hill 141. It was surprising that our men, laden with full equipment, had actually accomplished as much as they had, but even so, performance lagged far behind programme. At the close of the 26th our army, which we had hoped to see on the Krithia-Achi Baba Ridge, only occupied the preliminary covering positions along the crest line of the cliffs. All the men were so thoroughly worn out by the strenuous fighting and mental strain of the last two days that the grand attack had to be postponed till the 28th, so that the Turks were given three additional days to strengthen their defences.

Still in reserve on the 26th, the 5th Royal Scots had an opportunity to take stock of the ground leading up to Achi Baba. The most cursory examination revealed its manifold advantages for defence. Viewed from the sea the land stretching from Cape Helles to Achi Baba appeared as if it were under complete observation from the ships, but closer inspection showed that from Cape Helles and Sedd El Bahr the ground dipped into a broad shallow trough of which every yard could be seen by the Turks on Achi Baba, but which was screened from the eyes of our sailors by the crest of the cliffs, so that once our troops left the crest-line they could not be seen from the sea. From the trough the ground rose in a steady slope to the crown of the Krithia-Achi Baba Ridge. Numerous tree-filled hollows, where snipers and machine-gunners found convenient lairs, puckered the slope, which was furrowed by several watercourses known as nullahs. Except for a trickle of yellowish water these courses in the summer were dry gorges and the two largest of them, the Krithia and Achi Baba nullahs, falling down from the ridge in a direction roughly parallel to the coasts, broke through the crest-line and entered the sea at Morto Bay. These natural furrows seemed to provide a protected approach up the ridge, but they were of unequal depth and the Turks so sited their machine-guns that almost the whole length of the nullahs was commanded by their fire. Between these waterways ran the indifferent road which formed the normal means of communication between Sedd El Bahr and the village of Krithia, situated almost a mile due west of Achi Baba. Among the buildings of Krithia the Turks had a choice of a number of excellent observation posts and they used the woodwork of the houses to strengthen their dug-outs and trenches. Under German supervision the Turks had not been content to rely on the bounty of nature and had skilfully fortified their positions with strong earthworks plentifully protected by thick barbed wire. Before our landing was effected, we were aware that the enemy had entrenched the summit of the ridge between Krithia and

Achi Baba, but we were unpleasantly surprised to discover that he had spread his defences into the central depression, where it was almost impossible for us to detect the precise location of his trenches.

The British attack on the slope was fixed for the morning of the 28th April and the requisite preliminary movements were carried out during the afternoon of the 27th. After dark Lieut.-Colonel Wilson and "W" and "X" Companies of the 5th Royal Scots advanced for a distance of nearly two miles, without encountering any opposition, and dug themselves in. A brigade of French troops was landed at V Beach and came up into line on the right of the Twenty-ninth Division. The whole line of the Allies was thus swung right across the toe of the peninsula almost half-way to Krithia, the Turks, temporarily demoralised by the shattering fire from our warships, having withdrawn to their main defences in front of the village. This was our principal objective for the 28th, the attack being carried out by the French and the Twenty-ninth Division. The 88th Brigade was next to the French.

Covered by a heavy bombardment from the sea our attack was launched at 8 A.M. In spite of the intensity of our shelling the Turkish riflemen and machine-gunners were not silenced and with stoical steadiness continued to harass our infantry with a galling fire, which owing to the contour of the ground swept down the whole depth of the attacking force. Thus the 5th Royal Scots, in reserve, had advanced but a short distance when men began to drop. The Adjutant, Captain Hepburn, who was almost worshipped by the men and who was regarded by the whole battalion as the model of the perfect soldier, was suddenly struck down by a Turkish bullet, while he was directing the movements of the Royal Scots. In face of a veritable rain of lead the advance was doggedly carried onwards. Hostile counter-attacks were thwarted by the fire from our battleships and by noon the British and the French were only one mile from Krithia. Almost imperceptibly the 5th Royal Scots had now squeezed themselves into the firing-line, and with great dash heroically played their part in the last harassing stages of the advance. Weighed down by their heavy kits and exhausted by the strain and fatigue of four hours' continuous fighting and scrambling, the troops of the Allies were too spent to push on farther. The glorious effort had failed and Krithia remained beyond our grasp.

We could not even keep the line our troops had reached, for the whole of the communications were open to the fire of the Turkish guns, which commanded almost every inch of ground down to and including the beaches. There had been delay in landing the units that were responsible for maintaining supplies, and the British leaders were greatly perturbed about the ammunition and other stores which would be necessary for the troops in the firing-line. These considerations led to a slight withdrawal of our line; the right now rested on the hill just beyond Morto Bay, whence it was continued to the sea near Y Beach, our most advanced point being more than a mile from Krithia. Along this position, while a glorious sunset cast a strange radiance over the dappled battlefield, all the troops weary and worn commenced to dig in.

The losses of the 5th Royal Scots had been disquietingly high and many officers had fallen. Major MacDonald, the Second-in-Command, Lieuts. Sillars, A. Kerr, Green, and Sutherland were wounded; Lieuts. W. B. Hislop and W. E. Turnbull were missing, and it was ascertained later that they had been killed. Death also removed an outstanding personality in

R.S.M. F. J. Bailey, who during the period of training had given invaluable service to the battalion. Lieut.-Colonel Wilson was among the wounded; he was shot in the arm by a sniper at the critical moment when our line was retiring, and it was only by rare presence of mind and the favour of fortune that he did not fall into the hands of the Turks. Making his way through the gathering darkness in the direction of the sea, he encountered more than one Turk and once on reaching a path he walked into a party of wounded Moslems, who however made no effort to take him prisoner. More nerve-racking still was his experience in suddenly running into a hostile patrol. His only safety was in flight, and he managed to find refuge in a scrub-covered hole where he spent the remainder of the night. In the morning he had another adventure with a sniper, and having escaped by shamming death he at last succeeded in reaching our lines. The survivors of the 5th Royal Scots, now under Captain McLagan, passed uneasily a weary night and in spite of intense exhaustion few were able to sleep. All were relieved when darkness gradually vanished and the sun, bursting through the virginal mists, rose in a sky of sapphire blue and lit up the scarred slopes of the battlefield. Many figures lay motionless among the scrub, and the earth in the heat of the day began to suspire the unmistakable odour of death.

Meantime "Y" and "Z" Companies of the 5th had not been idle; they had been employed transferring stores from the ships to the beaches and much of their work was carried on under intermittent machine-gun and shell fire. Captain Mure's party landed at V Beach, where the bridge of boats leading from the *River Clyde* to the shore was still thickly smeared with the blood of those who had lost their lives in helping to build it. The willing labour soon wrought an amazing transformation in the appearance of the beaches, depots of stores of all descriptions being established in every suitable corner. In this highly necessary work Captain Mure and Captain MacIntosh with their companies were engaged till the first week of May.

After the battle of the 28th April only the incurable optimist could dream of Achi Baba being carried by a *coup de main*. The possibility of surprise had vanished after the landings were effected and a deadlock had arisen in Gallipoli which was to prove even more murderous than that in France. The Turkish positions could only be carried bit by bit, and for such a struggle the resources of Sir Ian Hamilton, especially in artillery, were utterly inadequate. Delay was necessary to allow plans to be excogitated and preparations made for a series of set attacks, but it contributed even more to the advantage of the enemy. The hostile position was within easy reach of reinforcements and every day enabled the foe to add new trenches and fortifications. Thus with the lapse of time the enemy tended to become relatively stronger, while we grew relatively weaker. At the same time it was clearly recognised that the enterprise could not be given up without a damaging blow being dealt to our prestige throughout the East. The chance remark of one of the officers of the 5th Royal Scots, "We have properly let ourselves in for it," concisely summed up the situation. Additional forces were urgently required but these, it seemed, could not be sent from France and had to be taken from Egypt, against which, however, the Turks could not make any serious attack so long as they were threatened in Gallipoli. From the land of the Pharaohs Sir Ian Hamilton could draw the East Lancashire Territorial Division and a Mounted Division under General Peyton. Meantime he received a welcome reinforcement in a brigade of Indian troops, and he was further cheered by the promise of a new French division.

Pick and shovel soon work a marvellous change on the appearance of a landscape, and by this time an elaborate trench system was spreading right across the toe of Gallipoli. Fire, support, and reserve trenches, with a few communication trenches running down to the beaches, marked off the ground in response to the labours of the men, at once protecting and circumscribing the routes from the coast to the firing line. The creation of this system was a tragic confession of our failure. Along with it developed the routine duties connected with the holding of trenches, and in many respects the discomforts of Gallipoli far exceeded those of France. The one abiding solace was the beauty of Eastern scenery: Gallipoli at its worst was never monotonously drab like the low country of Flanders. The play of sun on land and sea drew many pictures of varied hues. Most dawns were a sheer delight to the eye. Shot by the gleaming streak of the rising sun, the soft morning mists floating over Achi Baba transformed the ridge into a delicate pastel of purple film. The illusion of dawn lasted for a few brief moments and the sun, dissolving the mists, poured over land and water a fierce white light in which every object stood out with tyrannic definiteness. The hard blue of the sea and sky contrasted sharply with the rich amber of the earth. Then towards evening when the sun began its westering career, a glorious chromatic architecture unfolded itself to the vision until the colours faded away, leaving the earth in inky blackness under the jewelled canopy of the Eastern sky.

But the tragedy of war is that it makes so many

demands on the body that all zest is lost for the things of the mind. The material discomforts of Gallipoli were so aggressive that they occupied the greater part of a man's time and attention. Unceasing noise and the chance of death or wounds, being inseparable from war, were accepted as inevitable and were indeed accounted as trifling in comparison with the tortures fashioned by nature. The lightest breeze whispering through the scrub wafted a noisome stench that usurped the air; dust and sand, flitting everywhere, settled on the furrows of the forehead, filled the ears, nose, and mouth, and polluted the food; flies and mosquitoes, so densely massed that they appeared to form a wavering shadow round a man's head, explored every exposed part of his body; the sunshine in the middle hours of the day fell over the earth like a burning sheet, while the chill of night stiffened the limbs and defied sleep. An insatiable thirst tormented the soldier in his first experience of the East, but after a week the craving fortunately diminished. The water-supply was for some time a source of anxiety, for since every drop had to be fetched by sea, its use had to be strictly regulated. The water being primarily required for cooking and slaking the thirst, little of it could be spared for personal cleanliness. The troops at the beaches could wash in the Mediterranean, but those in the trenches suffered acute tortures; the excessive perspiration due to the scorching heat caused their garments to squirm into their flesh, and the consequent scrofulous misery was to many the most intolerable ordeal of the war.

A constant turmoil brooded over Gallipoli, and the men were never away from the booming of the guns. No region between the firing line and the sea was absolutely secure from Turkish bullets. In many respects it was safer to be in the front line than in reserve or at rest, since the snipers, the chief foe of the men in the firing line, could be thwarted by the exercise of reasonable caution, while the heaviest shelling invariably fell on the rear trenches and on the so-called rest camps near the beaches. During the early days of the enterprise there were snipers within our lines; our advances had swept over these men concealed as they were by scrub, and many forays, in some of which parties of the 5th Royal Scots took part, had to be organised before they were all accounted for.

On the night of the 1st May the Turks made a great effort to drive our troops into the sea. When the attack took place, the 5th Royal Scots were in reserve trenches astride the Achi Baba nullah and the Krithia Road. A violent bombardment suddenly burst on our trenches and the communications with the beaches, and at 10 P.M. the hostile infantry charged with such desperation that in several places they broke right through our lines. One of these breaks was in front of the 5th Royal Scots, but Captain McLagan restored the situation by a brilliant counter-attack. Leaping forward with fixed bayonets the Royal Scots bore down on the Turks, who scattered and fled before the onset. A few held on and were shot down by the men of Lieut. Swinton Paterson's platoon, which captured 4 prisoners (3 Germans and a Turk, all officers). Desperate and confused fighting raged till 3 A.M., when, having learned that the hostile stroke had been parried, Sir Ian Hamilton issued orders for the whole line to advance. Though tired and weary the men responded splendidly and swept the Turks in disorder before them, but they were too spent to penetrate the prepared positions of the enemy and fell back to their original trenches. The charge of the Royal Scots, observed by the Brig.-General, who in his admiration ejaculated: " By Gad! Well done, the Royal Scots!" was one of the most notable exploits during that night of fighting and proved beyond dispute that the Territorials were worthy comrades of the magnificent units of the incomparable Twenty-ninth Division. The loss of the battalion in officers was disproportionately heavy; Captain D. A. Lindsay, Captain W. Russell, and Lieut. J. M. Smith were killed in the dashing assault which established the reputation of the 5th Royal Scots.

On the following nights, the 2nd and 3rd May, other attacks were made by the enemy chiefly against the French, but these were repulsed with considerable loss to the foe. Except for the troublesome shelling the 5th were not affected. These repeated counter-attacks proved so costly to the enemy that General Von Sanders, who directed the Turkish defence, gave up the idea of expelling the Allies from the peninsula and issued instructions for the troops to devote their energies to strengthening the Krithia-Achi Baba position. Our observers reported that the Turks were busy with pick and spade, and it became apparent that if they were not interrupted this position would soon be made almost impregnable. Sir Ian Hamilton was still waiting for reinforcements and he had not yet received an adequate supply of ammunition, but he felt that the enemy could not be allowed to carry on his work without hindrance. Accordingly an attack was planned to be delivered on the 6th May at 11 A.M.

Meantime all the 5th Royal Scots were at last gathered together; on the 2nd May "Z" Company under Captain Mure rejoined, and two days later "Y" Company came up under Captain McIntosh, who took over the command of the battalion from Captain

McLagan. The Royal Scots occupied the firing line on the 2nd May with "W" and "X" Companies in the front trenches. On Monday, the 3rd, there was a short truce for burying the dead, since many of the corpses were decomposing rapidly under the torrid heat of the Gallipoli sun, and this unpleasant but necessary task was performed by the men of "Z" Company, for it is the general rule in the army to give the unsavoury jobs to the new arrivals. The assault on the 6th, though some ground was gained, did not achieve its main object. The 5th Royal Scots, who had been sent to rest trenches on the 4th May, were not involved until the attack had broken down. The battalion, taking advantage of the cover provided by the numerous dips and dry ravines, concentrated at the point where a tributary nullah falls into the Krithia nullah, a place which later became known as Clapham Junction. About 8 P.M. word was received for the Royal Scots to move forward, and amid a scurry of bullets the battalion took over the firing line between the Krithia Road and the Achi Baba nullah, the men having to dig with feverish haste to provide protection against the ceaseless rifle and machine-gun fire. The acting C.O., Captain McIntosh, one of the best loved officers in the battalion, was killed and Lieut. Gibson wounded. Captain McLagan again assumed command and chose Captain Mure as his Adjutant. The most useful progress on the 6th was made by the French on the right, where they strengthened their hold on the Kereves Ridge.

The turn of the Royal Scots came next morning and the date is memorable in the annals of the battalion, because it was the first occasion on which they attacked as a unit. Their numbers, however, had been sadly reduced and totalled little more than 600. The fighting on the 7th was part of the Battle of Krithia, though it will always be known to the 5th Royal Scots as the Battle of Fir Tree Wood, because this was the objective, in front of Krithia, which they were ordered to capture. The attack was launched at 10 A.M., but though the men sacrificed themselves unsparingly, they could not carry the wood. At one time they did penetrate it and to its southern fringe they clung on all day, while shells and bullets battered the wood, but after darkness the survivors of the battalion were reluctantly compelled to withdraw from the death-trap. Other units essayed the task with no better result. The 5th Royal Scots had now dwindled to little more than two companies and the battle deprived the battalion of other four experienced officers: Lieut. J. B. Aitchison was killed, and Captain J. W. S. Wilson, Lieuts. T. Darling and J. S. Geddes were wounded.

The most obvious cause of the frustration of our attacks on the 6th and 7th May was a cunningly concealed redoubt near Y Beach, from which the Turks poured an almost impenetrable enfilade fire along the left of our lines. Y Beach was actually in our possession on the 25th April and the abandonment of it proved little short of calamitous, for on the 8th, as on the two previous days, this redoubt remained our worst obstacle. A gallant attack by New Zealanders failed to carry it, and in desperation Sir Ian Hamilton sent up Australians from his reserve and a general advance was made along the whole line at 5 P.M. Even the magnificent charge of the Australians did not turn the fight in our favour and the battered ruins of Krithia still eluded our grasp. The 5th Royal Scots on this occasion were in support of the South Wales Borderers, but these were so few in number that the Royal Scots soon became merged in the firing line. "X" Company, now led by

Lieut. Swinton Paterson, seized a slight ridge in Fir Tree Wood, but Lieut. Paterson was wounded and his men were too few to keep all the ground gained against the superior numbers and the merciless machine-gun fire of the Turks, and the wood was once more abandoned to the enemy. In the fighting Captain F. W. Robertson was also wounded. Our desperate assault had only advanced our line a few hundred yards. From a mile up the western bank of the Kereves nullah the line extended right across the peninsula to the Zighin Dere opposite Y Beach, where our position took a sharp bend backwards owing to the Turkish redoubt established on the bluff near Y Beach.

The terrible truth could no longer be evaded that our plans for the capture of the Krithia-Achi Baba Ridge had collapsed like a house of cards. Throughout the campaign the enemy had exhibited the traditional tenacity that had always distinguished him in defence. A leaden gloom weighed down the British leaders, for none knew better than they how vital it was that the enterprise, once taken in hand, should be pushed to a victorious conclusion. Reinforcements were urgently required, but the Gallipoli leaders had no confidence that they would obtain the number that the situation demanded. More power, especially in artillery, was essential, but in this respect the needs of the Gallipoli force were never satisfactorily met, and time and again our troops had to advance against an adversary whose fire had not been wholly subdued by our bombardments.

The positions reached by our men on the 8th May were rapidly consolidated and woven into the trench system that stretched to the beaches. All were now accustomed to a semi-troglodytic existence. Keeping to the sunken corridors they baffled the sniper, secured comparative shelter from shell fire and in a measure protection from the scorching rays of the sun, and where the trenches had not to be kept clear for traffic a top covering helped to relieve a man from the attentions of obnoxious flies.

The fighting in Gallipoli made Achi Baba a familiar name at home; it represented the desire of our dreams and its capture would be hailed as the token of success. Similarly, a year later, we measured progress at the Somme in relation to Bapaume. Tidings of the exploits of the 5th Royal Scots drifted to Scotland, and the reputation won by the battalion was reflected in the manner in which the citizens of Edinburgh emphasised the connection of the unit with the Capital. But the folks at home would have been shocked had they realised how woefully the ranks of the 5th Royal Scots had been thinned by two weeks' fighting. More than half the original force had disappeared through death, wounds, or disease. After the fighting on the 8th May the battalion was withdrawn from the front line and till the night of the 16th/17th lived partly in rest and partly in reserve trenches. The rest trenches were all near the beaches, but the relaxation that they afforded was not what troops withdrawn from the line in France enjoyed. The beaches were spasmodically shelled by the Turks, and so long as a man was on the peninsula he could never get away from the din and discomfort of the battlefield. Repetition of sound, however, produces after a time a kind of mental deafness, and men could sleep under any noise short of a violent bombardment. But the wretched conditions of life, the stench that brooded over the hot earth, the sand and dust that defiled every mouthful of food and water, and the parasitic insects that tortured the skin, all combined to sap the health of the men and many succumbed to dysentery. But in the 5th Royal Scots the spirit triumphed over the weakness of the body, and it was through sheer grit and determination of will rather than any feeling of physical fitness that the men so heroically responded to the exhortations of their officers.

The position of the Allies on Gallipoli was improved on the night of the 12th May, when, by a brilliant feat, the Gurkhas captured the bluff at Y Beach. After this success our hold on the toe of the peninsula could be regarded as reasonably secure, and Sir Ian Hamilton had time to excogitate fresh plans for the campaign. Meantime he had not wholly abandoned hope of demoralising the Turks by a series of set attacks and of forcing them to retire from the Krithia-Achi Baba Ridge. But during the rest of May the 5th Royal Scots were not involved in the fighting.

From the 17th till the 26th a sojourn in the front line passed uneventfully and there were few casualties, but these included two officers: Lieut. C. J. Kemp was killed the night before the battalion was relieved, while Captain McLagan was hit by a bullet in the leg, the command of the battalion devolving on Captain Mure. Soon afterwards Lieut.-Colonel Wilson returned, looking far from well but having lost none of his keenness and enthusiasm. The Royal Scots now went to rest trenches near the ruins of a house, which, owing to the colour of its roof, was called Pink Farm, and here they were joined by their first reinforcements from Edinburgh, brought out by Lieut. Wetherall. Including officers the draft amounted to only 100, and was far from meeting the needs of the battalion, and new officers had to be obtained from other units. Bad luck as regards loss of officers continued to dog the Royal Scots, Lieut. R. Maule being killed by shrapnel on the 31st May. Working parties were provided nightly, and some of these were sent to Clapham Junction, which was earning a sinister reputation as one of the most dangerous spots on the peninsula. The gully formed by the junction of nullahs at this point afforded the sort of cover of which soldiers are naturally tempted to take advantage, and the Turks, well aware of this, sited machine-guns so that their fire swept right down the gully, which at times seemed to hum like a bee-hive.

Sir Ian Hamilton had now prepared his scheme for the continuation of the attack, and a general assault was arranged for the 4th June. The 5th Royal Scots were not to be at first engaged in the battle, but on the night of the 3rd June they were ordered to move up to the front line and occupy a position covering the front of the division. The battalion found itself back near Fir Tree Wood, of evil memory. The journey from Pink Farm to the front line had to be made in single file and the unit set out on its pilgrimage at sundown. These night marches were invariably unpleasant, for a man, burdened with full kit, always had the impression that the sides of the trenches were pressing in on him so that he could only move with difficulty. Dawn had crept in before all the 5th Royal Scots were in their allotted positions, and the leading company, under Captain W. Grant, who had come to the battalion from the Highland Light Infantry, would have been taken into the Turkish lines by a guide who had lost his way, had not the rosy light of early morn unfolded the danger of the position to Captain Grant, who curtly dismissed the guide and took his men into their proper place just as the sun rose clear in the sky.

The battle opened at 8 A.M. with a cannonade that lasted till 11.40, when there was a sudden lull and our troops made a demonstration as if to leave the trenches. This *ruse de guerre* achieved its aim, for the Turks, expecting an attack, rushed up fresh troops to the battle trenches whereupon our bombardment was resumed. The infantry advance followed at noon and the Royal Scots moving up behind the waves of the attack occupied the old front-line trench. The chief difficulty, as far as they were concerned, was to keep touch with the company on their right, at which flank Lieut. Wetherall was in charge. He had no trouble in finding the trench for the defence of which he was responsible, but he had been led to believe that he would have another unit on his flank. The trench, however, which his men occupied, faded away on the right into open country, and after an anxious personal reconnaissance, Lieut. Wetherall found that the unit, with which he was to maintain liaison, lay in a trench nearly 300 yards to the right and at least 50 yards behind the position of the Royal Scots. Under these circumstances liaison had to be secured by means of sentry posts. The losses of the Royal Scots were heavier than their passive rôle in the battle would have led one to expect, and this was almost entirely due to the fact that the enemy's bullets raked practically the whole of the trench zone.

The Allies were so far successful on the 4th June that hope soared once again and it was thought that the stubborn defence of the Turks was on the verge of giving way. The most satisfactory tidings were that the French had removed a great obstacle to our advance by capturing the work known as Haricot Redoubt on the Kereves Ridge; but our optimism was short-lived, for on the 5th the Turks recovered the Redoubt, from which they could enfilade our lines right across the peninsula. Thus our gains from the battle dwindled to a few hundred yards of ground. Furious counter-attacks were delivered by the enemy against our new trenches, but none of these broke through to the Royal Scots. On the 7th the battalion took over the new front line in the evening and remained there till the night of the 9th June, when it had the pleasure of being taken right down to the beach. Here indeed there was not much more safety than elsewhere, but the Mediterranean was at the disposal of the men for bathing, and a complete wash was the supreme height of luxury that Gallipoli afforded.

CHAPTER IX

GALLIPOLI

May to August 1915

The Fifty-second Division. Railway Disaster at Gretna. 4th Royal Scots in a collision at sea. Successful counter-attack by 5th Royal Scots on 19th June. Arrangements for 28th June. Action of 4th Royal Scots. Action of 7th Royal Scots. Effect of the success of 4th and 7th Royal Scots. Action of 5th Royal Scots. Share of 4th and 7th Royal Scots in operation of 12th July. The Suvla Bay project.

THE reinforcements for Gallipoli, sent out from home towards the end of May, included the Fifty-second Lowland Division, composed entirely of Scottish units. This division was known as the 2nd (from August 1914 1/2nd) Lowland Division and only received its new designation, under which it was to become widely known, on the 11th May 1915. Two battalions of the Royal Scots, the first lines of the 4th and the 7th, were in March 1915 relieved from their duties on coast defence and attached to the 156th Brigade, which was commanded by Brig.-General W. Scott-Moncrieff. The first intention of the authorities was evidently to send the division to the Western front, since the troops were issued with long Lee-Enfield rifles with the breeches strengthened to enable them to fire the Mark VII ammunition, but the awkward turn of events in Gallipoli led to its being despatched to the East. The old rifles were accordingly re-issued, and the numerous stores supplied to the division included sun helmets. In high spirits the troops entrained for the embarkation ports, but the start of the 156th Brigade was saddened by an appalling railway accident near Gretna, as a result of which the 7th Royal Scots were reduced to two companies. The battalion left Larbert in two trains on the 22nd May, the first containing Lieut.-Colonel Peebles with the H.Q. Staff and "A" and "D" Companies commanded by Major J. D. L. Hamilton and Captain A. M. Mitchell respectively. This train, running into some empty carriages of a local train, which through an oversight had been left on the main line, was overturned and wrecked. Horror was heaped on horror when a few seconds later an express, travelling northwards, crashed into the wreckage of the troop train, setting it on fire; three officers, twenty-nine N.C.Os. and one hundred and eighty-two men were killed or burned to death, and as many more suffered from injuries and shock. The officers killed, Major J. D. L. Hamilton, Captain J. M. Mitchell, and Lieut. C. R. Salvesen, were all well-known personalities in the 7th and had for years been associated with the work of the battalion. Among the injured were Lieuts. W. R. Kermack, J. A. Young, J. C. Bell, and 2nd Lieuts. N. G. Salvesen and T. G. Clark. The survivors, totalling only seven officers and fifty-seven other ranks, were taken by train from Carlisle to Liverpool. Deep and heart-felt grief spread over the port of Leith and the city of Edinburgh when the harrowing tidings of the ghastly tragedy were received.

It was a crippling blow to the 7th. Officers and men of such first-rate quality as those who had been lost at Gretna can never be replaced at a moment's notice. The effect of the shock was so overwhelming that when the survivors arrived in Liverpool all the N.C.Os. and men were sent home. The other Companies, "B" and "C," carried by a train which made a *détour* round the scene of the disaster, had already reached Liverpool, and Lieut.-Colonel Peebles embarked with only half a

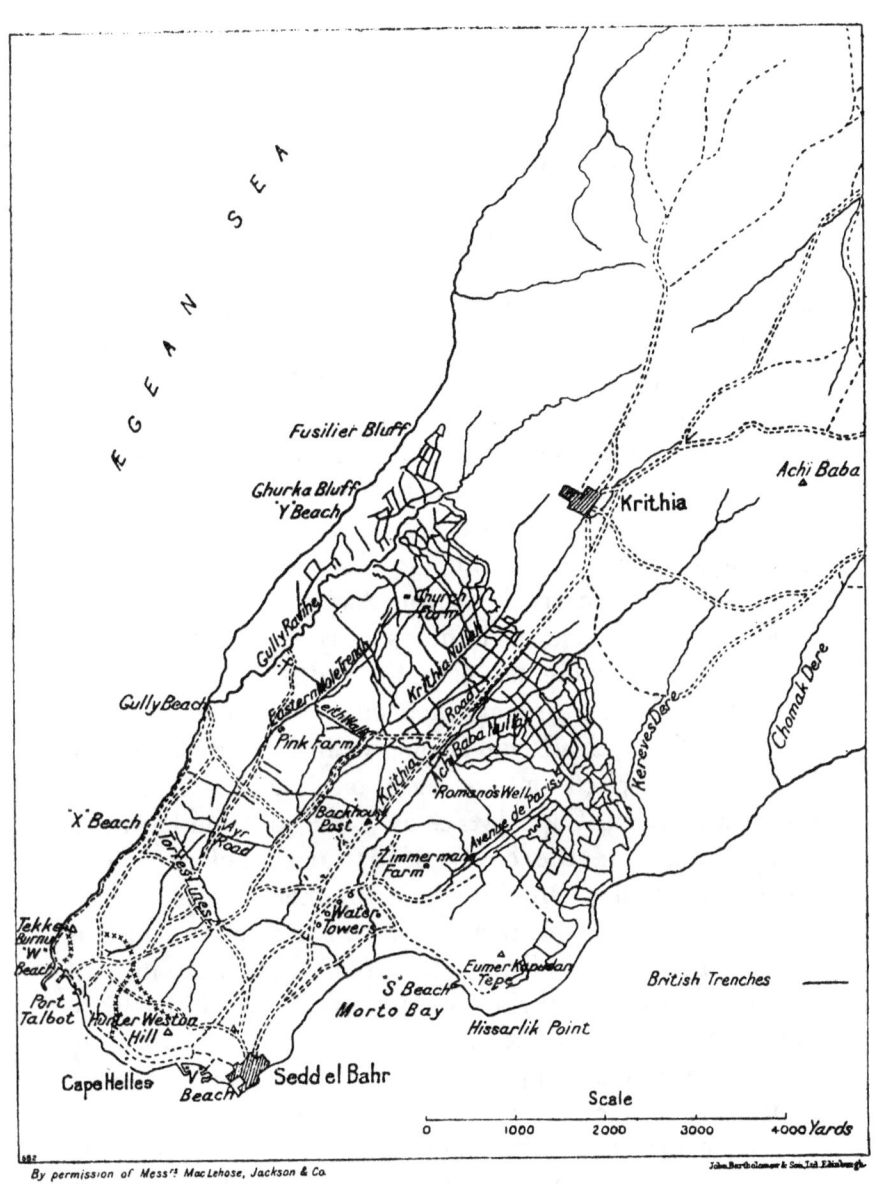

MAP VI.—Cape Helles, showing British Trench System.
(*See also* large scale Map at end of volume.)

K

battalion on the *Empress of Britain*, on board of which were also the 4th Royal Scots, whose journey to Liverpool had been uneventful.

After the inevitable trials of the first few days at sea the Royal Scots enjoyed a pleasant voyage, broken by a brief stay at Malta, and on the 3rd June the *Empress of Britain* sailed into port at Alexandria, whence the men after disembarking marched to Aboukir where they went under canvas. It was now the height of summer and the soft powdery sand, imprisoning the heat of the fierce Egyptian sun, seemed to scorch the very feet of the men through their boots. This was a foretaste of the ordeal that awaited them. The troops felt no regrets in leaving the land of the Pharaohs five days later. Returning to Alexandria on the 8th June they were carried by the *Empress of Britain* to Mudros on the Isle of Lemnos, arriving there on the 11th. On the same day Captain Rutherford, with "C" Company of the 4th, embarked on a transport for Cape Helles. The 7th Royal Scots, with the whole of the brigade stores, left on the 12th on board the *Carron* which arrived off Cape Helles at 7 P.M., but the battalion had to wait for the cover of darkness before it was allowed to land. On the whole the men were surprised by the aspect of the peninsula, which now spread out before their eyes. From the published accounts of our difficulties in trying to capture Achi Baba they had expected to see a frowning peak rising abruptly from the water, but instead they beheld a comparatively gentle slope culminating in a ridge stretching right across the peninsula, which for ruggedness and boldness could not be compared with Arthur's Seat. The darkness and a choppy sea lent some excitement to the process of disembarkation into trawlers, but there was practically no shelling, and part of the battalion, passing through the sides of the *River Clyde*, landed at V Beach while the remainder disembarked at W Beach. The men were then collected and led in artillery formation to a rest camp about two miles from the toe of the peninsula.

To their cost the 7th Royal Scots had experienced the perils of land; the 4th were now to encounter the dangers of the sea. Lieut.-Colonel Dunn and his Staff with "A" and "B" Companies left Lemnos at night on the 12th June on board the *Reindeer*, which steaming at full speed through a calm sea suddenly crashed into a hospital ship, the *Immingham*, which by good fortune was empty except for her crew. The *Reindeer* cut into the other boat so deeply that she was embedded in her side, and there was a serious possibility that the two vessels would go down together. Luckily the *Reindeer* was able to free herself before the *Immingham* went to the bottom, but it was doubtful if she could keep afloat for long. The troops, who paraded on deck with boots off, behaved splendidly; though there were no life-belts there was no panic and the men carried out unhesitatingly every order given to them, moving from side to side as commanded in order to "trim" the boat. At length the signals of the *Reindeer* attracted the notice of a French vessel, which stood by, while the wounded *Reindeer* steamed, stern first, slowly back to Mudros, where it was vigorously bombed by a hostile aeroplane, which fortunately failed to register a hit. At Mudros the troops re-embarked for the third time on the *Empress of Britain*. That no tragic consequences followed the collision was undoubtedly due to the magnificent discipline of the 4th Royal Scots; their conduct during the crisis not merely earned them a special mention by Sir Ian Hamilton, but showed that they could be relied on to meet any danger without flinching.

This accident caused a slight delay, and Battalion H.Q. and "A" and "B" Companies were not landed at W Beach till the 14th. "D" Company, under Captain Ross, had already preceded them and the whole unit was gathered together on the evening of that day. Both the 4th and the 7th Royal Scots were at first employed digging divisional dug-outs and working on reserve and communication trenches. The afflictions of a war conducted in a sun-parched land all too quickly made themselves evident. Bullets and shells claimed an occasional victim, but from flies, filth, sand, and disagreeable odours no man could escape, and the wastage due to sickness was alarmingly high. On the 19th June both battalions began their first tour of trench duty.

On this occasion the 4th relieved its sister battalion, the 5th, which had been holding the front line since the night of the 12th/13th June. The period passed quietly until the 18th, when an action took place in which the 5th Royal Scots once more greatly distinguished themselves. Darkness had descended, when suddenly a large body of Turks burst upon our lines, but Lieut. Wetherall had observed the rush and quickly gave the alarm. The Royal Scots mounting the fire-steps in their trench opened rapid fire, causing the Turks to drop into cover and crawl back to their own positions. No other attack was made against the Royal Scots, but later in the night the enemy rushed the trenches on the right of those held by the 5th and even pushed down a communication trench, with the result that the Royal Scots found themselves in a critical situation with hostile groups on their right flank and rear. Lieut.-Colonel Wilson, grasping what had happened, organised parties armed with bombs to keep the Turks at bay. Next morning, at 4 A.M., the greater part of the battalion, assisted by a company of the Worcesters, charged with the bayonet and expelled the Turks from the trenches which they had so daringly captured. The first man to jump over the parapet was Lieut. Russell who, heading his men, had just reached the Turkish trench, when he was shot, but Sergeant Westwater took his place and the platoon by a resolute dash seized the trench. The bayonet charge was vigorously backed up by the bombers, while Sergeant Chalmers, establishing the battalion machine-guns in an exposed position, scourged the opposing ranks with accurate enfilade fire. This well-organised attack, executed with unwavering determination, quickly broke down the resistance of the enemy, who, terror stricken, bolted back to his original position. But the action cost the battalion sixty casualties, a heavy loss considering its total strength, and these included four good officers, Lieuts. J. S. Merrilies, W. B. Russell, and C. N. Rundle killed, and Captain A. W. U. Macrae wounded. Lieut.-Colonel Wilson was now the only officer left who had gone out with the battalion, for Captain Mure, a few days before the battalion returned to the line, had been struck down by illness. Most of the casualties fell on "Y" Company; "W" Company was not engaged in the charge, but it gave valuable help by the accuracy of its sniping and compelled a party of Turks, who tried to dig in between the lines, to retire after suffering some losses. Thus the 5th Royal Scots were jubilant when they were relieved and marched down to X Beach.

The 4th and the 7th Royal Scots were in the trenches but a short time, when they learned that they were to engage with the rest of the 156th Brigade in a great attack which was to take place on the 28th June. There had been little change in the general position of the Allies since the 4th. Our left flank rested on Gurkha Bluff from which our line ran across the Krithia and Achi Baba nullahs to the Kereves Ridge. The Turks had most misgivings about the safety of their right flank, and between the sea and Gully Ravine, the name given to the nullah which ran down to Gully Beach, they had constructed no fewer than five lines of trenches, all thickly protected by barbed wire. Sir Ian Hamilton had by this time drawn up a scheme for attacking the adversary in another portion of the peninsula, but this plan had no chance of success unless the Turks were confirmed in the belief that our main attack was still to be directed from the toe of Gallipoli. Hence the battle of the 28th June was based partly on the need of keeping the attention of the Turks focussed on Cape Helles.

General Hunter-Weston, who was in direct command at Cape Helles, was in charge of the operation and his plan was as follows. Lying just west of the Krithia nullah was a tract of ground known as Worcester Flats, and keeping this point as its right the attacking force was to swing round till the left of our line had cleared the Turkish trenches between Gully Ravine and the sea. If success attended this movement, we would be firmly established on the sea flank of the village of Krithia. The hostile trenches were to be bombarded by our artillery from 9 till 11 A.M., at which hour the infantry were to advance to the assault. The operation was entrusted to the Twenty-ninth Division, to which the 156th Brigade was attached for the occasion. The assault along the coast between Gully Ravine and the sea, which seemed the most difficult part of the enterprise, was to be carried out by the 87th Brigade, on the right of which the 156th Brigade was to capture two lines of Turkish trenches situated on the east side of Gully Ravine.

The rôle of the 156th Brigade was to facilitate the advance of the 87th by protecting the right flank of the latter. Thus it was certain to have a rough passage since, the artillery preparation being used entirely to support the main attack along the coast, it would have to attack trenches garrisoned by men whose nerves had not been shaken by bombardment. Moreover, the information gleaned by our Intelligence Department about the Turkish trenches was misleading. Under the arrangements of Brig.-General Scott Moncrieff the attack of the 156th Brigade was to be carried out by three battalions, the 4th Royal Scots, the 7th Royal Scots, and the 8th Scottish Rifles from left to right, with the 7th Scottish Rifles in brigade reserve. The 4th Royal Scots were in a trench that formed an obtuse angle, with the nose pointing towards the enemy; on the east side of this nose the trench was labelled H10, and, except for a sharp bend called the Kink, ran straight to the position occupied by the 8th Scottish Rifles. Actually H10 was continued from the nose to the Gully Ravine in Turkish hands, and there was at least one other trench that had escaped our observation, so that on the front of the 4th Royal Scots four lines of trenches, and not two as given in the orders, had to be captured. The 7th Royal Scots held H10 on the right of the 4th for about 150 yards. The objectives were the hostile trenches known as H12A and H12, and in addition the 4th Royal Scots had to secure the communication trenches leading from H12 into Gully Ravine. The ravine itself was a sinister obstacle, for on its eastern flank the Turks had built a boomerang-shaped redoubt, close to the lines of the 4th Royal Scots, from which their fire could sweep all the ground between the British and Turkish lines to the west of the ravine. The capture of this fortification was so vital to the success of the operation that the 1st Border Regiment of the Twenty-ninth Division was detailed to attack it.

All the requisite preparations for the battle were efficiently carried through by the 4th and the 7th Royal Scots. In the front line Lieut.-Colonel Dunn had two companies, "D" commanded by Captain Ross and "C" commanded by Captain Rutherford, Major J. Gray, the Second in Command, exercising a general supervision over both companies. Major Henderson with "A" Company was in support and Captain McCrae with "B" Company was in reserve. The attack was to be in three waves. Half an hour before the assault "A" was to move up and join "C" and "D" Companies in the front line and "B" was to occupy the trench vacated by "A." When the leading companies attacked, "A" was to follow 70 yards behind them and "B" 70 yards behind "A"; "B" was to consolidate the first captured trench and "A" the second. As regards the 7th Royal Scots, Lieut.-Colonel Peebles put Major Sanderson in charge of the attack, which was to be led by "C" Company under Captain Dawson. Owing to the weakness of the battalion through the Gretna disaster, Lieut.-Colonel Peebles had only two companies, "B" Company of the 8th Highland Light Infantry under Captain D. Clark attached, which acted as support, and "C" Company of the 7th.

Our cannonade commenced punctually at 9 A.M., but no shells fell on the trenches to be attacked by the 4th and the 7th Royal Scots. The only effective covering fire was that provided by the machine-guns of the two battalions, but bullets cannot do more than force the enemy to keep his head down till the moment of assault; they can neither smash trenches nor bemuse a garrison. The men of the 156th Brigade probably did not realise that their task was in the nature of a forlorn hope,

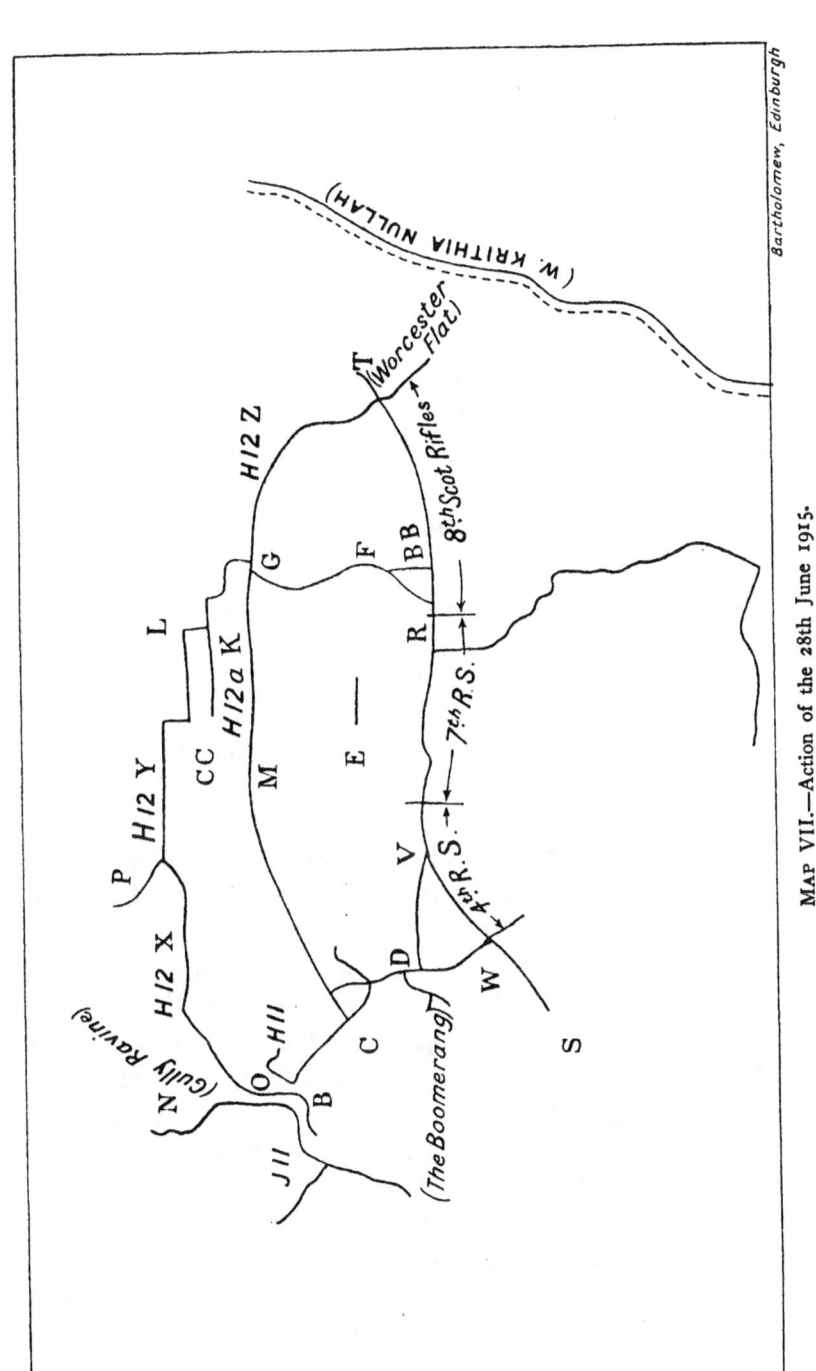

Map VII.—Action of the 28th June 1915.
(Reproduced from the Map issued to Lieut.-Col. Peebles.)

in that they were asked to attack trenches garrisoned by men over whom superiority of fire had not been obtained. Actually, before the assault took place, fire superiority was with the enemy. Vigorously replying to our bombardment, the Turks shelled not merely the trenches of the Twenty-ninth Division but also those crowded with the troops of the 156th Brigade, and many casualties were sustained before the hour of zero came.

Fortunately the attack on the Boomerang Redoubt, delivered a quarter of an hour before that of the 156th Brigade, was completely successful, and thus one formidable obstacle to the advance of the 4th Royal Scots was removed. The sun, high in the heavens by 9 A.M., threw down an intense heat on the parched ground, but after thirty minutes' bombardment its golden disc was veiled by thick clouds of smoke and dust that floated skywards, while the acrid smell of powder hung heavily in the air. The troops in the trenches, waiting with pent-up feelings for the approach of zero, hoped that they would acquit themselves like men and tried to crush all ignoble thoughts of self under a high resolve to follow the hard road of duty. At last the hour came and at the word, "Over you go, lads," the troops gave vent to one resounding cheer and, filled with the turbulence of battle, swarmed over the parapets into the perils of the open ground. Then the storm beat upon them; a rain of missiles smote their ranks, but slanting their bodies to the blast the survivors dashed on without flinching through the smoke and flame.

The losses sustained by the 4th Royal Scots in the first shock of the struggle were appalling. The left company had perhaps the most difficult task of all to perform, for after moving out some distance from its trench it had to swing half-right. The first few yards of the advance were thick with dead and wounded men.

Lieut.-Colonel Dunn was mortally wounded and Major Gray was killed before the first objective was reached, but nothing could stop the men animated with more than ordinary resolve. Most of the officers had fallen, before H12A, the first objective, was captured, but N.C.Os. at once took their place and where there were no N.C.Os. the men pressed on without any leaders. Encouraging the young soldiers by his marvellous coolness, Pipe-Major Buchan, although hit twice, gallantly held on until he reached the parapet of H10, where a Turkish bullet ended his brave life. The Turks were amazed by the heroic steadfastness of the Scots and many bolted before the approach of soldiers for whom death held no terrors. A few of the more fanatical, brave foes worthy of our steel, valiantly held their ground, and the pick of the Moslems found their way to Allah through a bayonet stab.

Thus the 4th Royal Scots fought their way to H12A, where "A," "C," and "D" Companies were now all mixed up. The men of "B" Company, which formed the third wave, noticing that their comrades were being enfiladed from the right, attacked the trench from which this fire was coming and expelled the enemy. Only three officers, Captain Sinclair, Lieut. Stewart and 2nd Lieut. Macrorie, were now standing, but the right company "C" had in C.S.M. Lowe a cool leader with experience in war. The final objective, H12, lay about 100 yards away, and C.S.M. Lowe, followed by about sixty men, sprinted over the broken and rugged ground, rushed into the trench and drove out the Turks, who were completely surprised by the dash of the attack. This forward party was now ahead of the 87th Brigade, which was operating on the other side of Gully Ravine, with the result that C.S.M. Lowe's men were harassed by a galling enfilade fire delivered from the western side of the gully. While a few of the men moved forward to ascertain what lay ahead, their comrades worked industriously preparing the captured trench for defence. No other trenches were within sight, but it was obviously out of the question for a small group of troops to advance without support to the summit of the ridge. The Royal Scots, however, had the consolation of finding an opportunity of avenging their fallen comrades. On the left, Gully Ravine, which was in this area little more than a saucer-shaped depression destitute of cover, was wholly exposed to their view and formed a trap where many Moslems were shot down as they were retiring in confusion before the attack of the 87th Brigade.

The Turks on Achi Baba Ridge were greatly perturbed by the extent of our gains, and with the object of preventing reinforcements reaching their bold assailants, they put down a heavy fire along Gully Ravine near H12A. The shrubs and gorse, so dry that a spark would have kindled them, burst into flames. Many of the wounded lay helpless within the zone of burning shrub, and their comrades braved flames and death to drag them into safety. In this self-sacrificing work Corporal Rankin, though feeble from wounds, gave up his life, which would probably have been preserved had he gone down to the dressing-station; not until he was unable to move a limb through sheer exhaustion did he abandon his noble rescue work and then his own life ebbed away through loss of blood. Private Byres twice risked almost certain death to bring in wounded under a murderous fire and many similar acts of heroism were performed by men whose names were not recorded. Others, like Private Lownie, valiantly exposed themselves by dashing into the open and beating out the flames with sandbags.

The burning gorse and shrub for a time formed a fiery wedge between C.S.M. Lowe's party and the remainder of the battalion, but volunteers were never lacking to keep communication open and several times Corporal Cowan, Private Lunn and Private Lownie dashed through the fire-swept zone with orders and messages. Meantime Lieut. F. B. Mackenzie, ably assisted by Sergeant Gunn, had done deadly work with his machine-gun. He had advanced 50 yards to the right rear of the leading wave and after the capture of H12 he mounted his gun on commanding ground, to the right of the part occupied by C.S.M. Lowe's force. From this position he obtained an excellent field of fire in practically every direction and many of the retreating Turks were laid low by his accurate shooting.

Thus though the odds had been heavily against them, the 4th Royal Scots, at a terrible cost, had accomplished what they had been asked to do. Only three officers escaped injury or death. Among the slain in addition to Major J. Gray were Major J. N. Henderson, Captains G. McCrae, R. E. Mackie, J. D. Pollock, J. Robertson, G. A. S. Ross, R. W. Rutherford, Lieut. C. Paterson and 2nd Lieut. W. J. Johnstone; Lieut. P. F. Considine was so badly injured that he died afterwards from the effects of his wounds. The wounded were Captain J. K. Hamilton, the Adjutant, 2nd Lieuts. J. Fleck, L. R. Grant, F. B. Mackenzie, J. Riddell, and the Quartermaster, Captain Smith; four officers were missing, Lieuts. C. F. Allan, A. Young, 2nd Lieuts. T. D. Aitchison and R. J. Gibson.[1] The casualties in other ranks amounted to three hundred and forty-five, which number included two hundred and four killed and missing. Many of the fallen officers had devoted years of their lives to the 4th and the 6th Royal

[1] Later it was ascertained that these must have been killed.

Scots and without them the battalion became sadly unfamiliar. It is impossible to exaggerate the gloom caused by the death of Lieut.-Colonel Dunn. As a soldier and a man he was worshipped by the whole battalion; he possessed that charm of manner that irresistibly sweeps up loyalty and love, and at his word officers and men would proudly have gone through any ordeal. The command of the unit now passed to Captain Sinclair. The Medical Officer, Captain Pirie Watson, had been laid low by sickness, but his place was taken by Lieut. Morham, who for forty-eight consecutive hours devoted himself to the care of the wounded.

On the right of the 4th, the 7th Royal Scots were equally successful. Major Sanderson advanced with "C" Company in the dash for the nearest opposing trench, lying about 300 yards away. The first objective was taken at comparatively small cost, for most of the Turks fled before the 7th reached H12A. After a short halt, during which the supporting waves of the Highland Light Infantry closed up, the advance on the final objective, H12, was begun. By this time the Turks, having recovered from their panic, delivered such a terrific fire that the Royal Scots fell literally in bundles. Half-way across Major Sanderson dropped and Captain Dawson and Lieut. Thomson were killed as they neared their goal, but the Turks were put to flight by the survivors, a stubborn few fighting to the death. Only three officers, of whom the senior was Lieut. Haws, and eighty unwounded other ranks now remained. The men were at once reorganised and steps were taken to adapt the captured trenches for defence. The battalion machine-guns, under Lieut. Elliot of the 8th Highland Light Infantry rendered most valuable support throughout the attack, and the fact that comparatively light losses were sustained in the first phase of the

Lieut.-Colonel S. R. Dunn.
4th Battalion, The Royal Scots.

attack was largely due to the skilful covering fire afforded by Lieut. Elliot's guns.

The price of success was deplorably heavy. Besides the officers already mentioned, 2nd Lieut. F. W. Thomson of the Royal Scots and Lieut. A. S. Elliot, the gallant machine-gun officer of the 8th Highland Light Infantry were slain. Among the wounded were Captain A. J. Wightman of the 7th, Captain J. R. Torrance and Lieut. J. Ballantyne of the Highland Light Infantry. Captain Clark, who commanded the Highland Light Infantry company, was mortally wounded, while Captain J. R. Peebles and Lieut. R. M. Galloway[1] of the 7th were missing. The total casualties in other ranks were two hundred and thirty, of whom one hundred and sixteen were killed or missing. Victory brought no end to the trials of the battle, for the captured positions became the target of hostile guns and so pitiless was the shelling that the utmost difficulty was experienced in maintaining communications throughout the battalion. The trained signal section of the 7th Royal Scots had been lost in the railway disaster at Gretna, but during the voyage Captain Wightman had organised a new section, which devoted all its leisure to mastering the intricacies of signalling work. Captain Wightman with Sergeant Rosie and 4 signallers attempted to run out a line from H12 back to Battalion H.Q., but practically every inch of the ground was under fire. Sergeant Rosie was killed and Captain Wightman wounded, but he did not cease his efforts until all his party had become casualties.

Unfortunately, on the right of the 7th Royal Scots, the 8th Cameronians fared disastrously. The hostile position which the latter had to attack was stiff with machine-guns, and since these had not been subjected

[1] These two officers were killed.

to our bombardment, their fire simply wiped out the attack. Still, as a whole, the 156th Brigade had discharged its function: the splendid work of the 4th and the 7th Royal Scots had substantially helped the battalions of the 87th Brigade on the west of Gully Ravine to advance our line in that quarter till it was west-north-west of the tumbled ruins of Krithia. Major-General de Lisle was so conscious of how materially the attack of his own division had been assisted by the advance of the Royal Scots that he sent them a message: "Well done, Royal Scots!" As far as the Royal Scots could see there was nothing between them and the top of the ridge, but in other parts of the battlefield the hostile resistance seemed far from succumbing to our blows, and not many minutes passed before both the 4th and the 7th Royal Scots found their own positions none too secure. Their left flank was safe owing to the success of the 87th Brigade, but their right was in the air. Lieut. Mackenzie accordingly took his machine-gun to the extreme right in order to help the 7th by covering that flank. Later in the day he was wounded in the neck by a sniper as he was bringing up a platoon of Cameronians to reinforce H12, but his Sergeant, John Gunn, proved a capable substitute, the accuracy of his machine-gun fire deterring the Turks from massing for a counter-attack. The garrison's sense of security was appreciably heightened when two machine-gun sections from the Border Regiment came up to support the 4th Royal Scots, but even after their arrival the position could not be viewed with complete satisfaction. The dust and sand that filled the air clogged the rifle-bolts, while the men were suffering from exhaustion and the terrific mental strain of their first fight; their mouths were so parched by heat and dust that their tongues swelled and they could scarcely swallow the rations that they had carried up; worst of all was the craving for water, and the troops endured long hours of agony before the precious liquid could be sent to them.

The action of the 28th June is a red letter day in the annals of the Queen's Edinburgh Rifles, because it was the only one in which the 4th and the 5th Battalions fought together. It was through the failure of the attack on the right of the 7th that the 5th Royal Scots came to be involved in the fight. From reserve trenches they were sent on the afternoon of the 28th to assault the position that had defied the 8th Cameronians. On arriving at the firing line the battalion found that the ground in front rose gently to a slight ridge lying between the British and Turkish positions. It was a ridge only by courtesy, but it seemed to provide a place where men could form up for attack without being observed. Two saps running from our front line into No-Man's-Land were the most convenient avenues along which the troops could be led to the shelter of the ridge.

The attack was launched at 4 P.M., when Lieut. W. H. Steel with a platoon of "Y" Company led his men up the right sap, while Lieut. Wetherall took up a platoon of "W" Company by the left one. The arrangement was that the former, having organised a line behind the ridge, should deliver a frontal assault assisted by a flanking attack by Lieut. Wetherall's platoon. The saps furnished a less easy route than had been anticipated; they were choked with debris and with the bodies of those who had fallen in the morning battle and the troops could move forward only with the utmost difficulty. Moreover, the Turks appeared to be expecting an attack, or they may have observed our preparations for it, for they maintained a heavy shell-fire, against which the rickety banks of the sap offered no protection, and when Lieut. Wetherall neared the hostile trenches he had only three men behind him.

The right sap ended abruptly in No-Man's-Land, but Lieut. Steel reached the ridge, on our side of which he rapidly formed up his men for the assault. The men charged forward with great gallantry, but as soon as they topped the ridge they were shot down by a withering fire from Turkish rifles and machine-guns; few of the Royal Scots survived the blast. Meantime Lieut. Wetherall with his scanty escort proceeded along the left sap till he was stopped by a barricade guarded by a Turkish sentry. There was a swift exchange of shots and the Turk fell dead; but Lieut. Wetherall, in a fleeting glance along the enemy's trench, caught a glimpse of many men with fierce bearded faces and he realised that to lead his three men against such a throng of foes would be an act of insane folly. Accordingly he withdrew and reported the situation to Lieut.-Colonel Wilson. Several other attempts with stronger forces were made to rush the hostile position but all to no purpose. Captain Grant of "W" Company exhibited lion-hearted courage. Though suffering from a painful wound in the foot, he strode into the open regardless of the storm of lead and encouraged his men to push on, but the men's plucky response only added to the casualty list[1] and the attack had to be abandoned.

The night brought constant alarms, but every attempt on the part of the enemy to mass for a counter-attack was smashed by our fire. Then the good news that they were to be relieved reached the 4th and the 7th Royal Scots, and during the night their trenches

---

[1] Besides Lieut. W. H. Steel, Captain T. A. Tressider and Lieut. W. O'Sullivan were killed; Captains Grant and Radcliffe, Lieuts. J. P. Elder, C. H. Jardine, and A. J. Wetherall, and 2nd Lieuts. D. S. Munro, B. Murdoch and F. M. Scott were wounded; the losses among other ranks numbered 270 in killed, wounded, and missing.

were taken over by the Hampshire Regiment and they withdrew to reserve trenches. The 5th remained in the line. No one could say for a certainty what had happened to all the men who had taken part in the abortive attacks on H12, and the 5th Battalion had no intention of leaving its wounded exposed to the hazard of bullets and shells, and the still more deadly effects of the Gallipoli sun. Bright moonlight silvered the desolate battlefield, so that no group of men could hope to move and escape detection, but Lance-Corporal Borthwick crawled out twice towards H12 in an attempt to ascertain if any of our wounded were lying near the fatal ridge. He came across several, too badly hit to be able to move, and with the assistance of Private Gordon he succeeded in bringing back ten men.

The frightful list of casualties sustained by the Royal Scots in the action of the 28th June plunged Edinburgh into mourning. There was such a slaughter of officers that people could only think that some unforeseen accident had happened. It was not then realised that the battalions had accomplished a feat rare in war, that they had, without any support from artillery, carried all their objectives against a resolute and gallant enemy. Few decorations came to the battalions for this action, but seldom did men more richly deserve them. Mere skill at arms could not have availed to take them through to their goal had it not been supported by an implacable determination to succeed at all costs, and it cannot be doubted that the soldierly desire to prove themselves as efficient as the men of the 5th Battalion counted for something in helping the 4th and the 7th Royal Scots to reach their objectives.

The toll of the war and the climate had reduced the 5th Royal Scots to the mere skeleton of a battalion. After only two months of fighting this fine unit had dwindled to less than a company, and the wastage due to shells, bullets, and disease was so colossal that the few drafts which came out from Scotland made no appreciable difference to its strength. None of the original officers except Lieut.-Colonel Wilson now remained, and others had to be procured from various regiments. It was clear that the battalion could not be brought up to anything like effective strength until it was withdrawn from the conflict. After being relieved from trench duty on the 2nd July, it spent four days at X Beach, returning for another spell of four days' trench duty from the 6th to the 10th. This virtually completed the active service of the battalion at Cape Helles, for on the 11th it returned to X Beach, whence it embarked on a transport for Mudros, where rest and training were undisturbed by the sound of guns.

The 4th and the 7th fared even worse than the 5th as regards wastage; within two weeks of landing the 4th were reduced to eight officers and 450 other ranks, while out of the two companies of the 7th only five officers and 170 other ranks remained. They were soon to be engaged in strife again, though on this occasion they were not destined to take the leading part. Owing to the great loss in senior officers suffered by the 4th on the 28th June they were combined as a composite battalion under the command of Lieut.-Colonel Peebles. After spending a few days in reserve the Royal Scots, on the 3rd July, relieved the Indian Brigade in the system of trenches at Gurkha Bluff. The one incident out of the ordinary occurred on the 7th, when early in the morning some Turks approached our lines under a flag of truce, bringing with them a sealed message for the British Commander-in-Chief. It contained a request for an armistice to bury the dead, but this was refused because we had received information that the Turkish officers could not induce their men to advance over the bodies of their fallen comrades who lay in heaps between the two lines. The trench tour of the Royal Scots ended on the 10th July and they returned to a rest camp.

Sir Ian Hamilton's plan for a landing in another part of Gallipoli had now been prepared, but in order to give the Turks the impression that the main threat on Achi Baba still came from Cape Helles, an attack in this area was arranged for the 12th July. On this occasion the objective was the system of hostile trenches between the Achi Baba nullah and the Kereves nullah, which was to be stormed by the Fifty-second Division in co-operation with French forces. On the southern side of the former nullah the Turks had constructed a fortified earthwork, which, owing to its shape, was known as the Horseshoe, and from this ran two main lines of trenches, both strongly wired, roughly parallel to our own front; these were known as E10 and E11, the former being at a distance varying from 100 to 200 yards from our front line. In addition to these trenches there were numerous smaller ones and at one part of E10 the enemy had dug a switch trench, which was indicated on our maps as A−0; it was with this switch that the Royal Scots were principally concerned. The attack was to be delivered by the 157th and 155th Brigades.

After spending a single night at the rest camp the Royal Scots marched at 3 A.M. on the 12th to Backhouse Road Post, and occupied a trench some 400 yards to the rear of our front line, where they lay in reserve to the two attacking brigades. After a heavy artillery bombardment the 155th Brigade attacked at 7.35 A.M., and would probably have met with complete success, if the leading troops had not gone on in accordance with their orders to assault a third Turkish trench which

L 2

did not exist. This deplorable mistake, which must be ascribed to a blunder on the part of the British Intelligence, caused the assailants to suffer unnecessary casualties and prevented the victory from being as decisive as it would otherwise have been. Our troops, finding that they had overshot their objective, were mowed down as they returned to E_{11}, and in the general confusion that followed, our arrangements for carrying on the battle were upset. Reserves were called for, and two companies of the 4th Royal Scots were sent up after 10.30 A.M. to fill a gap between the Royal Scots Fusiliers and the French, who had reported that they were not in touch with the British. But the French had been too hasty, for touch had never been lost, and the Royal Scots arrived at a section where the trenches were overcrowded with men. Turkish shells were falling all over the battlefield, and the Royal Scots had quickly to be squeezed into such space as was available.

It soon became apparent that the switch trench (A-0) with its tangle of communication trenches had not been thoroughly cleared by the attack, except on the right where it was subjected to a raking enfilade fire from machine-guns. Since it was vital that we should secure the whole of the switch, Lieut.-Colonel Peebles was instructed to send forward a company to clear and hold it. This task was entrusted to the company of the 7th under Lieut. Haws. During the advance Lieut. Haws was wounded and 2nd Lieut. D. Lyell took command. Having threaded their way with difficulty along the broken communication trenches, littered with rubbish and the bodies of the fallen, 2nd Lieut. Lyell and his men rushed headlong down the switch and cleared the whole of the trench. It was so battered that it gave but poor

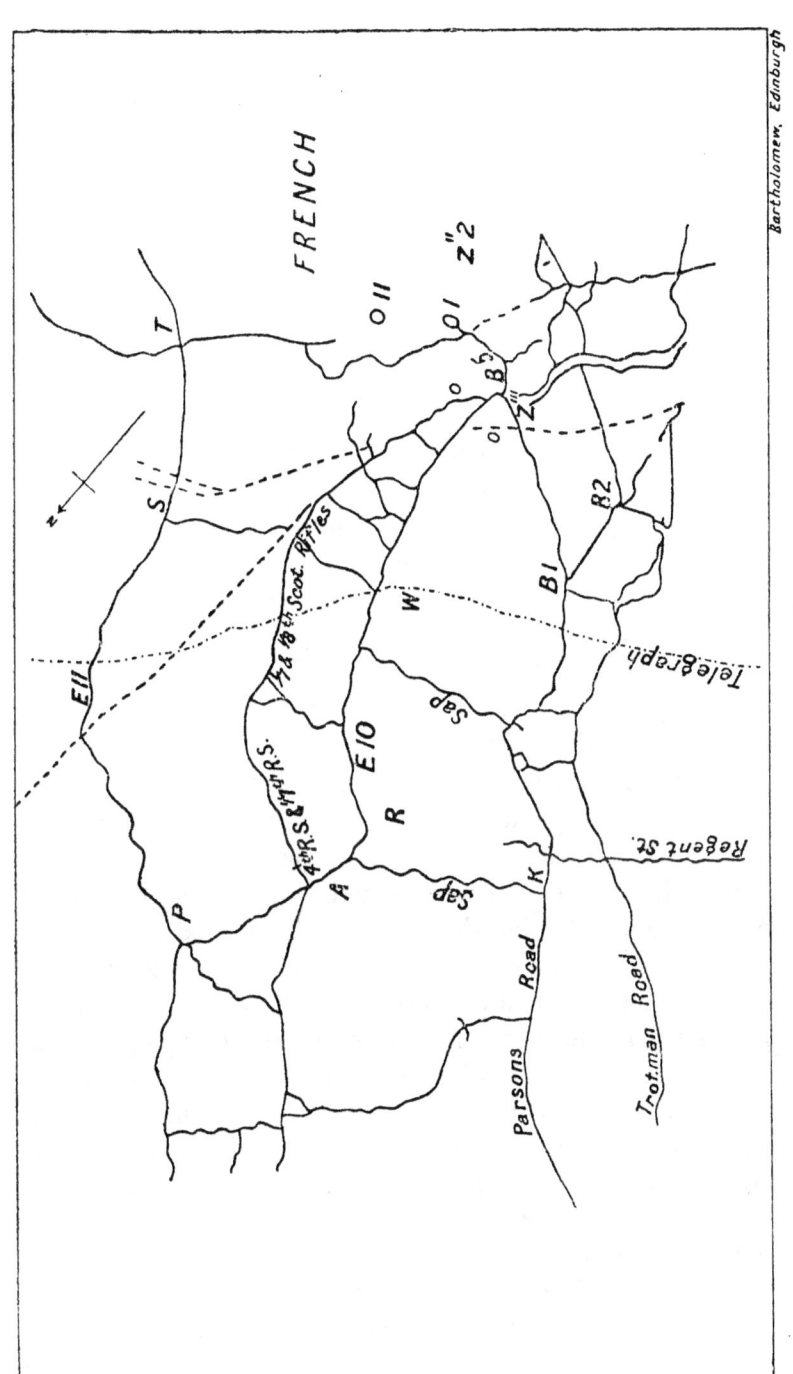

MAP VIII.—Action of the 12th July 1915.

protection, and while the men were deepening it and shoring up the parapet 2nd Lieut. Lyell, exposing himself too freely, was killed by a bullet. The only remaining officer, 2nd Lieut. McClelland of the 8th H.L.I. company, proved worthy of the serious responsibility that now devolved on him and under his supervision the switch was soon transformed into a fairly defensible position. Meantime the two companies of the 4th Royal Scots, acting along with the 4th Royal Scots Fusiliers, advanced on the right of the switch, and this gave us full command of E10 with its loop at A−0 and the ancillary communication trenches. Then a series of determined counter-attacks had to be met. Stealing along the numerous communication trenches, the Moslems repeatedly endeavoured to bomb their way into the switch, but their tenacity was surpassed by the stubbornness of the defence and our hold on the trench became more secure.

After the battle a night of feverish work had to be put in by every available man. The captured trenches had been so shattered in many places that they had practically to be reconstructed, and communication trenches had to be dug back to our old front line. By straining every effort the men completed all the essential work before dawn ushered in the 13th. Hostile counter-attacks had still to be repelled, but the Turks engaged in them had not their hearts in the business and usually retired at the first signs of opposition. Beyond the suggestion of liveliness that always immediately follows a battle nothing occurred on the front of the Royal Scots, but a machine-gun of the 7th rendered material assistance to the 7th H.L.I., by helping them to beat off an attack. The losses of the composite battalion were heavy considering that its part in the action was a minor one. The 4th Royal Scots were fortunate in losing no more officers, but they had seventy-four casualties in other ranks; the 7th, in addition to the officers already mentioned, had fifty-one casualties in other ranks. The Medical Officers, Lieut.-Colonel J. Mill of the 7th and Captain Pirie Watson of the 4th, laboured most devotedly throughout the engagement; they were at work for forty-eight hours on end in most exposed positions, tending the wounded. On the 15th the composite battalion was relieved and, after a day spent in clearing the trenches as far back as the Eski Trench line, went into a rest camp on the 16th July and till the end of the month was given a respite from trench warfare.

The 5th Royal Scots returned to Gallipoli on the 3rd August, wholly revived and refreshed by their tour at Mudros, but they were still far short of even half-battalion strength. Now opened the second phase of the Gallipoli campaign with the landing at Suvla Bay, which took place on the 6th and the 7th August. A series of demonstrations was made at Cape Helles, chiefly by the Twenty-ninth and the Forty-second Divisions, but in none of the actions were any of the Royal Scots battalions engaged. The drainage on their strength, however, from dysentery began to be alarming. Owing to the transference of many troops to Suvla Bay the garrison at Cape Helles was so reduced that all were required to undertake long spells of trench duty. On the 10th, the 7th gave a warm welcome to the officers who, having recovered from the injuries sustained in the Gretna disaster, now rejoined the battalion. The 4th and the 7th resumed their separate identities when on the 10th Lieut.-Colonel A. Young, accompanied by a number of officers, reached Gallipoli to take command of the former. It was very doubtful if he were fit to endure the hardships of an Eastern campaign, but his determination to share the dangers of a battalion, of which for many years he had been a prominent personality, carried him past all medical obstacles. In the 5th battalion there was a change in command. The excellent work performed by Lieut.-Colonel Wilson caused him to be promoted to the command of the 32nd Brigade of the Eleventh Division and Major White took over the 5th.

Unfortunately, after an encouraging start, the Suvla Bay *coup de main* failed, and the Twenty-ninth Division was transferred from Cape Helles to that area. On the night of the 20th/21st the 5th, embarking at V Beach, were put ashore at Suvla Bay in the small hours of the morning. Immediately they proceeded to an eminence known as Scimitar Hill, where under fire they began to dig in; here Major White was wounded. But pessimism was now invading the minds of the British leaders and it began subtly to affect the troops. Thus, as at Cape Helles, the position at Suvla Bay tended to drift into stalemate. The 5th took part in no attacks, but the cost of holding the line was undeniably great. On the 25th Captain McPherson, 2nd Lieuts. McDonald and Reid and three men were killed, while Captain McCloud, 2nd Lieuts. Gibson and Sinclair and thirty men were wounded. This was the most trying experience of the battalion during the month, and on the 30th it left the peninsula for the island of Imbros.

CHAPTER X

THE 2ND BATTALION AT HOOGE

April to October 1915

Lull on the British front in the West. 2nd Royal Scots at Railway Wood and at Hooge. German successes in the East. Reasons for the Battle of Loos. Attack of 2nd Royal Scots, 25th September. German counter-attack. Attack of "C" Company, 30th September. (See Map IV., p. 79, and large scale Map at end of volume.)

THE course taken by the war throughout 1915 rudely upset the complacent optimism prevalent in Britain at the opening of the year. A triumphant advance would, it was generally believed, be the inevitable sequel of our successful parry of the enemy's stroke in 1914. Consequently the report of every event on the Western front that suggested the beginning of the grand attack was scanned with hopeful expectation. But every assault from Neuve Chapelle to Festubert fizzled out after a few days, and the conviction was gradually brought home to our people that the German defences were more difficult to pierce than the language of the official communiqués had led them to imagine. Then attention was diverted to the Dardanelles expedition, on which so many important issues hung, and for a time optimism rose high, for people could not bring themselves to believe that soldiers, who had overcome the gigantic obstacles in the way of forcing a landing, could fail to capture Achi Baba. But when the tenor of subsequent reports was invariably to the effect that our army had captured so many lines of trenches, representing a gain of a few hundred yards of ground, people began to be uneasy; victory, it was now intuitively realised, had to be achieved quickly or the situation would drift into stalemate. This indeed was the case after the failure of our attack at Suvla Bay.

Still the idea remained fixed that the Allies would not allow 1915 to pass without attempting some big enterprise in France, where the chief armies confronted each other. But after the fighting at Festubert, weeks and months passed without anything unusual taking place, and for many of the Royal Scots battalions this was one of the quietest periods of the war. The 1st and the 9th Battalions after being relieved at Ypres spent, as we have seen, an uneventful time in the southern and more peaceful sectors of the British line. The 8th Battalion, having undergone a course of training in pioneer work, was transferred from the Seventh Division on the 20th August and moved to Bouzincourt in the Somme area, where it joined the Fifty-first Division, composed of Highland Territorial units. The 11th, 12th and 13th Battalions, as yet comparatively fresh to the work and anxious for an opportunity to show their mettle, took a keen zest in familiarising themselves with the routine of trench warfare. All three, at the beginning of September, were already in the districts where they were to have their first experience of battle. The 11th and the 12th occupied a sector of trenches east of Vermelles, while the 13th Battalion was farther south near Quality Keep.

The 2nd Battalion, which had not been engaged in any fighting since the 14th December, spent the greater part of 1915 in the most disagreeable sector on the whole British front. Mud and shell fire were the commonplaces of existence, and in April the unit lost two officers, Lieut. E. Molson being killed on the 1st and Lieut. J. Nisbet on the 15th. On the

Capt. J. Tait.　　Lt.-Col. Gemmill, Capt. B. M'Ewen, Capt. W. A. M'Crae, Lieut. Morgan, Capt. J. G. Pringle, Capt. J. Young.

OFFICERS OF THE 8TH ROYAL SCOTS AT BOUZINCOURT.

(Sketch by the late Lieut. W. W. Cowan.)

[*To face p.* 172.

1st May it formed a small drum and pipe band, the instruments which the battalion had taken out with it having been destroyed at Audencourt. On the 12th May it was transferred from the Kemmel sector to trenches north of Hill 60, and while here 2nd Lieut. Broad was wounded and Lieut.-Colonel Duncan took up a temporary appointment on the Staff, his place being filled by Lieut.-Colonel H. E. P. Nash. The next move of the battalion, on the 25th May, took it still farther north and was attended with no little difficulty, since the position near Railway Wood, which it had to take over, had been the scene of a recent local combat, and no one knew definitely how the trenches lay. But a matter like this caused no undue worry to the seasoned campaigners of the 2nd Royal Scots, and the required position was taken over and manned without trouble.

Probably owing to the recent liveliness the hostile shelling was unusually severe and the sector proved costly to hold. Within a short space of time four officers were wounded, Lieuts. J. Hill-Workman and the Hon. M. Bowes-Lyon on the 27th May, Lieut. the Hon. H. R. C. Balfour on the 4th June, and Lieut. Cole-Hamilton on the 15th. For an attack to be carried out by the 9th Brigade, assembly trenches were dug and the other preliminary arrangements were made by the Royal Scots, who left Captain Povah with the battalion machine-guns to assist in the operation. This took place on the 16th June, and Captain Povah, who had an intimate knowledge of the ground, by his skilful direction of the machine-gun fire rendered most valuable assistance to the brigade, which succeeded in capturing and holding the copse known, on account of its general shape, as Y Wood. Unfortunately, in the course of the action, Captain Povah was killed. After the battle, the Royal Scots returned and took over the newly captured line, which was littered with many of the dead and wounded. During the process of clearing up, three skulking Germans were discovered and taken prisoners. Other two officers became casualties, Lieut. J. M. Anderson being killed on the 17th and 2nd Lieut. Cleghorn being wounded. When the battalion was relieved on the 19th, it had been for twenty-five consecutive days in the trenches and was in sore need of the rest in billets that it now enjoyed till the 12th July. On that day it took over trenches north of Sanctuary Wood, where it was destined to go through much bitter fighting in September. The wood, which till the beginning of 1915 had been looked on as a kind of haven in the Salient, no longer deserved its name, and casualties were unpleasantly numerous. On the 14th July Lieut. B. P. Coxson was killed and on the 1st August Lieut. J. S. Lockhart was wounded. In September two officers, Lieuts. R. C. Blackwood and J. A. Turner, were wounded.

Meantime events in other theatres, as well as the failure of the Allies in France and in the Dardanelles to make any substantial progress, had aroused profound alarm among the people at home. It was no longer believed that the enemy was on the brink of defeat and that we were within sight of a decisive victory. Germany, confining herself to a defensive rôle in the West, where she retained just sufficient troops to keep her position secure, struck hard at Russia with the bulk of her forces. The resistance of the Russian armies was almost completely overwhelmed, and every day the Press recorded lists of fortresses toppling down before the rush of the foe. To the general consternation, Warsaw, and with it Poland, fell to the Germans on the 15th August, and there was a lively fear that

Petrograd would suffer the same fate. It was not convincing consolation to be told that the Germans were being frustrated in their main object—the destruction of the Russian field armies—for this was due not so much to the skill with which the Russian retreat was said to be conducted as to the fact that the enemy lacked the means to carry out the function, performed in previous wars by cavalry, of transforming a defeat into a rout by relentless pursuit. As the future was to reveal, the Russians, in 1915, had received a hammering from which they never recovered. Moreover, British lack of success at Gallipoli reacted calamitously on the situation in the Balkans, and there was strong reason for fearing that Bulgaria would enter the lists against us. As against these misfortunes the adhesion of Italy in May to the cause of the Allies counted for little, for she threw herself into a campaign which, designed to realise exclusively Italian aims, drew off only a fraction of the Austrian forces.

It was the Russian debacle that most affected the ordinary man who, from the national sense of sportsmanship, was exasperated at the passivity prevailing on the Western front. To help the Allies in 1914 Russia had sacrificed an army, and a like loyalty to their ally seemed called for on the part of the Western Powers in 1915. These considerations had their weight with the military leaders in France and Flanders. If it had been only a question of the Western front it is doubtful if the French and British armies would have embarked on an offensive after the summer of 1915, but a diversion in this quarter seemed imperative, if we wished to prevent the Germans from rendering Russia ineffective for the rest of the war. Possibly our purpose would have been best served by sending more troops and stores to Gallipoli. General Joffre was convinced of the necessity of assisting Russia, and he ultimately persuaded Sir John French to co-operate in a joint operation against the Germans.

A force consisting of the French Tenth Army and the I. and IV. Corps of the British Army was to advance eastwards in the direction of Valenciennes, while the French main attack was to be delivered from Champagne on Maubeuge. If no checks were experienced and the two forces were allowed to join hands, all the Germans within the salient, Rheims-Royon-Arras, would be cut off and compelled to surrender. The region selected for the British attack stretched from Haisnes in the north to Hulluch in the south. To prevent the enemy from sending reinforcements to the menaced sectors, arrangements were made for subsidiary enterprises to be undertaken in other parts of the line. In addition a general bombardment along the whole Allied front was to open at the beginning of September with a view to mystifying the foe as to where our blow would fall. The 25th September was the date fixed for the attack.

The Salient offered considerable scope for diversions, and the Third Division, holding the line near Hooge, was called on to take part in an enterprise. With the Fourteenth Division on its left it was to carry Hooge Château Wall and establish itself on Bellewarde Ridge. One company of the Royal Scots Fusiliers formed the right of the division, then came the 2nd Royal Scots, and on their left the 4th and 1st Gordons, and finally two battalions of the Fourteenth Division. The artillery bombardment was to begin at 3.50 A.M. and half an hour later the infantry were to advance. It was arranged also that four mines, run by sappers under the hostile trenches opposite the Royal Scots, were to be exploded the moment previous to the infantry assault.

The trenches occupied by the Royal Scots lay in Sanctuary Wood, south of the Ypres-Menin Road, and from their position the ground rose steadily towards Hooge. The battalion had three objectives to carry—the German front line, only 100 yards distant, then the support line, and finally, in the German reserve line, a natural hummock so thickly carpeted with sandbags that it was known as Sandbag Castle. Three Companies, "C," "B," and "A" were detailed by Lieut.-Colonel Duncan to make the assault, "D" Company being kept in reserve.

Our bombardment fulfilled its purpose, for the infantry on being unleashed carried all their objectives with little trouble. The point where the mines were exploded under the hostile trenches faced the position occupied by "B" Company, where our line, jutting sharply into No-Man's-Land, formed a salient. To avoid casualties from falling debris the company assembled some distance from the nose of this salient. There could be no plainer indication of zero than the thick cloud of earth that rose into the air when the mines were touched off, and with bayonets dulled in order that the advance might be as unobtrusive as possible the Royal Scots strode towards the German trenches. "B" Company, led by Captain Heathcote, was the only one to suffer seriously during the first stage of the assault; all its officers were lost before the German front line was reached. Having secured all their objectives the Royal Scots then commenced to consolidate the captured positions. So far the operation had passed off successfully; casualties were few, the enemy having offered only a feeble resistance, and the captures by the battalion included 116 Germans. The units on the immediate flanks of the Royal Scots experienced a similar triumph.

The Germans soon made amends for the ease with which they had allowed themselves to be ejected from their trenches, by the dash and skill with which they delivered their counter-stroke. They poured a galling and accurate fire on their old positions and inflicted on the Royal Scots more casualties than they had sustained while making the actual attack. This fierce counter-bombardment prevented "D" Company and the sappers from running a communication trench from our old to our new front line, our men being compelled to throw down their tools and dive for shelter into the nearest shell-holes. It soon became clear that our attack had not been uniformly successful. The 1st Gordons, on the left of the 4th, had run into a thick tangle of uncut wire guarding the German front line; hand wire-cutters were too puny to cope with such an obstacle and after suffering terrible losses, the Highlanders were forced to withdraw to their original trenches.

Thus the Boches opposite the 1st Gordons formed a pocket in our new position, and if they had been raw troops might have been overtaken by panic on realising that they were flanked by foes. But not being novices in the art of warfare, they saw that their position gave them a useful base for a counter-attack, which they undertook without delay. Headed by bombing squads, they burst on the left flank of the 4th Gordons who were soon engaged in a furious hand-to-hand combat. The enemy's strength was rapidly increased by reinforcements, so Captain Hay with "A" Company, on the right of the Gordons, disposed his men in such a position that they protected the left flank of the battalion.

The Germans adroitly and tenaciously pressed home their advantage. The general direction of their counter-attack was from north to south, their reinforcements arriving by a communication trench cutting across the

Menin Road. At this point they were exposed to the view of the Royal Scots who by machine-gun fire inflicted many casualties on them, but the advance was not checked. The German gunners co-operating skilfully with their infantry directed a heavy fusilade of H.E. shells on the left of the battalion, with such effect that "A" Company along with the 4th Gordons had to fall back to our old front line. The pressure growing more acute with each success now passed on to "B" Company which, bereft of all its officers, was also compelled to retreat.

Then came the turn of "C" Company which in addition to this attack from the north had to withstand an assault from the south, where the company of the Royal Scots Fusiliers, after being viciously bombed, had also found it necessary to retire. Captain Norman Stewart, in command of "C" Company, knew well his danger; his men were being attacked from three sides— the front and both flanks. A man in whom battle kindled a sense of high exaltation, he would have fought to the death and found joy in the conflict, but professional skill, and responsibility to his company and to his battalion forbade him to sacrifice his men from instincts of knight-errantry. As things stood retreat might be unavoidable, but that step would not be taken until the last possible moment. He sent back a concise report explaining the predicament of his company, but there was now no serious hope of arresting the enemy's progress. A company of the 4th Middlesex set off for the nose of a salient in the old front line of the Royal Scots, but it was delayed for half an hour by the accurate concentration of the Boche shell fire on our trenches. When no reinforcements appeared Captain Stewart reluctantly submitted to the inevitable, and by dint of stubborn fighting, skilfully extricated his company from the hold of encircling foes and led it back to our original line, where the survivors of the battalion were reorganised by Lieut.-Colonel Duncan.

At the end of the day not a yard of ground had been gained, but our object had been fulfilled by the attack. Possibly the Germans had expected our principal effort to be made in the Salient, since their counter-attack showed that they kept a large force in this area, and the assault of the Third and Fourteenth Divisions must have served to keep the enemy from sending assistance to Loos and Fosse 8. Containing attacks always make great demands upon the men engaged in them, for as their object is primarily to pin the enemy to his front, there is seldom the same artillery support for the infantry as when the main object is the capture of hostile positions. The glory and the fame are almost wholly monopolised by the principal enterprise, success in which, moreover, is often only possible through the self-sacrificing gallantry of those engaged in subsidiary fights. The 2nd Royal Scots suffered grievously at Hooge. In killed, wounded, and missing the casualties in N.C.Os. and men amounted to two hundred and forty-four; ten officers[1] were lost. 2nd Lieut. D. Pease was trying to establish telephonic communication between our front line and the final objective, when he was surprised by the Boche counter-attack and surrounded. 2nd Lieut. Mayo fell wounded in the afternoon, and the enemy's pressure was so menacing that it was impossible to bring him into safety.

After dusk the battalion was relieved by the 4th Middlesex and went back to reserve dug-outs about 300 yards in rear of the line, but its adventures in connection with this struggle were not yet over. On

---

[1] Killed—Lieuts. R. N. Strutt and G. Jack. Died of wounds—Lieut. R. S. Wilson and 2nd Lieut. C. O. Anderson. Wounded—Captain G. H. Hay, Lieut. J. A. Turner, 2nd Lieuts. C. B. Whittaker and R. N. Mitchell. Missing—2nd Lieuts. C. D. Mayo and D. Pease.

the following day the battalion snipers returned to the front line and with a grim, vindictive joy shot down many of the Germans, who could scarcely move along their battered trenches without exposing themselves. On the 27th September the battalion went into billets at Ouderdom and on the 28th it was inspected by the Corps Commander, General Allenby, who complimented the men on the manner in which they had carried out their task on the 25th and the very smart appearance that they presented after so much desperate fighting.

On the 29th the Royal Scots returned to the front line at a sector on the right of their previous position. "C" Company and the battalion bombers remained out, because they had been ear-marked to take part in a bombing enterprise. The Germans had blown a mine in the salient formerly occupied by "B" Company and had effected a lodgment at its nose. Since our lines would always be open to sudden raids if they were allowed to remain there, we determined to make an effort to drive them out. For this purpose "C" Company and the bombers were to co-operate with the 4th Middlesex Regiment in an attack, which after a short artillery bombardment was to be launched at 2.15 P.M. on the 30th. In this operation "C" Company was in the centre, supported on the right by a company of the Middlesex and on the left by a company of the 2nd Suffolks. Ultimately the enterprise was postponed for an hour.

The operation was almost entirely a matter of bombs, and progress was slow because the Germans, in anticipation of an attack, had taken precautions. They had constructed numerous steps and barricades, defended by groups of bombers, while the approaches over the open were covered by machine-guns. Under these conditions the fighting that ensued was of a fatiguing and desperate character. The bombers, advancing first, deluged a barricade with their missiles till it was thought that all behind it must be either killed or wounded, and then men armed with the bayonet went forward to clear the way to the next barrier. This combat proved that grenades were more noisy than deadly, for the bayonet men always found themselves confronted by a garrison which appeared to have suffered surprisingly little from their explosion. Owing to the confined area in which the struggle took place, no quarter could be asked or given, and after an hour's gruesome fighting the Royal Scots had won back only ten yards of trench. Captain Stewart fought like a paladin; he led first the bombers, then the bayonet men, and was always in the thick of the fray. There were no limits to his daring, and jumping out of the trench he began to throw bombs from the parapet. But a machine-gun bullet quickly cut short his life and with his death the whole attack collapsed. His loss was a calamity to the entire battalion. His glowing personality melted depression and kindled confidence, and in his presence the meanest man felt and behaved like a hero. In recording his death even the compiler of the battalion diary abandoned for one brief sentence his rigid devotion to the recital of bald facts: "In Captain Stewart the battalion lost one of its most capable officers; cool-headed in all difficulties, and as gallant as ever lived." After he fell, the fight degenerated into an exchange of bombs in which Lieut. Robertson, who commanded the bombers, was wounded, and the survivors of "C" Company commenced to build new bombing posts to maintain the ground that they had won. The enterprise had failed and had cost the Royal Scots sixty additional casualties. On the 1st October "C" Company and the bombers rejoined the battalion.

CHAPTER XI

THE BATTLE OF LOOS

25th to 28th September 1915

Objectives for 25th September. Nature of the terrain. Rôles of the Ninth and Fifteenth Divisions. Action of 11th and 12th Royal Scots, 25th September. The Attack on Haisnes. German counter-attack. Position at close of 25th. Events on 26th. Fosse 8 lost, 27th September. Fifteenth Division at Loos. Action of 13th Royal Scots, 25th September. Situation at nightfall. Attack on Hill 70, 26th September. German counter-attacks. Gallantry of Private Dunsire. Evacuation of Hill 70. Results of the Battle.

WHILE the veterans of the 2nd Royal Scots were engaged near Hooge, the 11th, 12th, and 13th Battalions were fighting in the main action. This was carried out by General Gough's I. Corps, which included the Ninth Division, on the left, and by General Rawlinson's IV. Corps, which included the Fifteenth Division, on the right. The object of the British force was to carry the system of German fortifications stretching from Haisnes in the north to Hulluch in the south, and then to continue the advance rapidly towards Carvin in order to protect the left flank of the French Tenth Army, which was to operate south of Lens. Rumours of a big attack had been afloat among our men since the beginning of August, but not until September were the final arrangements made, and the assault was ultimately fixed for the 25th. The men had abundance of warning that great events were impending, for they were set to prepare the faggots for their own martyrdom; every day and every night large parties were digging trenches, improving communications, and conveying stores to various dumps. Digging was never at any time popular, but on the whole men preferred it to carrying burdensome stores for what seemed miles along the slippery floors of cramping trenches. Most of all they disliked the task of taking up the heavy gas cylinders to the front line, not so much on account of the fatigue which the work entailed, as because of the nerve-racking fear that a chance shell would result in the asphyxiation of the whole party.

The attack was to be preceded by a four days' bombardment, and on the 25th September, after the gas had been discharged from our front, the infantry were to mount the parapets at 6.30 A.M. We hoped that our gas attack would be as effective as that of the enemy at Ypres in April, and that where our artillery failed actually to demolish obstacles, it would suffice to paralyse the defenders and prevent them from offering an energetic resistance.

The ground chosen for the battle was one of the ugliest and most grimy parts of France, but its value was not to be judged by its lack of beauty, for its sooty bosom covered a wealth of industrial resources, the deprivation of which seriously crippled France throughout the war. It lay between the two great industrial centres of La Bassée and Lens, and like most other prosperous mining districts it betrayed its association with modern industry by the squalor of its soil, its rows of petty cottages, and a multitude of spoil heaps. There was no scarcity of landmarks; wherever the eye turned it encountered mining shafts and dumps of debris. But these accretions of industry, though useful to the attack because of their aid to direction, were even more favourable to the defence, since each shaft and mound furnished a ready-made fortress admirably adapted for the siting of the deadly machine-guns.

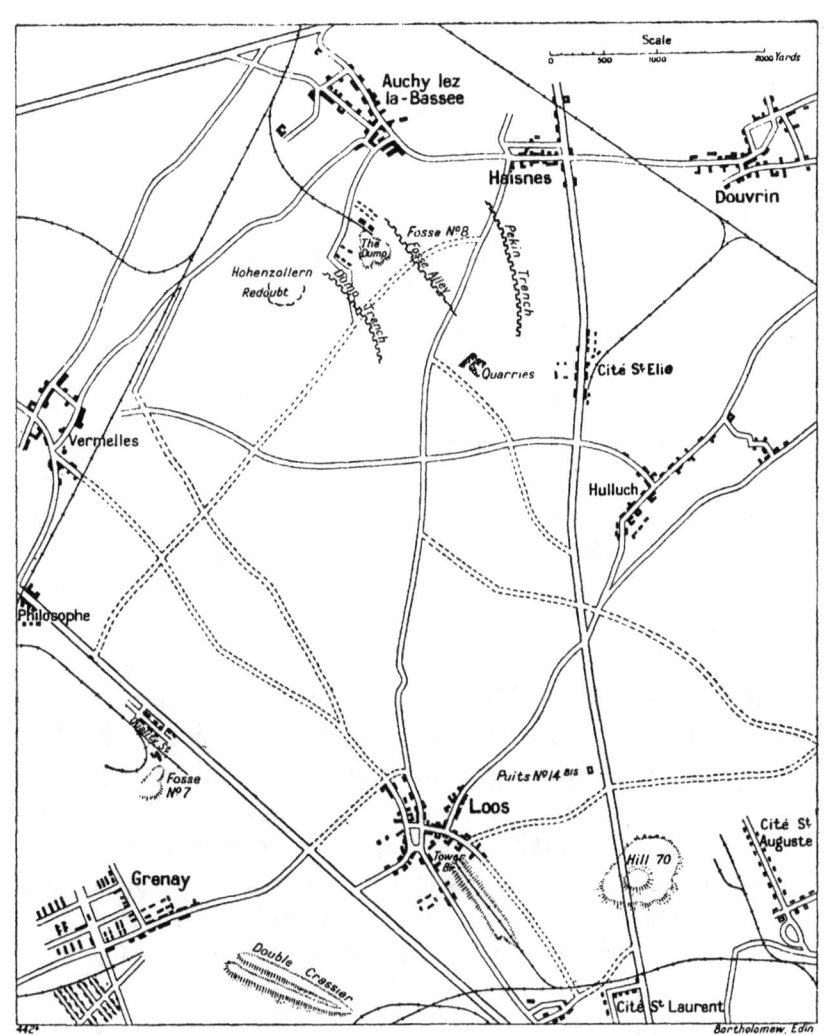

MAP IX.—The Battle of Loos, 25th to 28th September 1915.

Even apart from these features the Germans had a clear advantage. The general lie of the land was flat. From Vermelles in the British zone the ground rolled gently in a succession of slight crests which, being held by the enemy, enabled him to control his artillery fire by direct observation. In the German sector there stood out two most conspicuous and important tactical features, lying at the extremities of the area that the British proposed to attack. These were Fosse 8 and the Dump in the north, and the Double Crassier in the south. By capturing these positions the British could expect to command the whole surrounding district and would be able to assist the infantry by bringing up guns to their close support. If the operation resulted in our securing these positions, it would be well worth while. Apart from the slag heaps and pit-heads the country was open; nowhere could one trace a hedge, and the only trees that graced the landscape were those that lined the Hulluch Road.

The Ninth Division was involved in the northern and the Fifteenth Division in the southern portion of the battlefield. In each case the rôle assigned to the Royal Scots battalions was curiously similar. In the north the 11th and the 12th were with the 27th Brigade in reserve, and their part in the battle would therefore depend upon the fortunes of the two attacking brigades. These were to capture the Hohenzollern Redoubt, a maze of trenches which formed an insurance for the protection of the German front system, the Dump and Fosse 8, after which they were to seize Pekin Trench, the German line to the west of the village of Haisnes. To those of our men recruited from the mining districts of Lowland Scotland, the country in which they were operating was thoroughly congenial, for it seemed to them almost a replica of their homes near Broxburn or West Calder. If the 26th and the 28th Brigades were successful in all their objects, and if the Second Division, which was on the left of the Ninth, was able to capture Auchy, then the 26th and the 28th Brigades, closely supported by the 27th, were to continue the advance against Douvrin. If, however, as was very likely, Auchy was not taken, the two attacking brigades of the Ninth Division, after capturing Haisnes, were to form a defensive flank facing north-east.

In the south the objectives of the Fifteenth Division were the German front trenches lying about half a mile west of Loos, the second system of trenches and the northern portion of Loos, Hill 70, Cité St Auguste on the outskirts of Lens, and the high ground north of Loisons-Sous-Lens. The action of the 13th Royal Scots, in reserve with the 45th Brigade, would be determined by the fate of the 44th and 46th Brigades which were to lead the attack. The town of Loos, which gave its name to the battle, is tucked away in a shallow dip from which the ground rises to the coppiced slopes of Hill 70. The position of the town was clearly indicated to us by an iron-mining superstructure which, standing out in the distance with the delicacy of an etching, was happily christened by our men "The Tower Bridge."

The 25th September broke with a dun-coloured soggy sky casting a mantle of gloom over the battle-field. In the north the operations against the Dump and Fosse 8 were conspicuously successful, in spite of a grave check to the 28th Brigade and the Second Division. Regardless of bullets and shells, the Highlanders of the 26th Brigade, with traditional Celtic dash, flung themselves against the German fortifications and carried the Hohenzollern Redoubt, the Dump, and Fosse 8 in succession. Then they streamed eastwards towards Pekin Trench. Meantime, the units of the 27th Brigade were moving up from their positions in reserve, along trenches crowded from the first moment of the assault with wounded men and carrying parties. They had been scheduled to occupy the front trenches on the right of the divisional sector as soon as they were vacated by the 26th Brigade, but all the carefully drawn-up plans for the regulation of traffic in the communication trenches broke down during the stress of battle, and the advance to the front line was a dreadful nightmare. Not only were the troops exhausted by the halts which they were compelled to make every few minutes, owing to wounded men pushing their way down the same trench, but they suffered many casualties from the shells with which the enemy sprinkled our hinterland. The 11th Royal Scots, on the left, had the most arduous passage of all. The communication trench up which they advanced was more choked than the others owing to the collapse of the 28th Brigade's attack, and on reaching a point near the Vermelles-La Bassée Railway the battalion was obliged to turn into another trench, where fortunately it was able to make more rapid progress. On account of these delays the 11th Royal Scots were late in arriving at the front line, which they should have reached in time to follow the 12th Royal Scots, the leading unit of the brigade. Lieut.-Colonel Loch's men had already crossed into No-Man's-Land followed by the 10th Argylls, but the Highlanders halted to allow the 11th Royal Scots to pass through and take their allotted place.

The Royal Scots could hardly persuade themselves that the attack of the Highland Brigade had been successful, for as soon as they set foot in No-Man's-Land they came under a deluge of bullets. From the high ground on the left that the 28th Brigade had failed to capture and from Cité St Elie the Germans were able to sweep most of the ground up to our front line with rifle and machine-gun fire and every few yards of progress were purchased by a mounting list of dead and wounded, but gallantly led by their officers, the Royal Scots pressed on unwaveringly. At one point so murderous was the fire from the village of Cité St Elie that the men took shelter in a trench, but at the cry of Lieut.-Colonel Dundas, "Come on, Royal Scots!" the whole line surged forward again.

About 11 A.M. the 11th and the 12th Royal Scots, now formed into a single line with the latter on the right, reached Pekin Trench, where they came upon the most advanced troops of the 26th Brigade. The men had been marching for nearly five hours and their weary gait betrayed how much the unusual exertions had told upon them, but all were keyed up for a supreme effort, and after a scarcely perceptible halt they advanced against the village of Haisnes. If this could have been done an hour earlier, the village might have been secured, but the Germans had recovered from the shock of our assault and were sending up large forces for a counter-attack. Their garrisons maintained a continuous fire on the tongue of land between Haisnes and Pekin Trench, and the Royal Scots had to make their advance unsupported by any artillery fire. Their attack, skilfully conducted, was a striking proof of the efficiency of their training and would have done credit to a battalion of regulars. Working forward by small groups, each supporting the advance of its neighbour by covering fire, they swiftly lessened the distance between them and their goal by a series of short, sharp rushes, and a few sections even established themselves in the outskirts of Haisnes. But the Germans, most of whom were fresh troops, had a considerable superiority in numbers and after a stiff contest they succeeded in driving out our men. Hoping that new forces would arrive and thus allow the attack to be carried on, the surviving Royal Scots formed a line in the open about thirty yards east of Pekin Trench.

The 12th Battalion, on the right, was in touch with troops of the Seventh Division, but the position of the Royal Scots for the purpose of defence was hopeless. The raising of an arm, the slightest movement of the body, at once drew fire, and the discomfort of our men, condemned to lie still under drenching rain, became excruciating. But they would not surrender easily to an acknowledgment of defeat, and clinging to the hope that soon fresh troops must arrive, they refused to budge from their position, till dusk began to creep over the battlefield. Then having realised, with a despairing sense of frustration, that no help was to be expected, they withdrew to the shelter of Pekin Trench, where they had the Gordons of the 26th Brigade on their left. Shortly afterwards Brig.-General Bruce, the commander of the 27th Brigade, arrived, and learning that both Haisnes and Cité St Elie were strongly garrisoned he decided that an attack on the former was out of the question.

Defence was now the sole concern of the brigade. Pekin Trench offered poor protection against an attack from the east, being completely exposed to the fire of the Germans in Haisnes and Cité St Elie. The parapet rattled continuously from the impact of the bullets with which the enemy unceasingly sprayed our position, and no man could relish the prospect of peering over the top to see what was taking place. Our troops were virtually disarmed by the disadvantages of their position. Moreover, the whole of the trench was not in our hands, and in the northern portion of it the enemy, free from molestation, could mount a fresh attack at his leisure. Our men, soaked to the skin and benumbed by cold, were further handicapped by the fact that their rifles were so clogged with mud that they could not be fired without great difficulty, and the Béthune bombs were about as serviceable as stones, since their fuse lighters were so moist that they could not be ignited. In short, the position of the defenders was beset by almost every conceivable difficulty.

Fully alive to our weakness, the Germans emerging from Haisnes attacked the Gordons and overmastering their courageous defence drove them out of Pekin Trench. The plight of the Royal Scots was now desperate; unsupported on both flanks, since the troops of the Seventh Division had already been compelled to retire, they had to fight with fierce stubbornness to prevent the enemy from surrounding them. In this phase of the battle at least, they had the satisfaction of inflicting on the foe more losses than they themselves sustained; and drawing clear from the net in which the Germans were endeavouring to enmesh them, they fought their way back under the cool leadership of Lieut.-Colonel Loch to Fosse Alley, a trench running south from Fosse 8. Night was dropping veil upon veil of crape, and under the cover of darkness the Royal Scots were reorganised by Lieut.-Colonel Loch. The enemy had been so heavily punished that his attack was temporarily checked.

Thus our fortunes in the northern part of the battle-field had been chequered, but at the close of the 25th September the Ninth Division was still in possession of the Dump and Fosse 8, and if these places could be kept, the action would not have been fought in vain. They were manned by the 26th Brigade, the right flank of which was protected by the troops of the 27th Brigade, who were in touch on their right with the Seventh Division. Casualties among all ranks had been high, and the 11th Royal Scots had to mourn the great loss of Lieut.-Colonel Dundas, one of the best-loved officers in the Regiment, who probably fell during the advance on Haisnes.

The trend of the fighting, when night fell on the 25th, contained more than an echo-hint of trouble for the exhausted troops of the Ninth Division, and in fact the tide of fortune had set in strongly against them. Near Fosse 8 matters steadily and surely changed for the worse. All through the night the Germans kept up a harassing fire to prevent us from consolidating our captured positions, and before daybreak they had completed their plans for the recapture of Fosse 8 and the Dump. During the night the troops of the 26th Brigade were relieved by fresh troops, who had absolutely no experience of trench warfare, from the 73rd Brigade of the Twenty-fourth Division. The ordeal before these would have tested veterans, and to send in raw soldiers at the very crisis of the battle was a step that could only be justified if no other forces were available. The disasters that followed cannot fairly be attributed to the men of the 73rd Brigade. The position of the brigade was rendered very precarious by a hostile night attack which opened up its right flank. Creeping forward in the pitch darkness Boche skirmishers wormed a path between the Seventh Division and the 27th Brigade and suddenly assaulted the Quarries garrisoned by the former. Taken completely unawares the men of the Seventh Division had no chance to put up an effective resistance, and among the prisoners captured by the Germans at the Quarries was Brig.-General Bruce of the 27th Brigade. This disaster exposed the right wing of that brigade, the units of which were intermixed in Fosse Alley. German bombers, following up their success, began an attack along Fosse Alley, and Lieut.-Colonel Loch, now in command

Lieut.-Colonel R. C. DUNDAS, 11th Battalion, The Royal Scots.

[*To face p.* 192.

of the brigade, after consultation with the other C.Os., thought it expedient to withdraw to our original front line. This was safely accomplished, but the retirement exposed the Fosse and the Dump to assault from the south as well as from the front and the north. Inspired by their gains the Boches assailed these positions with ever-increasing weight and fury from three sides.

Major-General Thesiger, the commander of the Ninth Division, being anxious to keep the Fosse, could not allow Fosse Alley, the natural buttress of its southern flank, to fall into the hands of the enemy, so he ordered the survivors of the 11th and the 12th Royal Scots, on the morning of the 26th, to advance to Dump Trench, part of the original Boche front line, while the 10th Argylls and the 6th Royal Scots Fusiliers went on to reoccupy Fosse Alley. These measures were carried out, but an operation for the recapture of the Quarries was unsuccessful. The Fosse Alley garrison, however, easily repelled all frontal assaults, and there would have been little reason for misgiving, had it not been for the unsteadiness of the 73rd Brigade, which had suffered severely from the enemy's violent shell fire. Desultory encounters, chiefly between parties of bombers, livened the night and prevented sleep.

The strain of this persistent pressure was enormous, and ultimately proved more than the inexperienced troops of the 73rd Brigade could endure. Early in the morning of the 27th September they were driven out of the Fosse and their withdrawal left the Fosse Alley garrison in a sorry plight with both its flanks unprotected. A party of the 12th Royal Scots under Lieut. Rutherford was sent to reinforce it, and a magnificent but unavailing resistance was made against hopeless odds. Fighting every inch of the way, the garrison withdrew through Dump Trench, where the accurate fire of the 11th and the

12th Royal Scots checked the hostile advance. Straining every nerve, the Boches now threw themselves against the Hohenzollern Redoubt, but a splendid counter-charge by the 26th Brigade enabled us to maintain our hold on that strong point. In the defence of the Redoubt the bombers of the 11th and the 12th Royal Scots greatly distinguished themselves and rendered glorious service in keeping the enemy at bay.

The leading troops of the Twenty-eighth Division were now arriving on the battlefield and it became possible to withdraw the exhausted survivors of the Ninth Division. The relief was a lengthy process owing to darkness and confusion. Part of the 27th Brigade was clear by daybreak on the 28th, but the 12th Royal Scots remained in Dump Trench till about noon, while over 100 of the 11th Royal Scots, under Captain Wemyss Campbell, actively assisted troops of the Twenty-eighth Division in a series of bombing attacks and were not relieved till 9 P.M. The first rendezvous of the battered 27th Brigade was in the vicinity of Béthune.

We must now turn to the fortunes of the 13th Royal Scots near Loos where the Fifteenth Division achieved a remarkable success. The 44th and 46th Brigades in an irresistible charge bore down all opposition, and along with the Forty-seventh Division on their right drove the enemy from Loos and occupied the village. Scarcely halting they swarmed up the slopes of Hill 70, and if the advance had been stopped at this point the final results of the fighting would have been more satisfactory for us; but with orders to press on to Cité St Auguste the attackers, flushed with victory, strode down the eastern slopes of the hill and penetrated the outskirts of St Auguste. The Germans who had surrendered found themselves on the hill without a guard to look after them, and taking up their arms again, fired at the backs of their recent captors and made preparations to resist those who were coming to support the Highlanders.

Lieut.-Colonel MacLear's men did not share in the first stage of the attack, but their rôle was none the less strenuous. Without any of the stimulus engendered by the capture of a series of obstacles, they had to thread their way across ground continually pitted by the shells and bullets of the enemy, who was now recovering from the shock of the Highland charge. In the small hours of the 25th, the battalion left its assembly position near the village of Mazingarbe and had proceeded but a short distance when the men were alarmed by the sound of an explosion in their midst. A private had carelessly dropped a box of detonated bombs, which exploded, seriously wounding sixteen men. As the battalion was going along the trenches on the south side of Fosse No. 7, a sudden inferno proclaimed that our attack had been unleashed. But the trench walls were so high that the eager men could see nothing except where the sides had been smashed by shells and even then beheld only pale drifting mists of poison gas intermingled with fleecy shrapnel bursts. Curiosity was kept within bounds by a heavy shrapnel bombardment which caused some casualties in the battalion. Near Quality Street there was a halt for almost an hour and the men spent the time doing their utmost to ease the wounded, of whom many were lying on stretchers in rows at the little village. What news they heard was cheering, and the optimistic and confident accounts given by the wounded appeared to be well founded, for about 7.30 A.M. the hostile guns practically ceased firing and the rumour was circulated that the enemy was hastily extricating his guns in a headlong retreat.

Then the Royal Scots advanced to the old German front line and the men were set to work rebuilding the shattered trench. There seemed now to be a lull in the battle and the fear began to take root that the position in front was less promising than it had been. Lieut.-Colonel MacLear, whose wrist had been grazed by a bullet, strolled about the top keeping one eye on his men and the other on Loos. Something had gone amiss with the attack, for after 7 A.M. appeal after appeal for assistance was received by the Royal Scots from the assaulting brigades. Gladly would the battalion have responded to these appeals, but no instructions to advance from its position were received till 11.30 A.M. Had the order been given when the first call for help was received, it is quite probable that Hill 70 at least would have remained in our possession. The Royal Scots at any rate were convinced to a man that the outcome of the battle would have been entirely different, if they had been allowed to press on shortly after 7 A.M.

As matters stood, it was after midday before the battalion left the German front line and advanced towards the village of Loos, conspicuous by its tall twin towers. In extended order, the Royal Scots under heavy shrapnel fire went down the slope leading into the village, in front of which the wire defences were practically intact, and half the battalion had to proceed like sheep through a solitary gap in the wire before other approaches were discovered. The Royal Scots were amazed to find French civilians still in Loos who, shaken and terrified though they were by the ordeal through which they had passed, brought welcome gifts of hot coffee to our men.

All the units of the 44th and 46th Brigades were near Hill 70, which had now become the key-point of the battle. The universal impression in the Fifteenth Division was that a great opportunity of scoring an important victory had been lost. All knew that the attack was to be supported by the XI. Corps, and they felt that if it had been ready to advance when the Germans were pulling back their guns, the whole system of the defences to the north of Lens would have been shattered. This feeling finds expression in the diary of the 13th Royal Scots: "A whole Corps could have been moved up to Loos by now." The troops on Hill 70 were experiencing great difficulty in holding their ground and continued to ask for reinforcements. The Germans were no longer content to remain on the defensive; they were maintaining a heavy pressure on the hill and their gunners were putting down an unpleasant barrage to the north-west and west of Loos.

Lieut.-Colonel MacLear at once despatched "B" and "C" Companies to reinforce our line on the western slopes of Hill 70. From the Tower Bridge a large spoil heap ran to the south-east. Hugging its base for shelter "B" and "C" Companies advanced for some 200 yards, then climbing the steep and slippery sides of the slag heap, a platoon at a time, they quickly crossed the exposed surface and slithered down through the stunted shrubbery on to the western slopes of Hill 70, where the firing line was protected by a natural bank, rising breast high from the ground. About 4 P.M. the position of the Royal Scots was as follows: "B" and "C" Companies were on the hill, "A" was on the Loos-Hulluch Road, while "D" Company and the machine-gun section in reserve, in captured German trenches, were held in readiness to support the left flank of the division, which was endangered owing to the failure of the First Division to keep pace with the Fifteenth. By this time, from information supplied by Lieut.-Colonel Sandilands of the 7th Camerons, Lieut.-Colonel MacLear had a fairly accurate idea of what had happened. The daring groups that had entered St Auguste had been forced by the counter-strokes of the Germans to fall back on the north-west side of Hill 70, the crest of which was held by the enemy. At 7 P.M. men from practically every unit in the division were to be found on the hill, on a line running from the Dump on the south-east edge of Loos along the north-west slopes of the hill to the point where they were cut by the Lens-Hulluch Road, south of Puits 14 Bis. Both flanks were guarded by companies of the Royal Scots, "C" on the right, in touch with the Forty-seventh Division, and "B" on the left. In the centre were men of the Royal Scots Fusiliers and the 11th Argylls, and farther north some troops of the 46th Brigade were said to be beyond the pit known as Puits 14 Bis. The sorely battered 7th Camerons, reduced to less than 50 strong, were withdrawn and Lieut.-Colonel MacLear took command of our line on the hill. He was most uneasy about his unsupported left flank, against which it was certain that the German counter-thrust would be directed, and he requested a staff-officer to report how vital it was that some force should be sent up as speedily as possible to fill the gap between the First and the Fifteenth Divisions. German guns were now vigorously shelling Loos, and if help did not arrive without delay we would be in danger of losing the important positions that we had captured at so heavy a cost. Meantime Lieut.-Colonel MacLear strengthened his left flank by sending to the support of "B" Company a company of the 7th Royal Scots Fusiliers and some motor machine-gunners, and he made arrangements for tools to be supplied to enable the men to dig themselves in before daylight.

Thus by nightfall, on the 25th September, the situation at Loos was similar to that at Fosse 8. In the south we were in possession of the Double Crassier, Loos, and the western slopes of Hill 70, upon the fate of which the issue of the battle hung. But the élan of our attack and the importance and extent of our gains surprised not merely the enemy but our High Command, whose failure to send up reinforcements in time to take advantage of the success caused much bitterness among our men, who felt keenly that the gains procured by Scottish valour had been carelessly frittered away. "Thus ended the operations of the 25th," wrote an officer of the 13th Royal Scots. "The chance of a great victory was thrown away through the XI. Corps not supporting the IV. Corps immediately as originally intended; had this been done Lens would have been taken and the Germans forced to fall back from La Bassée and the Aubers Ridge." This may have been unduly optimistic, but no account of Loos would be true which ignored the impression prevalent among those who took part in the fight on the 25th September, that the fruits of a great victory had been allowed to slip from our grasp. But though the chance of a break-through had been irretrievably lost, the balance of advantage would be tilted in our favour if we could keep what we had won. Even to effect this reinforcements were urgently required.

During the hours of darkness the troops of the Fifteenth Division were feverishly engaged in consolidating their positions, but little effective work could be done owing to lack of tools and the incessant fire maintained by the enemy. There was no hostile infantry attack, but there were several sharp bombing encounters between "B" Company of the 13th Royal Scots and some German patrols, which crawled down from the crest of the hill to probe our line.

It required no gifts of vaticination to predict a fiery ordeal on the 26th. From the time that the first streak of light glimmered in the eastern sky, "B" Company, which held the post of danger, was subjected to a pitiless enfilade fire which caused the death of Captain B. D. Bruce and a number of his men. The only cheering episode was the arrival of the long awaited reinforcements of the XI. Corps. Shortly after midnight on the 25th/26th, two battalions of the 62nd Brigade reached the hill and relieved such troops of the 44th Brigade as still remained in the line. "D" Company of the 13th Royal Scots and the machine-gun section were also brought up and were established in reserve in the south-west outskirts of Loos, which had been savagely shelled all through the night. Then about 7 A.M. Lieut.-Colonel MacLear was informed that the 45th Brigade with the two battalions of the 62nd would attack the German position on the crest of the hill, and if the enterprise were successful, the Twenty-first and Twenty-fourth Divisions were to assault St Auguste.

To those on the spot such an operation appeared to be full of hazard. Our line near the hill formed a sharp salient exposed to a deadly enfilade fire from the enemy, and to make an attack under such conditions, without the support of covering fire on the flanks, seemed an act of folly. It appeared more reasonable that a thrust should be made on the left of the 45th Brigade, where assistance was urgently needed, and our troops on the slopes of the hill were in a favourable position to support such an operation by covering fire. Moreover, an unsuccessful assault on the crest might well result in our being driven off the hill altogether. The 45th Brigade however had to do its best to carry out orders. After half an hour's artillery bombardment the blow was to be delivered at 9 A.M. The 13th Royal Scots were on the left, with their right flank on the sunken road running east from Loos to Hill 70, where they were in touch with the Argylls in the centre. Three Companies, "A," "B," and "C," were to make the attack and were to be followed up by "D" Company carrying entrenching tools, and the machine-gun section. The time at the disposal of Lieut.-Colonel MacLear for issuing orders and framing a satisfactory scheme of attack was much too short, and it was nearly 9 o'clock before all the companies received their instructions.

Our worst forebodings were realised. The Germans bombarded our positions with furious determination from 8 A.M., and when thirty minutes later our barrage opened, it created such deadly havoc in "B" Company that it was unable to take part in the action. Our gun-fire did more harm to our men than to the Germans, but as an officer of the 13th Royal Scots mordantly remarked, "It was not likely that guns, which had not registered, would accomplish in half an hour what four days' bombardment and forty minutes' gas were considered necessary to carry out on the 25th." The operation was forlorn and hopeless, but the men never flinched from orders that could only involve them in death. As soon as "A" Company moved forward it was confronted by a tough wire entanglement and, after vainly endeavouring to tear a gap in it, had to return to its original position, having suffered great losses. The Germans had the range of our line to an inch, and as soon as "C" Company topped the parapet, Major G. D. Macpherson, Captain G. S. Robertson, and many of the men were shot down before they had moved a yard.

While these events were taking place on the left, the enemy, just before 9 A.M., began a dangerous counter-movement against the division on the right of the Fifteenth. Since our position on the western slopes of Hill 70 would be a death-trap if the right as well as the left flank were exposed, Lieut.-Colonel MacLear at once despatched two machine-gun teams to cover the streets leading into Loos from the south-east. This support was at least temporarily sufficient to establish the right flank. As an additional precaution "D" Company was sent to the right of the sunken road connecting Loos and Cité St Laurent, while a machine-gun was taken up by Corporal F. Whittle to the left of our line on Hill 70.

It was well that the hostile thrust on the right had been checked, for dire perils were accumulating on the left, where the foe never abated his pressure. The gallant and isolated parties of Camerons, who had grimly hung on to a wood east of Puits 14 Bis, were compelled to give way about 10.30 A.M., and the Germans were thus able to increase the weight of their fire against our left. Weak and dispirited troops might well have given up the game as lost. All the elements conducive to panic were present: our attack had spent itself, parties of our men were seen to be retiring, and the Germans were fighting with the full consciousness that they held the upper hand. But in the military qualities of tenacity and endurance the Lowland Scot is unsurpassed, as countless battles against the "auld enemy" have time and again proved; he is never quite as good as when things are at their worst. The most desperate forays of the enemy did not avail to shake the Royal Scots. When the Camerons evacuated the wood in front of Puits 14 Bis, Captain Penney of "A" Company calmly advanced with a platoon to reoccupy it, but he and many of his men were shot down before they had gone more than a few yards.

Then occurred an incident in lighter vein which helped to relieve the tension. The heroic gesture in modern warfare is not infrequently represented by an

Private R. DUNSIRE, V.C., 13th Battalion, The Royal Scots.

ordinary phrase transcending its customary meaning by a quality of the voice. Thus when an excited scout, feeling that the whole world was tumbling in chaos about him, shouted: "The Germans are coming!" Major Raymond, carefully fixing his eyeglass in his eye, calmly queried: "Germans? Where? I don't see any Germans." The commonplace acquires a tremendous significance when men are tuned up to expect the dramatic, and Major Raymond's remark had the bracing quality of a reproach and an exhortation; it warned the men not to build perils out of their imagination and to deal with emergencies only as they arose.

No regulars could have surpassed the work done that day by the quondam civilians of the New Army. Alike as regards individual pluck and concerted movements the men were admirable. But even on the 26th September, when deeds of heroism were common, an act of remarkable daring by Private Dunsire caused those who saw it instinctively to hold their breath. Lying in the fire-swept zone between British and Germans, a wounded man moved a limb as if in a despairing appeal for assistance, and Private Dunsire, heedless of the flood of bullets, crawled out to him and brought him back to safety. He had just returned when a shout for help drew his attention to a second wounded man, who also was rescued after a death-inviting sally by Private Dunsire. How he managed to escape without a scratch was a mystery, for the earth was madly dancing to the continuous thud of bullets.

By this time the Germans, having established themselves at Puits 14 Bis, were in a position to work round the left flank of the Hill 70 garrison, when to the joy of the Royal Scots more troops of the XI. Corps were seen in the distance. But these were mostly raw and inexperienced, and they entered the battle after it had turned in favour of the enemy. Under the circumstances their conduct was highly creditable. Ignorant of the precise positions of friend and foe they at first caused some casualties among the Royal Scots, who sought to indicate to the newcomers that they were friends by brandishing their balmorals on their bayonets. Then a heavy fire from the hostile machine-guns planted near Puits 14 Bis smote the reinforcements and compelled them to give ground. At the same time a Boche drive against our right flank was stopped by the fire of the Royal Scots machine-guns and a battalion of the 62nd Brigade.

The failure of the reinforcements to come up into line with the 45th Brigade settled the fate of our garrison on the hill. The position of our left flank was almost untenable, and an attempt by "B" Company to man a short stretch of the Loos-Hulluch Road was defeated by hostile machine-gun fire. Still the 45th Brigade clung obstinately to all its advanced posts, till at 4 P.M. it was ordered to withdraw from the hill. The retirement was carried out with remarkable precision, Corporal Whittle of the Royal Scots with his machine-gun covering the movement of the infantry, till Hill 70 was evacuated. The bulk of the 13th Royal Scots fell back on Loos, where they were relieved by the Third Cavalry Division; "D" Company remained in the village in support of the cavalry till about 11 P.M., while the remainder went back with the other units of the brigade to the Grenay-Vermelles trenches.

A few scattered parties remained on the hill till midnight. 2nd Lieut. Linton of "A" Company, on receiving instructions to withdraw, ordered his men to retire in small groups. The company was well down the slope when he noticed that Loos was being violently shelled, and, thinking that it would be wiser to keep his men where they were than to lead them to a place where they were certain to sustain casualties, he ordered them to halt. It is very doubtful if he could have continued the retirement in safety, for his men were in full view of the enemy and had to squat in shell-holes for shelter from the hostile fire. The fire became so hot that 2nd Lieut. Linton determined to return to his original trench, and on arriving there he found a number of men from various units still on the hill. Ably assisted by Sergeant Macalear, he assumed command of the whole party and organised a defence, but the German infantry fortunately made no attack and shortly after midnight reinforcements from the Cavalry Division began to appear on the hill. By this time the shelling had appreciably abated and 2nd Lieut. Linton led back his party, consisting of 19 men all told, through Loos to rejoin the 45th Brigade.

All three battalions of the Royal Scots suffered terribly in the battle. The 11th had eight officer casualties[1] and in other ranks the number of killed, wounded, and missing was three hundred and seventy; the 12th lost nine officers[2] and the casualties in other ranks totalled two hundred and eighty-five; the 13th lost fifteen officers[3] and three hundred and twenty-five other ranks.

[1] Lieut.-Colonel R. C. Dundas, Major K. McCloughlin, Captain A. H. Bell and 2nd Lieut. I. M. K. Brown were killed; Major N. M. Dryburgh, Captain J. Robertson, and Lieut. C. Dixon were wounded; Lieut. G. L. Brander was missing.

[2] 2nd Lieut. J. E. Ainslie was killed, the remainder, Captains G. D. Baillie-Hamilton, G. F. Faithfull, H. S. E. Stevens, Lieuts. F. L. Norton, J. R. Russell, 2nd Lieuts. G. Johnson Gilbert, F. J. Maloney, R. B. Stewart being wounded.

[3] Seven were killed—Major G. D. Macpherson, Captains I. C. Penney, B. D. Bruce, G. S. Robertson, Lieuts. C. B. Munro, R. A. Macfarlane, and 2nd Lieut. D. D. Brown. The wounded were—Lieut.-Colonel MacLear, Captains Buchanan and Glover, Lieuts. Christie and Underwood, 2nd Lieuts. Scott, Bramwell, Crowden, and Davies.

From start to finish Loos was a soldier's battle. The crusading spirit with which the men of the two Scottish divisions threw themselves into the fight, carried them over obstacles that might well have stopped veterans. But the ultimate results of the battle were disappointing. Loos remained in our hands, but Hill 70 and the important tactical points in the north, Fosse 8 and the Dump, were recaptured by the Germans. The success of the enemy in the north robbed our gains in the south of much of their value, for from the Dump and the Fosse the Germans commanded so extensive an observation that we were unable to plant our guns in the only valley from which they could effectively support the front-line positions in the newly-formed salient. For this reason the Loos salient was costly to hold, and in the north the Hohenzollern Redoubt remained a bone of contention between the two armies for many months. But whatever strictures may be passed on the conduct of the battle, none can apply to the men who fought in it. The New Army troops of the Ninth and the Fifteenth Divisions by their achievements won great and well-deserved credit. The 11th, 12th, and 13th Battalions of the Royal Scots had now proved themselves; they had shown a steadfastness, skill, and courage which made them worthy to take their place with the 1st and the 2nd in the glorious traditions of a famous regiment.

CHAPTER XII

THE EVACUATION OF GALLIPOLI

September 1915 *to January* 1916

Deadlock in Gallipoli. Trench life at Cape Helles. Attack on West Krithia Nullah by Royal Scots, 15th November. Turkish counter-attacks defeated. 5th Royal Scots at Suvla Bay. Winter conditions at Cape Helles. Decision to abandon Gallipoli. Difficulties with regard to Evacuation. Measures taken at Cape Helles. Incidents during the Evacuation, 8th January 1916.

THE failure of the Suvla Bay attack sealed the doom of our Gallipoli campaign. From that time a want of confidence clouded the minds of the leaders of the enterprise and it was not immediately clear what our next step should be. Unfortunately there was good reason for pessimism. The principal design of the campaign had been to circumvent the deadlock that had arisen on the Western front, and the most convincing evidence of its breakdown was the undoubted fact that a deadlock had also been reached in Gallipoli; opposing lines of trench systems as in France covered the ground at Cape Helles and Suvla Bay. It seemed that all our possibilities of effecting a surprise had been dissipated, and if we were to secure our objects by a series of trench-to-trench attacks we should require a far larger number of men and a much greater supply of heavy guns and shells than we had at the peninsula. But if this were the prerequisite of success, it was at least questionable if it were worth while persevering with the campaign. For the cost in life would necessarily be heavy, and it might serve our purpose better to concentrate on one front instead of two, and if this were so Gallipoli would have to be abandoned. It was at any rate sun-clear that we should not allow ourselves to drift into stagnation; we should either maintain a steady pressure until we had accomplished our purpose or we should abandon the enterprise. After the end of August there did ensue a period of stagnation caused by the fact that we had not finally determined our line of action with regard to Gallipoli.

Doubts and hesitations did not extend to regimental officers and men, who took it for granted that since they were dumped in Gallipoli they would not leave its shores until the command of the Dardanelles had been gained. But after August it was noticeable that no more big attacks were made and that all our enterprises were of a minor character. The 4th and the 7th Royal Scots were by no means apathetic and found much to interest them in the ordinary work of trench warfare. The latter soon had the satisfaction of becoming a battalion in strength as well as in name. On the 3rd September 12 officers and 440 other ranks, under the command of Captain W. T. Ewing, arrived at Gallipoli and made a vast difference to the appearance of the unit. Never again did the battalion receive such a large draft, which was ever after referred to by officers and men of the 7th as "The Five Hundred Draft."

Trench work, under the conditions that prevailed, was exacting. Fatigue in the front line was often forgotten in the interest that the men had in circumventing the Turkish bombers and snipers, and although the higher ground on which the hostile trenches were sited gave the enemy a natural advantage, our troops felt with good reason that they more than held their own in these little bickerings. But in support, reserve, or in rest, fatigue was the order of the day and even of the night. Since there were no roads, supplies had to be conveyed from the beaches to the front-line battalions by mule-carts or pack-mules along the dry water-courses that formed by no means ideal transport routes; and for much of the distance the supplies had to be man-handled by the weary troops. Dysentery was a merciless scourge and so consumed the strength of the 4th Royal Scots that at the beginning of November the battalion had to be reduced to two companies, the senior officer being Captain W. R. Cooper. Colonel Young was stricken down by fever and had to be evacuated, the 4th Royal Scots being attached once more to the 7th under the command of Lieut.-Colonel Peebles on the 4th November. At the beginning of December only two combatant officers and the Medical Officer remained of the forty-eight who had either gone out with the 4th Battalion to Gallipoli or had joined it with drafts from the 2/4th.

Much of our discomfort was due to the fact that the ground at our disposal was too limited in extent to permit of complete sanitary precautions being taken. The reek of ordure and sores lay heavy over the whole land, and such work in the way of hygienic arrangements as we were able to effect was neutralised by the fact that the Turks did not concern themselves at all about sanitation. Many of their dead were still unburied, and so much disease lurked in the earth and air that the peninsula became a huge lazar-house. Nor could our troops maintain health by the systematic training and recreation which were general in France, for since the whole of our area lay under the view of the enemy, no large party of men could be collected for training without drawing hostile fire. The men did contrive to play football on the comparatively level ground abutting on Morto Bay, but the games were usually punctuated by occasional shells. Bathing, while the weather remained warm, was the most popular exercise of all. Fortunately the troops were not troubled by gas attacks, but this was probably because the prevailing wind blew from our lines towards the opposing trenches. Risks could not be taken, however, and towards the end of the summer all ranks were issued with gas masks.

In the middle of September the tropical heat was mitigated by heavy downpours of rain which dispersed for a period the troublesome swarms of mosquitoes, but this relief was offset by discomforts of another kind, for the firm hard footing vanished with the arrival of softer weather, and the greasy surface of the clay subsoil upset the balance of heavily-loaded men moving up and down the narrow trenches. The lull in the active fighting was sometimes broken by sudden alarms. The tidings of our successes at Loos were greeted with general jubilation, and at a prearranged hour on the 27th September a great burst of cheering broke out along the whole length of the British line. The sound wakened up the Turks who, convinced that we were about to make an immediate attack, seized their rifles and blazed away thousands of rounds against our parapets. The thought of so much waste tickled the humour of the troops and a member of the 7th Royal Scots was inspired to pen a set of verses, of which the last stanza ran thus :—

> "And a despatch in pleasing wise
> Spoke of a daring enterprise
> Against some enemy supplies,
> Adding this tragic note :—
> The casualties of the force
> Were 60 men extremely hoarse
> And one severe sore throat."

October brought a foretaste of winter conditions. In the second week the men had their first real experience of Oriental rain. Falling so heavily that it seemed to form wires of steel in the air, the rain turned the dust into a thick gluey mud and filled up the burrows which the troops used as dug-outs in the rest camp. The men had waterproof sheets, but these were as useful as paper against the torrents of rain, and many of them, flooded out of their shelters, tramped about all night in an effort to quicken circulation. The cold was intense, and wherever they could find a half-dry nook, men huddled together for warmth and comfort. But these conditions had their compensations, for however direful they were to human beings they were fatal to flies, and after October there was a marked diminution in the number of these pests. This downpour was only a warning, an indication of the afflictions which the winter had in store for our men. After the second week the sun came out and dried up the trenches, but the air at night was too chilly to be altogether pleasant.

Since all ambitious operations had come to an end, units kept alive the fighting spirit by devising and making raids. Lieut.-Colonel Peebles prepared a plan for a raid on a Turkish trench running along the West Krithia nullah, but the battalion was relieved by the 7th Highland Light Infantry before there was a chance of putting it into execution. Our line near the vineyard, which had been the scene of much minor strife, was one of the spots where excitement could be had in unstinted measure. This was the part visited in October by the 7th Royal Scots, to whom the 1st Lancashire Yeomanry Regiment was attached for trench instruction, and there were several lively bombing encounters between the Royal Scots and the Turks, in which the latter were sharply handled. On the next occasion when the 7th Battalion took over the front line, Lieut.-Colonel Peebles had under his command the remnants of the 4th Royal

Scots as well, and before the tour was completed the Royal Scots dealt a shrewd blow against the enemy.

The Krithia nullah near the vineyard splits into two courses, known respectively as the East and West Krithia nullahs. The western bank of the latter stands about 40 feet above the level of the bed, but the ground on the east of the former slopes down more gradually to the floor of the water-course. Just at the bifurcation the wedge of land between the two branches runs up the ridge in a gentle slope. The Turkish trench system was skilfully sited on the cliffs overlooking the West Krithia nullah, then crossing the tongue of land, cut the slope on the east bank of the East Krithia nullah and moved on to the trenches in the vineyard. Since the nullahs formed the most tempting approaches up the hill —they had the irresistible appeal of the obvious—the Turks took care to construct their strongest works in their vicinity. The 156th Brigade made arrangements for an operation against the Turkish trenches on the east of East Krithia nullah and on the west of West Krithia nullah. Two companies of the 7th Royal Scots supported by two companies of the 4th were to undertake the latter attack, and the Cameronians, assisted by two companies of the 7th Royal Scots, the former. Hoping to take the enemy by surprise, we determined to dispense with the usual preliminary bombardment. The two operations were self-contained enterprises since our attacking forces were separated by the tongue of land between the two nullahs; 3 P.M. on the 15th November was the time fixed for the assault.

From the trenches of the 7th Royal Scots near the nullah jutted out saps where bombing posts had been established, and it was from the most forward post that the attacking groups were to embark on their adventure. What the 7th Royal Scots were asked to do was to capture a trench (H 11 A) running parallel to the nullah, as far as the point marked U, near which place a barricade was to be erected, and they had also to secure a trench (W-X) breaking off at right angles from H 11 A to the nullah. Bombing parties from Nos. 1 and 3 Companies of the 7th were to carry out these tasks, covered by the rifle and machine-gun fire of the two companies of the 4th Royal Scots. The signal for the attack was to be given by the explosion of a mine under a Turkish bombing station, when our bombers were to dash forward and our gunners were to shell the support and rear positions of the enemy.

Our careful organisation, in which not a detail was neglected, reaped complete success. A deafening crash and the sudden rise into the air of a pillar of smoke and debris formed a signal which none could mistake, and simultaneously with the opening salvos of our guns the bombers of the 7th, led by Lieut. J. Scott and Sergeant T. Berry, burst from our lines and dashed into the hostile trench. Most of the Turks were too shaken by the explosion of the mine to be capable of putting up a fight; some of them rushed from their shelters to ascertain what had caused the noise and these were disposed of before they had grasped the situation. Only a few quickly recovered their presence of mind; with these there was some brisk fighting, and during a rough-and-tumble *mêlée* a gigantic Turk, emerging from a dug-out, levelled his rifle point-blank at Lieut. Scott's head and pressed the trigger. Fortunately for the officer the bolt jammed, and before the Turk could discover what was amiss with his rifle he was shot by Corporal Kelly. Our bombers pierced so easily the resistance of the enemy that they passed beyond point U and reached another line fringed by the gleaming bayonets of the garrison. By this time Lieut. Scott

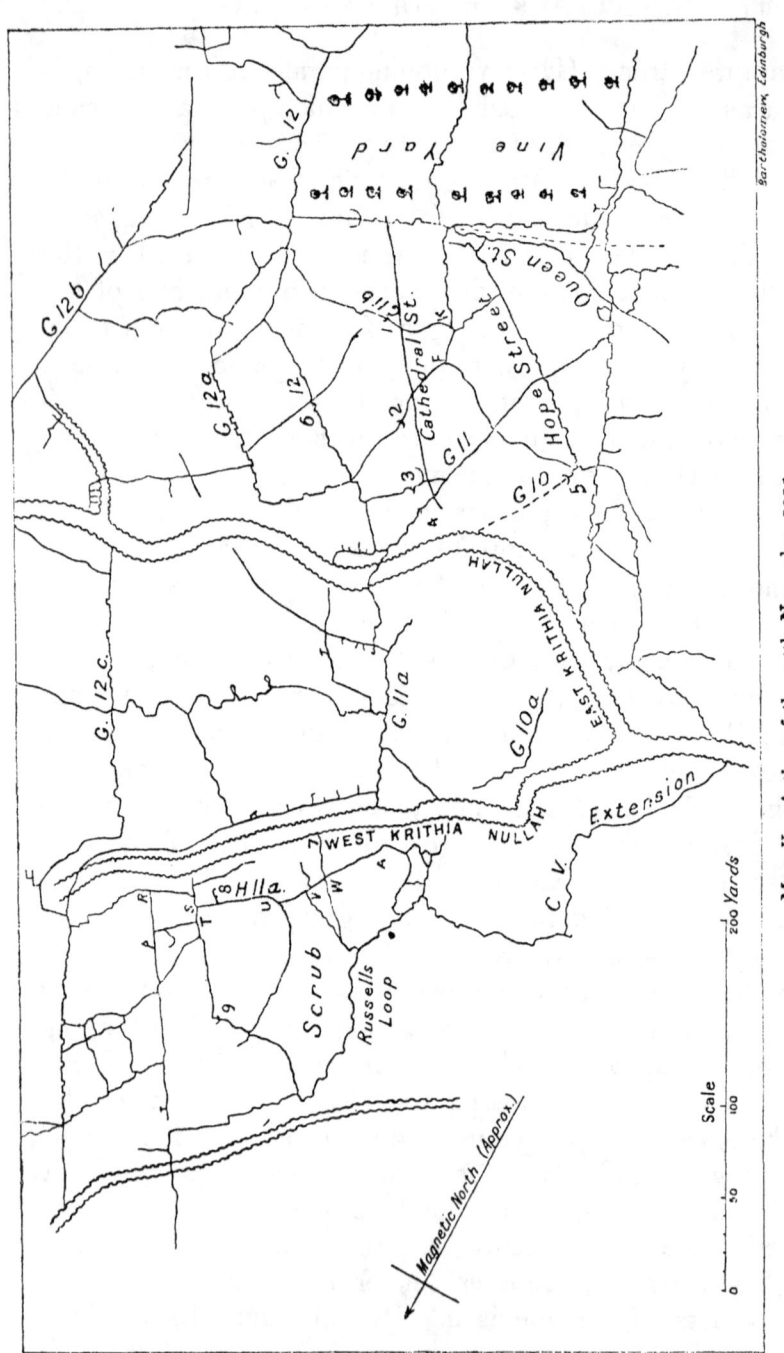

Map X.—Action of the 15th November 1915.

was aware that he had overshot his mark, and after his men had thrown a salvo of bombs into the Turkish trench, he led his party back to its proper position, a stout barricade being erected some distance in advance of it.

Meantime Sergeant Berry and his men proceeded unopposed down the trench W-X to the point where it intersected the nullah, and since this was the obvious avenue for a hostile counter-attack, the Royal Scots rapidly constructed a barricade at the junction of the trench and the nullah.

The brilliant success of this little affair was a reminder that mechanical devices and sheer weight of power are less effective servants of victory than surprise. Then followed the tribulations of consolidation. The hostile works having been almost entirely obliterated by the explosion of our mine, consolidation in this case was equivalent to reconstruction, and more than twenty-four hours of hard work with pick and shovel, under the supervision of Captain A. M. Mitchell, were necessary before the Royal Scots were satisfied with the results of their labours; over 10,000 sandbags were used in the building up of new parapets. By 6 p.m., on the 16th November, the captured area had been transmogrified into a remarkably compact and tidy position linked up with our old system by communication trenches. H 11 A was rechristened "Rosebery Street," in honour of Lord Rosebery, the Honorary Colonel of the 7th, while the communication trench that connected it with our old front line and was dug by the 4th Royal Scots was called "Forrest Road."

The discovery in the captured area of two mining shafts, both of which led under our lines, suggested that we had forestalled a Turkish attack. One was practically completed; the other, which ran under the bombing station from which our attack had been launched, was not in quite such an advanced stage of preparation, and from it we rescued two starving Turks who had been buried beneath the debris thrown up by the explosion of our mine. The entrances to both shafts were destroyed and barricades were placed in front of them. The enemy, probably annoyed to find that he had laboured to no purpose, made several attempts to regain possession of his lost mine shafts, but every assault was beaten back by the Royal Scots. The enemy's most pugnacious effort occurred on the 16th November about 8 o'clock, when some Turks, having crawled close to our lines by concealed approaches, made a sudden dash against the barricade in front of point U. Taken by surprise the bombers of the 7th, who had not expected an attack from the east, retired. The sentry on duty valiantly continued to fire through a loophole till, having discovered that he was alone, he also withdrew. The Turks were in the act of tearing down the barricade, when Lieut. Greenshields of the 7th Royal Scots, supported by Lieut. Neilson of the Ayrshire Yeomanry, rallied our men who scattered the assailants before they were able to accomplish their purpose. This episode caused the Royal Scots to draw back their barrier for a few yards to a position which gave the garrison a wider observation.

After this check the Turks lost heart and their later movements were more in the nature of demonstrations than serious attacks, and apart from shelling, which at this time was heavier than the normal, the Royal Scots were not greatly disturbed. The casualties of the 7th were slight and must have been considerably less than those suffered by the enemy. Lieut. J. E. Flett was killed by a sniper during the process of consolidation and Lieut. Neilson of the Ayrshire Yeomanry received a shrapnel wound. Sergeant Berry, who had led his party with fine resolution during the attack, was killed by a sniper on the 16th, when he was directing digging operations; seven other ranks were wounded.

In the successful action conducted by the Cameronians on the east bank of the East Krithia nullah the two supporting companies of the 7th Royal Scots were not involved in the fighting, but were employed in consolidating the captured positions and in linking them up with our original front. So quickly was the work done that four hours after the attack a communication trench had been dug sufficiently deep and wide to enable persons to pass in comparative safety from our old to our new front line. The composite Royal Scots battalion, justifiably pleased with the completeness of its success, was relieved on the 21st November by troops of the 157th Brigade and returned to a rest camp in divisional reserve.

Meantime the 5th Royal Scots had returned to Suvla on the 7th September. The motor lighter that carried the men ashore stranded on a reef in the bay and the battalion was compelled to spend the night at the Twenty-ninth Divisional Engineers' Dump. Next day it proceeded to the front line which, at Suvla Bay as at Cape Helles, was overlooked by the hostile trenches on the higher ridges. Our leaders had now virtually abandoned the enterprise and the troops were mainly employed in improving the trenches, a work which they carried out with such ardour and efficiency that they earned the honour of a compliment from Major-General de Lisle. During September Lieut. Malpas was wounded in the head, and on the 27th September one unlucky shell landing in a sap-head caused five casualties among the garrison, S. F. Munro, the R.S.M., being among the slain. On the 3rd October 2nd Lieut. W. Simpson, while in charge of a fatigue party, was killed by a stray bullet. So weak was the battalion, only about 100 strong, that it was doubtful if it could be maintained as a separate unit. The arrival of seven officers from the second-line battalion on the 4th, a number that would have been welcome to any ordinarily strong unit, gave the battalion a disproportionate strength in officers. On the 18th October the Gallipoli adventures of the 5th Royal Scots came to a close, and on that date they embarked on the s.s. *Sarnia* for Mudros.

The middle of November witnessed the arrival of typical winter conditions. Fortunately the men had been issued with warmer garments, particularly leather jerkins and wool-lined leather gloves, but it was impossible to erect huts or shelters, which alone could give the troops really adequate protection against the elements at night. On the evening of the Royal Scots' successful attack heavy showers of icy rain fell, and before the month passed blizzards of sleet and snow swept across the peninsula. The nullahs became frothy estuaries, and the swirling waters flooded the dug-outs and shelters that had been scooped in the banks. The erstwhile arid land after a stormy night was scored by torrents leaping down the slopes and forming lakes and lagoons in the hollows of the more level parts. The trenches became canals, and the men, careless of the sniper, balanced precariously on the narrow ledge of fire-step. One terrible storm lasted from the 26th till the 28th November and raged with a fury that threatened to destroy every living soul on the peninsula. Rain, sleet, and snow, whipped by a hurricane, beat madly on Gallipoli and seemed to pierce a man's body with a thousand needles of ice, while tumultuous seas boomed and crashed along the coast, smashing the piers and lighters, and littering the beaches with wreckage. This violent blizzard showed how insecure was our position. The unloading of stores at the tiny jetties on the beaches was a hazardous business even in moderate seas and would be utterly impossible during stormy weather.

The powers of human endurance defy calculation. Even though their blood is infected by fever, men compelled to live in the open air seem capable of enduring the utmost extremes of climate. The troops, after being grilled for weeks by a tropical sun, naturally suffered acutely from the wintry conditions, but invariably contrived to joke about the discomforts that afflicted them. They had already been instructed by the medical staff how to guard against frost-bite. The coming of winter was marked by an abatement of dysentery, but many of the men now began to succumb to jaundice, which though less deadly was no less unpleasant.

The composite Royal Scots battalion relieved a unit in the front line in the midst of the great storm in November. The march, accomplished in the teeth of a blinding blizzard of snow, was most exhausting, yet the men were probably better off struggling painfully up to the front line than shivering impotently in an attempt to woo warmth. Trench improvements formed almost the sole occupation of the troops, and there were few casualties. About this time the Royal Scots noted that the Turkish shells appeared to have improved in quality and increased in size. There could be little doubt that this was due to the Serbian retreat, as a result of which the command of the main Orient railways passed to our enemies who used them for the transportation of shells and guns to Gallipoli.

Before the end of 1915 the British authorities had decided to abandon the Dardanelles enterprise. In October Sir Ian Hamilton gave up the command to

General Monro, who reported that our military position at Gallipoli was bad and that our best policy was evacuation. With this verdict Lord Kitchener, after a visit to the Ægean, found himself obliged to concur, though none knew better than he the blighting consequences that our confession of failure would entail in the East.

It was recognised that to effect the evacuation of all the troops in the peninsula without loss would be a most difficult matter. The removal of the stores, guns, and troops could not be effected in one night, and at the worst, part of the force might have to be sacrificed to purchase the safety of the remainder. That risk had to be taken. Since the campaign had settled down to trench warfare, there were few clashes between the opposing troops and the hostile raids against our lines were desultory and as a rule half-hearted, while the Turkish shelling at night was too intermittent and indiscriminate to cause serious inconvenience at the beaches. Thus the first part of the evacuation was accomplished with little difficulty. Under cover of a demonstration by the Cape Helles garrison, in which the Royal Scots were not actively engaged, the forces at Suvla Bay and at Anzac were successfully borne away from Gallipoli on the nights of the 18th and 19th December.

The most critical part of the operation had now to be performed. Warned by what had taken place at Suvla Bay and at Anzac the Turks might be expected to devise measures to prevent the Cape Helles garrison from slipping off in the same fashion. Their plan might consist of repeatedly testing our lines by patrols and raids and of barraging the various beaches at frequent intervals during the night. If the Turks had done this it is beyond belief that the whole of the Cape Helles force could have got clear. If, since they had an abundance of guns and shells, they had even limited themselves to a systematic shelling of the beaches during the dark watches of the night, the embarkation of our troops would probably have been so interrupted that it could not have been completed by daybreak, when our project would have been disclosed. But the Turks did nothing, and their indolence or indifference was the one great slice of fortune that we enjoyed at the Dardanelles.

The opinion held by many people at home that the Turks were aware of and connived at the evacuation of Cape Helles may be dismissed as absolutely groundless. Nothing occurred to justify this assumption. Indeed the Turks seem to have been fully convinced that we meant to remain at Cape Helles, for on the night when the evacuation took place Captain W. R. Kermack of the 7th Royal Scots reported that in front of his position the Turks were strengthening and putting up fresh barbed wire entanglements.

It was just possible that the enemy thought that we meant to concentrate on an offensive from Cape Helles, and we therefore endeavoured to make him believe that this was our intention. To this end Lieut.-General Sir Francis Davies, on the 20th December, published a special order to the VIII. Corps informing it that our position at Cape Helles would not be abandoned. We surmised that this statement would reach the enemy through his spies. Even our own men were deceived, and rumours were spread that at Cape Helles we intended to construct a second Torres Vedras, an opinion strengthened by the fact that we continued to labour at the improvement of our defences. Then, on the 29th December, the VIII. Corps received a message to the effect that it would shortly be relieved by the IX. Corps. This news, we were certain, would filter through to the enemy and would prepare him for unusual activity at the beaches.

Provided that the Turks really believed that we meant to cling to Cape Helles, we had a tolerable chance of extricating at least the greatest part of our forces; in any case, our measures had to be based on that assumption. Guns continued to be landed during the day, new troops made their appearance, but under cover of darkness more stores and troops were taken from the peninsula than were landed on it during daylight. All the sick, except those likely to be fit again in a day or so, were evacuated, while contrivances were manufactured so that to observers from a distance or from the air no alteration in our daily round would be apparent. When all the sick had been sent away stuffed effigies took their place; sham guns filled the emplacements of those that had been removed; models of carts and motors were to be seen where genuine ones had previously functioned; even the clouds of dust created by the passage of vehicles and soldiers were raised by driving horses and mules from place to place. In the firing line some time previous to the final evacuation the British ceased firing about midnight and stillness wrapped our lines until dawn, when blasts of fire were poured against the hostile trenches. We desired the enemy to believe that our troops were anxious to enjoy their nightly rest without disturbance, and the Turks apparently were deceived by the device, though it had already been practised at Suvla Bay and at Anzac. These nightly lulls continued until the final evacuation took place on the 8th January.

Gradually the garrison at Cape Helles was thinned down till it became doubtful if we had kept sufficient weight to resist a serious attack. We could only trust that no chance raid would betray to the foe the bareness of our defences and that on the night selected for the final evacuation we would be favoured by propitious weather, for a sudden storm would upset all our plans. Happily the Turks never realised what was taking place. A raid which they made on the 7th January against the Thirteenth Division unexpectedly served our plans, for at the moment of attack our troops were engaged in a relief, so that we had an unusual number of men in the front line. The onset was decisively repulsed, and the heavy volume of rifle fire that proceeded from our trenches must have convinced the enemy that there had been no diminution in the strength of the garrison. Every possible precaution was taken to enable our last troops to secure their escape. The entanglements of the three front lines were secretly strengthened in order to retard any hostile advance, and in addition a fourth line stretching from Morto Bay to Gully Beach was stealthily constructed. Mine-fields and traps were laid; the routes to be taken by the troops on their way to the beaches were carefully selected, and every trench that we no longer used was filled with wire. Ingenious mechanical devices for firing rifles and flares were fixed up by sappers and every party made itself familiar with the particular route which it was to follow on the night of the evacuation. At junctions on the routes control posts with officers in charge were established, and it was the duty of each officer to remain there till every group in front of his position had been accounted for; then, having blocked the trenches with trestles of barbed wire, he was to telephone that all was clear, smash the machine, and conduct his party to the beaches. All the staff arrangements for the evacuation had been thought out to the last detail.

The 156th Brigade had the honour of acting as rear-guard of the Fifty-second Division. Since the 6th January every one had been aware that Cape Helles was to be abandoned, and from that moment all lived on tenterhooks until they were on board the transports. Fortunately there was plenty of work to perform and the troops applied themselves with relish to the construction of effigies to take the place of living men in the trenches. During the last night the strength of the garrison in the front line was one man to every four yards. The Royal Scots battalion occupied support and reserve trenches. The safety of the rear-guard depended upon the embarkation arrangements proceeding without a hitch and upon the absence of any hostile attack. Luckily there was no move by the Turks, and though the sea was not as calm as we had hoped the naval plans proved entirely adequate. Still, to the men waiting for their turn to proceed to the beaches every minute seemed an hour and every sound the herald of an attack. Nerves were atingle and could not be relieved by smoking, for on this fateful night all smoking was prohibited. "What a chance, if Johnny only knew," was the thought of more than one man. The men experienced an almost sickening feeling of suspense till their turn came to move and never did the road to the beaches appear so interminable. The trenches had been muffled with strips of blankets, and as a further precaution the troops enveloped their feet in sandbags in order to deaden the sound of their footsteps. The last party in the division to leave was a rear-guard force of 100 Royal Scots under Major A. M. Mitchell and these filed out from their posts in the Eski lines about midnight. The most trying time of all was when the men found themselves on the beach; there they had on their left the sea and on their right a wall of cliff, while occasional shells from "Asiatic Annie"[1] dropped into the water or fell near them. So densely

[1] So called, because this gun was posted on the Asiatic side of the Straits.

packed were the men at one time that they seemed to be making no progress, while shells continued to fall disconcertingly near; at any moment the Turks might find their target when there could be no escape. "We felt," said an officer of the 4th Royal Scots, "as if we were in a slow-moving theatre queue on a wet and chilly night." Most of the Royal Scots crossed a gangway erected over a sunken French ship at V beach and entered motor lighters capable of carrying 400 men tightly packed together, and from these they were transferred to the battleship *Prince George*, which had arrived in the roadstead after darkness. Major Mitchell's party, separated from the main body of the battalion, was taken off in a torpedo destroyer, the *Bulldog*. Faintly through the darkness the troops caught their last glimpse of Achi Baba poised like a guardian over the peninsula.

There was a universal sense of relief when our last man stepped off the soil of Gallipoli. So intense was the elation of all that a private might with impunity have slapped a "brass-hat" on the back. However sadly the reputation of generals may have been affected by the Gallipoli campaign, the martial exploits of our men at the peninsula will ever be recalled with pride. The evacuation of the Cape Helles garrison without a single casualty was a military feat which any nation would have been proud to accomplish, creditable alike to the staff that drew up the plans and to the men who loyally carried them out. It was a good end to an ill-omened enterprise. No one was sorry to quit the peninsula, but our joy in leaving the place was shadowed by the thought that it formed the tomb of many comrades, and that admirable as was the manner in which it was accomplished our departure was after all a confession of frustration.

Once on board the waiting ships the troops were

most hospitably treated by the sailors. Pillars of dancing flame, the pyres of stores that could not be carried away, lit up the sea at the beaches as the vessels moved off with their cargoes of troops to Mudros. The *Prince George*[1] was struck by a torpedo from a hostile submarine, but luckily it failed to explode and the main body of the Royal Scots without further adventure reached Mudros on the 9th January. That night there was some anxiety owing to the non-appearance of Major Mitchell and his party, but these rejoined the battalion next day, the *Bulldog* having had to put in at the port of Imbros on account of the submarine and rough weather.

[1] The battleship, while steaming slowly to-and-fro awaiting the lighters, had often come under the Turkish searchlight operating from Chanak, and this light assisted the Royal Scots to locate her; but it must at the same time have advertised her position to a submarine which was prowling about looking for a target.

CHAPTER XIII

THE BALKANS AND EGYPT

September 1915 *to June* 1916

Importance of Mediterranean Littoral. Reasons for Intervention in the Balkans. 1st Royal Scots at Salonika. Defences of the Allies. The Position in Egypt. 6th Royal Scots at Cairo. Expedition against the Senussi. 6th Royal Scots at Matruh. Action of 13th December. Action of 23rd January. Advance on Sollum. 6th Royal Scots at Sollum. The Battalion embarks for France. Eastern Defences of Egypt. 5th Royal Scots embark for France. 4th and 7th Royal Scots in Egypt. Turkish Attack on Dueidar. Routes across the Sinai Desert. Defensive Arrangements of Sir Archibald Murray. (See Map XV.)

THE Battle of Loos and the evacuation of Gallipoli completed the incidents of 1915 as far as the British were concerned. Thus ended a thoroughly unsatisfactory year in which the honours rested with the enemy. While keeping us at bay in the West and frustrating our attempt to secure the Dardanelles, he had administered a decisive defeat to Russia. His success was of such magnitude that it availed to win for him in October the alliance of Bulgaria, with the assistance of which he rapidly broke down the resistance of the gallant Serbians. There was a strong likelihood that the whole of the Balkans would fall under Teutonic control. We had nothing to offset these disasters. The effort of Italy counted for little in the war and her campaign against Austria seemed to many to be only a parochial affair. But the universal conviction that we had plumbed the depths of misfortune was a kind of inverted optimism. We were so deeply convinced that civilisation could only be saved by a victory for the Allies that we refused to contemplate defeat, and we felt that with the coming of 1916 our fortunes were bound to improve. Our most substantial reason for confidence was that the numbers of our men in the field and our supplies of guns, munitions, and stores had been vastly increased. Pride of race prompted the belief that these extra efforts on our part could not fail to achieve victory.

With the collapse of the Gallipoli enterprise the greater part of our attention was naturally devoted to the Western front. But Britain was clearly obliged to provide for the safety of her imperial communications; above all, she had to keep open the sea route between Britain and India through the Mediterranean and the Suez Canal. The danger of the Mediterranean was the immense scope afforded by the surrounding land for the harbourage of hostile submarines, and it was therefore necessary for us to limit the territory that might be used by the enemy. Gibraltar, France, Italy, Malta, and Egypt gave us the command of the larger portion of the Mediterranean littoral, but the eastern end of the sea was bountifully provided with islands and bays that could be profitably used by submarines. The Turks at the Dardanelles had successfully resisted our attack, and if the Germans should procure the alliance of Greece, by their command of the Turkish and Grecian ports and bays they would be strongly established on the flank of our communications at the very point where they were most vulnerable, the entrance to the Suez Canal. Motives of self-preservation, therefore, led us to intervene in the Balkans before they were irretrievably lost. In any case a sense of decency required that we should make some effort to help the hard-pressed Serbians, but for this purpose our intervention came too late.

The British expedition to Salonika included one

division composed of regular units, the Twenty-seventh, of which, as we have seen, the 1st Royal Scots formed one of the units. The battalion's experience of trench duty in France ended on the 24th October 1915, when it was relieved by a French force in the Cappy sector and marched to billets in an area west of Amiens, where it enjoyed an extensive spell of recreation and training that lasted till the 24th November. On that day it entrained at Longeau for Marseilles, at which port, on the 27th, it embarked on the *Ionian*. The vessel left the French port on the night of the 28th/29th November and after an uneventful voyage anchored off Salonika on the 8th December, but owing to the uncertainty of the military situation in the Balkans the troops were not landed till five days later.

A French force under General Sarrail had vainly attempted to succour the Serbians in November and had with difficulty extricated itself from the Bulgarian pursuit. Hopeful of securing the adhesion of Greece, the Bulgarians at first studiously refrained from advancing into Greek territory, and we were thus afforded an opportunity of completing our defensive arrangements without molestation. Landing at Salonika in winter the Royal Scots formed no very flattering impression of the city, the people, and the surrounding country. The first quarters of the battalion were at Lembet on the north side of the town, and till the end of the year the men had their time fully occupied in building roads, which were urgently needed. The mud surpassed even that of the Salient; it lay to such a depth that some men averred that it was stirred into motion like the waves of the sea when the wind blew. On the 3rd January the Royal Scots changed their quarters to Kalamaria on the east side of Salonika, and while they remained there they furnished a number of guards, including those over the

Austrian, Bulgarian, German, and Turkish Consulates in Salonika itself. These, being centres of hostile intrigue, had been cleared by General Sarrail on the 30th December, and the subsequent search of the premises afforded ample justification for this action.

The measures of the Allies for the defence of the Salonika base had already been taken. If we were to effect anything at all in the Balkans, it was obvious that we had to do more than keep a hold on the city alone, and our line was so arranged that the whole of the Chalcidean peninsula was included in our zone. It was not difficult to secure a satisfactory defensive position. Salonika, on the gulf of the same name, is situated on a plain, flanked on the west by the river Vardar, on the east by the river Struma, and guarded on the north by a bastion of mountains. The gulfs of Salonika and Orphani, into which the Vardar and Struma discharge their waters respectively, cutting off the Chalcidean peninsula from the rest of the mainland, formed the natural points on which we could rest the flanks of our defensive system. The Vardar, being unfordable, gave substantial protection on the west, and our line on the Gulf of Orphani on the east was guarded by the mouth of the Struma, while on the north we were assisted by the range of mountains. The west portion of the line was held by the French and the east by the British.

On the 21st January 1916 the Royal Scots left Kalamaria to take their position in the defensive system. Winter held the country in a firm grip, and acute discomfort was caused by the intense cold. There were no roads and the battalion, during a heavy snowstorm, laboriously threaded its route by mule paths through the mountains until, on the 23rd, it arrived at Gomonic, a squalid village on the northern slopes, where it bivouacked behind a strongly wired line of defences overlooking the Langaza Valley, which runs between Lake Langaza and Lake Besik. Till March 1916 the battalion, with the other units of the 81st Brigade, worked vigorously to strengthen the defences and found time for a certain amount of training. The high standard of discipline, which it was the aim of Lieut.-Colonel Callender to uphold, was never allowed to relax. Before long everything was in readiness to meet the onslaught of the Austrians and the Bulgarians, which the Royal Scots desired rather than expected; but as the enemy made no attack our troops were never called on to man the Salonika defences. Thus the battalion remained in peace at Gomonic till the month of June.

More vitally important to us than the Balkans was the safety of Egypt, where we had to maintain an adequate force to guard the Suez Canal. The menace especially to be feared was a Turkish invasion from the east, and one such attack was beaten off in the spring of 1915. This danger became slight while the Gallipoli campaign was in progress, since the Turks were obliged to employ the greater part of their forces in guarding the entrance to the Dardanelles. We could not afford, however, to neglect any precautions, and we were bound to ensure that our defence of the Canal was not complicated by any risings within Egypt itself that would distract our attention, for there were many in the country who sympathised with the Turks and who, if opportunity offered, would stir up trouble against us. This hostile influence towards the end of 1915 won over the Senussi, a religious fraternity of Mohammedan tenets, thereby causing us some uneasiness about the western frontier of Egypt.

On the west of Egypt lies Tripoli, which had passed to Italy as a result of her war with Turkey; but Italian influence was confined to the coast and had never been extended into the hinterland where the natives retained their allegiance to Turkey. The most organised and formidable inhabitants were the Senussi tribesmen who, after the outbreak of the great war, were at first friendly towards Egypt. But Turkish agents working on the religious prejudices of the tribesmen soon wrought a change in the attitude of the Senussi, who by a series of unfriendly acts compelled us to send an expedition against them.

The 6th Royal Scots were the only unit of the regiment engaged in the Senussi campaign. This battalion was the last of the Royal Scots Territorials to leave Edinburgh. This was entirely due to the fact that it had contributed nearly half of its strength to the 4th and the 8th Battalions, and time was required to make good this loss in trained men and officers. Ultimately, about the end of 1914, Lieut.-Colonel Turnbull determined to form an Imperial Service Battalion, and after sanction had been given for this step the first line of the 6th Royal Scots was formed on the 6th February 1915. Most of the training was carried through at Selkirk and Peebles, and the unit on the 4th August returned to Edinburgh, where it was billeted in the Olympia in Annandale Street. Here its sojourn was brief, for on the 15th it was ordered to prepare for foreign service in the near East, and on the 4th September it entrained at Princes Street Station for Devonport. Lieut.-Colonel Turnbull having been transferred to the command of a battalion of the Rifle Brigade, the unit was placed under the command of Lieut.-Colonel A. O. Jenney. On the evening of the 5th it embarked on the *Ceramic* which, after touching at Malta where officers and men had an opportunity of visiting Valetta, arrived at Alexandria on the 14th.

Disembarkation took place on the next day and the battalion proceeded to the Abbassia Camp in Cairo.

The 6th Royal Scots thoroughly enjoyed the ten weeks that they spent at Abbassia. For a few days the men were unpleasantly affected by the climate, but they soon became accustomed to the new conditions of life. Training was carried on systematically but did not absorb the whole of the time, and all ranks paid frequent visits to the pyramids, the citadel, and the numerous places of historical and archæological interest that make Cairo one of the world's greatest tourist centres. The British soldier was a type of visitor of which the Arab guides now had ample experience, and their vocabulary was enriched by many phrases that cannot fail to astonish and amuse the post-war traveller. The most imposing ceremony in which the 6th Royal Scots were required to take part was on the 1st November when the battalion furnished a Guard of Honour under Major Milligan at Abdin Palace in honour of the Sultan's arrival in the city from Alexandria. By the end of October the battalion was in first-rate trim and was capable of performing long marches through the sands without distress. But though the stay at Abbassia was for the men a delightful experience they were not displeased when, on the 21st November, they were ordered to proceed to Alexandria, where they learned that they were to form part of the expedition that General Maxwell was organising for operations against the Senussi.

Egypt has a long land frontier on the west, but the greater part of this is effectively guarded by the impassable Libyan desert, so that the approaches from the west are limited to a belt lying along the coast in the north and forming the Libyan plateau, well garnished with oases, which afford natural resting stations in the caravan routes between Egypt and Tripoli. A railway ran west from Alexandria to Dabaa, and from Mersa Matruh a track, made by clearing the surface of rock and scrub, led to Sollum on the Egyptian frontier; this road, known as "The Khedival Road," though rough and unmacadamised, was capable of bearing motor traffic. The hostility of the natives compelled us in November to abandon Sollum and draw in our frontier posts to Matruh, where our expeditionary force was to assemble.

Besides the 6th Royal Scots, the Western Frontier Force comprised horse artillery, yeomanry and other details, but the expedition had been collected so hastily that the various units had very little knowledge of each other. On arriving at Alexandria the Royal Scots were quartered in Wardian Camp, where they remained till the 26th November, when "D" Company boarded two Granton trawlers and one Egyptian coastguard cruiser and after a roughish voyage was landed at Matruh. On the following day "C" Company, embarking on two trawlers and one coastguard cruiser, had a terrible passage. The sea was lashed into gigantic waves by a violent gale; nearly every man was sick and it was not till the 30th that the last boat put in at Matruh. The storm continued to swell in fury, so that "B" Company, which with the battalion H.Q. set off on the 28th, was even more buffeted than "C." In ordinary weather the voyage was performed in sixteen hours, but the vessel that carried H.Q. had a narrow escape of being wrecked and took three days to reach its destination. "A" Company, leaving in December, was the most fortunate of all and arrived at Matruh up to time after a pleasant voyage.

The appearance of Matruh was most fascinating. The harbour, though small, was beautifully shaped and was not marred by unsightly buildings, while the water possessed such richness of colour that the men at once dubbed it "The Blue Lagoon." Matruh itself was a tiny coastal village deserted by most of its polyglot inhabitants who, on the approach of the Senussi, had fled to Alexandria. The camp of the Royal Scots lay little more than a mile from the harbour quay and the outpost line was formed on a ridge which overlooked the village and also the desert to the west. Ordinary garrison duties occupied the attention of the battalion till the 11th December, when two companies and the machine-gun section were ordered to hold themselves in readiness to march on the following day. On the 11th a small force under Lieut.-Colonel J. L. R. Gordon had moved out of Matruh and successfully engaged parties of the Senussi at Wadi Senaab, but air reconnaissance revealed that the enemy was in considerable strength near Ras Manaa and our column had, therefore, to be reinforced.

"C" and "D" Companies and the machine-gun section, the whole under the command of Lieut.-Colonel Jenney, left Matruh at 10.30 A.M. on the 12th to join Lieut.-Colonel Gordon's expedition which was encamped near Um Raknum. The march to this place through the retarding sand was a wearisome ordeal and the rear-guard did not arrive at the camp till after midnight. On the 13th the battalion had its baptism of fire. The column broke camp at 8.30 A.M. for the purpose of attacking the Senussi at Ras Manaa, and a platoon of "C" Company under Lieut. Jardine was sent out by Lieut.-Colonel Jenney to the left to act as flank guard. The march had barely commenced when strong clusters of the enemy were encountered. While crossing a deep gully, the Wadi Shaifa, the flank guard was suddenly fired at by parties of Senussi lying in ambush and Lieut. Jardine was wounded. He immediately ordered his platoon to fall back on the main body and the enemy followed in pursuit. Practically the whole of our force had crossed the Wadi with the exception of the flank guard, so that the Senussi were established in a dangerous position in our rear and "a sharp and somewhat critical action developed."[1] The main body of the Royal Scots facing to the left to meet the attack moved forward and seized a ridge overlooking the Wadi. Captain Turner and a party, followed by another body under 2nd Lieut. Wallace, crossed to the far side of the Wadi, where they were joined by the C.O. A Senussi machine-gun, planted at the head of the Wadi, caused some casualties among the Royal Scots as they dashed across and among the wounded was Major Milligan; so violent and accurate was the enemy's fire that our men could not raise their heads to reply to it. Fortunately reinforcements[2] from Matruh arrived and turned the battle in our favour. At the same time the Adjutant of the 6th, Captain Gillatt, took a platoon by a wide detour to succour the Royal Scots on the far side of the Wadi, and the column was in a favourable position to take the initiative when the Senussi, who had suffered about 250 casualties, hastily decamped. The rapid descent of night unfortunately prevented us from pressing on in pursuit. After the action the column withdrew unmolested to the camp at Um Raknum, where it remained during the night, and on the following morning it returned to Matruh. In this action the losses of the 6th Royal Scots were light; in addition to Major Milligan and Lieut. Jardine, 2nd Lieut. N. Henderson was wounded; of the other ranks three were killed and fourteen wounded.

[1] Despatch of Sir John Maxwell, 1st March 1916.
[2] Two guns Notts Royal Horse Artillery and two squadrons Australian Light Horse.

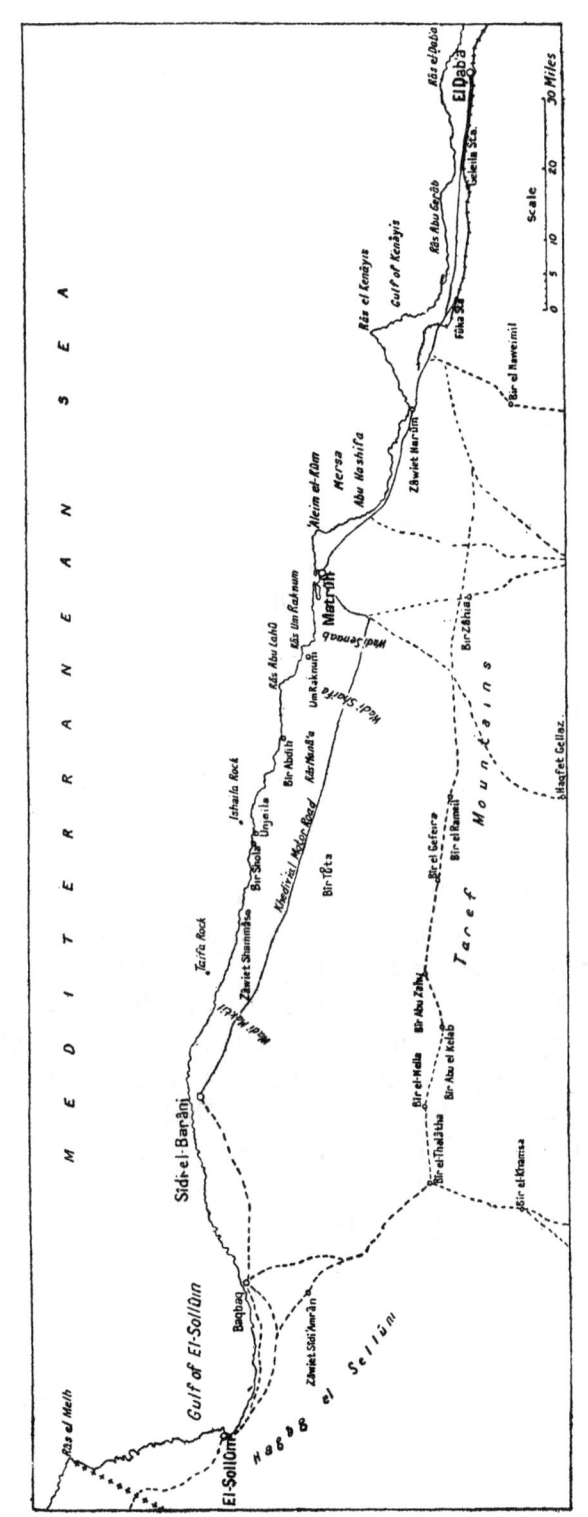

MAP XI.—The Senussi Campaign, 1915-1916.

The force at Matruh was strong enough to hold the Senussi in check, but the experience of our operations against them on the 11th and the 13th December proved that it would have to be considerably augmented if we were to achieve rapid and decisive victory. Hence ensued a lull while reinforcements were being collected, and till the end of the year the Royal Scots were engaged in garrisoning and strengthening the defences of Matruh. On Christmas Day an expedition under Major-General A. Wallace, in which the Royal Scots were not included, defeated a concentration of the Senussi near Gebel Medwa, with the result that the enemy retired to Unjeila and Bir Tunis. This victory gave us time to clear all the country between Matruh and Dabaa, and in January fresh units arrived to augment the Matruh force. On the 19th January our air service reported that the Senussi were encamped 23 miles west of Merjid, and Major-General Wallace determined to attack them as soon as possible in order to prevent further concentration and by striking a decisive blow to discourage the Arabs from embracing the Senussi cause. Accordingly an expedition in two columns left Matruh on the 22nd January. "A" and "B" Companies of the 6th Royal Scots accompanied this force as reserve, the other two companies remaining at Matruh. Our troops on establishing contact with the enemy on the 23rd, some miles west of Bir Shola, at once attacked and drove in his centre, but the resistance of the Senussi was most skilfully conducted and they made repeated attempts to drive in both our flanks. This led to the Royal Scots being brought into the battle, for at an early hour in the afternoon they were called on to stop an outflanking movement by the enemy on the right. With "B" Company leading and "A" in support a model attack was delivered, the men advancing with great steadiness, and the Senussi were compelled to retire. Leaving a small force to hold what had been won the remainder of the Royal Scots returned to reserve.

Then an assault on the 15th Sikhs caused a company of the Royal Scots under Major J. W. Adams to be sent to their assistance, but the battle was practically over by the time it reached the Sikhs. The enemy's camp was carried by a charge in the centre, but our men were too exhausted by their efforts to be capable of carrying on a sustained pursuit, so Major-General Wallace resolved to bivouac his force about 2 miles east of the captured position. An important but not decisive victory had been won. Our success would probably have been complete had it not been for the abnormal rainfall during January which, by converting the whole country into a quagmire, had seriously interfered with the operations of our mounted troops. The men passed the night in considerable discomfort, since the transport having been stuck in the mud, neither supplies nor blankets could be brought up and the weather was intensely wet and cold. On the 24th the force moved back with great difficulty to Bir Shola; so thick was the mud that every vehicle had to be man-handled, while such of the wounded as were unable to ride had to be carried by stretcher. Fortunately the transport was met some 3 miles west of Bir Shola, and the infantry were relieved of their burden. On the 25th, under more genial conditions, the march was continued back to Matruh.

The 6th Royal Scots acquitted themselves with great credit on the 23rd. The men had responded promptly to every command and their counter-attack had been carried out with skill and dash, so that their casualties were slight, one man being killed and five wounded. After this little affray there ensued another spell of picquet duty at Matruh for the battalion, and it was not till the 20th February that operations against the Senussi were resumed. By that date a formidable expedition had been collected and placed under the command of Major-General Peyton, who was directed to complete the defeat of the Senussi and reoccupy the town of Sollum.

Accordingly on the 20th February, under Brig.-General T. Lukin, a large force which included the 6th Royal Scots set out from Matruh. A strong wind made the first day's march exceedingly trying, sand filling the air and causing the eyes to smart. The first halt was at Ras-um-Rakum where the expedition bivouacked; the next day's journey brought it to Bir Abdih and on the 22nd February Unjeila was reached. This place had already been prepared for defence by the 1st South African Regiment, and the Royal Scots were annoyed to learn that the battalion was to be split up. The bulk of the unit was left at Unjeila and only 350 under Major Adams proceeded with Brig.-General Lukin's column to Barani. On the 24th the force camped at Wadi Maktil, which was shelled on the following night by the Senussi. On the 26th news was brought by our air service that the enemy was at Agagia and Brig.-General Lukin at once advanced to engage the tribesmen, but in the successful action that was fought the Royal Scots had no part, for, to their keen regret, they were left to guard the supply base.

The campaign against the Senussi was completely victorious, and within three weeks of the setting out of the expedition Sollum was reoccupied by our troops and the war was at an end. It was the misfortune, and in no sense the fault, of the Royal Scots that their part was mainly passive. From February to April they were on the lines of communication between Matruh and Sollum, various detachments performing guard duties at the depots of Sidi Barani and Unjeila. Two companies, "A" and "B," accompanied as convoy escorts the force which under Major-General Peyton entered Sollum in March, and about 150 of the men, under Captain Mowat, had the satisfaction of entering the town.

By the end of March the battalion was back at Matruh, but remained there for only a short period. On the 2nd April "A" and "B" Companies under Major Adams were conveyed by five trawlers and the warship *Veronica* to Sollum. The remainder of the battalion landed at Sollum on the 6th, and until the 3rd May the Royal Scots were kept employed building sangars, constructing roads, and erecting barbed-wire defences. The town rejoiced in a spacious harbour which the Germans had used as a submarine base, hundreds of empty petrol tins being found by our men on their entry into the town. The one touch of colour was the blue of the sea which contrasted sharply with the dingy brown of the land. Bathing was the only real recreation afforded by Sollum, and the troops soon grew tired of the monotony of garrison duty, some declaring that they would die of melancholy if they were kept for any length of time in the place.

This garrison duty ended on the 3rd May and next day the battalion was conveyed by sea to Alexandria, from which city it marched to a camp at Sidi Bishr, and a few days later, on the 8th, it embarked on the *Saxonia* for France. Those who served with the 6th Royal Scots from September 1915 till May 1916 will always retain a kindly memory of Egypt with its pyramids, mosques, its palm trees, and the unparagoned Nile. Many of the battalion regarded the palm trees as the most typical and the most welcome sight of the country, for they were what travellers looked for in the desert; where they stood out clearly on the horizon against the hard blue sky men could feel assured that a well lay somewhere near.

The satisfactory completion of the Senussi campaign permitted us to concentrate on the eastern defences of Egypt, for now that the Gallipoli campaign was at an end there was every likelihood of a Turkish attack against the Suez Canal. The only battalions of the Royal Scots which were for any considerable time with the Egyptian force were the 4th and the 7th. The 5th Battalion after leaving Gallipoli in October remained at Mudros till the end of December. But few drafts came to it from home and there seemed no prospect of the unit attaining the strength with which it had left Edinburgh in March 1915. On the 7th January it was transferred to Egypt, where with the rest of the Twenty-ninth Division it was concentrated near Suez. There it sojourned till March, when with the other units of the division it embarked at Port Said on the 10th and was conveyed to Marseilles.

The 4th and the 7th Royal Scots remained at Mudros for rather more than a week, a rest which enabled officers and men to recover from the severe strain to which they had been exposed at Cape Helles. On the 15th January the advanced party of the Fifty-second Division left Mudros for Egypt and by the 21st the whole of the 156th Brigade was concentrated in the Abbassia suburb of Cairo. The 4th and the 7th resumed their separate identities on the 20th January, when Colonel Young returned from hospital to take command of the former. The period was devoted to rest, training, and refitting, and when the battalions were reclothed with new issues of cotton drill they presented as smart an appearance as could be desired. Cairo was a fascinating haunt for the men who grasped the opportunity, which would never have come to most of them but for the war, of visiting the principal attractions of the land of the Pharaohs. There was one slight alarm when detachments from the 4th, the 7th, and the Scottish Rifles were sent to suppress a mutiny of Egyptian reservists at Abbassia barracks, but happily the trouble was smoothed over without bloodshed. On the 16th February the brigade was transferred to Ballah on the Suez Canal, where training and recreation were methodically carried on. At this place the Royal Scots had their first experience of a sand-storm. The fine sand, whipped up by the gale and filling the air "like a pea-soup fog," carried everything before it, tearing down tents and canvas; it clogged the eyes, ears, mouth, and nostrils, and seemed to enter the pores of the body. Generally speaking, however, the weather was good and all ranks enjoyed bathing in the Canal. On the 21st February Major J. G. P. Romanes, the Adjutant of the 7th, who had spared no pains to make the battalion as efficient as possible, received a well-earned promotion when he was appointed to command the 7th Scottish Rifles in the same brigade. In March the brigade was transferred to the important station of Kantara; the name is an Arabic word meaning a "bridge," since the town stands on the threshold of the desert linking up Egypt with one of the principal caravan routes from Asia. Here the men were occupied mainly in training and in strengthening the defences of the Canal until the 23rd April, when some excitement was caused by a Turkish raid on Dueidar.

The great continents of Africa and Asia are connected by the peninsula of Sinai, of which only the northern portion is passable for men and transport. This traversable area is bounded on the south by a belt of mountains, bare and almost waterless, between which and the sea lies an expanse of desert broken by oases and sprinkled with dunes and shrub. This area has an enormous strategical value since it is the causeway between the two continents, and it was the one avenue by which the Turks could attack Egypt. There were two feasible routes. The southern one lay along the northern margin of the mountainous tract, but it was so lacking in water-supply that no large force could be taken along it, and a Turkish invasion by this route in the spring of 1915 had been easily repulsed. The northern route follows closely the line of the coast, running from oasis to oasis and terminating at Kantara. About 30 miles from that place lies an important group of oases at Katia where a considerable army could be permanently maintained.

In our first arrangements for the defence of Egypt we had formed our main line of resistance on the west bank of the Suez Canal, so that the enemy would have to undergo the ordeal of traversing the desert before he established contact with our forces. But the defect of this plan was that the Turks, if they were permitted to come close to the bank, could employ artillery fire to prevent ships from passing up and down the Canal; in their attack in the spring of 1915 they had shelled several of our vessels. Consequently, in order to maintain intact our sea communications with India, we now determined to push our defensive line well to the east of the Canal.

Sir Archibald Murray, who succeeded Sir John Maxwell as Commander of the Egyptian Expeditionary Force, decided to occupy and hold the Katia oases, and to this end made plans for the construction of a railway from Kantara to that place. The enemy had no intention of allowing us to establish our forces at Katia without molestation, and a hostile raiding force of 3500 men made an attempt to overwhelm our frontier posts and to cut the railway. One of these posts was at Dueidar, and it was in connection with the attack on it that the 4th and the 7th Royal Scots were hastily despatched from Kantara on the 23rd April. Both battalions were conveyed by rail to the vicinity of Pelusium, which in ancient times had been a notable town on the caravan route but had fallen into decay when the branch of the Nile on which it stood dried up. At Pelusium there was no adequate shelter for the Royal Scots, who were too hot during the day and too cold at night. The men were obliged to restrict themselves to a scanty supply of water, which was sent up in tanks to the rail-head, whence it was conveyed by camels to the troops. There was no need for fighting since the Dueidar garrison had beaten off the Turks.

On the 11th May the 4th Royal Scots were transferred from Pelusium to Mahamdiya, about 3 miles north of Romani. The intense heat and glare of the sun, the deep powdery sand, which holding and reflecting the sun's rays scorched feet and ankles, made this march a tribulation. On the following day the 7th Royal Scots undertook the same weary pilgrimage, and both battalions were employed in outpost duty and in constructing defence works. The extreme heat of summer lay heavy over the land and in the middle of the day it was torture to move even a limb; no man, however hardy he be, can exist with comfort in an oven-like atmosphere. The hateful Khamseen, a wind from the south, gathering heat in its progress over the burning sands of the desert fell on the flesh like a searing blast, and during the day the temperature often rose to 125° in the shade, of which there was virtually none. The training to which the men were now subjected proved invaluable later. They became inured to marching long distances through the hot yielding sand, and each man became accustomed to limit himself to the contents of one water-bottle per day. Not that this restriction was acceptable; an unlimited store of liquid which could be imbibed without stint or hurt was ever the yearning desire of the troops, and one officer remarked that his most delightful dream was of a land where a straight line consisted of "the shortest distance between me and the next pub.!" Without this training in stamina and self-control no force could hope to accomplish anything in a desert campaign. There was no trouble with the enemy during May and June, and the occasional bombardments of our lines by hostile aeroplanes were the chief indication that there was a war. About the end of June Colonel Young was forced, through ill-health, to resign his command, and the new C.O. of the 4th Royal Scots was Lieut.-Colonel Darroch of the 5th Argyll and Sutherland Highlanders.

CHAPTER XIV

EVENTS IN THE WEST

October 1915 *to June* 1916

German Offensive against Verdun. 2nd Royal Scots in the Salient. Tribute to Major A. E. Everingham. 11th and 12th Royal Scots in the Salient. "Plugstreet." 11th Royal Scots raided, 13th May. 13th Royal Scots in Loos Salient. Death of Lieut.-Colonel MacLear. The Battalion raided, 11th May. 8th Royal Scots at the Somme and Arras. 9th Royal Scots at Vaux and Arras. First Experiences of 15th, 16th, and 17th Royal Scots. The 15th and 16th at the Somme. 5th and 6th Royal Scots formed into one Battalion. Plans of Sir Douglas Haig for 1916. Significance of Battle of the Somme.

THE main issues of 1916 hung upon the course of events on the Western front. The Germans had been so far successful in their 1915 campaign that they required only a small force in the East, and they were now ready for a gigantic effort to break through the lines of the Allies in France. A great attack was unleashed against Verdun in April, and after five days' fighting the enemy was within easy reach of the fortress. Fortunately, the French were braced up for a desperate defence, and under the masterly generalship of Pétain ultimately stopped the German thrust. But the Boche attack was continued with great perseverance, and even at the end of June Verdun was still being strongly pressed by vast hordes of the enemy. To the British forces the ordeal of the French brought a temporary relief; for the German offensive against Verdun was an assurance that other parts of our line in France and Flanders would be reasonably safe from any serious attack, but the degree of immunity that a battalion in the line enjoyed depended upon the tactical importance of the locality which it was holding.

The 2nd Royal Scots found their second winter in Flanders less arduous than their first, and during the month of October 1915 the losses of the battalion near Sanctuary Wood from shell fire were trifling. The unit was represented by two officers and twenty men in a composite battalion of the Third Division that was inspected by H.M. the King at Reninghelst on the 27th October. For the greater part of November it was out of the line, but an accident during a demonstration at the Army School at Terdeghem cost it the services of three officers, Captains B. H. H. Perry and J. C. A. Grant and 2nd Lieut. N. J. Bennett being wounded by a rifle grenade.

On returning to the line on the 29th November the 2nd Royal Scots took over trenches near St Eloi, and during the month of December the battalion lost two officers, 2nd Lieut. H. Parsons being hit on the 5th, and 2nd Lieut. S. E. Coffin being mortally wounded on the 18th. A hostile gas attack on the 19th affected the northern part of the Salient but fortunately did not trouble the Royal Scots. An important change in the personnel of the battalion occurred on the 30th, when Lieut.-Colonel Duncan, who had been C.O. since the Battle of Le Cateau, was promoted to command the 165th Brigade. Another of the original officers of the battalion, Captain E. P. Combe, left in February to take a Staff appointment. After the departure of Lieut.-Colonel Duncan, Major H. L. Budge commanded the unit until the 17th January, when he was succeeded by Lieut.-Colonel Dyson. The diary is almost a blank during this period, but records with some relish that the Germans celebrated the 1st January 1916 not wisely but too well, and exposed themselves so freely that the snipers of the Royal Scots secured ten victims.

March was reckoned an unwholesome month. The battalion took over trenches at the Bluff, one of the famous cockpits of the Salient, and numerous parties of the men were engaged in burying the corpses, both British and Germans, with which the area was littered. The trenches were waterlogged and the weather was so inclement that during the four days that the battalion spent in this sector more than two hundred men were evacuated to hospital suffering from exhaustion and trench feet. The next tour was in the St Eloi district, where Captain R. R. Davidson and 2nd Lieut. J. W. M. Rainie were killed while the battalion was moving up to take over trenches which had been captured by the 4th Royal Fusiliers. The Royal Scots had four more casualties among officers before they finally left the Salient, Lieut. J. S. Lockhart being killed, while Lieut. J. L. Donaldson and 2nd Lieuts. J. Bennett and R. Scott were wounded.

Throughout the service of the 2nd Battalion in France and Flanders the men had been well catered for as regards food, equipment, and baths, and no unit could possibly have had a better Quartermaster than Major A. E. Everingham. He was one of the outstanding personalities in the battalion, esteemed by officers and men alike, and he was honoured throughout the Regiment as a sterling soldier and a man whom it was a privilege to claim as a friend. Consequently, the news that he had been awarded the D.S.O. was greeted with general enthusiasm, and Lieut.-Colonel Dyson marked his appreciation of the distinguished position that Major Everingham held in the Regiment by inserting in the diary for the 6th June the following notice: "The Commanding Officer has great pleasure in announcing to the battalion the award of the D.S.O.

to Major A. E. Everingham, and feels sure that all ranks will desire to join with him in offering their sincerest congratulations to one whose difficult duties have been carried out in such a brilliant manner since the commencement of the campaign. The Commanding Officer takes this opportunity to express to Major Everingham the gratitude of all ranks for his unsparing efforts for their welfare and comfort." This was a tribute which Major Everingham cherished more highly than the award.

The 2nd Royal Scots left the Salient on the 20th June 1916 and proceeded to a training area near St Omer, where they prepared for the part that they had to play in the impending Battle of the Somme.

The 11th and the 12th Royal Scots, after being withdrawn from Loos, sampled the miseries of the Salient for three months. The perpetual rain, the leaky shelters, the ubiquitous mud, the unsightly ruins, and the general gloom and untidiness of the Flemish landscape, even if there had been no shelling, would have predisposed the mind to melancholy. It required an effort to rise above the depression caused by the evidences of decay that seemed to brood over Ypres and its surroundings, and it was possibly a blessing in disguise that the sodden ditches, which passed for trenches, necessitated unflagging labour on the part of the Royal Scots to prevent them from tumbling in. Systematic training was impossible on account of the mud, and the men kept themselves fit by the daily exercise which they derived from the wielding of pick and shovel. For many weeks most of the companies were commanded by mere boys, second lieutenants, who balanced their lack of experience by an abundance of enthusiasm. Neither the 11th nor the 12th Battalion was engaged in close conflict with the Boches, but both ever afterwards looked back on the sojourn in the Salient as their most unpleasant experience of trench warfare. The 12th lost two officers, Captain Barras being wounded on the 30th November, and 2nd Lieut. J. P. Halcrow on the 19th December. The 11th, in December, welcomed a new C.O. in Lieut.-Colonel W. D. Croft, who, as the Commander first of the 11th Battalion and then of the 27th Brigade, was connected with the Ninth Division till the close of the war. The most serious alarm occurred on the 19th December, the day before the division was relieved, when the Germans, after subjecting the whole of our front line to a very violent bombardment, let loose clouds of gas. But the attack was expected, and the rapidity with which our guns opened fire on the hostile trenches stopped any assault by the infantry if such had been intended.

Relieved on the 20th December the 11th and the 12th Royal Scots proceeded to billets in the neighbourhood of Merris, where they carried out a programme of systematic training, varied by recreation, till the 26th January 1916. Then they went into the Ploegsteert Wood sector for a tour of trench duty that lasted till the end of May. As usual the trenches required continuous work, but whereas in the Salient no amount of labour appeared to effect any appreciable difference, here the men flattered themselves that as a result of their efforts their trenches were the best in France. Many parties too were engaged in carrying loads for sappers who were preparing a mine, which doubtless was exploded when we captured Messines Ridge in 1917. No-Man's-Land was patrolled by parties every night, but owing to inexperience neither battalion succeeded in bringing off a successful raid. Lieut. Bellamy of the 11th discovered a gap in the enemy's wire, and near it a Boche sentry apparently half asleep, so he returned to our lines to organise a kidnapping party. But the sentry must have been more wide-awake than he appeared to be, for on approaching the wire again Lieut. Bellamy and his men were fired on by machine-guns and the party returned with a loss of three men.

On the 13th May the 11th Royal Scots had one of their most thrilling experiences in trench warfare. The mine which entailed so much wearisome labour for our troops was being run under the trenches opposite those of the Royal Scots. At this point the German trench formed a pronounced salient, so lavishly protected with wire that it was known by our men as "The Birdcage." Probably suspecting our mining designs, the Boches, on the evening of the 13th May, violently bombarded the trenches of the 11th with heavy shells and trench-mortars and shortly afterwards sent out large raiding parties in the confident expectation that the garrison would be too dazed by the effects of the bombardment to be capable of putting up any resistance. They must have been amazed by the warmth of their reception; the Royal Scots fought like tiger-cats, and a counter-attack led with utter abandonment by Lieut. Henry and Private Holland completely routed the Germans, who fled hastily to their own trenches. The losses of the 11th were caused mainly by the bombardment, sixteen being killed, sixty-one wounded, and eight missing; ten German corpses were left in our trenches and the raiders probably sustained other losses as they scurried back across No-Man's-Land. The Boches failed in their principal object; they did not succeed in destroying the mine-shaft.

In spite of this episode "Plugstreet" was held in high esteem by the Royal Scots, who were as keen and as fit as when the battalion arrived in France. During this period Lieut.-Colonel Loch of the 12th was promoted to command a brigade in the Fifty-sixth Division and

Lieut.-Colonel H. MacLear, D.S.O.
13th Battalion, The Royal Scots.

he was succeeded by Lieut.-Colonel H. L. Budge. The advance of summer, betrayed by the festoonery of green that laced the trees, brought with it a feeling of optimism that made the men desirous of another tilt at the enemy. Their wish was soon to be gratified. At the end of May the 11th and the 12th Royal Scots departed from the Ploegsteert area to quarters near Bomy, whence after a spell of training they were transferred to the Somme area in the vicinity of Vaux-en-Amienois.

Following their ordeal at Loos, the 13th Royal Scots had no easy time during the winter of 1915-16. Their district was the Loos sector, which was more disturbed by shelling than most other parts of our front, but alarming though the shelling was the men were of the opinion that it was harder work fighting the weather than the enemy. Casualties were frequent, and universal regret prevailed throughout the battalion when Private Dunsire, who had so greatly distinguished himself at Loos, was killed on the 31st January. Another melancholy event occurred on the 16th March, when the respected and loved C.O., Lieut.-Colonel MacLear, was killed by a German bullet, a loss that was mourned by the whole division. His admirable handling of the critical situation during the Battle of Loos had stamped him as a most skilful leader, and he would probably have risen to a high command but for his untimely death. The command of the unit passed first to Major H. F. M. Worthington Wilmer and later to Lieut.-Colonel R. B. C. Raban of the 1st Lancers (Indian Army), who arrived in April.

On the 11th May the 13th Royal Scots were holding the line near the Hohenzollern Redoubt, with "C," "B," and "A" Companies in the front and support trenches and "D" in reserve. Shortly after 4 o'clock in the afternoon a terrific bombardment opened on our trenches and a shell, plunging into the dug-out where H.Q. were established, killed or wounded the whole of the Staff. Lieut.-Colonel Raban, Major Wilmer, Captains I. A. Ferguson, A. C. Jekyll, and C. W. Yule were killed; Captains C. T. Francis and 2nd Lieut. A. Linton were wounded. About 5.15 p.m. the bombardment slightly slackened, and observers in our support line noticed groups of German infantry moving against our position. Then the cannonade swelled in fury and trenches and dug-outs became a chaos of tumbling earth under the cascade of shells and mortars. The earth continued to heave and groan under the savage pounding, while the men crouched quivering on the floor of the trenches, dumbly hoping that the nightmare of horror would soon pass away.

When, after what seemed an eternity, the cannonade died down after 6 p.m. the German infantry attacked our lines. On the left "A" Company was able to stand its ground, but in the centre where the trenches had been most smashed and flattened, the Boches succeeded in entering and holding our front system. Major Tomlinson, now in command of the battalion, on seeing the waves of Germans press into our lines, rallied the few survivors of "B" Company and took them back to a support trench close in the rear, from which heavy rifle and Lewis gun fire was poured into the Boches, inflicting on them many casualties. More than one effort was made in vain by the enemy to reach our support trenches. Major Tomlinson quickly drew up a plan for a bombing counter-attack, but unfortunately on going forward to reconnoitre the hostile position he was mortally wounded. The command then devolved on Captain H. S. E. Stevens of "D" Company, and the bombing attack was pressed with great vigour, but the enemy clung tenaciously to his gains.

At midnight it was apparent that the lost trenches could not be recaptured by grenade parties alone, so it was decided to launch an attack across the open from our support trench. After a brief artillery bombardment the Royal Scots, consisting of half of "C," half of "D," and a few men of "B" Company assisted by a company of the 7th Royal Scots Fusiliers, charged over the space between the two lines at 1.30 A.M., but the Boches were ready for this move and shattered the assault by the accuracy of their fire. The enemy's success had given him a firmer grip on the Hohenzollern Redoubt, which had been a veritable cockpit ever since the 25th September 1915. Mining, counter-mining, and infantry clashes were almost a matter of daily routine in that perilous neighbourhood, and those who lived in the vicinity of the Redoubt never lacked material with which to fill their correspondence. It was clear that the Germans could not be ejected from their gains without a desperate effort, and it was not deemed worth while to mount an attack for the purpose of restoring our original line. Our position therefore was consolidated along the support trench, where the enemy's advance had been stemmed. The losses of the 13th Royal Scots were very heavy: in addition to the officers of the H.Q. Staff and Major Tomlinson, Captain A. M. Macdonald and 2nd Lieut. A. Taylor were killed, Captain M. Halcrow and 2nd Lieut. A. Wemyss were wounded, and 2nd Lieut. L. D. Collins was missing; the casualties among other ranks totalled two hundred and twenty-six.

After the disaster of the 11th May the battalion spent a comparatively peaceful time, and on the 19th Lieut.-Colonel G. M. Hannay took over the command. On the night of the 27th/28th June a small raiding party, led by 2nd Lieut. Tingle, met with a warm reception from an alert enemy; 2nd Lieut. Appleby was killed, 2nd Lieuts.

Ferguson and Tingle were wounded. The 13th Royal Scots remained for a few more weeks in the Loos salient, and therefore had no part in the first phase of the Battle of the Somme.

To the 8th and the 9th Battalions the months from September 1915 to July 1916 were more uneventful than any similar period in their history. Since becoming the pioneer battalion of the Fifty-first Division the former had distinguished itself by the quality of its work and the speed with which it was accomplished. It remained in the Somme area making roads, digging trenches and dug-outs, and constructing shelters until the 6th March 1916, when after a long march it entered the Arras area, where it was fated to serve for many months at different periods of the war. The famous Labyrinth, the scene of many furious combats between the French and the Germans in 1915, was not a healthy place to work in, and companies of the 8th in digging new trenches or in clearing out old ones frequently unearthed dead bodies. Labour was constantly interrupted by hostile shelling and trench-mortar fire, and occasionally a piece of work that had occupied the battalion for a month was demolished in the course of a few minutes. The Labyrinth was an active mining area, and the 8th Royal Scots often rendered a service to the division by the quickness with which they consolidated craters formed by mine explosions. The battalion excelled particularly in the ease and rapidity with which it could erect wire entanglements, and on the 4th April when a mine was exploded, two platoons, under 2nd Lieuts. Sharp and Sutherland, speedily formed a wire protection round the crater which was quite close to the enemy's lines. But in spite of shells, trench-mortars, and mines, the losses of the battalion were not numerous and only one officer, Lieut. W. T. Gray, was wounded.

The 9th Battalion spent only a short time with the Fifth Division. During December 1915 and the first few days of January 1916 it held the front line near Vaux on the Somme. This sector was interesting, partly because it was for many months the extreme right of the British line and partly because the conditions there differed totally from those prevailing in other parts of the British front. The line from Fargny to Frise, where the French area began, lay along extensive marshes abutting on a loop of the Somme. Only at Fargny were trenches possible, and south of it the line consisted of isolated platoon or section posts ensconced in the drier parts of the marsh-land, and connection between the posts and between the battalion and the French had to be maintained by patrols. On the 12th January the popular Adjutant, Captain R. M. Dudgeon of the Camerons, left the battalion on being appointed Second-in-Command of the 16th Warwickshire Regiment. February brought the 9th Royal Scots their greatest immunity from danger, because they were then employed as Third Army troops, and this was the only period during which the battalion did not figure as a front-line unit. On the 1st March it was attached to the 154th Brigade of the Fifty-first Division at Pierregot and accompanied the division to the Arras sector, where no unusual incidents disturbed the routine of trench warfare. In April there was another change in personnel, when Lieut.-Colonel A. S. Blair was appointed Commandant at Abancourt and his place in the battalion was filled by Lieut.-Colonel P. T. Westmorland, C.M.G., D.S.O. Within a few days this officer left to command a brigade, and the 9th Royal Scots then received as C.O. Lieut.-Colonel W. Green, D.S.O., a former Adjutant of the battalion.

Three new battalions, the 15th and the 16th with

the Thirty-fourth Division and the 17th with the Thirty-fifth Division, arrived in France at the beginning of 1916. All three units had experienced a longer spell of training than they deemed necessary, and they were unfeignedly glad when at last orders came for them to proceed overseas. The two former battalions, under Lieut.-Colonels Urmston and Sir George McCrae respectively, crossed the Channel on the 8th January, landed at Havre, and concentrated near the town of St Omer. Along with the 11th Suffolks and the 10th Lincolns they formed the 101st Brigade commanded by Brig.-General H. G. Fitton. Their apprenticeship was passed under conditions that were as congenial as could be expected in war, for they were stationed in the Armentières sector, generally regarded by the troops as one of the "bon" spots in the line. Both units were in the best of trim when in April the division withdrew from Armentières to the neighbourhood of Tilques, where they put in some strenuous training for the Battle of the Somme. Early in May the 101st Brigade returned to the line east of Albert, and the 15th and the 16th had an opportunity of making themselves familiar with the district where they were to have their first experience of battle. The 4th June was the most exciting day prior to the opening of the battle. On that date, as the 15th Royal Scots were being relieved, the Boches violently shelled our trenches and a few bold raiders even penetrated our lines, but they were speedily ejected. On the night of the 28th/29th June a small party of the 16th Royal Scots, led by 2nd Lieut. T. M. Miller, went out to raid the opposing lines, but failing to get through a thick tangle of wire that lay concealed in a valley, was obliged to return. The expedition, however, was not fruitless, for the location of the wire, which had hitherto escaped our notice, was reported with such precision that our gunners were able to destroy the obstacle before the 1st July. The preparations for the battle made heavy demands on the infantry, the 15th and the 16th Royal Scots being nightly required to furnish large working and carrying parties.

The 17th Royal Scots, who left Southampton on the 31st January, concentrated at Wardrecques on the 3rd February. Their first trench tour as a unit began on the 7th March, and from this date till June the battalion held at different times the front line south of Armentières, at Fauquissart, Neuve Chapelle, and Festubert. The last was perhaps the most disagreeable of these sectors, and among the casualties sustained there was 2nd Lieut. E. R. Craig, who was killed near the end of May. In the middle of June the battalion rested and trained at Oblighem for twelve days, and early in July proceeded south to the Somme area.

As we have seen, the 5th Battalion under Major Griffiths left Egypt on the 16th March. It arrived at Marseilles on the 22nd, and after some travelling was quartered at the village of Arquèves, where on the 6th April it was joined by Major D. C. McLagan, who took over the command. Had the battalion been up to strength it would in all probability have maintained its connection with the Twenty-ninth Division, but it was so weak in numbers that during the months of May and June it was engaged in duties on the lines of communication.

The 6th Battalion on reaching Marseilles on the 8th May was put into quarantine for a month owing to a suspected case of typhus. Its losses had not been heavy, but it was patent that Edinburgh could not make good the wastage of both the 5th and the 6th, so on the 15th June the two battalions were combined under Major McLagan as the 5th/6th Royal Scots. On the

11th July Lieut.-Colonel J. T. R. Wilson joined and took over the command of the composite battalion, which towards the end of that month was attached to the 14th Brigade of the Thirty-second Division.

Before the opening of the Battle of the Somme an important change had been effected in the organisation of infantry battalions. The Vickers machine-guns, it was discovered, gave more valuable service when grouped in companies, and they were therefore formed into companies under the command of brigades. Thus battalions lost their machine-gun sections, but they were compensated by receiving the lighter Lewis guns. Some units, like the 11th and the 12th Royal Scots, had been armed with these weapons during the Battle of Loos, and before fighting on the Somme began there was a sufficient supply of Lewis guns to allow four, one per company, to be issued to each battalion. This establishment was gradually increased till, by the end of the war, each platoon had two Lewis guns, while the battalion had an additional four for anti-aircraft work. Previous to the Battle of the Somme the steel helmet, popularly called the "tin hat," became the battle head-gear of the Army and provided valuable protection against shell-splinters. The balmoral might be worn out of the line, but on all ceremonial occasions and in the trenches the wearing of the steel helmet was compulsory.

The comparative immunity experienced by the British during the period that we have traced was due to the Battle of Verdun and, as this action developed, hasty critics at home impatiently wondered why the British armies remained so passive. But no time in fact was being wasted, and Sir Douglas Haig[1] was busily engaged in completing his preparations for a great

[1] British Commander-in-Chief since December 1915.

ARRANGEMENTS FOR ATTACK

counter-offensive. These preparations were of a most comprehensive nature, and were carried through with great thoroughness. Sir Douglas Haig was convinced that a systematic scheme of training for the troops in France was absolutely necessary, and the whole hinterland teemed with schools and training centres. Stores and guns of all kinds had to be got ready for the campaign which he had planned, and the wonderful organisation of the British Army was devoted to that end. The lessons of previous battles had been taken to heart and a system of tactics excogitated which had the eminent merit of being logical.

All these preparations were made with a view to taking the strain off our French allies, who had been engaged in heavy fighting since April. Moreover, the course of events in other theatres of the war suggested the need of immediate action on the part of the British forces in France. Austria had counter-attacked Italy with such vigour in the Trentino that Russia, which had apparently recovered from the effects of her disasters in 1915, in June launched an offensive brilliantly conducted by General Brussilov, which resulted in sensibly relieving the Austrian pressure on Italy. With the Russian campaign in full swing, it was advisable to prevent Germany from transferring troops from the west to other fronts, and this could only be done by an Allied attack in strength in France. In order to assure the effective co-operation of British and French the district chosen for the great attack was Picardy, the junction of the two armies.

The Battle of the Somme is one of the towering landmarks of the war. For months after July 1916 the manner of conducting a battle was stereotyped, and war seemed in process of being transformed from a profession or a science into a business. The preliminary bombardment, the limited objectives, the "creeping" barrage[1] were the salient features of the "set" battle, and as a general rule the enemy appeared to know when, where, and with what strength we were going to attack. Thus the power of our artillery to flatten entrenchments and chloroform the surviving defenders supplanted the element of surprise as the basis of success.

The unfortunate infantryman became a mere marionette, and his task, though straightforward, was singularly unenviable. To capture a definite number of trenches was a rôle that demanded dash and endurance rather than skill. Moving forward in accordance with a fixed time-table against a position directly in front, the troops were given little scope for manœuvre and were employed as a sort of human battering-ram. The horrible deadliness of this type of warfare preyed on the minds of the more intelligent, for they felt that they were in no sense the masters of their fate; either they charged over tortured ground picking up a few demoralised captives, or they ran into a storm of bullets that swept across the earth like leaves before a hurricane. If the attack was broken there was mourning for lost comrades, and if it was successful jubilation was short-lived. In the early days of July a platoon commander in his first and, as it chanced, his last battle, on reaching the final objective, exclaimed in a burst of rapturous enthusiasm, "Now, we are all right!" To this his company commander with memories of the aftermath of Loos remarked, "Victory brings more perils in its train than defeat." Counter-attacks and incessant shell fire frequently caused

---

[1] The "creeping" barrage jumps rather than crawls. The artillery play on a line for a certain period and then switch on to successive lines usually 50 yards apart. The "creeping" barrage, which was first employed at the Somme, was thenceforward used by the British Army in all its attacks.

greater slaughter among the conquerors than that sustained during the actual attack.

Any illusions cherished by men about the romance of war were dissipated by one experience of the Somme. Hard knocks were more common than glory, and the glamour surrounding war, of which the combatant was but faintly conscious, was really invented by the war correspondent. "The enemy's position was carried by the bayonet" was a journalistic rather than an accurate description of the finish of a fight. It is questionable if, throughout the war, there ever was a clash of cold steel between the adversaries before one side or the other gave way and fled; the triumphant bayonet charge that carried a battalion to its victorious goal encountered only isolated enemies, drugged into a stupor by the fury of our bombardment. Like the grenade, the bayonet was found to be mainly a "moral" weapon, and men sometimes wondered why so much time was devoted to instruction in its use; it produced its effect by terrifying and not by stabbing the foe. So conscious was a highly esteemed adjutant of the Royal Scots of the rarity with which the bayonet was used that he once recommended that it should be discarded in order to lighten the soldier's burden.

Another circumstance that gave a peculiar character to the fighting in 1916 was that the fury of the war was then at its zenith, and though individual acts of chivalry were not uncommon, British and Germans regarded each other with a passion and rancour that over-mastered the promptings of pity and mercy. Exulting like inquisitors at the burning of a heretic, men expressed a barbarous joy in the sufferings of their opponents.

Troops on being withdrawn from the Somme felt that they had been vouchsafed a glimpse of the horrors of another world. "You don't know what war is until you have been in the Somme," said a veteran to a young soldier who joined the 12th Royal Scots in August. There could now be no doubt that the holding of a trench system outside the battle area was almost reduced to the level of an innocuous occupation. It is not, however, the habit of the British soldier to dwell upon stark and gruesome things, and his capacity for sheer irrelevance was the most potent anodyne against moroseness and despair. From the wreckage caused by war he picked up splinters of pure humour, and the banal flippancy of British marching songs was to a certain extent a measure of the gravity of the struggle.

Few individuals would have gone back to a "set" battle of their own accord. Yet after a few weeks' rest, which sufficed to diminish the sense of horror, men not only returned to the battle but did so with marvellous cheerfulness. Some seemed to look on the war as a kind of grotesque art and professed to find a symphonic dignity in a bombardment. Others (extremely few) were addicted to the horrors of war as a degenerate is to a drug; these experienced an unholy pleasure in wearing the hair shirt, the evidence of pride rather than humility. The vast majority, however, were inspired to return from motives of self-respect and pride in their unit, and will led them to challenge that from which the flesh shrank; for the soul of a battalion kept alive a heroism far surpassing that of any individual.

CHAPTER XV

THE BATTLE OF THE SOMME—LA BOISSELLE, DELVILLE WOOD, AND LONGUEVAL

July 1916

Description of Terrain. The German defences between the Somme and the Ancre. Three phases of the Battle. Sector of Thirty-fourth Division. Objectives of 15th and 16th Royal Scots. Attack of 15th and 16th Royal Scots. Importance of La Boisselle. Wood Alley. Situation at nightfall, 1st July. Sir George McCrae at Wood Alley, 2nd July. Capture of Scots Redoubt. Events on 3rd July. Achievements of Thirty-fourth Division. Relief of 15th and 16th Royal Scots. 11th and 12th Royal Scots at Montauban. The 12th at Bernafay Wood, 3rd July. 2nd Royal Scots. Longueval. Arrangements for Attack on 14th July. The Assembly. Action of 11th Royal Scots. Attack on Longueval by 12th Royal Scots. 2nd Royal Scots in Action, 14th July. Gains of the Battle. Continuation of Attack on Longueval, 15th July. 11th Royal Scots attack Longueval, 16th July. Heroism of 2nd Lieut. Turner and Sergeant Allwright. Longueval, 17th July. Relief of 11th and 12th Royal Scots. German counter-attack. 2nd Royal Scots.

THE main object of the British attack was the irregular ridge slanting across Picardy from the south-west to the north-east. This ridge, rising at its highest point to more than 500 feet above sea-level, forms the watershed between the Somme on the one side and the rivers that drain the flats of south-west Belgium on the other. Throwing out on both sides a succession of spurs and valleys it forms a typical part of the landscape of Picardy. Undulating and irregular, it merges into the horizon in an infinite variety of shapes, and its grassy slopes, splashed at intervals by the darker hue of spacious umbrageous forests, bore smilingly the hamlets of the French peasants. The first impression conveyed by the scenery was one of agricultural well-being and of bucolic tranquillity. But only those in the habit of forming hasty judgments could describe the view that stretched before them as peaceful. The sunshine and loveliness which lapped Picardy in the summer of 1916 gave to the battlefield a satiric sinister flavour. What were once happy villages had been transformed into fortresses, from the chimneys of which no hospitable smoke curled upwards to the sky, while in the pleasant woods of peace now lurked all manner of death-traps. The opposing lines of trenches, forming snaky waves across the country, proved to be crude obstacles compared with the hamlets and woods, whose names recall to us the most thrilling episodes in the drama of the Somme.

The principal effort of the British was directed against the section of the ridge lying between the Somme and the Ancre. The Germans occupied a position that was in itself naturally strong, and having been unmolested in this area for nearly two years they had, in their quiet industrious manner, systematically improved it until they might be pardoned for thinking it all but impregnable. Their first system ran along the southern slopes of the ridge fronting the British trenches from the Ancre to the Somme; their second line of defence lay along the highest part of the ridge; and behind that they were constructing other fortifications. It was obviously no light task that the British had before them, but if they could carry the ridge they would be in a position to threaten the enemy's hold on that important centre of communications, Cambrai.

The battle has been described by Sir Douglas Haig as dividing itself into three phases: in the first stage, which lasted till the 17th July, we attacked and captured the southern crest of the main plateau between Delville Wood and Bazentin-le-Petit; during the second stage,

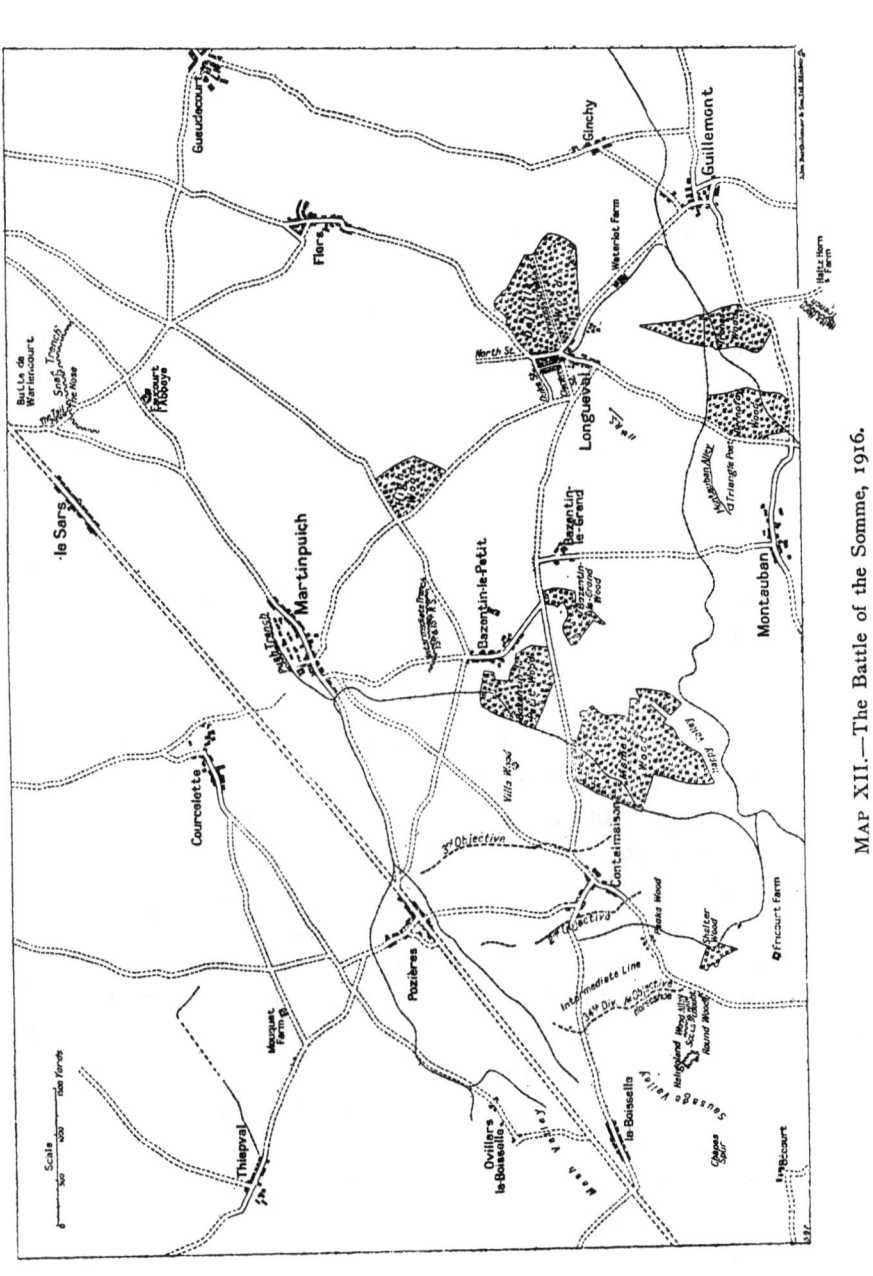

MAP XII.—The Battle of the Somme, 1916.
(*See also* large scale Map at end of volume.)

which continued till the first week of September, we had to fight desperately to maintain our hold on these gains; then, the German counter-attack having been defeated, came the third stage in which we carried the whole plateau from Morval to Thiepval and pushed our advance down the farther slopes.

In the first phase our attack between the Somme and the Ancre was not uniformly successful. The frontage was approximately 20,000 yards, and the assault was preceded by a tremendous bombardment of the hostile positions which lasted for six days. The infantry attack took place on the 1st July, and in the south, as far north as Fricourt, was strikingly successful, but beyond that point only local gains were made. Two of the Royal Scots battalions, the 15th and the 16th, took part in the fighting of the first few days of the battle.

The Thirty-fourth Division, lying astride the great main road between Albert and Bapaume at the point where it begins to ascend towards the watershed, had been in its position for sufficient time to allow it to become thoroughly acquainted with the chief features of the country over which the attack was to proceed. In this neighbourhood the watershed fans out in four spurs to the west. North of the road and running parallel to it, is the spur on the southern slopes of which the ruins of Ovillers-La Boisselle formed the most conspicuous object. Then Chapes Spur, with the main road skirting its northern selvage, extends beyond the village of La Boisselle, where the German fortifications projected like a spear-head from their front line, almost to the northern apex of Bécourt Wood. Between the two spurs nestles the valley, marked on our maps as Mash, which after bending round towards Bécourt Wood turns in a north-easterly direction, and under the name of Sausage Valley narrows as it gradually ascends the ridge. The southern slopes of Sausage Valley are formed by the spur that runs south towards Fricourt. From this village a path wanders northwards along a deep cutting terminated by a cluster of trees known as Round Wood, whence continuing in a north-easterly direction it cuts across a valley, where it is shaded by Peake Wood, and mounts the fourth spur to the village of Contalmaison.

It did not require a soldier's eye to see that the hostile positions, with their forward trenches lying along the western slopes of the first three spurs, were enormously powerful. The villages of Ovillers-La Boisselle and La Boisselle were clearly places of quite exceptional strength, and no force could expect to pass safely through the space between them unless the enemy's machine-gunners, hidden in their ruins, were almost completely subdued. The key of the German position was La Boisselle, where the fortifications extended into No-Man's-Land like a peninsula, from the point of which the trenches bent back north and south in rough semi-circles, so that the machine-gunners lurking in the village could sweep with their fire an extensive tract of No-Man's-Land on both flanks. We made careful arrangements for dealing with this fortress. The sappers burrowed four mines which were to be exploded in its vicinity, and a heavy trench-mortar barrage was to be maintained on the village till such time as parties of bombers from the 102nd Brigade had reached points from which they could attack La Boisselle from both north and south.

Apart from these fortified villages the hostile defences consisted of a front, support, and reserve line, together forming the front system, and a trench on the west side of Contalmaison. All the trenches were bountifully protected by entanglements of barbed wire. The two Edinburgh battalions in the forthcoming battle were to operate on the right flank of the division, with troops of the Twenty-first Division on their right and the 11th Lincolns on their left. The first objective, comprising the German front system, was the task of the 15th Royal Scots. This meant that the 15th had to carry four lines of trenches: the front line with the lozenge-shaped strong-point known as Heligoland and a shorter stretch of trench leading south from it; then the support line; and finally the reserve trench. The most noticeable feature in this trench was a strong-point shaped like a triangle which, lying just west of Round Wood, marked the right boundary of the battalion; it was prophetically termed Scots Redoubt. After this position was taken the 16th Royal Scots were to go through the 15th, and, passing over the Intermediate Line with its right flank including Peake Wood, were to capture and consolidate the strong line that formed the immediate protection of Contalmaison on the west. From this point troops of the 103rd Brigade were to carry the line to the east of that village.

Strong though the German positions undoubtedly were, both the 15th and the 16th Royal Scots were confident that the attack would be successful. They were aware of the extensive preparations that we had made and in which they had taken some part, and they were inspired by the optimism that comes to men who know exactly what they have to do.

Eventually the opening of the attack was fixed for 7.30 A.M. on the 1st July. On the 25th June our preliminary bombardment commenced, and from that date till the end of the year the turmoil of the guns brooded over Picardy. During these six days the 15th and the 16th Royal Scots speculated vaguely as to

THE ATTACK OPENS

what was taking place behind the hostile lines; the bombardment appeared to them so ruthless that it could not fail to demolish the German gun positions, and the more optimistic believed that they would meet with little opposition. On the morning of the 1st July our cannonade swelled in volume and the earth shook under the frenzied roar; the eastern sky became a sheet of light and flame in which the puffs of bursting shrapnel formed a variety of distorted arabesques; the mines near La Boisselle were touched off and the air was black with flying debris and smoke. Then came the moment for which the men were waiting, and at 7.30 A.M. the first waves of the 15th Royal Scots climbed the parapets and advanced into No-Man's-Land.

It was soon realised that our arrangements, comprehensive though they were, had not fulfilled their purpose. Our bombardment, though it seemed tremendous to our own troops, had silenced neither the guns nor the machine-guns of the enemy. The explosion of the mines from which we had hoped so much, failed to demoralise the garrison of La Boisselle, and the village surpassed our worst expectations. The brigade on the left of the 101st could make no progress in face of the blast of bullets that swept it from Ovillers-La Boisselle and La Boisselle, and this failure reacted on the attack of the 101st Brigade. From the moment that our first wave of troops scaled the parapets a heavy barrage descended upon our trenches and many were killed before they could spring clear of their own trenches. Owing to the inability of our artillery to keep down the fire of the defenders, our chances of achieving complete success became very faint. At first nothing could be heard above the crash of exploding shells, but as the Royal Scots, catching their breath and with heads bowed as if to escape a deluge of rain, pushed on, they heard the sharp patter of the even more fatal machine-guns, and men fell so thickly that of the long waves that first moved off only tiny clusters of figures could be seen.

The most deadly fire came from the concealed fortifications of La Boisselle and from the high ground to the left of the battalion, and only men who were tuned up to sacrifice themselves for their cause could have made any progress. There could be no finer testimony to the resolution and devotion of the two Royal Scots battalions than the splendid unwavering advance which they made under conditions that were all against them. First the 15th were buffeted by the storm of shells and bullets, then the 16th; and it was probably at the exposed zone just in front of our parapets that many of the officers and men made the supreme sacrifice. The flood of fire from the north inevitably caused our advance to veer in a southerly direction, but in spite of that the 15th Royal Scots secured the greater part of their objectives and were the only unit in the division that did so. "C" Company, under Major Stocks, plodded grimly on and, crossing Scots Redoubt, reached Peake Trench. There Major Stocks found that only a handful of his men, joined by a few from the 16th Royal Scots and the Suffolks, now remained, and on the flanks there were none to give support. Ultimately this scanty group succeeded in establishing touch with troops of the Twenty-first Division, but being exposed to attack from the north it could not maintain its hold on Peake Wood and was driven back about 300 yards from it. Major Stocks, assisted by Lieut. Robson, did his utmost to re-form his command, and with such success that when the Germans counter-attacked with overwhelming numbers his men drew off in good order to the reserve line. Unfortunately, during this desperate fighting,

Major Stocks was severely wounded and fell into the hands of the enemy.

The command of the party was now taken over by Lieut. Robson, who was joined later by Captain Brown of the Suffolks. Here at Wood Alley, the strip of trench adjoining Scots Redoubt, Lieut. Robson met a group of "B" Company of the 16th under Lieut. R. C. Lodge. The 16th, following the 15th, came under a murderous fire when they reached our front line, and Lieut. Lodge, dominating his men by his own imperturbability, rallied them and led them through the turmoil of shells and sputtering bullets to Wood Alley. At this point there were probably less than 100 men in all under three officers, Lieuts. Robson and Lodge of the Royal Scots and Captain Brown of the Suffolks, and upon the leadership of these depended issues greater than probably they were aware of. For the retention of Wood Alley was vital to the security of the Twenty-first Division, which had made a successful attack on the right of the Thirty-fourth. Retirement was not even contemplated, and the officers of the Wood Alley garrison took every precaution to safeguard their position. Nothing contributes more to shore up resolution than the quality of leadership that evokes the spontaneous confidence of troops, and the three officers splendidly satisfied the most searching test that they had yet been called upon to undergo. Lieut. Robson, brisk and energetic, seemed to exude assurance, while Lieut. Lodge's easy nonchalance, a mask concealing the keenness with which he took stock of the position, led his men to believe that there was really no cause for alarm. His platoon was greatly surprised that he was still alive; 6 ft. 8 in. in height, he must have been one of the tallest officers in the British Army, and there was a rumour in the 16th that picture post-cards showing his head and shoulders above the trenches were on sale in the streets of Berlin.

When night descended on the 1st July, the position of the advanced party was far from being secure. The leaders knew that their force was almost surrounded by the enemy, but they kept this knowledge to themselves. The right flank was tolerably safe, being protected by the Twenty-first Division, but otherwise all round were Germans. The enemy had regained his hold on his front trench, with its strong-point known as Heligoland, and so cut off the Wood Alley force from direct communication with our original front line. It was very doubtful if our advanced group could withstand any serious counter-attack and it was impossible to reinforce it quickly, since the only means of communication was by a trench in the area of the Twenty-first Division. This avenue was wholly inadequate to meet the needs of two divisions, and throughout the night of the 1st/2nd July it was so congested that movement along it was almost impossible. The Staff-Captain of the 101st Brigade, Captain R. Greig of the 15th Royal Scots, volunteered to lead a water-carrying party to Wood Alley. In pitch blackness and under heavy shell fire he and his men laboriously forced a way over the corpses that now formed the floor of the trenches, and ultimately they clambered on top and proceeded across country in the direction of Scots Redoubt, till they found a trench occupied by a company of the Twenty-first Division. By this time Captain Greig who had started off with twelve had only three men, so he gave his supplies to the Twenty-first Division and returned after several adventures to Brigade H.Q. Fortunately for the troops in Wood Alley, another party under Lieut. Ash of the R.E., with bombs and other stores, succeeded in reaching them during the night, and rendered much valuable assistance by consolidating the trench.

Although the attack of the Thirty-fourth Division had been only partially successful it had shaken the Germans, who seem to have been too nervous about their position to make a counter-attack. Brig.-General Gore of the 101st Brigade took immediate steps to strengthen our hold on Wood Alley. Acting on his instructions, Lieut.-Colonel Urmston and Sir George McCrae had not gone forward with their men, but in the evening, orders were sent to the Battalion H.Q. instructing the C.O.s. to join their advanced posts and clear up the situation. Owing to some misunderstanding only Sir George McCrae received the orders, and at 9.25 P.M., accompanied by Captain Robertson and Major Warden, he left his H.Q. A very heavy hostile barrage forced them to take cover for some time, and they did not reach the forward troops till near daybreak. By this time Lieut. Lodge had been joined by 2nd Lieut. Hamilton, and the former had now about 150 men of the 16th Royal Scots under his command. Sir George McCrae first ascertained the strength of the Wood Alley garrison. In addition to these 150 men, Lieut. Robson had 85 men and one officer with him, while there were also troops of the 10th Lincolns, 11th Suffolks, and 27th Northumberland Fusiliers, the force amounting in all to 11 officers and 293 other ranks. Not far to the rear, under Captain Armit, was the remainder of "B" Company of the 16th Royal Scots, which in the fighting on the 1st July had established itself in a trench some distance behind Wood Alley. In spite of the severe ordeal to which they had been subjected, the men were in good spirits, but all were showing signs of exhaustion and were in sore need of food and water. Most of them had received no water since the dawn of the 1st, and all had consumed the emergency rations that they had carried with them into the fight. It was well that there had been no hostile thrust, for the supply of grenades and ammunition was too scanty for any protracted battle.

The arrival of Sir George McCrae exercised an almost magical effect upon the Wood Alley garrison, and perhaps his most cherished souvenir of the war is a letter which he received later from one of his men, thanking him for the confidence which he spread among his troops by the cheerful unconcern of his bearing. At once he realised that the expulsion of the Boches from Scots Redoubt was absolutely necessary for the safety of his own force, but he had to wait until his men had been fed and bombs and ammunition brought up before this could be effected. By noon all his arrangements were complete, and an hour later the 15th Royal Scots, armed with grenades and led by Lieut. Robson, with great dash attacked and carried the Redoubt, capturing 50 prisoners. Then a force of the 16th Royal Scots, under 2nd Lieut. Hamilton, attempted to clear the Boches from a trench, called the " Horseshoe " because of its shape, which extended from Scots Redoubt to the north. It gained about 150 yards of this trench, but was then held up by a stout barricade where the Germans had established a bombing post.

The success of these brilliant attacks did not render wholly secure the position of Sir George McCrae's force. The Germans were in great strength on his left flank, and from Heligoland and the adjoining trenches still menaced him from the left rear. Brig.-General Gore however had already made arrangements to attack Heligoland by two companies of the 7th East Lancashire Regiment of the Nineteenth Division, and before darkness fell Sir George McCrae had the satisfaction of knowing that there was no longer any danger of a German onslaught from the left rear. With Heligoland in our hands it was possible to establish direct communication between Scots Redoubt and our old front line, so that reinforcements and stores of all kinds could now be sent up with greater ease and rapidity. There was vigorous shelling during the night of the 2nd/3rd July, and the Boches somewhat tardily began a series of counter-strokes in the hope of regaining their lost positions, but they accomplished nothing against the stonewall resistance of our men. Reinforcements, to the total of 400 officers and men from units of the 101st and 103rd Brigades, arrived during the night at Scots Redoubt and the "Horseshoe," while carrying parties brought up ample supplies of food, water, and bombs. The Quartermaster of the 16th Royal Scots, Lieut. D. W. Gray, in spite of colossal difficulties, managed to send up a full supply of freshly cooked meat, so that the men of the battalion were able to enjoy the luxury of a good square meal for the first time since the opening of the battle.

When the 3rd July dawned the position of Sir George McCrae's force was perfectly secure, and the 16th Royal Scots, without any difficulty, beat off a counter-attack. On this day the Divisional Commander, General Ingouville Williams, visited the Redoubt, and his eyes gleamed moist with tears as he praised and thanked the men for all that they had done. Their achievements were not to be measured by the amount of ground they had gained. The attack of the Thirty-fourth Division was delivered at the point that formed the boundary line between success and failure, and but for the resolution of the Royal Scots in holding on to Wood Alley, the area of our success must have been considerably diminished. The troops of the Twenty-first Division, the left flank of which was buttressed by the Royal Scots, gratefully acknowledged how much they had been assisted by the attack of the 101st Brigade and commended especially the performance of the two Edinburgh battalions. Moreover, sufficient ground had been gained by the right of the Thirty-fourth Division to enable us to assault the village of La Boisselle, which fell to the Nineteenth Division on the 3rd July.

In the evening the wearied but indomitable garrisons of Scots Redoubt and Wood Alley were relieved by troops of the Twenty-third Division and marched back to Bécourt Wood, arriving there early on the morning of the 4th July. By their deeds in the fighting during the first three days of July, the 15th and the 16th Royal Scots firmly established their reputation as first-class fighting units, but the price of victory was woefully high. The 15th lost eighteen officers[1] and six hundred and ten other ranks in killed, wounded, and missing. Of the 16th[2] three officers were killed, three were missing, and six were wounded; of the other ranks four hundred and sixty were killed, wounded, or missing. Perhaps one of the saddest consequences of the battle was that the intimate connection with Edinburgh could no longer be maintained. Hitherto, the personnel of the 15th and the 16th Royal Scots, both in officers and men, had been drawn principally from the Scottish capital,

---

[1] The officers killed were—Majors J. R. Bruce and H. L. Stocks; Lieuts. W. A. Hole and R. Reid; 2nd Lieuts. J. L. Brough, J. B. Dougal, A. Elder, J. Grant, and E. M. Pinkerton; while Captains G. E. Gee and J. L. Lawrence died from the effects of their wounds; among the wounded were Lieut. G. P. Douglas and 2nd Lieut. Brown.

[2] Captains P. Ross, L. G. Coles, and 2nd Lieut. G. S. Russell were killed. It was ascertained later that 2nd Lieut. W. L. Crombie, who was wounded and missing, had been killed. Captain A. Whyte was wounded and missing, 2nd Lieut. R. M. Pringle, missing, and Lieut. H. Rawson, 2nd Lieuts. T. H. Bell, J. McKenzie, W. A. McMichael, T. M. Millar, and J. G. P. Stevenson were wounded.

but after the 3rd July the gaps in the ranks were filled by newcomers drawn from all parts of Scotland. Nevertheless, the circumstances of their origin caused the citizens of Edinburgh to continue to take an especial interest in the doings of the two battalions.

While the 15th and the 16th Battalions were being withdrawn from the battle, three other units of the Royal Scots, the 11th, 12th, and 2nd Battalions, were preparing to enter it farther south. On the 23rd June the two battalions in the Ninth Division, fit and eager after a spell of rest and training, assembled near Corbie. Most of the officers and men had been long enough in France to acquire the imperturbability of the "old soldier." The mass of stores and dumps of every description that littered the hinterland formed an unmistakable warning that a great battle was impending. From the 24th June the men of the 11th and the 12th Royal Scots lived in an atmosphere of bustle and noise; parties were engaged in carrying all kinds of stores up to dumps near the front, and every gun was belching messages of iron into the German positions. On the night of the 30th June the units bivouacked in Billon Copse, but few slept because of the din of the guns which seemed to be placed all round the wood. The whole sky quivered with the lightning of war, and the earth throbbed under the beat of marching men and the grinding of wagons. In the morning all turned their eyes towards the east, wondering what was happening behind the sheet of smoke and flame which was all that they could see. Then joyful tidings began to filter through from the attack. The Boches had been chased from Montauban and Mametz was in our hands, but nothing definite was gleaned about the outcome of the battle farther north.

At nightfall the 12th Royal Scots went up to help the Eighteenth Division to consolidate its gains, but this errand turned out to be wasted labour, for the men who acted as guides to the battalion lost their way in the darkness and after a blasphemous tour the unit returned to its quarters without having accomplished anything. On the night of the 2nd/3rd July the 11th Royal Scots left Billon Copse to take over Montauban. The village could be clearly discerned and Lieut.-Colonel Croft could have taken his men straight to it, but being anxious not to complicate the relief, he entrusted his companies to the guides who had been detailed to lead the battalion to its position. The guides lost their way and then their heads, and the Royal Scots were being led into the village of Longueval when the company commanders angrily dismissed the guides and brought their men into Montauban just as the sun began to climb the eastern sky. The positions held by the 11th lay along the eastern side of the village; the western was guarded by the 9th Scottish Rifles, while the 12th Royal Scots were in reserve.

Montauban was not a place for nervous or timid men. It was one of the favourite targets of the German gunners, who at frequent intervals and with great accuracy poured salvos of 5.9s on the battered hamlet. Every day the air was thick with the flying debris of the village. Under these conditions movement had to be restricted as much as possible and the chief relaxation came after dark when the men could go out patrolling. The 11th had forty casualties at Montauban, while four officers of the 12th (Captains Sanderson and W. Skinner and 2nd Lieuts. G. Middlemas and A. T. McLaren) were wounded.

Fronting the village was the hamlet of Longueval and between them lay the forests of Bernafay and Trones, and it was clearly essential to occupy these two woods before launching an attack against Longueval.

From Montauban towards Longueval the ground dipped gently to a shallow valley, then climbed gradually to a plateau which from Longueval and Delville Wood threw out two arms, one leading due west to the two Bazentins, the other running north-west to the high ground crowned by High Wood, which could be plainly seen from Montauban. Between these two arms the ground sagged to a slight depression.

From the Montauban defences a trench (Montauban Alley) led towards Bernafay Wood, and to prevent the Germans from closing in on the village, bombing sections from the 11th Royal Scots and the 9th Scottish Rifles worked their way along this trench to a strong-point known as Triangle Post, which they garrisoned early on the morning of the 3rd July.

In the afternoon orders came for the 27th Brigade to capture Bernafay Wood, and the 12th Royal Scots and the 6th K.O.S.B. were detailed for the task. Each battalion, forming up on a one-company front, assembled at a trench to the east of Montauban, and the direct assault was supported by a flanking movement along Montauban Alley carried out by "B" Company of the 12th Royal Scots. The attack, delivered at 9 P.M. after a brief bombardment, proved to be an unresisted advance. The few Boches in the wood made no attempt to fight, and the 12th found four deserted field-guns and one machine-gun. The flank attack along Montauban Alley was equally gainful, but the wood once in our hands proved to be a dismal prize, for the Germans shelled it with extraordinary violence, causing numerous casualties among the Royal Scots and the K.O.S.B. Raked daily by hostile fire, the wood, after a week, presented a woeful spectacle; before the 3rd July a man on the fringe of it could see only a few yards in front of him, but after two or three days of German shelling he could see without difficulty the far end. The garrison had to dig for dear life. The 12th Royal Scots held the west and north sides of the forest and were more fortunate than the K.O.S.B., who sustained grievous losses. The work of consolidation was often interrupted by bursts of fire, but progress continued to be made, and "D" Company of the 12th, under Lieut. Crowden, performed a very creditable piece of work when, with much labour, it cleared away the suffrutescent undergrowth and dug a formidable strong-point in the middle of the wood.

The other forest, Trones Wood, was the scene of most desperate fighting which, however, did not directly concern the men of the Royal Scots. The attacks were carried out by the Thirtieth Division, which made its first attempt on the 8th July, and the 12th Royal Scots helped this division by covering its left flank with machine-gun fire. While this action was in progress, Private J. Stevenson of the 12th spotted a German sniper in the act of firing at men of the 90th Brigade and, carrying a Lewis gun into the open, engaged the sniper; though he failed to kill him he prevented the Boche from interfering with the assailants of Trones Wood.

On the night of the 8th/9th July, the 11th and the 12th Royal Scots were relieved and marched back to Billon Valley. Meantime the 2nd Battalion had arrived in the Somme area and on the night of the 6th bivouacked in the forest of Les Celestins. From that place the 2nd Royal Scots proceeded, on the 7th, first to Bronfray Farm and then to trenches near Montauban. The Third and the Ninth Divisions were to be neighbours in the continuation of the grand attack, which was ultimately fixed for the 14th July. In this action the task of the Ninth Division was to capture the key-point of the Longueval plateau—that is, the village and Delville Wood, while the Third Division on its left was to seize the remainder of the western arm of the plateau from Bazentin-le-Grand to Longueval.

Before the war Longueval, tucked close into the west side of Delville Wood, must have been an attractive spot, but the very features that gave it charm were also those that made it a most formidable fortress. Delville Wood, which overshadowed it, was its chief protection on the east. The hamlet itself was built along three roads, the junction of which formed the centre or main square. From this point one road, indicated on our maps as North Street, extended north to meet a path midway between High Wood and Flers; the second branched to the south-west skirting the west border of Bernafay Wood; the third veered in a south-easterly direction towards Guillemont. From the square the street that branched west towards Bazentin-le-Grand was known to us as Clarges Street; parallel to it and about 300 yards to the north of it was Duke Street. These two streets were both cut by a lane, Piccadilly, running parallel to North Street, and these four streets formed a rectangle enclosing the orchards of Longueval. The hostile front trenches skirted the south of the village and then turned off towards the south-east, past Waterlot Farm and on towards Guillemont.

On the front of the Ninth Division the 11th Royal Scots and the 9th Scottish Rifles were to capture the German trenches in front of Longueval, after which the 12th Royal Scots were to pass through the Scottish Rifles, and the two Royal Scots battalions together were to complete the capture of the village. On the front of the Third Division no definite rôle was assigned to the 2nd Royal Scots, who formed on this occasion the reserve battalion of the 8th Brigade, which was to attack on the left of the 27th.

The most important of the preliminary arrangements

for the attack on the 14th July was a difficult night operation which was performed with signal success on the night of the 13th/14th. The entire attacking force, covered by patrols, moved over the open and assembled between 300 and 500 yards from the German front line. Thanks to the careful arrangements made by all the Staffs concerned and to the excellent control and discipline of the troops, the movement was effected without the enemy suspecting what was taking place. The men had been warned that the outcome of the battle depended absolutely upon the secrecy and silence with which they moved up to their assembly positions, and they did their part of the work magnificently.

In the Ninth Division Lieut.-Colonel Croft, shortly after midnight, led the 11th Royal Scots up to Montauban, which was being vigorously shelled by the Boches. On reaching the village the whole battalion, in single file, stealthily advanced to its assembly position close to the German trenches in front of Longueval. The 11th completed the preliminary movements without suffering any losses, but the 12th Royal Scots were not so lucky. In passing the western outskirts of Montauban they were caught by the hostile shell fire, and though the casualties were few, they included the C.O., Lieut.-Colonel Budge. Most of the men were unaware that their popular commander had been slain, and some time elapsed before Major Macpherson realised that he was in command of the battalion. Both units formed up in their assembly positions in good time and the preliminary arrangements were carried out with similar success.

At 3.20 A.M. our barrage opened and five minutes later the infantry advanced against the hostile positions. The 11th Royal Scots on nearing the first trench found that a considerable area of the protecting wire was uncut, and though they were played on by machine-gun fire they

Lieut.-Colonel H. L. BUDGE, 12th Battalion, The Royal Scots.

[To face p. 284.

began rapidly to cut and pull aside the wire in order to force a passage into the trench. During this very trying period the officers set a fine example of self-control and coolness; but thereby they attracted the attention of Boche snipers, and Captain J. A. Henry and Captain J. D. C. Cowan were both killed while assisting to clear away the wire. To cut the wire by hand would have been impossible, had not Lieut. Winchester with his Lewis guns engaged the German machine-guns and by the accuracy of his fire silenced them. Happily, too, a platoon of "A" Company had found an unimpeded passage on the right flank, and entering the trench, the men bombed their way down it, distracting the Boches and enabling their comrades to complete the demolition and removal of the wire. The capture of the trench was then quickly effected, and two parties, headed respectively by 2nd Lieuts. Turner and Fleming and aided by Lieut. Winchester and his Lewis guns, after a combined bombing attack, succeeded in rounding-up and capturing 63 prisoners. After clearing the first trench the 11th Royal Scots met with little opposition and easily secured their first objective. This attack was notable, not so much because of the gallantry as on account of the skill with which it was conducted. The co-operation between the various parties had been wholly admirable, and reflected great credit on the thoroughness with which Lieut.-Colonel Croft had trained his troops in the art of soldiery.

After the objective was reached, expeditious work soon converted a German communication trench into a fairly strong support trench. A patrol was sent out, but never returned. A larger party, with a Lewis gun, then went out and spotted several groups of Germans with machine-guns in cornfields close to Longueval, and they must have been responsible for the disappearance of the first patrol. Thus early were we warned that the Boches were not going to leave Longueval without a fight.

The first objective had been taken in less than an hour from the opening of the attack. The second phase of the battle, during which the 11th and the 12th Royal Scots were to complete the capture of Longueval, was of the utmost importance, since the possession of the village and Delville Wood was an essential preliminary to our contemplated operations against High Wood. Owing to the situation of the village the attack on it was beset by more than ordinary difficulty. The advance to the first objective had been in a north-easterly direction, but the rectangle of orchards between Piccadilly and North Street lay almost at right angles to the first objective, so that from that point our troops would have to make a wheel, pivoting on the right. The project of the 27th Brigade was as follows : The 11th Royal Scots, up to this point the right of the brigade, were now to become the left attacking battalion, with the 12th on their right. The former were detailed to take Duke Street from its junction with Piccadilly to its junction with Pont Street, which ran roughly parallel to Piccadilly ; the latter were to storm the key position of Longueval, the enclosure of orchards in the rectangle. The task of the 12th Royal Scots was by no means easy, and it was a great misfortune that a hostile shell had deprived them of the experienced leadership of such a soldier as Lieut.-Colonel Budge. Moreover, the battalion had already sustained serious losses in the advance to the first objective, for during the delay caused by the uncut wire in front of the 11th Royal Scots, many of the 12th had become interspersed with the attacking battalion and several officers had already been killed or wounded.

At 4.15 A.M. our barrage lifted from the village and

the two Royal Scots battalions resumed the assault. The 11th made satisfactory progress and dug in on a line south of Duke Street; further advance mainly depended upon what happened to the 12th on the right, upon whom fell the burden of the second phase of the attack. Our bombardment unfortunately inflicted little damage on the village defences, while the Germans, protected from the worst effects of our barrage by the ruins of the houses, were thoroughly keyed up to offer an obstinate resistance. Concealed in ruins and orchards, they opened a murderous fire on the advancing 12th Royal Scots, who dropped in swathes, but the survivors held grimly on till only a handful was left. The enemy seemed to have the ground marked off to an inch and to make a movement invited death or wounds. Hugging the ground the Royal Scots scraped a shallow ditch just 200 yards from Piccadilly. The right flank of the battalion rested on Clarges Street, where it was in touch with the 10th Argylls of the 26th Brigade, and on the left it was linked up with the 11th Royal Scots. The men felt as if they had been fighting for hours, yet it was not 7 A.M.; in this short time the battalion had lost nearly 50 per cent. of its strength, and only seven officers, all of them second lieutenants, were in the front line.

Two of these, 2nd Lieuts. A. Noble and G. McGregor, held a hurried council of war and decided that at all costs the attack on the village should be pressed on. "A" and "D" Companies accordingly, at 7 A.M., made a fine charge and actually got within 50 yards of fatal Piccadilly when the cascade of bullets from the hostile machine-guns once again brought them to a halt and compelled them to dig in. Baffled but not beaten, the battalion paused merely to recover its breath before it made another effort. It was sun-clear that a frontal assault against Piccadilly was suicidal, so the 12th next tried to carry the rectangle by an advance from Clarges Street. 2nd Lieuts. Armit and Noble, having mustered three sections with one Lewis gun, attacked Piccadilly and North Street from the south. The principal attempt was directed against North Street, at the junction of which with Clarges Street we had erected a barrier. Passing through this the Royal Scots came under a withering fire as soon as they entered the hostile area. Every ruin housed at least one machine-gun, and to escape the sputtering lead the men had to cower under the broken masonry that lined both sides of the street. The Boches had every advantage; they occupied positions that could not be precisely located, and they commanded all the cleared spaces that the assailants had to traverse if they intended to push home their attack. The 12th had no option but to retire, and it was not without incurring many perils that they reached the friendly side of the barricade.

The orchards and ruins of Longueval had now revealed themselves as a fortification of quite exceptional strength, and Major-General Furse, the commander of the division, arranged for the village to be bombarded by field-guns and trench-mortars before another thrust was made against it. But the rectangle was impervious to any improvised barrage, and when at 11 A.M. the 12th Royal Scots again attacked, they were immediately halted by a vigorous concentration of rifle and machine-gun fire. The battalion was too spent to make further efforts, and employed the remainder of the day in reorganising its ranks and in consolidating its position.

Despite this check the results of the day's fighting were very satisfactory, for the Ninth Division had won a firm hold on the southern portion of Longueval and had forced a lodgment in the western area of Delville Wood.

The onslaught of the Third Division on the left was markedly successful. At 12.30 A.M., on the 14th, the 2nd Royal Scots silently left Carnoy, and without a single casualty dug themselves in on their assembly position in four lines. Though in reserve to the 8th Brigade the battalion played a prominent and distinguished part in the action. On advancing to the attack the leading units came up against intact barbed wire, and while endeavouring to cut gaps through it, sustained great losses. The check was so serious that the Royal Scots were ordered to pass through and carry the trenches. Lieut.-Colonel Dyson, aware that a frontal attack would probably pile up the losses of his battalion without effecting his object, decided to make his onset from a flank. The 9th Brigade on the left had fortunately cleared the trenches opposite it, and taking advantage of this Lieut.-Colonel Dyson despatched the bombers and snipers of the 2nd Royal Scots to work their way up from these trenches. This movement, backed up by a similar attack carried on by the Royal Scots Fusiliers from the right, proved completely effectual. 2nd Lieut. Greenwood the sniping officer was killed, and 2nd Lieut. Taylor who led the bombers was wounded, but once the flanking attack was under way, the hostile resistance speedily collapsed and the trenches opposite the 8th Brigade were rapidly cleared; 284 Germans, including four officers and four machine-guns, were captured. The operation was a very smart piece of work, a good example of skilful leadership as contrasted with mere dash.

The final objective of the 8th Brigade, consisting of the German second line, was then seized without difficulty, and the 2nd Royal Scots, who had suffered the fewest casualties in the brigade, took over the new front with "C" and "D" Companies under the command of Captain Perry. In the afternoon "B" Company was also ordered up to the front line and had the misfortune to lose its commander, Captain R. J. Malcolm, who was mortally wounded by a shell. For a time we dared to hope that the enemy's resistance had collapsed, and our cavalry which had been massing in the valley galloped through, while the Fifth Division attacked High Wood. But the Boches were hardly ripe for cavalry yet, and after rounding-up a few prisoners the cavalry, fired on by the Germans in Delville Wood, were compelled to return. After darkness fell, "A" Company, under Captain the Hon. J. G. Stuart, also moved up to the firing-line taking over the right front of the brigade, where it was in touch with the Ninth Division in Longueval. Another stroke of bad luck befell the battalion during the afternoon when Captain G. W. J. Chree, the Adjutant, was killed by a shell. Throughout the day the hostile shelling was very severe and accurate, and though the losses of the Royal Scots during the advance had not been heavy, they mounted up in most alarming fashion after noon.

In the action of the 14th July the British troops in General Rawlinson's Fourth Army won a substantial and meritorious victory. On the 1st July, when we secured Montauban and Mametz, the enemy in this area of the battlefield had been taken by surprise, but our assault on the 14th must have been anticipated by the Boches, and the solid material gain that we achieved was therefore a testimony to the skill of the Staff and the indomitable courage of the troops. On a frontage of 6000 yards we had obtained a footing on the main ridge. This frontage was too narrow to permit of a general attack being continued along our whole line, so local operations had to be conducted with a view to widening it. The ground that we were attacking was vital to the enemy, who if he allowed himself to be thrust from the main ridge would be driven back to positions not nearly as strong as those that he held at the commencement of the battle. Consequently there now ensued a terrific struggle between the British and the German forces, and since, from the nature of the situation, there was very limited scope for manœuvre, the contest became a stubborn and protracted trial of strength in which victory would rest with those who displayed the greater endurance and tenacity. These considerations explain the ferocious and exhausting nature of the fighting that marked the Battle of the Somme from the 14th July till September.

Throughout the night of the 14th/15th July the noise and screams of bursting shells formed a sinister counterpoint to the activities of the troops in the battle area. In the trench systems men were at work with pick and shovel, while in the hinterland hordes of parties carrying stores and rations braved numerous gusts of shell fire as they carried out their missions. It is to the credit of the Quartermasters and the Transport Officers and their staffs that they never allowed any difficulties to prevent them from delivering the food and other stores that they knew were urgently needed by the men in the trenches. Under the prevailing conditions sleep was practically impossible for anyone near the front, and when the 15th July dawned the crinkled faces of the troops showed how heavy was the strain to which they were being subjected.

On that day the 12th Royal Scots received more punishment as a result of attempts to carry Longueval. The village had been fruitlessly attacked by South African troops during the night, and early on the 15th the 12th Royal Scots were instructed to make another assault. After a bombardment by guns and Stokes mortars they advanced at 11 A.M., and in spite of the exhaustion caused by their efforts on the previous day they threw themselves into the fray with unabated ardour, though only five officers now remained with the unit. Three sections, under C.S.M. Geddes, made the attack. Two of these essaying the North Street route made most amazing progress, and it seemed that the rectangle was at length to be carried by the persevering Royal Scots. The third section, operating from the west, was soon located by Boche snipers and compelled to retire. Meantime the North Street party, bombing from house to house, dropped small garrisons to hold each position as it was won and ultimately reached a point almost half-way to Duke Street, where it was stopped at a clearing amid the ruins of the houses. The Boches had removed all obstructing fragments and rubble to form this open space which they could sweep from end to end with their fire. To cross this zone in face of a vigilant and determined foe was a sheer impossibility.

The effort of the 12th Royal Scots, however, availed to give us a footing in the rectangle, but this important gain was not maintained, for the German gunners shelled the portion of North Street held by the Royal Scots with such ferocity and accuracy that the garrisons were compelled in the early evening to retreat to the shelter of the barricade.

Even after this reverse the 12th made another attack. Led by 2nd Lieut. Noble three sections, at 7.30 P.M., plunged straight into the orchards from Clarges Street, while two sections, under 2nd Lieut. Armit, advanced up North Street. The former group, moving with some difficulty through the tangled undergrowth, had progressed about 100 yards when it reached a thick hedge beyond which it was impossible to advance. The first men who tried to wriggle through it at once became the target of rifle and machine-gun fire. The North Street thrust was also a failure, but 2nd Lieut. Armit and his party had the satisfaction of dropping a number of the enemy by the fire of a Lewis gun. The battalion had now reached the limit of exhaustion, but though the men were too weary to assault they were still able to deal shrewdly with any attack that was directed against them. About 11 P.M. some Germans issued from the rectangle with the intention of making a counter-attack, expecting probably that the Royal Scots would be so discouraged by their repeated rebuffs that they would not offer any effective resistance. They were rudely disillusioned; the Royal Scots opened such a galling fire that the attack swiftly melted away.

As regards the 11th and the 2nd Royal Scots the 15th July passed uneventfully except for the ceaseless shelling which repeatedly interrupted the work of consolidation. During the day the 11th sent out a patrol to form a strong-point at the road junction half-way between High Wood and Longueval, but it was unable to fulfil its purpose owing to the alertness of the enemy. The night was rendered extremely disagreeable by the hostile gun fire which fell with deadly effect on Delville Wood, in which the South African Brigade had effected a lodgment, and on the south and south-west portions of Longueval. The ferocity and exactness of the German shelling during the fighting in July 1916 will remain in the memory of all who had any experience of it with the persistence of an evil dream.

On the 16th July came the turn of the 11th Royal Scots to be involved in the Longueval fighting, when they were detailed to co-operate with the 1st South

African Regiment in an attack on the rectangle at 10 A.M. After a preliminary bombardment by 2-inch trench-mortars the assault was to be delivered from the line of Princes Street-Clarges Street by two companies of the South Africans and "C" and "D" Companies of the 11th, while "B" Company of the latter was to create a diversion by attacking from the west.

The 11th Royal Scots were valiantly led by 2nd Lieut. Turner of "C" Company, but the rectangle had been rendered even more formidable since the failure of the last attack by the 12th Royal Scots. The area would have been difficult to penetrate even without fighting, since it was seamed with rows of thick and prickly hedges, and there was a profusion of tough undergrowth that wound round a man's legs like tentacles. The Germans had strengthened these natural obstructions by erecting belts of barbed wire concealed by the foliage and hedges. These barriers rendered a direct advance through the orchards well-nigh impossible, and 2nd Lieut. Turner and his men tried to turn the hostile defences by working up North Street as the 12th Royal Scots had previously attempted. The clearing that had baulked the 12th on the 15th again proved an insuperable obstacle, and an attempt of the 11th to dash across it in extended order was easily frustrated by the Boche snipers and machine-gunners.

Thus the attack broke down, but it forms one of the memorable episodes in the annals of the 11th Royal Scots owing to the heroism of 2nd Lieut. E. G. Turner and Sergeant Allwright. Amid the broken shrubbery of the rectangle, and within close range of the enemy, lay some wounded Royal Scots with the strong sun of Picardy beating mercilessly upon them. The task of rescuing these was fraught with many perils, but 2nd Lieut. Turner was loath to abandon them without making some effort to bring them in. He and Sergeant Allwright therefore crept cautiously into the orchards and hoisting the wounded men on their backs crawled with them into safety. Gusts of bullets stirred the undergrowth as they performed this noble feat, but by rare good fortune neither the officer nor the sergeant were hit.

Still another enterprise against the rectangle, in which the 11th Royal Scots were to co-operate with the 6th K.O.S.B. and the 1st South African Regiment, was projected for the early morning of the 17th. During the night, parts of our front line were temporarily vacated by the garrison while our heavy guns bombarded the rectangle and the northern portion of Longueval. Unfortunately this bombardment, owing to various delays, lasted for little more than an hour, and as it was directed without the aid of observation it is doubtful if it made any marked impression on the opposing defences. The infantry attack with the 11th Royal Scots on the left took place at 2 A.M. Lieut.-Colonel Croft entrusted the main assault to " A " Company supported by two platoons of " B "; another platoon of " B " was to attack the cross-roads of Piccadilly and Duke Street, while the fourth was to advance from the west and endeavour to force a lodgment in the rectangle about 100 yards north of Clarges Street.

Even this concentration of attacks failed to achieve its object. It was very dark and wet, and in a nightmare kind of combat " A " Company advanced from house to house up the west side of North Street, while the K.O.S.B. cleared the other side. In the pitch blackness the work was done mainly by the bayonet, but in this type of conflict the Jocks excelled, and both Royal Scots and K.O.S.B. hacked a passage almost up to the junction of North Street and Duke Street. But the route was strewn with casualties, and in the gloom many groups of Germans were passed over. These, recovering from their surprise, began to attack their adversaries from the rear, and the Royal Scots were reduced to a tiny handful by the time they neared Duke Street. Captain B. H. Whitley of "A" Company was shot dead by a sniper, and 2nd Lieut. Tredgold, who then assumed the command, had the greatest difficulty in maintaining liaison with the Borderers on the other side of the street. Bullets continued to pour along the streets and every movement was a challenge to death. The enemy's position had not really been captured. By dint of sheer pluck and dash the assailants had pushed their way up North Street until they formed merely an insignificant pocket in the German position.

This brilliant feat of arms could only be turned to account if it were aided by the other attacks, but these unfortunately were repulsed, though Sergeant Allwright, who led the charge into the rectangle, actually forced an entry into that sinister jungle, assisted by the friendly darkness. With the aid of Very lights the Boches directed a raking fire on Sergeant Allwright's party and finally compelled it to retire. With the failure of this attack the position of "A" Company became untenable, but as it retreated it picked up all its wounded before returning to the shelter of Clarges Street.

On the 17th July terminated the part played by the Royal Scots of the Ninth Division in the fighting at Longueval. They had added enormously to their reputation by their resolute and heroic conduct during three days of strenuous struggle. Where they failed, as in the attack on the Longueval orchards, they did so because they had not the slightest chance of success. Over a month of gruelling and desperate fighting was required before Longueval and Delville Wood passed into our undisputed control. At the close of the 17th July both the 11th and the 12th battalions, utterly exhausted, were relieved and withdrew to Talus Boise near our old front line of the 1st July. The slaughter among the battalions was terrible. The 11th lost thirteen officers (six killed[1] and seven wounded) while the casualties in other ranks amounted to three hundred and eight; the 12th also lost thirteen officers (seven killed[2] and six wounded) while their losses in other ranks totalled three hundred and four.

The 2nd Royal Scots during the period from the 15th to the 18th July were engaged mainly in consolidation. Early on the morning of the 18th the 76th Brigade of the Third Division attacked Longueval and gained a footing in the northern part of it, but the enemy had for some time been preparing for a great counter-stroke, which after a terrific bombardment, lasting from 8 A.M. till 2 P.M. on the 18th, was delivered against Delville Wood and Longueval. Only by the most frantic efforts was this shock withstood, and though the greater part of Delville Wood and the northern portion of the village were wrested from us we still retained our grasp on the main ridge. In this counter-attack none of the Royal Scots battalions were involved, though in the evening of the 18th the 12th Royal Scots were sent up to garrison part of the old German trenches in front of Longueval. The Ninth Division, however, was relieved on the 19th, and the 11th and the 12th Royal Scots, after a short period spent in refitting and recuperation, proceeded to a less lively part of the front.

The 2nd Royal Scots were also relieved on the night of the 19th/20th, and the battalion suffered a serious loss

[1] Captain J. J. Maybin, Lieut. F. Lemmey, and 2nd Lieut. A. B. M. Bogle in addition to those already mentioned.
[2] Lieut.-Colonel H. L. Budge, Captain F. J. Maloney, Lieuts. C. Young, A. Watkinson, H. Parsons, D. E. Gordon, and A. W. F. Glendinning.

as it made its way down from the front line to the support trenches in Montauban Valley. Many gas shells were fired by the enemy during the relief, and the effects of these caused Lieut.-Colonel Dyson and his Adjutant, 2nd Lieut. E. B. Swinton, to be evacuated to hospital. The command of the battalion was taken over by Captain Perry. The manning of trenches in the battle area proved a costly business, the losses of the 2nd Royal Scots in killed and wounded amounting to one hundred and seventy-six, of which number only seventy-seven were sustained during the battalion's attack on the 14th.

CHAPTER XVI

BATTLE OF THE SOMME—GUILLEMONT, HIGH WOOD, MARTINPUICH, AND THE BUTTE DE WARLENCOURT

July to October 1916

Third Division at Guillemont. Assaults of 2nd Royal Scots, 22nd and 23rd July. Battalion relieved. 17th Royal Scots at the Somme. Fifty-first Division at the Somme. Happy Valley and High Wood. Attack of 9th Royal Scots, 23rd July. Adventures of Major Moncreiff. Relief of Fifty-first Division. 15th and 16th Royal Scots near High Wood. Attacks on Intermediate Trench, August. 17th Royal Scots. Fifteenth Division arrives at the Somme. Situation at beginning of September. Arrangements for attack on 15th September. Effect of wet weather. 11th and 12th Royal Scots at Vimy Ridge. The Butte de Warlencourt. A difficult relief. Incidents at Snag Trench.

IN the dogged struggle that raged for many critical weeks during July and August the Germans proved themselves to be worthy and valorous opponents, but the supreme capacity of the British troops for standing a heavy pounding finally gained them the verdict. During the titanic conflict which ebbed and flowed over Longueval and High Wood, the aspect of the country was altered in a fashion almost beyond belief. The lush greenery of the meadows was blotted out by a succession of terrific bombardments, and the once leafy forests were battered into masses of broken timber. Between the contending armies the earth was pitted by a myriad of shell-holes that intersected each other, and men on beholding the spectacle for the first time could hardly believe that it was possible for anyone to go through a barrage and escape being hit. The rural hamlets had been shattered into gaunt mounds of brick dust, and everywhere the mellow sun of Picardy lit up a scene of untidy ruin and decay.

The most difficult part of the British position to maintain was the salient poking its nose into the German lines near Longueval and Delville Wood. Under observation of the enemy's position from High Wood to Guillemont it offered itself as a tempting object for counter-attack, and it was only after the most obstinate fighting that our position there was firmly established. It became expedient for us to flatten out the salient by advancing our line on the flanks, especially on the right where the village of Guillemont had to be carried, and while this operation was in progress a steady pressure was kept up along the rest of the line.

The Third Division was part of the force detailed for the attack on Guillemont, and the 2nd Royal Scots, after spending a few hours in the support trenches in Montauban Valley, moved up on the night of the 20th/21st July to the captured German trenches near Waterlot Farm and Trones Wood. Captain Perry posted "B" and "D" Companies in front of the wood, "A" between the wood and the farm, and "C" in the farm. The move had not been long completed when instructions with regard to the offensive arrived. The battalion was detailed to carry the network of trenches lying between Waterlot Farm and Guillemont, but as ill-luck would have it there was no time to study the hostile position, for the assault was timed to take place at 2 A.M. on the 22nd.

Had it been possible, Captain Perry would have delivered the attack without any preliminary bombardment on the chance of taking the Boches by surprise, but a patrol brought in the report that the opposing trenches were too powerful to be captured without the assistance of the guns. Accordingly, the hostile entrenchments were methodically plastered by our artillery before the infantry assault took place on the morning of the 22nd. It was still very dark when two platoons of "C," followed by the remainder of the company, set out on their mission. Uncertain as to the exact location of the Boches, they groped their way down a trench running parallel to the road in the direction of Guillemont Station, and had proceeded for a considerable distance when they became aware by the sound of voices and of firing that Germans were occupying a trench on their right. Hastily emerging from their trench, the Royal Scots in extended order advanced across the open in the direction of the enemy, but they were met by a murderous fire which seemed to come from more than one quarter, and they were compelled to retire as best they could.

An attack on a larger scale in conjunction with the Thirtieth Division was organised for 3.55 A.M. on the 23rd. The objectives of the Royal Scots were the same as on the 22nd, and this time the operation was entrusted to "B" and "D" Companies. Unluckily the smoke barrage put down to cover the advance of the Thirtieth Division dropped short, some of the smoke bombs exploding in our own trenches, and this mischance gave rise to a great deal of confusion, causing the assaulting units to lose touch with each other. In consequence most of them had not even reached their assembly positions when zero came. The Royal Scots however were ready, and the right company "D," under Captain Cochrane, started off punctually and reached its objectives. But the attack as a whole was spoiled through the breakdown of the assembly arrangements. "B" Company of the Royal Scots was delayed by other assaulting troops entering its trench, and, when at length it shook itself free, was unable to reach its goal. Consequently "D" Company, being totally unsupported, sustained numerous losses from the fire concentrated on it, and when it realised that no help was forthcoming retired to its original position. Captain Cochrane was wounded, and his three subalterns and the battalion bombing officer, Lieut. C. B. Whittaker, were among the slain.

 The confusion on the left which had interfered with the attack of " B " Company almost beggared description. One officer of another unit on reaching the Royal Scots' trench was evidently under the impression that he had stumbled on the enemy, for, pulling out his revolver, he called on his men to charge the Royal Scots, but happily he discovered his error before any damage was done. Owing to the loss of direction and the consequent delay, the whole attack was a fiasco and no tangible advantage was gained. The Royal Scots had some compensation for their losses when they virtually annihilated a party of Germans who were gathering for a counter-attack against their left flank. In the afternoon some Royal Scots snipers creeping out from our trenches detected a number of the enemy carrying boxes from the direction of Ginchy and shot down two of the party. In 1916 the Germans, as a nasty incident in the afternoon showed, would stick at nothing in order to snatch an advantage. From a ruined barn abutting on the main road leading into Guillemont, a few Boches, with their arms turned skywards in token of surrender, approached the lines of the Royal Scots, but when some of our troops went out to bring them in the Germans suddenly opened fire, killing and wounding several of the men. The ruse was tried a second time, but the angry Jocks were not to be taken in twice and shot down the offending enemy. Against this example of trickery should be set an act of chivalry by the foe. A night patrol of the Royal Scots picked up several of the men who had been wounded during the fighting in the early morning. Among these was one who had been discovered by some thirsty Boches to whom he offered the contents of his water-bottle. These accepted his gift, and to his amazement instead of taking him captive wished him good luck and a safe return to his lines.

Throughout this arduous and chaotic period R.S.M. Pugh performed magnificent work by contriving to have all the rations and water taken up to the companies every night. The battalion had practically no one to spare for carrying work, yet nightly comparatively large bodies of men wended their laborious way along the horrible communication trench carpeted with German corpses that led to Waterlot Farm. How so many troops were available for carrying remained a mystery until it transpired that R.S.M. Pugh had personally commandeered them from a neighbouring division. His presence was so austere and his tone so imperious that these parties stopped their own work or rest and meekly carried up the rations of the 2nd Royal Scots over a most difficult and unwholesome country.

This was the last operation undertaken in July by the 2nd Royal Scots. The line was held till the 25th, during which period serious casualties were caused by the continuous and carefully directed shell fire of the enemy. Its adventures in the neighbourhood of Guillemont cost the battalion five officers, four killed [1] and one wounded, and one hundred and seventy-six other ranks. It was relieved on the night of the 25th/26th July and marched back to Happy Valley, whence it proceeded on the 26th to Méaulte.

[1] Lieuts. H. M. Jardine and C. B. Whittaker, 2nd Lieuts. F. D. T. Cooper and M. L. Robinson.

Meantime the 17th Royal Scots of the Thirty-fifth Division were sampling the manifold troubles and discomforts of the Somme hinterland. During the action of the 14th July the battalion was quartered at Talus Boise, and from that date was employed principally in supplying large parties for work near the front line. The experience of the unit throughout the Somme fighting was most disheartening, for it was frequently exposed to shell fire without having a chance of retaliation. Since the attack on the 14th the whole region between Delville Wood and Montauban was constantly barraged by the enemy, and in this perilous zone Lieut.-Colonel Cheales and Captains R. C. Barry and E. E. Ruddell, who were engaged in reconnoitring the approaches to Delville Wood, were wounded on the 17th July, the command of the battalion passing to Major G. F. F. Foulkes. On the 19th it bivouacked in Caftet Wood, and four days later occupied trenches in Montauban and its neighbourhood. On the following day two companies advanced to the northern end of the twisted mass of splintered boles that marked the site of Bernafay Wood, and on the 25th the battalion returned to the bivouacs in Caftet Wood. Next day it had another bout of trench duty, during which Major Foulkes injured his knee so badly that he had to be evacuated to hospital, the command of the unit devolving on the Adjutant, Captain Scougal, and on the 27th it returned to Caftet Wood. So far the 17th had sampled only the disagreeable side of war and had not known the feral joy that comes from taking part in a "set" attack. Officers and men in their keenness were sorely disappointed that the battalion had not been afforded an opportunity of showing what it could do in battle.

On the 29th July it seemed that the 17th Royal Scots were at last to have a chance of proving their mettle, because then the Thirty-fifth Division received orders to co-operate in an attack on Guillemont which was fixed for the 30th. But the bad luck of the Royal Scots still persisted, for they were not put in the forefront of the fight. The attack was a failure. On the 30th, the battalion marching up from Bernafay took up a position in trenches near Maltz Horn Farm in support of the 89th Brigade, but beyond this point no advance was possible owing to the congestion of troops between the battalion and our front line. The Royal Scots remained in readiness to move forward as soon as opportunity presented itself, but they were not required to do anything, and at 9 P.M., after being relieved, returned to the now familiar Caftet Wood.

We have seen that the high ground of the Longueval plateau with its arm stretching to High Wood was the scene of almost fanatical fighting. High Wood, like Delville Wood, earned a sinister notoriety as one of the great cockpits of the battle, and four Royal Scots battalions, the 8th, 9th, 15th, and 16th, have good reason to remember the grisly fighting in its neighbourhood.

The tour of duty of the 9th Royal Scots at Arras terminated at the beginning of July, and on the 13th the battalion marched to Chelers. Progressing by easy stages, on the 20th it reached Méaulte, one of the centres of the Somme hinterland. On the same date the pioneer battalion of the Fifty-first Division arrived at Ribemont and moved the next day to Mametz Wood. On the evening of the 21st the 9th Royal Scots marched through Fricourt and Mametz to take over the front line in the vicinity of Bazentin-le-Grand Wood, from which the more famous High Wood could be plainly seen.

High Wood owed its immense tactical importance to the fact that it crowned the loftiest point of Picardy.

As a result of weeks of fighting we had established a footing in the wood sufficient to deprive the foe of the wide observation that he had enjoyed while High Wood remained in his undisputed possession. For the enemy's lines now lay on the reverse slope of the plateau, so that all the country lying to the south-west of the wood was screened from his direct gaze. Nevertheless the approach to the position taken over by the Fifty-first Division was extremely dangerous to traverse. The route, by which troops went up to the line and by which all stores and rations were brought, was an indifferent path along the valley just south of Mametz Wood, and the Boches were fully aware of this. The road was never empty of men or vehicles at any hour of the day or night, and, though the Germans were deprived of direct observation, they could, by means of their balloons, see much of what was going on in Happy Valley, such being the inappropriate name by which it was known to our men. The clouds of dust raised by the tramp of feet and the grinding of wheels would have been sufficient in any case to warn the Boches when unusual movement was taking place in the valley, which was viciously bombarded by them at frequent and irregular intervals. So great, as a rule, was the congestion in Happy Valley that a battalion, condemned to go through it during a barrage, was almost certain to sustain big losses.

The trenches held by the 9th Royal Scots lay rather more than 1500 yards from the north-west corner of High Wood, and consisted of joined-up posts that previous attacking troops had dug during the battle. The battalion had practically no time to become acquainted with the features of the region, when it was called upon to take part in an action on the 23rd July. The goal allotted to it was the far side of the road connecting High Wood and Martinpuich, which meant that the battalion in making its attack had the wood on its right front. On its right flank were the 4th Gordons and on its left was a unit of the Nineteenth Division. The onslaught was to be carried out by "B" Company commanded by Major Ferguson, and "C" under Major Moncreiff. Officers and men of the 9th who took part in this operation had, and still have, a suspicion that the assault was hardly expected to be successful, and that it was designed to prevent the enemy from sending reinforcements to Pozières, where we did make a successful attack on the 23rd. It is highly probable that they were right in this conjecture, since all the arrangements had to be made very hurriedly. There was a most unusual feature as regards zero. It was fixed for 1.30 A.M., and was the hour at which the assailants were to arrive at the objective, not the time when they were to leave their own trenches. Battalions made their own arrangements as regards starting, and 12.45 A.M. was the hour fixed by Major Moncreiff for the 9th Royal Scots.

This divergence from customary practice is to be explained by the fact that the width of No-Man's-Land varied very considerably from point to point. The opposing lines lay almost cheek by jowl in High Wood, where the Boches had a strong redoubt at the northeast corner, liberally garnished with machine-guns mostly sited so as to fire to the right flank. The German line continued from the wood towards Martinpuich, but our trenches veered away from it to Bazentin-le-Petit, so that on the front of the 9th Royal Scots the opposing trenches lay nearly 1000 yards away.

Previous to the attack, "B" and "C" Companies were in reserve, the line being held by the other companies. Each was to advance in four waves on a platoon front, with "B" Company on the right. The two companies reached the front line just in time to escape one of the appalling barrages with which the Germans were wont to devastate Happy Valley, and at 12.45 A.M. they threaded their way through prepared gaps in our wire. Terrific machine-gun fire met the Royal Scots as soon as they were free of the trenches, and a violent hostile barrage split up the formations and caused "B" and "C" Companies to lose touch with each other and with the Gordons on the right. Our barrage was so ragged and indifferent that it did nothing to disconcert the enemy, who, from his skilfully sited machine-guns in the High Wood redoubt, sprayed with bullets the open ground which the Royal Scots were traversing. All the officers[1] were hit and only a handful of men returned from the fatal enterprise.

Major Moncreiff had an odd experience, and in getting back to his own lines he was greatly blessed by fortune. Advancing with his third wave, No. II platoon commanded by Sergeant Blyth, he was hit in the neck, shoulder, face, and left hand by fragments from a shell when the German barrage came down. He collapsed into a shell-hole, but later, having somewhat recovered from the rude shock, he stood up to see how his company was faring. At this point consciousness deserted him and everything remained a blank till he realised that he was digging furiously with an entrenching tool in a shell-hole where were also Lance-Corporal Baxter and two men of "B" Company. From the spot where he was wounded he must have wandered about half a mile diagonally across and even beyond the area of "B" Company till he dropped into the shell-hole, which was but 30 yards away from a German sap. It was still

---

[1] Major Ferguson and 2nd Lieut. Gibson of "B" Company were wounded and missing; Major Moncreiff, Lieuts. A. M. Ballingall and H. M. Wardrop, and 2nd Lieuts. F. B. Moncreiff, W. B. Bentley, and A. D. Lyall were wounded.

dark, being only about 2 A.M., and this was in truth a stroke of luck, for aided by the illumination cast by their flares, Boche snipers were potting vigorously at the semi-fortified shell-hole. On the Germans ceasing to send up their flares Major Moncreiff and his companions, spreading out fan-wise in order to give a more difficult target to the enemy, began to crawl towards our line. The odds were that none would escape, but only Lance-Corporal Baxter failed to get back. Before reaching safety Major Moncreiff received another wound in the right elbow from a bullet.

The slaughter was not limited to the attackers, for in "A" and "D" Companies were many victims of the German shell fire, among them being the Adjutant, Captain S. Fraser, Lieut. W. Morris, and 2nd Lieut. Gellatly, who were all wounded. The list of casualties in other ranks contained one hundred and sixty-two names. In the evening the battalion was relieved by the 7th Argylls and marched back to Mametz Wood. On the following day it provided parties to carry for the battalion holding High Wood, a most unpleasant task, but after another day at Mametz Wood it moved back to the tolerably safe vicinity of Bécordel, where Captain Rowbotham of the 8th Royal Scots joined it as Second-in-Command.

The 8th Royal Scots, being pioneers, were not actually engaged in the struggle near High Wood, but they assuredly suffered more than any other infantry unit in the division from the periodic tempests of shells that disturbed the peace of Happy Valley. The failure of the attack on the 23rd saved the battalion from carrying out the work of consolidation that it would otherwise have had to perform. From noon on the 22nd till noon on the 23rd the 8th sustained more than one hundred casualties from shell fire, including 2nd Lieuts. T. Meek,

W. Constable, and A. Douglas, all wounded. In the afternoon of the 24th Captain Rowbotham and four men went up to the front and at great risk taped out in broad daylight a trench from a windmill near Bazentin-le-Petit to High Wood. When darkness fell this new trench was cut by "C" and "D" Companies, and on the night of the 25th "D" Company fringed it with barbed wire. Virtually continuous work was also done by the battalion in improving a communication trench known as High Alley, which ran from Bazentin-le-Grand Wood to High Wood, while "B" and "C" Companies began a new communication trench named Thistle Alley.

On the 7th August the Fifty-first Division was relieved, and the 8th and the 9th Royal Scots, after the now customary respite for training and refitment that followed a battle, moved north to a sector near Armentières.

The 15th and the 16th Royal Scots became interested in the High Wood sector just as the Fifty-first Division was preparing to leave that ill-omened spot. The merciless punishment inflicted on the Thirty-fourth Division during the first three days of July caused temporary alterations to be made in its organisation. For a time the 102nd and 103rd Brigades were transferred to the Thirty-seventh Division, and their places were filled by the 111th and 112th Brigades of that division. The 101st Brigade had been hit too hard to be in form for immediate action, and remained at Hénencourt absorbing drafts and refitting till the end of the month. While it was thus employed, the sad news was received that Major-General Ingouville Williams, C.B., who had really created the Thirty-fourth Division, had been killed on the 22nd July, while reconnoitring ground in the neighbourhood of Mametz. Next day he was buried in the cemetery of Warloy, the pipers of the 15th and the 16th Royal Scots being in attendance.

By the end of July the 101st Brigade was again ready for action, and after marching to Bécourt Wood on the 30th took over on the following day the front line from the east of Bazentin Wood to High Wood inclusive. Our troops in going forward to the trenches were enormously cheered to notice how far east our line had been advanced since the 1st July. The 16th Royal Scots occupied the front trenches to the left of High Wood, to the eastern outskirts of which the Boches were still clinging, and the 15th[1] lay in brigade reserve at the north end of Mametz Wood. Seldom have troops had to occupy a more anxious line than that taken over by the 16th Royal Scots, for in consequence of an only partially successful attack, delivered some time before, the trench which they held was shared by the enemy, the 16th being on the right and the Germans on the left, separated from each other by two barricades in the centre. In the annals of the Thirty-fourth Division this trench which lay not far north from Bazentin-le-Petit is referred to as the Intermediate Trench.

The situation was without doubt as uncomfortable for the Boches as it was for the Royal Scots, but the 16th felt that they could never spend an easy night while the enemy lay at their very gates, and Sir George McCrae determined to evict his unwelcome neighbours. To this end no fewer than five bombing attacks were made on the night of the 1st/2nd August by "D" Company, but all were abortive. The Germans had taken precautions against being rushed, so a careful plan for an assault on the following night was organised by "D" Company. Magnificently led by Captain Hendry, parties of bombers burst through the enemy's barricade, and after some brisk exchanges captured about 150 yards of territory. This success was unfortunately marred by the loss of Captain

[1] Commanded since 6th July by Lieut.-Colonel H. A. Rose.

Hendry, who was so badly injured that he died the next day. The Germans were not disposed to take lying down what knocks we chose to give, and they delivered a series of bombing attacks in an attempt to regain the lost ground, but the 16th's bombers refused to relax their hold on what they had won.

On the night of the 3rd August the 16th were relieved by the 15th Royal Scots, who had not been wholly pleased with their Mametz quarters, for not only were they frequently shelled, but the wood and all around it seemed to be thick with corpses. They were therefore not reluctant to leave this polluted spot for the unknown perils of the front line. Though relieved from the firing trenches, the 16th were asked to complete the work that they had so well begun by co-operating in an assault fixed for the night of the 3rd/4th August. After a preliminary bombardment of the Boche position two companies of the 16th and two of the 11th Suffolks were at 1 A.M. to attack the portion of the Intermediate Trench held by the enemy. For this business Sir George McCrae selected "A" and "B" Companies under Lieut. J. G. Mackenzie and Captain N. Armit respectively. Unfortunately the plan miscarried. The Royal Scots and the right company of the Suffolks lost their way in the darkness and day had dawned before they had reached their assembly positions. Thus the attack was delivered by only "B" Company of the Suffolks, which actually secured a footing in the Boche trench and held on to its gains with praiseworthy pluck. Owing to their belated arrival, the Royal Scots and the other Suffolks company had to make a daylight advance under the direct observation of the enemy's machine-gunners. The intended night attack might have achieved its object, but an advance in the clear light of the morning simply supplied the Boches with targets that they could hardly miss, and the assailants paid a heavy penalty for the blunders that had delayed them. Captain Armit was killed, and of the assaulting force Lieut. Mackenzie alone got as far as the German trench and he reached it only to be shot dead. After this repulse it was impossible for " B " Company of the Suffolks to maintain its position, and after putting up a brave fight it returned to its original trench.

Next came the turn of the 15th Royal Scots. It was arranged that at 10.15 P.M. the 10th Lincolns, reinforced by 60 bombers of the 15th Royal Scots, should deliver a frontal attack, while 2nd Lieuts. F. F. Watson and C. Hodgson of the Royal Scots with a bombing party stormed the hostile position from the flank. The frontal attack however was not even attempted, owing to a paralysing barrage put down on our lines by the foe, and, though the flanking party pushing along the trench did not spare itself, it gained but a meagre 50 yards of ground. The casualties were fairly heavy, and included both officers, 2nd Lieut. Watson being killed and 2nd Lieut. Hodgson wounded. Another effort was arranged for the following night, but just as a bombing party under Lieut. Tempest left our trenches it was met by a Boche counter-attack, which in the first shock secured for the enemy a footing in our lines. In the darkness there was a wild and prolonged *mêlée*, but the Royal Scots outwore the resolution of their opponents, and by daylight no living German remained in our trenches.

After this episode the Somme adventures of the 15th and the 16th Royal Scots soon came to an end. On the night of the 6th August the 101st was relieved by the 112th Brigade, and after another brief spell of trench duty near High Wood the whole division was relieved on the 15th August. The Thirty-fourth Division then went north to Armentières, where the 111th and 112th

Brigades left to join their own division and the 102nd and 103rd returned to the Thirty-fourth.

The sojourn of the 17th Royal Scots in the Somme also terminated in August. The battalion had its worst experiences near Maltz Horn, where from the 21st to the 26th August it had to supply nightly large parties ranging from 100 to 500 men for work near the front line. On two successive nights these parties were under the command of Captain W. A. Douglas, who had served with the 6th Royal Scots against the Senussi and had been transferred to the 17th when his own battalion was amalgamated with the 5th Royal Scots. During the second night, the 24th August, a concentrated barrage fell upon the party, causing the deaths of Captain Douglas and 2nd Lieut. H. R. Fraser, while of the men eight were wounded and one missing. Captain Scougal was wounded on the following night, and the command of the battalion then passed to Captain W. Simpson. On the 26th August the battalion was withdrawn to a camp in Happy Valley, where it received a new C.O. in the person of Major Weston of the 18th Lancashire Fusiliers, and four days later it left the Somme area for the Arras sector.

The next Royal Scots battalion to appear in the Somme was the 13th. From the end of June there was comparative tranquillity in the Loos salient, though before the battalion was relieved it lost three officers from wounds —Captain H. S. E. Stevens being hit on the 1st July, 2nd Lieut. J. R. Mitchell on the 2nd, and 2nd Lieut. R. Armstrong on the 12th. The relief took place on the 21st July, and the journey to the Somme from the Hulluch sector was performed nearly all by route march. On the 8th August the 13th Royal Scots were at Peake Wood, where the 15th had so greatly distinguished themselves on the 1st July, and on the 9th they occupied a support position at Contalmaison. The next day they entered the firing line, and on the following night Lieut. Jardine, with a reconnoitring patrol, ran into some Germans and brought back four prisoners. The Germans opposite the 13th appeared to be poor-spirited troops, for during the night of the 12th four Boches belonging to a Saxon regiment gave themselves up to the Royal Scots.

When the battalion was not in the front line, every available man was employed on working parties, especially on the roads, which required constant tinkering to enable them to bear the enormous burden of traffic that passed over them every day and every night. On the 27th August the 13th Royal Scots took over the front line from the 11th Argylls. The trenches were rickety and unstable and were kept under almost ceaseless shell fire by the Germans, who from their observation posts near High Wood could detect any sign of movement. Thus the daily toll of casualties was alarmingly high, averaging nearly thirty a day, and among those wounded were Captain P. Turner, Lieut. Jardine, and 2nd Lieut. Buchanan. On the 29th August the Royal Scots were relieved by the 6/7th Royal Scots Fusiliers, and retired to the vicinity of Villa Wood. Torrents of rain near the end of the month transformed the region into a morass, and the 13th Royal Scots in their next spell of duty during the first week of September found themselves wallowing in a gigantic mud pie. On the 4th September the Fifteenth Division was withdrawn to the east of Albert, where arrangements were completed for a great attack on the 15th September in which the division was to participate.

Before the close of August it was clear that the obstinate and protracted trial of strength, which had been raging since the 14th July, for the possession of the main ridge was turning in our favour. By the end of the first week of September the Germans had been driven from the ridge along a front roughly extending from Delville Wood to Mouquet Farm, on the road running north-west from Pozières. Moreover, British troops had firmly planted themselves on the high ground stretching east from Delville to Leuze Wood. The second phase of the great battle had ended satisfactorily for us, and Sir Douglas Haig judged the time ripe to deliver a grand general attack on the weakening enemy. This was planned for the 15th September. On the right our chief goal was the hamlet of Morval, and on the left the objectives were the villages of Martinpuich and Courcelette.

The Fifteenth Division was on the left wing of the battle front. There was no preliminary intense bombardment, but from the 12th September the hostile entrenchments were subjected to a steady and constant shelling from guns of all calibres. On the 13th September the 13th Royal Scots, leaving their bivouacs near Albert, advanced to the neighbourhood of Shelter Wood and Fricourt Road, and on the next night they moved forward to their assembly positions in the front line some distance east of the ruins of Pozières. Their objective was the hostile trenches in front of Martinpuich, and they were disposed for the attack in two waves, the first consisting of "B" and "D" Companies, the second of "C" and "A." Zero was 6.20 A.M.

By 4.40 A.M. the battalion was ready, and at zero our barrage opened with such violence and proved so accurate and deadly that the Germans offered a most feeble resistance to our infantry. The 13th Royal Scots in fact suffered less from the enemy's fire than from the shells of our own guns, the men in their impetuosity pressing too close to the barrage. The objective was carried with amazing ease, and many bemused prisoners, including a battalion C.O. and his Adjutant, fell into the hands of the Royal Scots. Three hours after zero our barrage lifted beyond Martinpuich, and a strong patrol, entering the village, unearthed nearly 200 prisoners who were still too dazed from the effects of our cannonade to be capable of offering any resistance. Exploiting this success, the Royal Scots went right through the village to a trench on the far side known as Push Trench, which was later occupied by the 6th Camerons who had followed the Royal Scots. In the evening " A " and " D " Companies moved forward in support of the Camerons, and " A " Company contrived to gain touch on the right with the Fiftieth Division, which had also made a very successful attack. This was the action in which the enemy was surprised and bewildered by our tanks, which made an impressive first appearance in the war; one of these assisted the assault of the Fifteenth Division, but it did not leave our front line till after the infantry had started, and when it reached Martinpuich the village was already in our hands.

We gained more by the attack on the 15th September than in any single operation since the commencement of the Battle of the Somme.[1] The 13th Battalion had good reason to plume itself on the completeness of its success, and considering the magnitude of the victory its losses were not disproportionately heavy. In killed, wounded, and missing, the casualties among the men amounted to two hundred and sixty-three, while nine officers[2] were wounded. The enemy had been so savagely pounded that he did not venture to make any counter-attack, but

[1] See Sir Douglas Haig's Despatches, p. 42.
[2] Captains R. J. M. Christie, M. C. Fitch, Lieut. Jardine, 2nd Lieuts. G. H. Berry, W. Cowie, R. Gellatly, W. R. Lawrie, J. Ogston, and T. Smith.

contented himself with shelling our positions. Despite the shell fire, however, all our gains were expeditiously consolidated. The 13th Royal Scots remained in the trenches near Martinpuich till the 18th September, when under a deluge of rain the battalion was relieved and marched back to Mellincourt. During this period two officers, 2nd Lieuts. J. F. G. Turner and A. Brown, were wounded by shell fire.

By the time that the 13th Royal Scots returned to the line on the 10th October, the successes of the 15th September had been vigorously followed up. The obstinate resistance of Thiepval, which had been chiefly responsible for holding up the northern British attack on the 1st July, was at length broken down on the 27th September, while on the immediate front of the Fifteenth Division the village of Le Sars was now in our hands. Except for a few isolated posts, the Germans had been ejected from the whole of the ridge lying between the Tortille and the Ancre, and it seemed that we could not fail to reach Bapaume, the capture of which would be looked on by every British soldier as the seal of success. Unfortunately just when the efforts of the British Commander seemed on the verge of being crowned with complete triumph, the weather utterly broke down, and throughout the whole of October scarcely a day passed without rain. The soft country roads, already deeply rutted by the never-ending traffic, dissolved into ribbons of liquid mud, through which the indispensable stores for the artillery and infantry could be dragged only with the greatest difficulty. The trenches were rendered almost uninhabitable. In the worst spots the depressing amphibian conditions caused both sides to give up sniping; parties of British and Germans squatted on the parapets, and neither loosed off a shot at the other, since this would mean that every man would be condemned to stand all day up to the waist in a muddy fluid. These well-nigh intolerable conditions mostly favoured the defence, and from the end of September the fighting was of the give-and-take nature that followed the action of the 14th July.

Just as after the Battle of Loos the Fifteenth Division remained for months doing trench duty at the scene of its victory, so now after the capture of Martinpuich it was destined to spend the winter in the dismal swamps between Le Sars and the Butte de Warlencourt, where the men suffered more from cold, damp, and exposure, than from the activity of the enemy. For a fleeting period the division was partnered in October by the Ninth Division, which, since its relief from the Somme in July, had been engaged in holding trenches on the Vimy Ridge. The sojourn at the famous ridge, though the casualties of the division during that spell were trifling, was not relished by any man, owing to the mining that seemed to be the normal industry of the region. An odd incident, with a touch of comedy in it, occurred on the 19th August, when the Germans set off a small mine on the front of the 12th Royal Scots, who were now commanded by Lieut.-Col. Fargus, D.S.O. Major-General Furse was going round the lines at the time and just missed being caught in the explosion, but two men and a sapper were buried in the crater. Some Germans were also imprisoned by the debris, and both sides observed an informal truce while the victims were dug out of the rubbish. As regards raids neither the 11th nor the 12th were very fortunate, the nearest approach to success being on the night of the 3rd September, when Lieut. Lockhart and Lieut. Collins with some men of the 12th made a sally into the Boche trenches, but though they killed a few Germans they secured no identifications. Trench-mortar bombardments were of daily occurrence, and at all times men had to beware of the Boche snipers, who in this region were extremely skilful. As regards sniping, however, Jack was as good as his master, and the Boches probably loathed the sector as much as our men did. There was no hint of sadness in the feelings of the men when at last they bade farewell to the ridge, though they must have known that the Somme, towards which they now directed their steps, held greater perils in store for them.

The journey to the south began on the 25th September and proved a trying pilgrimage, particularly for the Lewis-gunners. The establishment of battalions had by this time been increased to ten guns, but the transport, provided for these and for the necessary ammunition and magazines, was wholly inadequate. The hand-carts supplied for the purpose might have been suitable for good roads, but they were too flimsy for the strips of deep mud that had once been paths in the Somme. The carts were fitted so that they could be drawn by mules, but even these could not drag their loads through the clinging mire, and the weary men usually had to man-handle them for a considerable part of the distance, arriving at their destination with strained backs and limbs like lead.

A respite came for the 11th and the 12th Royal Scots when the 27th Brigade, on the 10th October, bivouacked at Mametz Wood. For nine days the men were employed in repairing the roads, while the other two brigades were engaged in attacking the positions in front of the Butte de Warlencourt. On the 19th orders arrived for the 27th Brigade to take over the whole of the divisional front.

This lay just north of the ruined Abbey of Eaucourt.

The whole battlefield was a chaos of slime thickly strewn with British and German corpses, and the air was rank with the odour of corruption. The fighting in this neighbourhood had been fierce and prolonged, and the position of the enemy's trenches could be located only with difficulty. The one conspicuous feature was the Butte de Warlencourt, a cretaceous mound about 50 feet high, which stood out with all the particularity of a picture in a frame. It lay at the far end of the spur that ran from the main ridge through Flers, and was flanked by the tree-lined Albert-Bapaume Road. From our front line the ground rose in a long slope to the Butte.

The night of the 19th/20th October, when the relief of the South African and 26th Brigades by the 27th took place, was one of undiluted horror. The units started on the morning of the 19th from Mametz Wood under torrential rain, and marched first to High Wood where the mud was already ankle-deep. The task of the 11th Royal Scots in relieving South African troops in support trenches was not attended with any exceptional difficulty, but the ordeal of the 12th Royal Scots and the 6th K.O.S.B., who were required to take over the front trenches, beggared description. Dante never pictured torments more dreadful than those which afflicted all who were involved in that relief. The trials began as soon as the troops plunged into the canals that had a few hours previously been dry communication trenches, the laden men struggling along with aching backs and galled shoulders. While they were thus painfully floundering towards the front line, the Germans, who may have suspected what was taking place, put down a sustained barrage on all our approaches. Whole sections were annihilated in a moment, the sides of the communication trenches were blown away, and the men were subjected to a succession of horrors more diabolical than they could have conceived in their wildest dreams. But most of them were so utterly exhausted in body that they were reduced to a state of abandonment in which they were almost beyond caring what happened to them. The ground subsided beneath their feet, and several men were bogged almost up to their necks, unable to extricate themselves without assistance; not a few of the wounded who fell in the trenches were suffocated in the mud and were trampled under foot by those who came after them. The Black Watch, who were relieved by the 12th Royal Scots, were in a pitiable plight, many of them being so dog-tired that they tore off the kilts that absorbed mud and water and weighed down their leaden limbs. It was not surprising that the relief was not complete till 6 A.M. on the 20th October.

The 12th Royal Scots occupied the firing trenches with three companies in the front line and one in support, and their worst trials were over when they were established in their positions. The ground in front was thick with corpses and among them were found many wounded men, the victims of previous attacks, and seldom did a patrol return without bringing back men who had been lying helpless for several days amid the shell-holes of the wasted land between the opposing positions.

The 11th Royal Scots were called on to play a more active part than their comrades of the 12th. The front taken over by the K.O.S.B. consisted of a trench called Snag Trench, part of which, including a communication trench known as the Tail running towards the Butte, was held by the Boches. The junction of the Snag and the Tail formed a strong-point known as the "Nose," which had defied several efforts by the South Africans. On the night of the 20th October the capture of this strong-point by the K.O.S.B. brought the whole of Snag Trench into our possession, but owing to weakness in numbers the gain was temporarily evacuated by the Borderers, and "B" Company of the 11th Royal Scots under Captain Winchester was sent up to retake the "Nose." Misled by its guides, "B" Company was kept floundering for six hours in the mud, losing several men from the hostile shelling, and when Captain Winchester at length reached the "Nose," he discovered that the K.O.S.B. were once more in possession of it. "B" Company, though very wearied, relieved the K.O.S.B. and explored a considerable stretch of the Tail without encountering any Germans. Unfortunately, Captain Winchester, who had been with the 11th Royal Scots ever since the formation of the battalion, was seriously wounded in the chest by a bullet. On the night of the 21st the remainder of the 11th Royal Scots arrived and relieved the K.O.S.B. in the front line. It was some solace to them to find that our artillery and machine-gun fire had caused great havoc among the Boches, and Lieut.-Colonel Croft estimated that there were about three hundred German corpses near the "Nose." Many recumbent figures, however, bore British uniforms and all were not dead. The 11th Royal Scots rescued a wounded South African who had been lying not far from the "Nose" for six days and nights; another wounded South African had evidently crawled down into a dug-out near the "Nose" where he was discovered, still breathing, with a pick through his skull.

Till the evening of the 24th October the units of the 27th Brigade were busily employed in consolidating our position, "shaping the mud pie," the men called it, and in digging new assembly trenches in preparation for an attack on the Butte. All the men in the Ninth Division were so worn out by their experiences that they were unfit to take part in an arduous battle, and the whole division was relieved late on the night of the 24th October. Though neither the 11th nor the 12th Royal Scots could be said to have joined in any action near the Butte, they had sustained severe losses considering the comparatively short time that they had been in the line. The 11th Royal Scots lost four officers wounded, and one hundred and fifty-six other ranks; and the 12th three officers wounded, and ninety-six other ranks; but these numbers were far from representing the total wastage, for at least as many more were evacuated to hospital suffering from exposure and trench feet. After leaving the Somme the 11th and the 12th were transferred to the neighbourhood of St Pol, where for several weeks they were occupied in training and refitting.

CHAPTER XVII

THE BATTLE OF THE ANCRE—BEAUMONT HAMEL AND SERRE

October 1916 to February 1917

13th Royal Scots near Martinpuich. 17th, 11th, and 12th Royal Scots at Arras. 8th and 9th Royal Scots near Armentières. 15th and 16th Royal Scots at Bois Grenier. 2nd Royal Scots in the Hulluch Sector. 5/6th Royal Scots. Beaumont Hamel and Serre. Situation at the Ancre and preparations for Attack. Raids by 9th and 2nd Royal Scots. Work of 8th Royal Scots. Attack on Beaumont Hamel, 13th November. Attack of 2nd Royal Scots at Serre, 13th November. 5/6th Royal Scots near Beaumont Hamel. 8th and 9th Royal Scots at Courcelette. Successful enterprise by 2nd Royal Scots at Serre, 5th January.

FROM the middle of October 1916 the wide barrier of mud that lay along almost the whole length of the Somme battle-front precluded for some time any operations of the same scope as those of the 14th July and the 15th September. The lull in the fighting provides a convenient opportunity to review the activities of the Royal Scots battalions in the different parts of the Western front.

There is nothing outstanding to chronicle in the doings of the 13th Royal Scots during the winter. Officers and men stoically endured the discomforts of the Somme area, and the gossip of the messes dealt chiefly with the comic side of adventures or mishaps in the mud that befell individuals or parties. The losses from shell fire and bullets were probably less than those sustained during a similar period of time in the Loos salient. One officer, 2nd Lieut. A. Young, was killed, and two,

2nd Lieuts. W. D. Howat and H. F. L. Lowery, were wounded. The battalion's long spell of trench duty near Martinpuich and Le Sars came to an end at the beginning of February 1917, when the Fifteenth Division was relieved and moved northwards to Arras.

Away from the Somme, and even there when circumstances were favourable, dress was once more exalted to the dignity of a ritual in the British Army. It is easy to deride the "spit-and-polish" school, but the enormous importance attached to appearance by the British military man has been thoroughly justified by experience; the well-turned-out unit is always a reliable fighting unit. Even the most casual visitor would have noticed how spick-and-span was the appearance of the troops in the Arras sector, which served as a convalescent home for several Royal Scots battalions.

The 17th Royal Scots experienced no unusual incidents while they sojourned near Arras. About this time doubts began to be entertained as to the wisdom of maintaining a Bantam division, and these may have been responsible for the relief of the Thirty-fifth by the Ninth Division at the beginning of December. At any rate, until February 1917, the Bantam units remained in the Arras hinterland, being employed in making preparations for the offensive that was to take place in the spring. Another change occurred in the command of the 17th Royal Scots, Lieut.-Colonel C. B. J. Riccard of the 2/6th Essex Regiment arriving as C.O. on the 12th December.

The 11th and the 12th Royal Scots were destined to serve in the Arras sector till June 1917. At first a prodigious amount of labour was expended in improving the trenches, to such effect that the men passed the greater part of the winter in the line in tolerable comfort. Careful attention was also devoted to training, especially in the use of the rifle, and the Ninth Division Infantry Fighting School, organised and supervised by Lieut.-Colonel Croft of the 11th Royal Scots, played no inconsiderable part in promoting the efficiency of the various units. Complete mastery was achieved over the enemy as regards patrolling, raids, and artillery duels, and a spirit of the utmost confidence imbued all ranks of the division. This was partly due to the indisputable fact that we were supported by a greater weight of artillery than was the enemy, but even more to the fact that nearly all our raids were fruitful while those of the enemy failed. At the very beginning of December, when the 12th Royal Scots first took over the front line, "C" Company, without difficulty, beat off a German raid by rifle and machine-gun fire. The most successful raids of the division were carried out by other units, but the 12th Royal Scots had reason to complain of bad luck when, on the night of the 2nd January, a party effected an entry into a German trench without encountering any of the garrison. Harassed by the aggressiveness of our troops, and unable to engineer any gainful raids, the Boches retaliated by bombarding our lines with trench-mortars and aerial torpedoes, the latter weapon especially proving destructive to life; it was from one of these torpedoes that Major F. Anderson of the 12th received a mortal wound on the 26th January.

Armentières vied with Arras as a kind of health resort, and there the 8th, 9th, 15th, and 16th Battalions were sent to recuperate. All units greatly benefited by the unwonted tranquillity which was their lot for several weeks, and in the annals of the 8th Royal Scots it is remarked that Armentières was "associated not so much with work as with happy and pleasant times." The infantry battalions in the line gave proof of their fitness by organising raids against the hostile trenches, and the

9th Royal Scots had the satisfaction of carrying through a very successful one on the 16th September. At 8.10 P.M. a party of 6 N.C.Os. and 27 men of "A" Company, led by Lieut. A. H. Douglas and 2nd Lieut. F. M. Ross, left our front line and reached the parapet of the German front trench, where Lieut. Douglas was shot dead. 2nd Lieut. Ross was wounded at the same time, but rallying his men he headed them in a wild charge into the trench and the garrison fled before them. The Royal Scots, after bombing a machine-gun emplacement and killing at least three Germans, brought back the body of Lieut. Douglas. The Fifty-first Division was relieved from the Armentières sector on the 25th September, and in October returned to the Somme battlefield in the neighbourhood of Beaumont Hamel, where the various units began to gird themselves for another strenuous struggle.

The experiences of the Thirty-fourth Division near Armentières in the Bois Grenier sector were as uniformly agreeable as those of the Fifty-first. Both the 15th and the 16th Royal Scots were gradually brought up to strength in officers and in men, and the wastage resulting from bullets and shells was small. At this period Sir George McCrae was invalided home, and though he returned again to his battalion it was obvious that his health could no longer stand the strain of active service, and in November he left the 16th Royal Scots to take up duties at home. His successor was Lieut.-Colonel A. Stephenson, M.C.

The even tenor of trench life was broken by active patrolling and a number of raids. Three raids, after careful arrangement and rehearsal, were carried out by the 16th Royal Scots; in the first two, the Royal Scots were prevented from forcing their way into the German lines by uncut wire, but in the third one Lieut. Rawson

BREASTWORKS AT ARMENTIÈRES.
(Sketch by Capt. D. M. Sutherland, M.C., 16th Royal Scots.)

[*To face p.* 328.

with a patrol entered the German front trench, which proved to be unoccupied. An ambitious foray was made on the 8th November by a party of the 15th Royal Scots. The raiders, consisting of Captain H. J. Selby, 2nd Lieut. Sandison, and 42 other ranks, under cover of an artillery and Stokes mortar bombardment, left our parapets at 1.35 A.M. and on reaching the opposing trenches split into two groups. One under Captain Selby, veering to the right, was stopped by a barricade, with the garrison of which the Royal Scots waged a fierce bombing combat without being able to carry the obstacle. In this part of the hostile trenches there was a concrete dug-out, apparently full of Boches, but the Royal Scots could not force open the concrete door. One of the enemy rashly opened it to throw a grenade, but he was killed by a bullet before he could effect his purpose. Captain Selby, exploring a communication trench, was suddenly confronted by three Germans whom he shot dead; in the scuffle he received a blow from a rifle, but was able to make his way back to our own trenches. The other group under 2nd Lieut. Sandison and C.S.M. Park, turning to the left, had experiences very similar to those of Captain Selby's party; it also was stopped by a barricade, but it slew several Boches and destroyed a trench-mortar. The whole raiding party, having played considerable havoc with the enemy's trenches, reached its own lines at 2.18 A.M.

The Thirty-fourth Division was relieved from the Bois Grenier sector about the end of January 1917, and after spending some time near Meteren, where a strenuous programme of training was carried through, went to Arras at the beginning of March 1917.

The 2nd Royal Scots from the 26th July till the 10th August spent a happy and profitable time at Méaulte. From that date till the 20th August they supplied numerous parties for work in the Somme battle area, and many losses were sustained; then after returning to Méaulte, they were transferred to the Hulluch sector on the 31st August. This district was much quieter than it had been when the Fifteenth Division held it, and there was only one casualty, 2nd Lieut. R. F. Scott being severely wounded in the head by a sniper's bullet. Relieved on the 8th September, the battalion was again favoured with a long rest from the line, and under the direction of Lieut.-Colonel A. F. Lumsden, who assumed command on the 25th August, it very rapidly attained a high degree of efficiency. Lieut.-Colonel Lumsden, who had been with the 1st Battalion, knew only one standard, the highest, and as he spared himself even less than his subordinates he soon won the whole-hearted respect and loyalty of all his officers and men. His favourite reminder to those who served with him, "You are here not to do your bit, but your all," epitomised his conception of the soldier's duty. On the 8th October the 2nd Royal Scots returned to the left wing of the Somme battle front, being accommodated in huts in Acheux Wood, and like the 8th and the 9th were thereafter engaged in making preparations for the operations that took place near the end of the year at Beaumont Hamel and Serre.

The 5/6th Royal Scots as a unit had no exciting adventures during 1916. After the amalgamation took place the battalion entered the line in the Cuinchy sector on the 5th July. On the 15th September a bombing party under Captain McCloud raided German trenches which proved to be unoccupied except by one Boche corpse. At the end of September the battalion was withdrawn from the line and accompanied the Thirty-second Division to the Somme. When on the 15th November it arrived at Mailly-Maillet in the hinterland of Beaumont Hamel, there was a general expectation that more serious business was on hand than the holding of trenches, but the task of the 5/6th Royal Scots proved to be much tamer than had been anticipated.

Owing to the breakdown in the weather in October, the Battle of the Somme, as we have seen, to some extent languished, but all along the battle-front minor operations continued to be carried out, the general result of which improved our position. Even before October, the Germans had been expelled from the whole of the ridge lying between the Tortille and the Ancre, and the hostile stronghold at Beaumont Hamel had been uncovered on its southern flank. These successes in the south paved the way for an operation against the fortresses of Beaumont Hamel and Serre, which was ultimately fixed to take place on the 13th November, by which time the weather had become dry and cold.

The valley leading up from the river Ancre on which stood the ruins of Beaumont Hamel formed a natural pucker created by the junction of several uplands, and consequently the ground in the vicinity was more broken and difficult than in most parts of the Western front. The ruins of the village itself provided unusual facilities for defence, since it was honeycombed by extensive caves, capable of sheltering several battalions from the effects of our artillery fire, while the numerous sunken roads seemed as if they were intended for the construction of secure dug-outs. South of the village ran the long and deep "Y" Ravine with almost precipitous banks, which threw out its two arms from the main stem in the direction of the British lines. Bristling with dug-outs and intersected by several trenches, it could hold a large garrison which could be easily reinforced from the trenches or from the Station Road which, hidden from our view, connected the village with the River Ancre. On the north side of Beaumont Hamel was a valley flanked by the Beaumont Road running parallel to "Y" Ravine, the whole of the high ground between the ravine and the valley being generously protected by thickly wired defences. The Boches had made the most of their topographical advantages, and had good reason for thinking that Beaumont Hamel was as nearly impregnable as any place could be.

Serre, the other famous fortress, stood on the loftiest ground in the whole district, and the most casual glance at the place was sufficient to convince one that the village, or rather the site of it, was the key to all the surrounding country. Our lines lay some distance from the crest, and our infantry in making the attack would have to advance over ground every inch of which was commanded by the enemy's fire.

Weeks of fighting at the Somme had taught us many things, and we realised particularly how vital it was that our artillery preparation should be absolutely thorough. The prospect of victory would be poor unless the wire defences of the Germans were demolished, and to effect this the infantry were required to co-operate with the gunners, though such co-operation was feasible only as regards the wire guarding the front entrenchments of the enemy. While the gunners shelled the hostile positions, the infantry were expected to examine the wire, report on its condition, and prevent the Germans from blocking such gaps as had been cut. Thus a very important duty of the 2nd and the 9th Royal Scots, when in the front line, was the scrupulous patrolling of the Boche wire. As regards the wire that could not be visited by infantry patrols, the gunners had to rely upon observation from the air and upon the study of air photographs of the hostile lines.

With a view to gaining identifications and so discovering with what formation the Boches were holding their defences, several raids were organised. One attempt by a party of 52 men of "B" Company of the 9th Royal Scots, led by Captain A. Taylor and 2nd Lieuts. J. R. Black, A. H. M. Moir, and I. M. Maclennan, on the night of the 7th/8th November, was not successful, because the ground was so water-logged that the men found it almost a physical impossibility to make any progress at all and so failed to get through the German wire. The 2nd Royal Scots had better fortune on the night of the 3rd November. A small group of volunteers, including Private Robson, V.C., under the command of 2nd Lieut. Callender, reached the enemy's first line and drove back a hostile listening-post. The party then proceeded to the next line which was found to be strongly manned. 2nd Lieut. Callender and his men, having taken careful stock of the Boche position, then commenced to withdraw, and though the foe kept up a heavy rifle fire and threw numerous grenades, they arrived back at our lines without a casualty.

Apart from patrolling and raiding, the infantry units helped to forward the battle arrangements by supplying working and carrying parties, and by keeping the communication and other trenches fit for traffic. As regards work, the heaviest burden naturally fell upon the pioneer battalion, and the 8th Royal Scots excelled themselves by the rapidity and the thoroughness with which they completed their tasks. They vastly improved the existing trenches and constructed a large number of dug-outs for "battle H.Q." and dressing-stations in a chalk cliff about 40 feet in height, which, seen from the rear, appeared as a white stroke across the country, and was therefore known as "The White City." On the 9th November the whole battalion excavated a new communication trench up to our front line, and during the night of the 10th/11th November it prepared the front line for the assembly of the assaulting units.

The preliminary bombardment of the hostile positions began on the 11th November, and was continued up to the moment of the assault, which was timed for 5.45 A.M. on the 13th. The attack on Beaumont Hamel and Serre formed one operation, but the assaults on the two villages may be conveniently treated separately.

The objectives of the Fifty-first Division were Beaumont Hamel and a trench beyond it, known as Frankfort Trench. The 9th Royal Scots, being in reserve at Mailly Wood, took no leading part in the action. The early news brought back by wounded was of a most satisfactory description. Four lines of hostile trenches including the village were carried, and hordes of prisoners were captured. Nevertheless the resistance of the foe was not negligible, and at "Y" Ravine he put up a very gallant fight. By the time that the whole of the village with the ravine was in our hands, the barrage had been irretrievably lost, and the attack on the farther objective, Frankfort Trench, was not attempted. Shortly after noon, the 9th Royal Scots, who were waiting impatiently at Mailly Wood, received instructions to assemble along the railway line south of Auchonvillers. At 4.35 P.M. "A" and "D" Companies were ordered to go to a position near the south-west outskirts of Beaumont Hamel in support of the 153rd Brigade, and two hours later they were joined by the remainder of the battalion.

In the small hours of the 14th, "D" Company, under Captain Cowan, moved up to Leave Avenue, a trench on the far side of Beaumont Hamel, in order to co-operate with the 7th Argylls in an attack on Frankfort Trench,

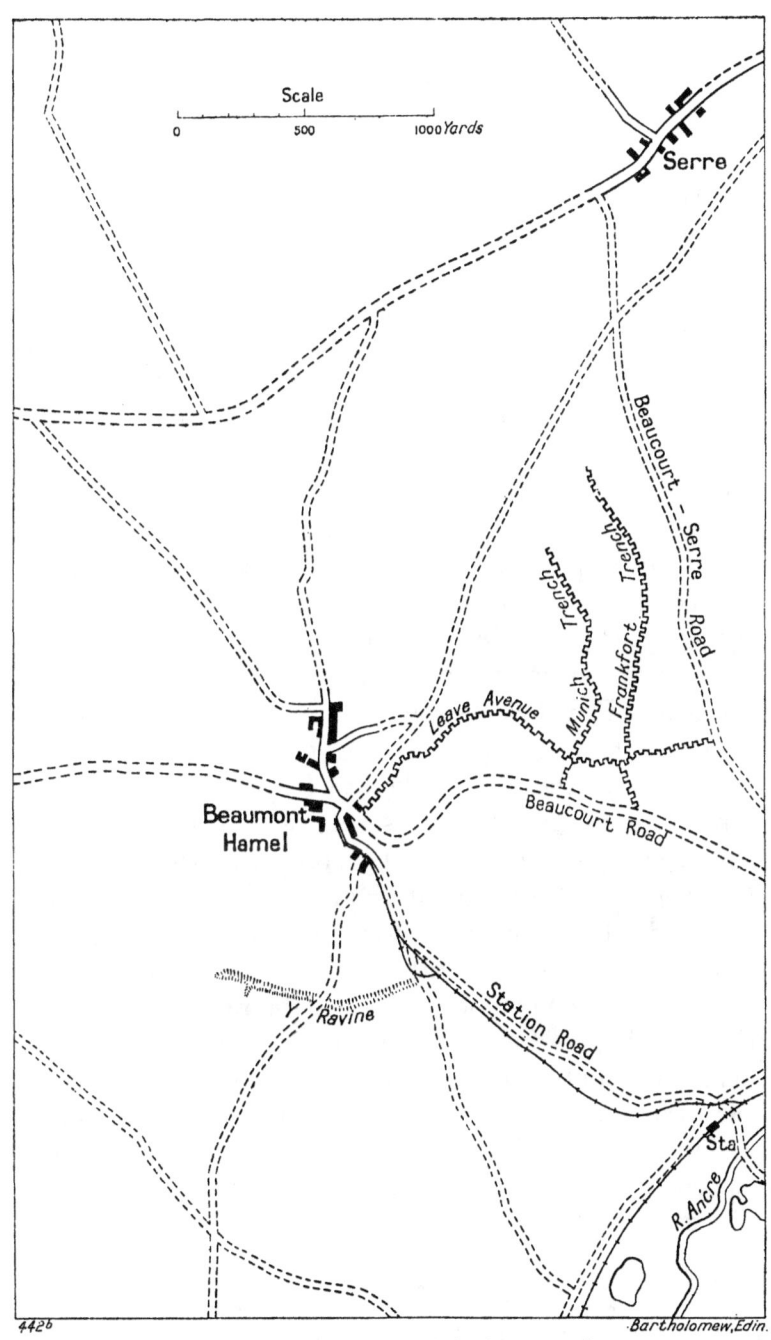

MAP XIII.—The Battle of the Ancre, 1916.

but this operation was cancelled by the 153rd Brigade.[1] Shortly after noon Captain Cowan was joined by Captain P. A. Blair with "A" Company, and both joined with the 7th Argylls in a brilliant charge which carried Munich Trench overlooking the ruined village. Unfortunately the violence of the hostile shell fire rendered permanent habitation of this newly-captured position impossible, and the Royal Scots and the Argylls turned their attention to Leave Avenue, which they sought to bolster up for defence. During the night half of "A" and half of "C" Company of the 8th Royal Scots, under Captain T. B. Mitchell, arrived in the front line for the purpose of consolidating Munich Trench, but finding it now reoccupied by the Boches, the pioneers, gladly assisted by Captain Cowan's men and the Argylls, dug a trench, the New Munich Trench, which Captain Cowan and his company occupied, while "A" Company of the 9th Royal Scots remained in Leave Avenue near Beaumont Hamel.

Meantime the rest of the 9th Royal Scots remained in position to the south-west of the village. Early on the morning of the 15th, "D" Company, being relieved, moved back to Beaumont Hamel. In the afternoon "A" and "D" Companies were withdrawn to dug-outs some distance to the south-west of "Y" Ravine, while the other two companies occupied the ravine in support of the 4th Gordons. Next morning "B" and "C" Companies took over the front line near Station Road from the Gordons, the remainder of the battalion moving up to "Y" Ravine. This continued to be the dispositions of the 9th Royal Scots till the 19th, when on relief by the 5th Seaforths they returned to Mailly Wood.

[1] "During the night a telephone message, spoken over a faulty wire, was misunderstood, and the attack was cancelled instead of being postponed."—*History of 51st (Highland) Division*, p. 118.

Throughout the battle the 8th Royal Scots worked at high pressure. Under constant shell fire they not merely continued to improve the captured trenches, but they constructed a light railway up to Beaumont Hamel, which proved of inestimable value in taking up stores and rations to the forward troops. Assisted by the sappers, the battalion, in spite of the enemy's attentions, wired the whole of the new front of the division, a really magnificent feat. Under the circumstances it is not surprising that the 8th lost more heavily than the 9th Royal Scots. The former had sixty-two casualties, including four officers—Lieut. R. Weir was killed by a shell, and Lieut. W. Lowson and 2nd Lieuts. G. O. Wilson and J. R. Dodds were wounded. Lieut. Lowson who, before the war, had established his reputation as one of the most promising of the younger advocates at the Scottish Bar, was so severely injured that he died from the effects of his wounds. In the 9th Royal Scots one officer was wounded, seven men were killed, and thirty-eight wounded.

The attack on Serre was a failure. "B" and "A" Companies of the 2nd Royal Scots were detailed by Lieut.-Colonel Lumsden to lead the advance up the slope to the hostile positions. The preliminary arrangements were carried through like clock-work, and the troops were in their proper positions by 5 A.M. Had the routes to the gaps in the Boche wire been marked by tapes, it is just possible that the attack would have succeeded, for part of our troubles was due to troops losing direction. The morning was thick with fog, and at zero it was impossible for anyone to see more than a few yards ahead. Moreover, it soon became apparent that the wire along the German front had not been cut to the extent that had been reported, and practically the only force of the assaulting units to break through to the hostile trenches was "B" Company of the Royal Scots with the right half of "A." The enemy was not taken unawares, and poured a heavy fire on our men as soon as they began to advance. Indeed the amazing thing was that, with the Germans alert and far from being demoralised, any troops should have been able to reach the hostile entrenchments at all. "B" Company, under Captain Spafford, carried not only the enemy's front trench but his second one as well, but being totally unsupported it was viciously counter-attacked from both flanks. Nevertheless the men clung to their gains, until the sad truth could not be evaded that the attack elsewhere had failed, and with great difficulty they retired, suffering heavy losses as they did so.

The left half of "A" Company under Captain Strange, struggling through the mud, reached a forest of wire without a single path through it. German rifles and machine-guns kept up a malevolent chatter, and the Royal Scots were forced to drop for shelter into shell-holes about 50 yards from the hostile front trench. "C" and "D" Companies, advancing in support, were met by a withering blast of fire, a sure token that the attack had been hung up, but they plunged through the hail of bullets till they came up against the German front trenches. Unfortunately they had been pushed to the left by the troops of the division on their right, so that they struck the trenches at the point where the advance of "A" Company had been checked. Finding it impossible to get through the wire, they joined with the survivors of "A" Company in establishing a firing line 50 yards away from the Boches. The command of this group was taken over by 2nd Lieut. G. T. McGill of "C" Company, who displayed remarkable coolness and resource throughout the battle.

The hostile shell fire was now exceedingly heavy, and a mixed body, consisting of some troops of "A" Company and men from other units, returned to our shattered front line, where they were re-formed and reorganised by Captain Strange and Lieut. A. C. Scott. This party and that commanded by 2nd Lieut. McGill rendered most valuable service by keeping down the enemy's machine-gun fire, though both were exposed to pitiless shelling from the direction of Puisieux. The accuracy of their fire was probably responsible for the failure of the Boches to deliver a counter-attack under conditions that seemed to invite one. The explanation of our reverse was simple—the hostile position was so strong that the prerequisite of success was the demolition of the wire entanglements, and since this had not been effected, our troops had no chance of getting to grips with the foe. Yet that the Germans had been cowed by the assault was demonstrated by their reluctance to counter-attack, and the 2nd Royal Scots held their position unchallenged till nightfall, when they were relieved by a battalion of the 9th Brigade, and retired to billets in the village of Bus. The slaughter was heavy: Captain A. D. D. Spafford and 2nd Lieut. R. T. Dawson were killed and ten officers were wounded; of other ranks nineteen were killed, ninety-two missing, and one hundred and fifty-one wounded.

The Medical Officer with the 2nd Royal Scots, Captain F. A. Hampton, had during the July fighting earned the respect of the whole battalion by the coolness of his bearing under the heaviest fire. Throughout the action at Serre he displayed the most wonderful bravery and stamina, constantly moving forward to succour the wounded wherever they were, and showing an Olympian disregard for danger; but for him many injured Royal Scots would have been left to perish in No-Man's-Land.

The action of the 13th November had on the whole been crowned with success. The enemy still had Serre, but he had been ejected from Beaumont Hamel and the spur that overlooked it, and our victory gave us the command of the Ancre valley on both banks of the river.

The 5/6th Royal Scots, as we have seen, came into the battle area on the 15th November when they reached Mailly-Maillet, but they took no part in any action. On the 16th they furnished parties for carrying rations and other stores to the units in the front line. Two days later there was a local operation against Frankfort and Munich Trenches, conducted by the 97th assisted by the 14th Brigade; this kept the battalion on the alert, but its services were not required for fighting, and after supplying parties for fatigues, it passed a cold and miserable night in a chalk quarry near the Serre Road. On the next day it returned to Mailly-Maillet, and on the 21st, 300 officers and men under Major Macrae and Captain J. McCloud joined with the 16th Northumberland Fusiliers in relieving the 1st Dorsets in the front line. These Royal Scots on the 23rd assisted a minor attack of the Northumberland Fusiliers by passing up bombs to the front troops. On the 24th the whole battalion mustered again at Mailly-Maillet, and throughout the month of December it was free from trench duty and carried through a course of training near Pernois.

The Fifty-first Division did not linger long in the Beaumont Hamel sector, and early in December the 8th and the 9th Royal Scots marched to Courcelette, where the rest of the winter was spent. The condition of the trenches in this district was so terrible that the men of the 9th wore trousers instead of kilts. The 8th put in a great amount of work, wiring the front line, repairing roads, and constructing dug-outs. After nearly two months of trench duty, training, and working, the two battalions moved north with the division to the trench system in front of Arras.

The 2nd Royal Scots, who remained in the Serre sector till the 9th January, carried through a brilliant raid on the night of the 5th January. The raiders, consisting of two officers and 23 other ranks under the command of 2nd Lieut. Casey, left our parapet at 5.45 P.M. and separated into small groups on reaching the enemy's trenches. The party under 2nd Lieut. Casey, though fired at by Boche sentries, got into the trench and collected a number of terrified Germans, who emerged from the entrance of a dug-out with their hands up, shouting "Pardon! Kamerad!" On learning that other ten Germans were skulking in the dug-out, 2nd Lieut. Casey accompanied by Sergeant Lawson went down the steps. Two Boches who tried to induce their comrades to resist were shot down, and the others meekly surrendered. Then 2nd Lieut. Casey, having established his men in good fire positions, was proceeding to explore another part of the hostile trenches, when a party of fifty Boches advanced to counter-attack. He allowed them to come within 50 yards when, at his word, the Royal Scots opened a sudden fire which broke the attack, about twenty Germans being seen to fall. A second attempt by the discomfited foe was equally unsuccessful. The captured position was maintained and consolidated; it was adequately equipped with dug-outs, and its situation afforded an admirable field of fire across the Serre valley. At the cost of one officer, 2nd Lieut. Northam, and five men wounded, an important tactical point had been won, while eight Germans were captured and at least twenty-three had been put out of action.

Thus the 2nd Royal Scots on leaving the area on the 8th January were full of elation, and after a well-earned period of rest at different places behind the line, moved up to Arras at the end of February.

By the end of December 1916 the Battle of the Somme was virtually at an end. Sir Douglas Haig had achieved all his principal objects, but he had had the misfortune to be robbed of many of the fruits of success by the heavy rains of the winter. Had the season been propitious, the British forces would have been in Bapaume before the close of the year.

CHAPTER XVIII

EVENTS IN THE EAST

June to December 1916

Events in the Balkans, 1916. 1st Royal Scots at the Struma. Operations against Bala and Zir, 30th September. Attack on Homondos, October. British preparations in Egypt. The Position at Romani. Turkish Attack on Romani. Part played by the 7th Royal Scots, 4th August. Defeat of the Turks. March across Sinai begins, 11th October. El Arish reached, December.

THE protracted and critical struggles at Verdun and at the Somme kept all eyes fixed on the Western front during 1916, and only intermittent attention was bestowed on events in other theatres of the war.

The district that probably caused our rulers the greatest preoccupation was the Balkans, where the unfriendly attitude of the Greek monarch caused considerable anxiety to General Sarrail, who commanded the Expeditionary force of the Allies. In December the intrigues of King Constantine compelled the Allies to insist on a partial demobilisation of the Greek army. Some time elapsed before there was any fighting with the Bulgarians, and the 1st Royal Scots were nearly a year in the Balkans before they were required to fire a shot in battle. Had it not been that they were quartered in an alien country amidst an inhospitable populace, officers and men might have found it difficult to believe that they were at war. Few liked the country or its inhabitants, and the climate was trying. The intense cold of the winter was succeeded by a torrid summer, which was accompanied by swarms of tormenting mosquitoes. Under these circumstances, where there was no stimulus arising from the prospect of a brush with the foe, the responsibility of all the officers and N.C.Os. was heavy, and it speaks volumes for their zeal and devotion to duty that the discipline of the battalion was never allowed to relax.

On the 18th June 1916, the battalion at last made a move from Gomonic. The heat at this season in Macedonia was so intense that practically all marches took place during the night, and after three nights the Royal Scots arrived at Stavros, to the north-east of Salonika and close to the delta of the River Struma. After spending five days at Stavros, where some useful training, including musketry practice, was undergone, they marched on the 16th June to the Hortakos Plateau, and here a Spartan programme of training was carried out till the 11th August. At this period, too, the difficulty of taking limbers through the defiles of the Balkan hills led to the adoption of a system of transport by pack-mules. By this time all the battalions in the 81st Brigade had become inured to the rough marches and knew how to make themselves as comfortable as possible in camp, while the result of their training was so satisfactory that the Commander of the Brigade, Brig.-General Widdrington, wrote that the battalions "on the field were looking what regular battalions ought to look like."

August brought some excitement and relieved the tedium of training. For in this month Rumania entered the war on the side of the Allies, and to prevent it from being taken in the flank by Bulgaria, General Sarrail was instructed to engage the armies of the latter. But the plans of the French General were upset by the Bulgarians adopting the offensive on the 17th August,

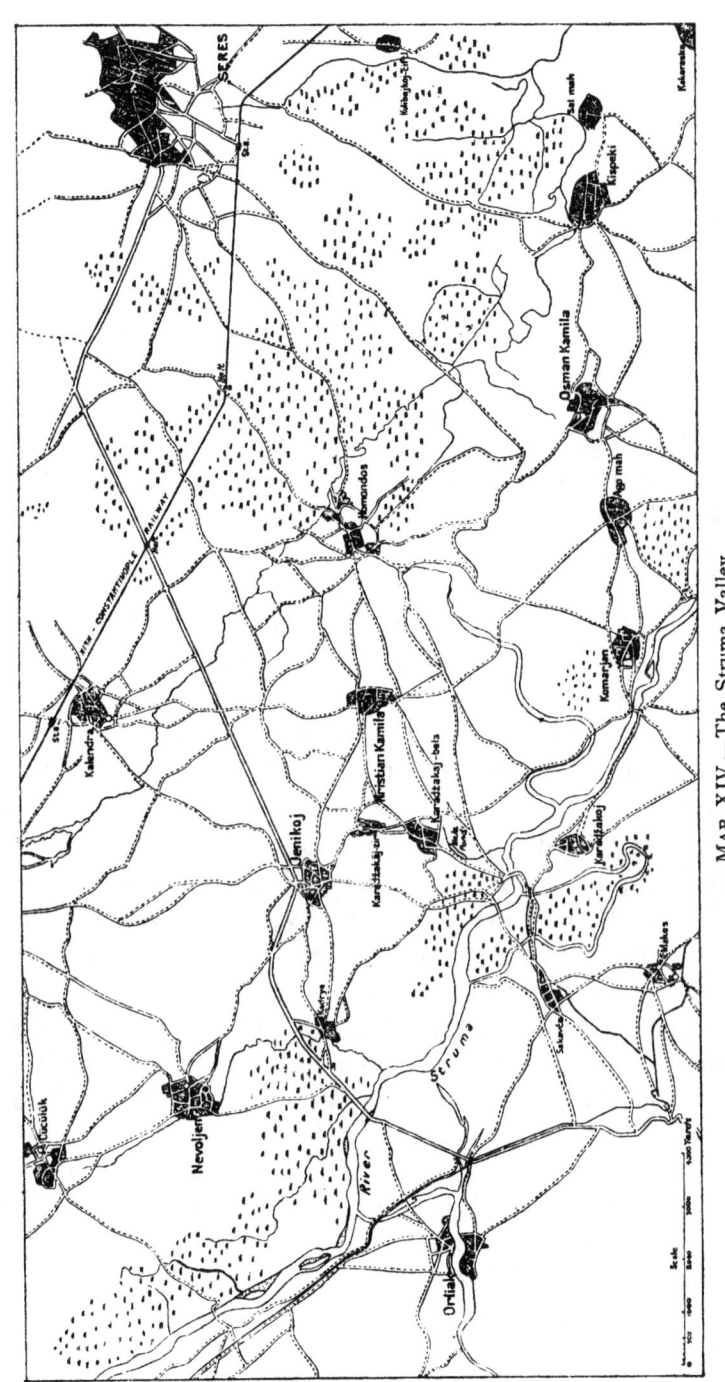

Map XIV.—The Struma Valley.

when their forces gained some ground on the flanks of the Allies. On the west the Bulgarian advance was ultimately held at bay by the Serbians near Ostrovo; in the east the enemy, advancing towards the Struma Valley, captured the forts of the town of Kavala and threatened the town of Seres on the Nish-Constantinople Railway. Near the Struma the Bulgarians secured the whole of the plain lying north of the river and put it into a state of defence. These events made it impossible for General Sarrail to deliver any attack by way of the Vardar or the Struma Valleys, but while concentrating on defence in the east, he decided to carry out an offensive against Monastir, conducted chiefly by Serbian forces. To facilitate this operation, he entrusted the whole of the Salonika defences, from the Vardar eastwards, to the British forces under General Milne, who was to do his utmost to prevent the Bulgarians on his front from sending reinforcements to Monastir.

With the Balkan front astir, the Royal Scots looked forward to some fighting. On the 6th August Lieut.-Colonel Callender, having completed his period of duty as C.O., left the battalion, and his successor was Lieut.-Colonel R. R. Forbes of the Argylls. It was vital that the British should keep a firm grip on the southern Struma, and on the 22nd August the 81st Brigade commenced to march towards the Krusha Balkan mountains, a great bastion, running east and west, that overlooked the Struma Valley from the south and formed an almost impregnable position. After its arrival at the village of Paprat, the battalion was temporarily formed into two groups, H.Q., "A" and "C" Companies proceeding on the 29th August to Turica and "B" and "D" Companies to Butkova. These villages commanded an extensive view of the Struma plain opposite the Rupel Pass, and from the positions taken over from the 83rd Brigade the Bulgarian positions at Elisan, Cuculuk, Nevolven, and Belas Lake Ridge could be observed. From Turica patrols were sent out to explore the plain in front of these positions, and they drew hostile fire on the battalion for the first time since its arrival in the Balkans. On the 25th September both groups of the battalion were relieved and gathered together on the 27th on the Salonika-Seres Road.

During their month's sojourn on the hill-tops overlooking the Struma, the officers of the Royal Scots from their eyrie had studied with their glasses the topography of the district, but they had no opportunity of inspecting the plain at close quarters. Brig.-General Widdrington, however, with his Staff and his C.Os. visited almost every part of the river line, and on one occasion, as a party was walking along the right bank of the Struma, it was suddenly saluted by a volley from the far bank at a range of not more than 100 yards. If the Bulgarians had not been execrable shots, they would have secured quite a good "bag"—a couple of Brigadiers, several Staff officers, and a few C.Os. and Adjutants—but they failed to record a single hit. The battalion also had an opportunity of witnessing the results of raids carried out by other units against the villages on the plain occupied by the enemy. Generally the objective of a raid was reached, but the Bulgarians invariably counter-attacked strongly, and our men usually had to return home more quickly than they had intended. Favoured by the sunken roads in which the plain abounded, the Bulgarians, screened from our view, advanced in close formation, and appeared with such suddenness that they seemed to rise up out of the ground in front of our men who, taken completely by surprise, had to retreat. Although the objectives had been secured, many of our raids were discounted by the effectiveness of the enemy's admirably executed counter-attacks, and the opinion gained ground that such raids were more likely to increase the morale of the Bulgarians than that of our own men.

Accordingly it was decided that certain villages on the plain should be captured and permanently held by a strong force of troops. Those selected were Karadzakaj-Bala and Karadzakaj-Zir, hereafter referred to as Bala and Zir, on the left bank of the Struma, and the force entrusted with the task of capturing and holding them was the 81st Brigade. The attack was originally planned for the 29th September, but Brig.-General Widdrington, in order to allow his brigade a brief rest after assembling, obtained the postponement of the operation for twenty-four hours. On the 28th September the brigade mustered on the heights at the point where the Seres Road descended to the valley of the Struma. Brig.-General Widdrington was able to hold a conference with his C.Os. on the morning of the 29th, when he explained his plans for the attack, which was to be led by the 2nd Gloucesters and 2nd Camerons, with the 1st Argylls in support and the Royal Scots in reserve. While the assault was in progress, one company of the Royal Scots was to clear the ground east of Bala Pond, and after doing this join the main attack. This diversion might be expected to deceive the enemy, who was accustomed to demonstrations from that direction, and might conclude therefore that he had to deal merely with a foray; moreover, the flanking party would be able to tackle some hostile machine-gunners, probably Germans, who were known to be located on that side.

The attack was timed to begin at dawn on the 30th with a preliminary bombardment by the Twenty-seventh Divisional Artillery, augmented for the occasion to a total of ninety guns, and after dark on the 29th the brigade marched down the Seres Road to the bottom of the hill, and rested for an hour, during which period steel helmets were issued to all ranks. The advance was then continued through Mekes to Artillery Bridge, which had recently been thrown across the Struma between Orljak and Komarjan. In spite of some delays, due to faulty work by guides, the leading troops started up to time, and then our guns opened. The Gloucesters and the Camerons carried all before them, killed and captured a large number of Bulgarians, and established themselves in their allotted positions at Bala. Meanwhile "C" Company of the Royal Scots under Captain T. Bell, which had been sent to clear the ground east of Bala Pond, accomplished its task without difficulty. Bala was in our hands by 7.15 A.M., and then the attack on Zir was led by the Argylls.

This phase of the operations was more difficult, since by this time the Bulgarian artillery was in full blast, and shells poured down from the front and from both flanks. But the heaviest losses of the Argylls were caused by a murderous machine-gun fire which raked them from the right flank, and after making some ground the troops halted, because Brig.-General Widdrington had been instructed that the attack was not to be pressed if it seemed likely to involve severe casualties. Meantime the Royal Scots in reserve had advanced in successive lines of companies until within some 500 yards of Bala, when, coming under devastating shrapnel fire from the Bulgarian guns, they closed up under cover of a sunken road running from east to west across the front, and then, turning to the east, followed the road into Bala. Battalion H.Q. were established in the village, while the companies were disposed so as to frustrate any hostile attempt to recapture Bala.

About 4 p.m. Brig.-General Widdrington received from the Corps a peremptory injunction that Zir was to be taken at all costs, and he thereupon ordered the Camerons to advance through the Argylls and attack the village. But the former were not in a convenient position for making the assault, and on realising this, he instructed the Royal Scots to undertake the task. All this time the Royal Scots had been drawn up to the left rear of the Argylls and were positively itching to take part in the fight. Discarding their packs, the men formed up in successive lines in a sunken road in front of battalion H.Q., with the C.O., Second-in-Command, Adjutant, and pipers in front, followed by the leading company and platoon commanders. To the skirl of the pipes the battalion advanced to the attack with "B" Company in front, followed by "D," "A," and "C," there being a distance of 150 yards between each company.

Covered by the fire of the Camerons, which served to make the enemy's marksmanship erratic, the Royal Scots sustained few casualties during the first stages of the advance. The road between Bala and Zir, however, ran diagonally across the line of the attack, and, when the battalion was clear of Bala, the right flanks of the companies suffered losses from shell and rifle fire, which came from the direction of Hristian Kamilla. Lieut. F. Spinney, who had recently joined the unit, was mortally wounded, and Captain W. Harris was hit by a bullet in the leg. Nevertheless, with almost incredible speed, the Royal Scots traversed the 1000 yards between the two villages and ejected the enemy from Zir; over eighty prisoners, including one officer, were taken. Darkness was creeping on, and measures were promptly taken to put Zir in a state of defence. The need to do so was emphasised by a Bulgarian counter-attack which was sharply repulsed. Entrenching material was brought up, and as soon as possible barbed-wire entanglements were fixed round the west, north, and east sides of the village. No less than five counter-attacks were delivered during the night, but all were baffled by the fire of the defenders, the brunt of the fighting falling on "B" Company commanded by Captain D. R. Currie.

Lieut.-Colonel Forbes throughout the battle gave a magnificent lead to his men by his marvellous coolness under fire, and in this respect an account by Brig.-General Widdrington, who during the night visited the battalion at Zir, is worth quoting. "As soon as I could get away that evening, I went up to the front line and found Colonel Forbes with some of his officers standing in the road at the south side of Zir in the full glare of a burning house. He told me that the Bulgars were still quite close and that they could be heard talking and shouting, which was true enough. I asked why they did not shoot and he replied 'they do,' and just then a volley crashed out from quite close. It appeared to amuse the Royal Scots, so I had to pretend that I liked it too, but found urgent business elsewhere."

Besides Lieut. Spinney, another officer, 2nd Lieut. J. Mudie, was killed. Thirty-nine N.C.Os. and men were killed and nearly one hundred wounded. The work of consolidation on our new line was constantly interrupted by vigorous counter-attacks. At 1.45 P.M. on the 2nd October a very gallant effort by the enemy was defeated, and at 3 P.M. he made another thrust. On this occasion the Bulgarians charged with such dash that they penetrated the defence at one or two points, but after some brisk fighting they were finally driven off. The failure of their counter-attacks, which up to the Battle of Bala had almost invariably been successful, evidently depressed the Bulgarians, and after the check on the 2nd the fighting degenerated into mere patrol encounters.

A brigade of the Tenth Division on the left of the 81st Brigade attacked and held the village of Jenikos on the 3rd October, and this success rendered it necessary for the Royal Scots, pivoting on Zir, to swing up their left flank across the open plain in order to continue the new line held by the 30th Brigade. This manœuvre was carried out in the face of galling shell fire in a cool and methodical manner that earned the admiration of all who watched it.

The Battle of Bala may be said to have ended on the 5th October. The troops of the 81st Brigade who took part in it were either continuously on the move or engaged in fighting from dusk on the 29th September till dawn on the 5th October, and, considering how the heavily laden men were exposed alternately within a few hours to great heat, wet, and bitter cold, their victory must be deemed a first-rate military achievement, which could not have been performed, except by thoroughly trained and disciplined soldiers in a high state of morale. The battle was an action in open warfare, carried out with very little warning or preparation, giving therefore the Royal Scots and the other units of the 81st Brigade an opportunity of demonstrating how well versed they were in the science of soldiery.

On the night of the 5th/6th October the Royal Scots were relieved and withdrew to bivouacs behind the River Struma to refit. Disheartened by their reverse at Bala, the Bulgarians evacuated the Struma plain and retired to the foothills in the north. When the enemy's retreat was perceived, orders reached the 81st Brigade to advance and occupy Hristian Kamilla and Homondos on the plain, the latter of which villages was destined to play a large part in the lives of all ranks of the brigade. The direct road to it lay through Hristian Kamilla. Before war visited the Struma valley in 1916, the village was probably an attractive spot, but during the ebb and flow of the struggle on the plain it was gradually battered to pieces, and most of the Royal Scots came to look on it as a place of ill-omen, though the Bulgarian memories of it must have been even more despondent than our own.

Homondos was held alternately by Bulgarians and British for several months at a time, and was the scene of many raids and patrol encounters. Its position, when used as an advanced post by the enemy, was roughly 3 miles from the trenches on both sides, and, when held by our troops, was about a mile and a half in front of our line. This comparative isolation naturally provoked many raids. When first occupied by us in October 1916, the village formed an advanced post to our defensive line and was garrisoned by a company. The company on this duty enjoyed no sinecure, for owing to the extent of the village, the posts had to be well strung out, and it took an officer from three to four hours to walk round them on a dark night. There was always the feeling, too, that a really determined attempt by the enemy to retake it could hardly be frustrated. Consequently the strain on the garrison company was very severe, and reliefs took place every three or four days. Fortunately there was at this time no serious opposition from the hostile forces, which appeared to be very disorganised, and were too busy preparing a defensive line along the foothills on the north of the plain to undertake any offensive action.

Thus during the winter months of 1916 the Homondos

garrison was comparatively immune from danger. There were occasional skirmishes between the scouts of the Royal Scots and those of the enemy, in which the former nearly always secured the mastery. Ultimately Homondos was included in our general defensive line, and, since it formed a large salient, the strength of the garrison was increased to an infantry battalion, while advanced posts were pushed out as far as the railway line. There was greater liveliness when some of the Bulgarian troops were relieved by Turkish regiments, the latter signalising their appearance by sending out a patrol of about 15 men to bring prisoners from Homondos, which then happened to be garrisoned by the Royal Scots. The patrol, when about 150 yards from the village, opened fire, but met with such a volume of rifle and machine-gun fire from the forward companies that it fled in haste, leaving behind a number of fezes and rifles. The Turks were more enterprising in reconnaissance work than the Bulgarians, and the Royal Scots had more than one encounter with them, the general effect of the skirmishing, however, being to convince the enemy that we held the upper hand on the plain.

Meantime the possibilities of the Allies in the Balkans undertaking any ambitious offensive had been dissipated by the complete defeat of Rumania at the hands of the Germans. Nor had General Sarrail sufficient forces at his command to make any diversion that would assist the Rumanians. He had only been able to carry out an attack against Monastir, and this was so far successful that the town was in our possession before the end of the year, but this campaign had not affected in the slightest degree the German attack on Rumania. Thus at the end of 1916 the Germans controlled the whole of the Balkans except the part of Greece which was

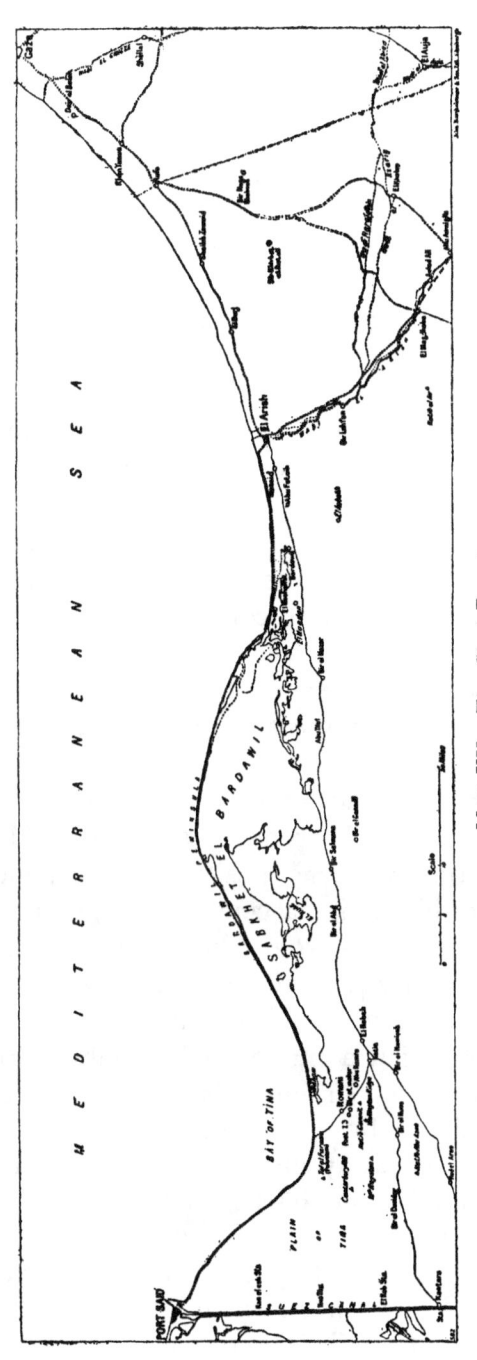

MAP XV.—The Sinai Desert.

(*See also* large scale Map at end of volume.)

dominated by the armies of the Allies under General Sarrail.

In Egypt, however, the course of events in 1916 turned out favourably for us. The British, as we have seen, were not content to maintain a passive defence along the line of the Suez Canal, and had decided to push eastwards into the desert by the ancient caravan track in the north, the only route that was feasible for a large army. In olden times commissariat difficulties had been met by establishing granaries at the oases dotted along the track. Modern methods were now applied to transform the route into a convenient highway, and, under the protection of the infantry and the mounted forces, a railway line, a water-pipe line, and good roads, were constructed with all possible speed along the caravan track. Early in 1916 Sir Archibald Murray had determined to advance to El Arish in October, and by the summer the railway line had been carried to Romani.

Near Romani lay our main line of defence, where a range of sand-hills running south from Mahamdiya gave us a naturally strong position. The dominating height was Katib Gannit, a conspicuous mound of sand rising about 250 feet from the desert, which afforded us excellent observation over the ground to the east. Slightly east of this line was a row of lesser dunes, in front of which a number of redoubts formed our main position. On our immediate front was a belt of oases, distinguished by tall, graceful palms, and beyond it the desert rolled away interminably, bathed in a clear blaze of sunshine, monotonous, and motionless; its apparent flatness was broken by a multitude of tiny dunes, about 3 feet high, formed by the soft sand drifting against the scrub and camel weed which littered the desert.

South of Katib Gannit our line of posts swung round

the waste of high dunes to the north-west. At Dueidar, some 10 or 12 miles south-west from Katib Gannit, we had fortified another line. Between our two positions lay a number of dunes, some of considerable height like Mount Royston and Canterbury Hill, all unguarded except the latter. This unprotected gap was left as a trap for the enemy in case he should attack.

It was generally expected that the summer would pass quietly, but the whole British force was galvanised into activity when, on the 19th July, our aeroplanes reported that there was a large Turkish force, estimated at over 10,000 strong, in the neighbourhood of Bir-el-Abd. Its immediate goal was obviously Katia, with its abundant water-supply, lying some 9000 yards east-south-east of Katib Gannit. We learned later that the total Turkish force was 18,000 strong and was under a German commander, Colonel Kress von Kressinstein.

When the presence of the Turks was reported, the 4th Royal Scots were at Chalnas and the 7th at a rest camp near Alexandria. Both were sent at once to the scene of danger. The former were taken by rail to Romani, arriving there on the 19th July, but being in reserve, took no part in the action that was fought at the beginning of August, and suffered only one casualty.

The 7th Royal Scots moved from Alexandria to Kantara on the 20th July, whence they were hurried up the line to Romani, reaching there early next morning. Both battalions laboured hard, digging and wiring and making other preparations for defence. On the 27th No. 1 Company of the 7th, under Lieut. J. C. Bell, reinforced by a Lewis gun section, took over the outpost line at El Maler, hitherto held by troops of the Anzac Mounted Division, in order to free the latter for reconnaissance, while No. 2 Company, under Captain W. T. Ewing, garrisoned Post 23 to the north-east of Lieut. Bell's company. On the night of the 27th/28th July the Turks began to swing forward their left wing, and, since it was considered probable that the enemy would attempt to cut the railway line behind Romani, half of No. 3 Company of the 7th was sent on the 28th to take up a position north-west of Post 23 and between it and the railway, while on the night of the 3rd August No. 4 Company was detailed to act as escort to the heavy guns near Romani Railway Station.

It was soon apparent that the Turks aimed at cutting off the Romani force from its water-supply, and to this end the enemy began a movement to outflank our right wing. But this manœuvre had been anticipated, and while the Turks, confronted principally by our mounted and mobile troops, pressed on, General Lawrence and Sir Archibald Murray completed their preparations for the destruction of the foe, once he was in the gap between Dueidar and Romani, by a counter-attack delivered from the west and north-west. In general, the battle followed the course expected by the British commanders, whose measures were almost completely successful.

The 7th Royal Scots came into the contest at dawn on the 4th August, when heavy Turkish rifle and shell fire was directed against the southern posts of the Romani position. The enemy was apparently plentifully supplied with artillery, for long-range H.E. shells were fired at our dumps near the rail-head, while German aeroplanes vigorously bombed all the camp areas, but the 7th Royal Scots had not to cope with any infantry attacks, since the posts held by them lay to the rear. Nevertheless they were kept under rifle fire from Wellington Ridge, a high sand-dune, which the Turks captured early on the 4th. So impetuous was the advance of our opponents that Lieut.-Colonel Peebles reinforced the post manned by half of No. 3 Company with the other half. Battalion H.Q. joined No. 2 Company at Post 23, while the remainder of the 156th Brigade was mustered in the same neighbourhood, which had now become the threatened flank of the defence; for the Australians and New Zealanders, gallantly contesting each ridge, were nevertheless being gradually forced back by the superior numbers of the Turks. The hostile fire grew hotter, and about midday Battalion H.Q. and No. 2 Company were strung out to fill a gap between the mounted troops and No. 1 Company, which had sustained several casualties, including Lieut. Bell, from the enemy stationed on Wellington Ridge. No. 3 Company took the place of No. 2 in Post 23.

The enveloping movement of the Turks, however, crumpled up before our counter-attack, delivered from Dueidar by mounted troops, and from the north-west by the Forty-second Division, which had detrained at Pelusium. The very extent to which the Turkish left wing had penetrated—as far as Canterbury Hill—contributed to the undoing of the enemy, for he was so utterly exhausted by his efforts under a scorching sun that he had not the pith to offer any effective resistance against the counter-stroke which we unleashed against him. The hostile left wing was absolutely smashed, and after dark the 7th Royal Scots, in conjunction with the 8th Cameronians, dug themselves in on the north edge of Wellington Ridge, which was still held by the enemy. When morning dawned, the Turks on the summit, girt round by confident foes, saw that their plight was hopeless, and without courting further unpleasantness hung out the white flag. Over 800 prisoners, with rifles, machine-guns, and a mountain battery, surrendered to the 8th Cameronians.

After the recapture of Wellington Ridge the bulk of the 156th Brigade returned to Romani to rest, but the 7th Royal Scots at 11.30 A.M. were ordered to rendezvous near Katib Gannit and assist the 155th Brigade in clearing the palm grove of Abu Hamra. This operation was commenced at daybreak on the 6th August, and no opposition being encountered, the troops, in artillery formation, advanced and occupied in turn Rabak and Katia. A torment of heat lay over the desert, and owing to this and the scarcity of water, the march though unopposed was exceedingly exhausting, and it was with feelings of unbounded relief that the Royal Scots at nightfall took over part of the outpost line covering the advanced position; here the battalion remained till 4 A.M. on the 7th August, when it was relieved and returned to Romani.

The results of the action at Romani were decisive. Our victory put an end for ever to any danger of the invasion of Egypt from the east, and cleared the way for the advance of our own troops. This had been arranged to begin in October, and mounted troops and infantry led the way, a railway, a water-pipe line, and a road being constructed in their wake. The road consisted simply of wire netting laid on the flat expanse of sand, an arrangement which proved very effective, the netting preventing the foot from sinking more than an inch or two into the hot sand, so that the labour of marching was considerably diminished. The benefits of this road were chiefly experienced by later arrivals, for the troops of the 156th Brigade were among the pioneers that tramped in front of the track and laid the wire netting, their legs sinking to the ankle in the soft yielding sand of Sinai.

By this time the men of the 4th and the 7th Royal Scots had become quite familiar with the conditions of bivouac life in the desert, and had added to their vocabulary a weird collection of Arabic words and phrases learned from the native camel drivers. The most abusive of these words, such as "Majnum," were usually applied to the camels which the Jocks had more opportunity of studying at close quarters than they relished. The operation of loading these animals was a delicate business and provoked amusement or abuse according as one was spectator or worker. "Occasionally," wrote Lieut.-Colonel Peebles, "when a camel about to be loaded broke loose, the methods by which for a while it succeeded in holding off its pursuers, while chasing men and officers in turn and even the Regimental Sergeant-Major, kept a whole battalion in merriment." But these were only incidents in the general routine of work and training, and before the advance began both battalions had attained a very high degree of efficiency. Until October they were either at Mahamdiya or Romani.

By the 11th October all our preparations were complete, and the trek of the Fifty-second Division across the desert was commenced. So disheartened were the Turks by their defeat at Romani that they put up but a feeble opposition, and our mounted troops had no difficulty in clearing the villages and hamlets up to the Palestine end of the desert, without calling on the infantry for assistance. Yet though there was no fighting, the march to El Arish was an exacting test for the men, who responded admirably to every demand that was made on them. With every step the troops kicked up a white pall of loose sand, which in the burning stillness of the desert air caused a feeling of enervating and oppressive discomfort, "a form of Turkish bath which," said one, "ought to be reserved for sybarites in the world of the damned."

On the 13th October Bir-el-Abd was reached, the 156th Brigade taking up an outpost position north of the railway. By the end of the month the advance had been pushed to Ganadil, where there was a long halt while the necessary engineering work was being carried on. Meantime there had occurred a change in the command of the 4th Royal Scots. Lieut-Colonel Darroch left the battalion on the 17th October, his place being temporarily taken by Major J. O. Taylor, and when Ganadil was reached, Major Goldthorpe of the 1/1st Welsh Yeomanry took over command. The 7th Royal Scots were cheered by the arrival of a pipe band, originally the Camelon and District Pipe Band, which had enlisted in the reserve battalion in 1915 for the purpose of filling the gap created by the loss of all the battalion's pipers in the Gretna disaster.

Towards the close of November the march was resumed, and on the 1st December the 156th Brigade encamped at Abu Tilul. El Mazar was reached on the following day, and here another long stay was made, the battalions carrying on their training. The only retaliation attempted by the enemy during all this period was by means of his aeroplanes, which frequently came over our camps and dropped bombs without inflicting any serious damage. When news was brought by our aircraft that Turks were holding a strongly entrenched position at El Massid, some 5 miles on our side of El Arish, it looked as if the infantry would have at least one fight before the desert was crossed. But the enemy did not wait for them. On the 20th December the 154th Brigade halted for the night at Madaan, and on the 21st, by a forced march, it reached Meshalfet, where Captain Pirie Watson, the M.O. of the 4th Royal Scots, left the battalion to take a surgical appointment in the 54th C.C.S.; his successor was Captain Hepburn.

After a brief stay at Meshalfet the brigade left at sunrise on the 22nd December, its objective being El Arish. This was in many respects the most trying day's march that the men were ever called upon to perform. There was no wind, the heat was almost insufferable, the dunes were like rolling billows 20 to 50 feet high, and the sand was very hot and powdery, filling the boots and rising up in fine dust to torture the eyes. At length the minaret of El Arish appeared in view and the men were buoyed up with the thought that the end of their journey was at hand. But such was the illusion created by the clear desert air that, when the crest of the next dune was topped, the minaret seemed as far off as when it was first seen. After several such experiences the men declared that the Turk was taking the mosque with him. The last climb was the stiffest of all, but at last the 156th Brigade, the first infantry to arrive, entered El Arish shortly before noon on the 22nd. The rate of progress made by the heavily-burdened men during this forced march, $2\frac{3}{4}$ miles per hour, was a remarkable speed under the conditions. On the following day our mounted troops, without waiting to carry water with them, engaged and defeated a strong force of Turks at Magdhaba, and during the night Lieut. Pender of the 7th Royal Scots led a convoy of 250 camels laden with water for the Anzacs. Never was anyone so warmly welcomed as was Lieut. Pender by the cavalry.

When El Arish was reached, the desert was bridged, and thanks to the indefatigable labour of sappers and infantry our communications with the Nile had been securely established. Thus at the end of 1916 not merely was the safety of Egypt assured, but we were favourably placed for carrying the war into the enemy's country in the next campaign.

CHAPTER XIX

THE SECOND BATTLE OF GAZA

December 1916 *to April* 1917

Gaza. Entry into Palestine. Preparations of 156th Brigade for Attack on Gaza. Dispositions of 4th and 7th Royal Scots. The Attack, 19th April. Failure of the Attack.

EL ARISH in pre-war days was the Government post on the boundary between Egypt and Palestine.

A squalid village of the usual Oriental pattern, it owed its importance to the fact that it lay at the Sinai margin of the desert which the Fifty-second Division had taken almost a year to cross. Its surroundings afforded a welcome haven to the Lowlanders of the 156th Brigade. Only those who have dwelt for some time amid wastes of sand can appreciate how gratifying to the eye is a hint of green. The village was encircled with fertile greenery, and in the palm groves that lined the Wadi-el-Arish the troops could spend their leisure in comfort greater than they had known for months. Moreover, there was a good supply of drinking water, supplemented by wells sunk by the sappers on the beach, while the blue waters of the Mediterranean were within easy reach for those—and they were legion—who desired to bathe. For over a month the 4th and the 7th Royal Scots remained near the mouth of the Wadi, in a district which, compared with the places they had been in since the march began, seemed to them paradisial.

Work, of course, was not neglected, and the Royal Scots performed their share in preparing a strongly fortified

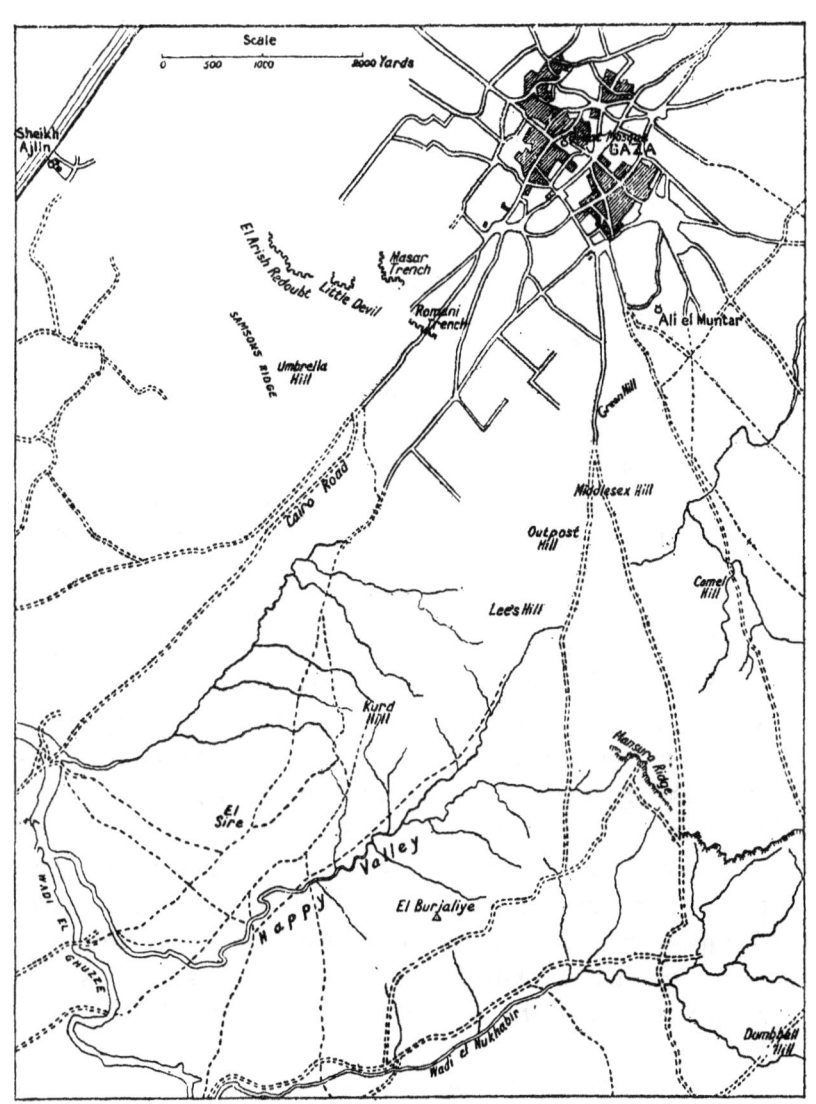

MAP XVI.—Gaza.

zone round the village, but there were some opportunities for recreation and the men played football with real zest and vigour. The weather was excellent, except for a short spell of boisterous wind and torrential rain at Christmas. During this gale a mine-sweeper was wrecked on the beach, but with the help of the officers and men of the 156th Brigade, who formed a living chain extending into the sea, all the crew were saved. A boxing tournament held on New Year's Day was interrupted by a visit from hostile aeroplanes, which sprayed the palm groves with machine-gun fire. Several brigade manœuvres, comprising exercises in open warfare, night attacks, counter-attacks, and rear-guard actions, were practised, so that the battalions were well prepared for the fighting that lay ahead of them.

From El Arish our next goal was clearly the city of Gaza, 50 miles away, but between the two places there was no large supply of water on the caravan route. Gaza itself was amply provided with water. Of the supplies within its vicinity that which lay nearest to us was at the Wells of Shellal on the Wadi Ghuzzee, some 15 miles south of the town. These wells, lying about 10 miles from the caravan route, would have to be seized by us as a preliminary to any enterprise against the city.

Tucked in a fertile valley, Gaza was separated from the Levantine coast-line by a zone of sand-hills nearly 2 miles in breadth, and was overlooked on the east by an extensive plateau which, throwing out spurs and ridges to the south of the city, stretched inland to the lofty heights of Judea, purplish-blue in the distance. The outcrops of the plateau extended as far south as the Wadi Ghuzzee, so that in approaching the city from this side our troops would have to force a passage over broken and difficult ground. From the Wadi ran a series of spurs, parallel to the coast, met by ridges farther north running at right angles to them. The spur of greatest tactical importance was that of El Sire which was carried up to the south-eastern side of Gaza and culminated in a gigantic rock, 272 feet high, known as Ali-el-Muntar. This rocky eminence, the highest point to the south, was the key to Gaza. The spurs were separated from each other by puckered dips, from 10 to 20 feet deep, presenting the type of country with which the Royal Scots had been familiar in Gallipoli. Divorced from El Sire by the Happy Valley Nullah ran the El Burjaliye spur, which was met by the Mansura Ridge, carried on to the east by the Abbas Ridge.

Viewed from the spurs or ridges, Gaza was a study in white and red, enriched and harmonised by its delicate minarets and groves of palm trees. Round the city lay a belt of fertile land, nearly 3 miles deep in the south, dissected into numerous fields and gardens, marked off by thick and high cactus hedges which formed obstacles even more impenetrable than barbed-wire entanglements. "We never expected war to be a bed of roses," said a Royal Scots officer, "but we did not bargain for it being a bed of cactus hedges." Supervised by their German task-masters, the Turks had taken full advantage of the facilities for defence afforded by the city and the high ground surrounding it.

It was some time before the work on the railway was sufficiently advanced to allow us to move on Gaza, and till March the time of the Royal Scots was mainly occupied with toil and training. A very strongly entrenched position, about 2 miles north-east of El Arish, was quickly completed. On the 7th March the battalions advanced to El Burj, where they spent the night, and on the following day they proceeded to Sheikh Zowaid. Here nearly three weeks were spent in building fresh entrenchments to protect the railway and pipe lines which were being constructed and in laying wire roads. With a feeling of chagrin the troops of the Fifty-second Division watched the Fifty-third Division march past them over the roads which they had made but which they had never had the privilege of using. Universal was the relief when the fatigues came to an end; and on the 25th the 4th and the 7th Royal Scots set out on the advance that brought them at last into the enemy's country, and to the tune of "The Blue Bonnets over the Border" they passed the political boundary of Egypt at Rafa, a police-station on the frontier marked by a couple of granite columns. The strong entrenchments near Rafa, from which the Turks had been ejected only the day before by the Australian cavalry, seemed admirably adapted for a prolonged resistance, and caused the troops to wonder why the enemy had bolted so hastily. It was well, however, that there was no occasion to fight, for the going was bad, the sand in patches being soft and deep, and the march was the most exhausting that the men had experienced for weeks. For the last 3 miles the white dust was so thick that a man could distinguish only with difficulty his fellow in front. The desert journey terminated when Khan Yunus, on the borders of Palestine, was reached, and an outpost line was established round the village. In the morning the men found to their delight that they had arrived at a pretty and attractive country-side; the trees, the variety of colours, the enclosed patches of cultivated ground with their cactus hedges, above all the cool greenery, refreshed the eyes and spirits of men tired of gazing over illimitable wastes of sand. The troops had a kindly feeling for the hard ground that now supported them.

From this spot Gaza was about 6 miles away. The association of the city with biblical and historical events, the glamour and sanctity that tradition had cast over the land on which their feet were now planted, inspired the men with more than a touch of the crusading spirit. The feeling that they, after the lapse of centuries, had the opportunity of succeeding, where the crusaders had failed, in winning back Palestine for Christianity, was a stimulus that added to the morale of all but the completely unimaginative.

The first attack on Gaza was made on the 27th March by the Fifty-third and Fifty-fourth Divisions, assisted by the mounted troops, and ended in failure. The Fifty-second Division was not involved in the battle and suffered no casualties. During the fight the 155th and 157th Brigades were at the Wadi Ghuzzee, while the 156th Brigade guarded the lines at Khan Yunus. Having failed to take Gaza by a *coup de main* we could achieve our object only by more deliberate methods. Both sides set to work, the one preparing for attack, the other for defence, and the appearance of numerous strong trenches testified to the industry of the enemy.

We required almost three weeks to complete our preparations, but by the 16th April all was ready. On the 30th March the 156th Brigade rejoined the rest of the division at Wadi Ghuzzee, both sides of which were fortunately commanded by us. The operations were to extend over three days. On the 17th April the Fifty-second Division, employing the 155th and 157th Brigades, was to capture El Sire Ridge as far as the point known as Kurd Hill and also the Mansura Ridge; on its right the Fifty-fourth Division was entrusted with the attack on Abbas Ridge. The 18th was set aside for consolidation and the bringing up of all necessary stores for the grand assault, which after a preliminary bombardment was to take place on the

19th. To the Fifty-second Division fell the task of taking El Muntar and its group of hills, and when this was accomplished the Fifty-fourth Division was to swing round the right of the Fifty-second and seize the hills in rear of Gaza. Meantime the Fifty-third Division on the left was to attack along the coast, its chief objectives being Sheikh Ajlin and a prominent sand-hill known to us as Samson's Ridge. For the protection of the inland flank of the attack there were available the mounted troops, some of which were also stationed near Shellal to watch a Turkish force at Hereira.

The 156th Brigade was in reserve for the first phase of the battle, and on the night of the 16th the 4th and the 7th Royal Scots dug themselves in on the north of the Wadi Ghuzzee. The operations on the 17th were entirely successful, Kurd Hill and the Mansura and Abbas Ridges being captured with great dash by our troops. Despite the enemy's artillery fire the consolidation of these positions, which gave us a convenient jumping-off point for the decisive assault, was rapidly effected. The infantry attack in the all-important operations of the 19th was to begin at 7.30 A.M. On the left of the divisional front the 155th Brigade was responsible for capturing El Sire Ridge as far as Green Hill, to the south of El Muntar, while the 156th on its right was to advance over Mansura and attack El Muntar from the plain. The movements of the 156th were largely dependent upon the fate of the 155th Brigade, for unless the group of hills to the north of El Sire Ridge, particularly Outpost Hill, was captured by the latter, the advance of the former on Muntar would be swept by the fire of the Turkish defence.

After dark on the 18th the units of the 156th Brigade moved up from the Wadi Ghuzzee to Mansura Ridge, the order from left to right being the 8th Cameronians,

4th Royal Scots, 7th Royal Scots, with the 7th Cameronians in brigade reserve. The Royal Scots battalions were formed up for the attack in eight lines or waves, the 4th having "A" and "B" Companies in front with Major Taylor in command of the firing-line, and the 7th No. 2 Company in front with Major Mitchell in command of the firing-line.

The issue of the battle hung on the attack of the 155th Brigade. At 5.30 A.M. our bombardment opened, and two hours later the infantry were unleashed. At first all went well, and for over a mile the advance was carried on without a check, but the Turkish garrison of Outpost Hill, fighting with magnificent resolution, successfully stemmed the assault of the 155th Brigade, and the 156th had to stop in conformity with its neighbour. When the check came, the troops of the 156th Brigade had reached the plain to the east of El Sire Ridge, with the right of the 7th Royal Scots about 700 yards south-east of Green Hill. The attacking troops lay in extended order across the open, exposed to heavy artillery fire, and at the mercy of the Turks on the commanding heights, to whose machine-gun fire they were unable to reply. The situation was bad, and the 7th Royal Scots had an exposed right flank to guard, for the Fifty-fourth Division after some initial successes had also been repulsed. For nearly six hours the men were but human targets, and matters became very serious when, about 2.45 P.M., Turkish artillery opened fire on the rear of the 7th Royal Scots from Tank Redoubt[1] and the south-east. Lieut.-Colonel Peebles saw that it was necessary to readjust his line and withdrew his leading company from its exposed and untenable position on

---

[1] A tank which fell into the hands of the Turks at the first Battle of Gaza.

Camel Hill. The manœuvre, a very difficult one, since it had to be carried out under heavy fire, was performed in a manner that reflected the greatest credit on the discipline of the men and the leadership of the officers. Shortly after readjustment was completed Major Mitchell was wounded, his place as commander of the firing-line being taken by Major Ewing.

After a desperate combat the Turks not merely kept Outpost Hill, but were even able to launch an attack against the 8th Cameronians on the left. Bullets were pouring into the troops of the 156th Brigade from nearly every quarter, and it was now patent that the attack had spent itself. Accordingly the brigade withdrew to a more tenable position, the movement being carried out most skilfully, companies retiring by platoons. On becoming aware that our men were in retreat, the Turks essayed a counter-attack, but it was shattered by our artillery fire. At nightfall the left flank of the brigade rested about 500 yards south-east of Outpost Hill and the right lay near Camel Hill, where touch was secured with the Fifty-fourth Division.

Our attack might have been successful had it been supported by a greater weight of artillery fire. The barrage was accurate, but proved too thin to ease the task of the infantry, who had been detailed to make a frontal assault on positions of quite exceptional strength. Officers and men had behaved splendidly, and had shown most creditable coolness and steadiness during the action. Our losses were heavy, but the enemy also must have suffered severe punishment, for he did not dare to make any counter-attack during the night.

After the action the 4th Royal Scots retired at midnight to the rear slope of Mansura, while the 7th remained for other two days near Camel Hill before they also withdrew to Mansura, where a strong line was

1917] LOSSES OF 4TH AND 7TH BATTALIONS 373

entrenched and wired. Most of the gains that we secured in the battle were retained, especially Lees Hill, which gave us a better jumping-off place for our next assault.

The casualties of the Royal Scots, though not light, were under the circumstances less heavy than might have been expected. This was partly due to the extended formation adopted for the attack, there being about four paces between each man. In the 4th one officer, 2nd Lieut. G. B. Cave, was killed and six[1] were wounded; thirteen men were killed, one hundred and ten wounded, and four missing. The 7th Royal Scots being on the exposed right flank suffered more seriously; Lieut. G. Pender was mortally wounded and in addition Major Mitchell and other six[2] officers were wounded; twenty men were killed and one hundred and twenty wounded.

The repulse on the 19th was so serious that months elapsed before we were ready for another enterprise against Gaza. Meantime we will turn to the Western front and trace the fortunes of the other battalions of the Royal Scots during 1917.

[1] Major Taylor, Lieuts. Soutar, Sturrock and Winchester, and 2nd Lieuts. Dalgleish and Wallace.
[2] Captains Bell, Kermack and Weir, and Lieuts. Evans, Innes and Waterston.

CHAPTER XX

THE GERMAN RETREAT AND PREPARATIONS FOR THE BATTLE OF ARRAS

February to April 1917

Situation at beginning of 1917. Plans of Sir Douglas Haig. German Retreat to Hindenburg Line. Advance of 5/6th Royal Scots. Advance of 17th Royal Scots. Situation at Arras. Royal Scots Battalions at Arras. Raid by 16th Royal Scots, 7th April. Daylight raid by 13th Royal Scots, 5th April. Reconnaissance by 11th Royal Scots, 21st March. Gallantry of 2nd Lieut. Storey. The struggle for air supremacy. Arras. Arrangements for the Battle. Objectives.

(*See* Map XXII.)

At the beginning of 1917 the soldiers of the Allies on the Western front were animated by a confidence greater than they had experienced since the opening of the war. Our numbers had visibly swollen and were still increasing; since the 1st July 1916 our flying men had dominated the air, while in guns and munitions we had achieved an undoubted advantage over the enemy; and, most potent influence of all, we were at last beginning to reap the fruits of our victory at the Somme. A general feeling was abroad that the Germans would be forced to bow to defeat before the year closed. The trials and hardships of the fighting at the Somme were forgotten, and our troops looked forward with lively zest to the commencement of the campaign.

At a conference held at the French G.H.Q. in November 1916 it was arranged that on all fronts a series of offensives should be carried on with a view to "depriving the enemy of the power of weakening any one of his fronts in order to reinforce another."[1] The first concern of Sir Douglas Haig was naturally to round off his success at the Somme by cutting off the salient between the Rivers Scarpe and Ancre into which the enemy had been herded during the course of the struggle, and this could be effected by a converging attack, delivered by the Third Army from Arras and by the Fifth Army operating on the Ancre front. At the same time the First Army was to storm the Vimy Ridge, the capture of which would expose to our direct observation the wide plains stretching from east of the Ridge to Douai. Beyond securing these objectives Sir Douglas Haig did not expect that the Arras campaign could produce any great strategical results, and therefore he purposed to transfer his main offensive to Flanders after having forced the enemy to use up his reserves at Arras.

The British Commander, unfortunately, never had the opportunity of putting his plan into execution. The increase in the number of his troops was offset by the fact that he had to take over a considerable portion of the line hitherto held by the French. Still more serious in its effects on his plans was the arrangement made by the British Government to subordinate the action of the British forces to the projects of General Nivelle. Thus the Arras offensive, instead of being the immediate preliminary of an attack in Flanders, was now to serve the schemes of the French General by engaging and holding as large a proportion as possible of the German forces. These modifications resulted in the Battle of Arras being continued beyond the point that suited the purpose of Sir Douglas Haig, and in the principal British offensive being postponed till late in the season.

[1] See Sir Douglas Haig's Despatches, p. 81.

Even without these alterations, the prospects for 1917 were marred by the retreat of the German forces from the threatened salient between the Ancre and the Scarpe, and by the Russian Revolution, by far the most important event in the war. The military consequences of the latter were sufficient to prevent us from realising our sanguine expectations, by instilling fresh courage into the enemy, and by unyoking large German forces from the east for employment on other fronts. The immediate result of the retreat was to cheat us of one of the prizes that should have been the guerdon of our victory at the Somme.

Alarmed by the persistence and extent of our attacks in 1916, the Germans laboured zealously throughout the campaign to prepare a new haven for their armies, and by the end of that year they had practically completed a formidable system of entrenchments in front of Cambrai (The Hindenburg Line). The enemy was thus able to frustrate the schemes of Sir Douglas Haig by withdrawing his forces from the Scarpe-Ancre salient before the British could deliver their attack. Our army following in pursuit had to observe continual caution, because the hostile forces, intact and under full control, would not let slip any chance of launching a counter-attack which might possibly turn our pursuit into a disaster. In consequence, there was little actual fighting during the retreat of the Boches to the Hindenburg Line.

Two Royal Scots battalions, the 5/6th and the 17th, were involved in the pursuit, but neither was engaged in a serious grapple with the foe.

The 5/6th Royal Scots remained near Serre and Beaumont Hamel till February, without having any direct part in the bickering that went on in this district. In January Lieut.-Colonel Wilson, whose name is honourably linked with the actions of the 5th Royal Scots in

Gallipoli, left France for service at home and was succeeded by Lieut.-Colonel J. M. Gillatt, formerly Adjutant of the 6th Royal Scots. The Thirty-second was one of the divisions sent to take over the extension of front from the French, and consequently the 5/6th Royal Scots found themselves at the end of February south of the River Luce. The nervousness of the Boches had been apparent for some time, and it created no surprise when they began to give ground. The advance of the 5/6th Royal Scots lay through Le Quesnel, Liancourt Wood, Nesle, and Voyennes, and on the 19th March the Thirty-second Division held an outpost line across the Somme on a ridge in front of the last-named village. Thence the route was continued through Quivières and Ugny l'Equipée, less than 10 miles from the town of St Quentin. Many tales were afloat of ingenious booby traps laid by the retreating Boches in the deserted villages, but the only mishap suffered by the 5/6th Royal Scots occurred when the battalion was marching through the hamlet of Lanchy, the wall of a ruined house suddenly giving way and killing two of the men. Near the end of March a quiet, unassuming cavalryman, Major J. Fraser, reported for duty as Second-in-Command. The newcomer became a great personality in the battalion, and his fame spread even beyond the gossip of the Thirty-second Division.

By the 1st April the division was within easy reach of St Quentin, having established itself in the Bois de Savy, and on the 2nd the 5/6th Royal Scots took part with the rest of the 14th Brigade in a successful attack, which secured for us the villages of Francilly-Selency and Holnon. After this, however, the hostile resistance hardened, and it soon became apparent that the foe had no intention of relaxing his hold on St Quentin.

Farther north than the 5/6th, who were operating on the extreme southern wing of the British Army, were the 17th Royal Scots who, on leaving Arras in February, moved down to Beaucourt. When the Boche retreat began, they were not engaged in any fighting, but did much hard work in repairing roads and in filling up the mine craters by means of which the enemy sought to impede our advance. On the 23rd March they had the pleasure of welcoming back Lieut.-Colonel Cheales, but the effect of the wound that he had received near Delville Wood proved more baneful than was expected, and he was obliged to relinquish his command on the 13th April. On the date when the Battle of Arras opened the battalion, which had ceased to be a Bantam unit, was established near Monchy le Gache.

While the German retreat disconcerted our generals, it acted as a fillip to our soldiers, who took it as a good omen that Bapaume was now firmly in our hands. To them this was the most convincing proof that the sacrifices of 1916 had not been in vain. It was confidently expected to be the forerunner of greater triumphs, and the pick of the British troops, now assembled near Arras, were eager to be unleashed against the weakening foe. The marked efficiency of our troops at this time was probably due in part to the character of the training now in vogue, in which the bomb, not unfairly described as "the windy man's weapon," was relegated to a very subordinate place as compared with the rifle. At any rate it is certain that in every part of the Arras front our troops had achieved a clear mastery over the adversary, and the tally of successful raids was heavily in our favour. Whether battalions were in or out of the line, work and training were carried on with an ardour that promised and deserved handsome results. Our front trenches boasted a neatness and cleanliness foreign to those of the Germans, and as the winter proved to be the driest one since the commencement of the war, the health of our troops was all that could be desired. The precautions taken to prevent "trench feet" were so efficacious that scarcely a single man had to be evacuated for this reason. In January and February 1917 an unusually severe frost set in, which, while holding the trenches together, proved in other ways very unwelcome since there was at the time a great scarcity of fuel, and it is not surprising that wood and furniture were occasionally looted from the deserted houses of Arras, to produce a modicum of warmth amid the arctic conditions. With the thaw that followed, parapets dissolved in liquid mud, and prodigious exertions were required to keep the trenches habitable. The temporary discomfort, however, created little depression among the men and even inspired a company commander of the 12th Royal Scots to record his impressions in the trench log-book thus:—

> "Sing a song of trenches,
> Trenches full of mud,
> Five-and-twenty 'Minnies'
> And not one 'bloody dud.'"

There were no fundamental changes as regards the equipment of battalions; but the firing power of each was greatly increased by the issue of additional Lewis guns, each platoon now possessing one of these weapons, while the "box" respirator, which about the end of 1916 supplanted the gas helmet, gave the men more adequate protection against gas attacks.

The feeling that things were going well with us put a razor-edge on the keenness of the troops, and each battalion vied with its neighbours in an effort to show that it was the pick of a first-class lot. The veteran 2nd Battalion looked with confidence to the skilful leading of Lieut.-Colonel Lumsden and Captain the

Hon. J. Stuart, than whom there was no more popular or stimulating Adjutant in France. Lieut.-Colonel Gemmill of the 8th and Lieut.-Colonel Green of the 9th Royal Scots were almost worshipped by their men. All in the pioneer battalion, it need hardly be stated, were kept hard at work, and during February and March they reconstructed old and dug many new trenches and dug-outs. The same happy and confident spirit affected all the battalions. Lieut.-Colonel Croft of the 11th was willing to maintain that no C.O. had better officers and men than he. The C.O. of the 12th was now Lieut.-Colonel H. U. H. Thorne, Lieut.-Colonel Fargus having been compelled, through ill-health, to return to England in March 1917. This battalion boasted in Captain James Murray one of the outstanding personalities of the Ninth Division: gifted with a whimsical sense of humour, he countered the German Hymn of Hate by framing a Catechism of Blood, and acting as High Priest he chanted the questions while his company, as one man, shouted the responses. Lieut.-Colonel Hannay had established himself firmly in the affections of the 13th Royal Scots, and he had the fortune to be assisted by a number of officers young in years but experienced in war. In the 15th and the 16th Royal Scots were still many officers and men connected with Edinburgh. Lieut.-Colonel Stephenson had won an assured place in the esteem of the 16th, but owing to a breakdown in the health of Lieut.-Colonel Rose there occurred a change in the command of the 15th after the unit arrived at Arras. The new C.O. was Lieut.-Colonel W. J. Lodge, who had just returned to France after recovering from a bout of trench fever. He suddenly found himself confronted with a great responsibility. The plans for the battle had already been prepared and numerous instructions had been issued, but Lieut.-

Colonel Lodge readily grasped what was required of his battalion and allowed no detail to be neglected.

Most of the Royal Scots units took part at some time in the raids that kept the garrisons of the Boche trenches in a continual flutter. Three particularly notable operations were carried out by the 16th, 13th, and 11th Battalions. On the night of the 7th April, Captain A. C. Cowan with 125 officers and men left the 16th's trenches, invaded the German lines and captured three prisoners. The joy of the unit, however, was marred through Captain Cowan being wounded and falling into the clutches of the enemy.

The 13th Royal Scots distinguished themselves by an audacious daylight raid, executed on the 5th April by two platoons of "C" Company, commanded by Captain J. A. Turner. The objects of this expedition were to ascertain if the foe was holding his front trenches, to find out to which formations our opponents belonged, and to examine the effect of our bombardment on the hostile positions. The raiders were aided and shielded by a "box" barrage put down by our field-guns, reinforced by trench-mortars and Stokes mortars. The two platoons under 2nd Lieut. J. Davie and 2nd Lieut. G. L. Stewart doubled across No-Man's-Land at noon and formed into four groups on reaching the Boche positions, which they entered and occupied for a period of twelve minutes. All dug-outs were systematically smashed and blown in, and eight Germans, one of whom was severely wounded, were taken captive. It was discovered that the Boches were not holding the front line, but were occupying posts along their second line. All their objects having been accomplished, the raiders returned to their lines, having incurred losses to the extent of four men wounded.

The noteworthy operation of the 11th Royal Scots prior to the battle was not a raid but a reconnaissance in force. The German withdrawal in the south to the Hindenburg Line fostered a suspicion that the hostile garrisons on the Arras front might slip away in similar fashion before we had time to deliver our stroke. The 11th Royal Scots were accordingly called upon to make a reconnaissance in force against the enemy's trenches with a view to ascertaining his intentions. This enterprise took place at 3.30 P.M. on the 21st March. The assembly of the 11th was unfortunately spotted by a hostile aeroplane, and the foe therefore was ready for the Royal Scots as soon as they appeared over the parapets. Trench-mortars were fired into our lines, and bullets from rifles and machine-guns spattered all around, but the Royal Scots with fine resolution sprinted across No-Man's-Land and entered the Boche positions, where for a brief period a desperate struggle ensued. In this tussle our men had the best of it. The Germans trusted chiefly to grenades, but the Jocks, putting their faith in rifles, perched themselves on the top of the parapet and shot at the Germans at point-blank range. The Boches could only avoid the bullets by suffocating themselves in the mud, which was more than waist-deep in the trenches, and the Royal Scots amply revenged themselves for the losses that they had sustained while traversing No-Man's-Land. With Lieut. Smith leading the way on the right and 2nd Lieut. Tredgold on the left, they beat the Germans back to their second line. The battalion's task was accomplished; there could be no longer any reasonable doubt that the foe was prepared to defend his position before Arras in force: so Lieut.-Colonel Croft broke off the engagement. So severely had the Boches been handled that the Royal Scots were allowed to return practically unmolested to their lines. Considering the desperate nature of the mission which they had been asked to discharge, the casualties of the 11th—five officers and seventy other ranks—cannot be considered unduly high, but the officers and men lost were of a quality that could ill be spared. Among the fallen were Captains J. W. Brown and J. Fleming, who had greatly distinguished himself at the Somme, and 2nd Lieuts. J. G. Sandilands and H. C. Lunn. Sergeant-Major Francis, who was also slain, was one of the best N.C.Os. in the battalion.

In the night the Germans took their revenge. At 5 A.M. on the 22nd, after a short preliminary bombardment, a small party of the enemy swooped down on a Lewis gun post and made off with three prisoners. This was a blow which had to be returned, and on the night of the 23rd Lieut. Matthews, accompanied by two men, crept into the opposing trenches and killed four Boches. Unluckily, one of these made an outcry, which aroused his comrades, and the tiny group of Royal Scots was attacked before it could decamp. One man escaped, and on his return to the trenches he stated that his comrade had been killed, but he did not know what had happened to the officer. During the day some sentries reported that they could see a body lying near the enemy's wire, and Lieut.-Colonel Croft gave orders that a patrol should go out after dusk and bring it in. 2nd Lieut. Storey, who was now in command of the company, was under the impression that the patrol was to go out without delay, and since no force could leave our lines in broad daylight without drawing fire, he felt that he could not reasonably ask his men to undertake the task. Accordingly he went out alone. Skilfully crawling through the grass, while German machine-guns chattered ominously, he got sufficiently near to the Boche lines to be able to discern that the so-called body was but a piece of sacking.

As far as the Arras front was concerned, the only

matter that dimmed the confidence of our men was the fear that we could not maintain our supremacy in the air. After February 1917 the dove-tailed aeroplanes of the enemy patrolled the sky constantly, sailing far over our hinterland and boldly challenging conflict with our aircraft. The "circus" of the famous flyer, Von Richtofen, consisting of from 30 to 50 machines, speedier and more manageable than ours, proved more than a match for any combination of our aeroplanes, and the numerous individual combats that took place between the rival airmen usually resulted in the triumph of the enemy. We were buoyed up by the belief that the new and swift machines, which it was known were being manufactured at home in great numbers, would arrive in time for the battle and turn the scale in our favour.

There was no secret about the impending offensive; evidences of preparation for battle abounded everywhere. All the roads leading into Arras droned nightly with the grinding of laden vehicles and the beat of feet and hoofs, while guns filled every patio and sheltered grove or field. Working parties from nearly every unit were required to push on the preparations. Instructions for the various battalions were issued in good time, and in most cases models of the ground to be attacked were constructed and studied, so that officers and men knew the names of the German trenches that they had to capture. All the troops that were to open the attack put in several days of intensive training in our hinterland, where areas corresponding as closely as possible to the hostile systems which were to be assaulted had been marked off. Seldom were men so thoroughly prepared for a battle as for that of the 9th April.

Arras was the centre from which our blow was to be delivered. The city had been the scene of furious fighting in 1914, but since then it had scarcely been molested except by occasional shells. Most of the inhabitants had fled in terror, and our troops on first entering the town experienced a feeling of depression on witnessing the signs of destruction and decay that everywhere met the eye. Arras presented all the incongruities of a city both ancient and modern. In the centre of the town, which was entered by gates of mediæval pattern, the streets were narrow and bordered on each side by high houses, and the general impression was such as would be conveyed by the Royal Mile of Edinburgh, if it were deserted by all its denizens. Here and there the broken walls exposed to view the contents of rooms, whose occupants had hurriedly collected a few things and fled before the menace of war. Such civilians as remained belonged chiefly to the skulking and parasitic population which infests the purlieus of every large town. There were a few who made life vastly more pleasant for our soldiers by opening small restaurants and cafés which became the popular rendezvous of all in their hours of leisure. Towards the suburbs Arras broadened out into spacious thoroughfares and boulevards, flanked by the commodious houses of opulent merchants and professional men. The natural centres of the city, the Grande and the Petite Place, had been ruined by hostile bombardments, and hardly a day passed without occasional shells being dropped into these places. Here all that was oldest and best of Arras had suffered irreparable injury from the fury of war. The magnificent Hotel-de-Ville stood a melancholy yet fascinating ruin near the Grande Place, while the jagged remains of the Cathedral suggested the destruction of a grandeur that it had never possessed. Our troops gazed at the jumbled mounds of broken masonry with something of the deep awe that one might feel on beholding the majestic remains of ancient Rome, but the most poignant chords in their hearts were touched by the spectacle of the neglected and dismantled houses which French people of their own class had been obliged to abandon. It was then that they most acutely realised how much their own land had been spared by its freedom from invasion.

The town had a value beyond its æsthetic treasures, for it was the nexus of a considerable railway system which the Allies could not use till the Germans had been driven far from the city gates. Lying in the valley of the River Scarpe, which flowed past its northern faubourgs, Arras was overlooked on practically every side. The highest point near it was the ridge occupied by the Boches, which in the north merged into the Vimy Ridge, and so extensive was the view commanded by the enemy that we had erected canvas screens along the road leading from the Baudimont Gate to St Pol. The railway towards the south ran to Bapaume and Albert, both in our hands, but the northern extension to Lens was firmly held by the Germans; and they would have to be driven off the vantage ground from which they overlooked Arras, before even the southern part of the railway could be used by the Allies. The drawback of disemboguing troops from a town within easy range of hostile artillery fire was overcome by a careful organisation of routes, to prevent confusion and congestion among those going up to the battle, and by making use of the extensive system of underground vaults and catacombs which honeycombed Arras.

After several delays the attack, which was to be covered by the customary creeping barrage, was arranged for 5.30 A.M. on the 9th April, and was to be preceded by a preliminary bombardment commencing on the 5th. For some time previously our guns and trench-mortars had been used to cut the Boche wire, and the gaps formed in it were nightly inspected by infantry patrols in order to prevent the enemy from closing them. The artillery arrangements were made with the utmost thoroughness, with a view to accomplishing three important ends: to silence hostile batteries, to force the front line Germans to grovel under cover until it was too late for them to train their rifles and machine-guns in position, and to cut the wire so that the infantry would have an unimpeded entry into the hostile trenches.

The terrain selected for the attack was cut by the valley of the River Scarpe. North of the river the main tactical point was the Vimy Ridge, which was continued in a slightly lower ridge through the Point du Jour to the Scarpe Valley between Athies and Fampoux. South of the river the general lie of the ground consisted of a succession of parallel spurs, thrown off from the main watershed and sloping gently down into the Sensée Valley. The principal feature in this part was the upland which was crowned by the village of Monchy le Preux.

The general objective of our attack was clearly indicated; it consisted of the Vimy Ridge and its continuation to the Scarpe, and south of that river the spur which ran from Feuchy southwards towards the Cojeul river. Our advance was to be made in three bursts, the breaches into the enemy's position being marked off by three objectives. The first, the Black Line, was a deep, heavily-wired trench that ran along the reverse slope of the eastern ridge overlooking Arras. The second objective, the Blue Line, in the area with which Royal Scots battalions were concerned, was the Lens-Arras Railway and the ground south of it from Railway Triangle. The third objective, the Brown Line, was the Vimy Ridge, the Point du Jour, the village of Athies, and the Feuchy Line. Immediately north of the Scarpe was a fourth objective, the Green Line, which included the village of Fampoux.

North of the Scarpe were the 11th, 12th, 15th, 16th, 8th, and 9th Battalions of the Royal Scots; south of the river lay the 2nd and the 13th. Of these the 13th, 12th, 16th, and 9th were to take part in the assault on the Black Line; the 2nd was to carry the Brown Line; the 11th was set to attack both the Blue and the Brown Lines, while the 15th was to pass through the 16th on the Blue Line and carry the advance to the final objective. All the battalions were in a high state of efficiency, and their confidence was increased by the smoothness with which the arrangements for the assembly were carried through. Before zero every unit was in its allotted position awaiting the crash of the barrage.

CHAPTER XXI

THE BATTLE OF ARRAS

9th to 13th April 1917

Action of 12th and 11th Royal Scots. Action of 16th and 15th Royal Scots. Action of 9th Royal Scots. Blangy captured by 13th Royal Scots. Action of 2nd Royal Scots. Gains of the 9th April. The struggle south of the Scarpe, 10th to 13th April. Events north of the Scarpe. Abortive attack by 11th and 12th Royal Scots, 12th April. Work of 15th, 16th, 9th, and 8th Royal Scots.

SHORTLY before zero rain was falling in a gentle drizzle, but none could then have been expected to predict how banefully weather was to intervene between promise and performance. To the waiting men the last few minutes appeared to drag wilfully before the synchronised watches recorded 5.30 A.M.: then along the whole front our barrage opened like the crack of doom. The earth danced and heaved as if from the shock of an earthquake, and the eastern sky rose up in a grotesque wall of smoke and dust flecked with crimson patches, through which wriggled at intervals the bright signal rockets of the Boche garrison frantically invoking the assistance of their gunners. But our artillery had done its work, and many of the hostile batteries were silenced before they had time to fire a round, with the result that the counter-barrage, slow in being put down, was so thin and straggly that it was virtually ineffectual. The wire protections of the enemy's front trenches were cut into ribbons, and along the whole line the rush to the first objective was a tremendous overwhelming triumph. Those of the Boche infantry who survived the deluge of projectiles were too shaken to be capable of using their weapons, and within forty minutes from the commencement of the battle the front system of the enemy's trenches was captured. The action thus auspiciously begun was continued with almost unbroken success, and at the end of the day all our objectives, except for a few points of no great importance, had been secured.

In the following account it has been found convenient to describe first the fighting on the north side of the Scarpe, then that on the south side.

North of the Scarpe the Divisions with which we are concerned were from right to left, the Ninth, Thirty-fourth, and Fifty-first, all in the XVII. Corps, commanded by Sir Charles Fergusson.

The Ninth Division was responsible for the capture of the German system from the Point du Jour to the village of Athies, the 27th Brigade being on the left flank. The 12th Royal Scots were the right assaulting battalion, formed up in two waves, each consisting of two lines, and each followed by a line of "moppers-up" from the 9th Scottish Rifles. The left assaulting unit was the 6th K.O.S.B., drawn up in similar formation and supported by "moppers-up" from the 11th Royal Scots.

Our troops, mustered in the mine craters fringing the front trenches, during the first three minutes of the barrage swarmed into No-Man's-Land, fanning out into the formations in which they were to carry on the attack. With the first lift of the barrage the entire line swept forward, and the only difficulty experienced by our troops was in recognising the hostile trenches, which had been so completely flattened by our barrage that in many places they were scarcely distinguishable from the cavernous holes scooped by our heavy shells. Owing to this and the hazy atmosphere, the "moppers-up"

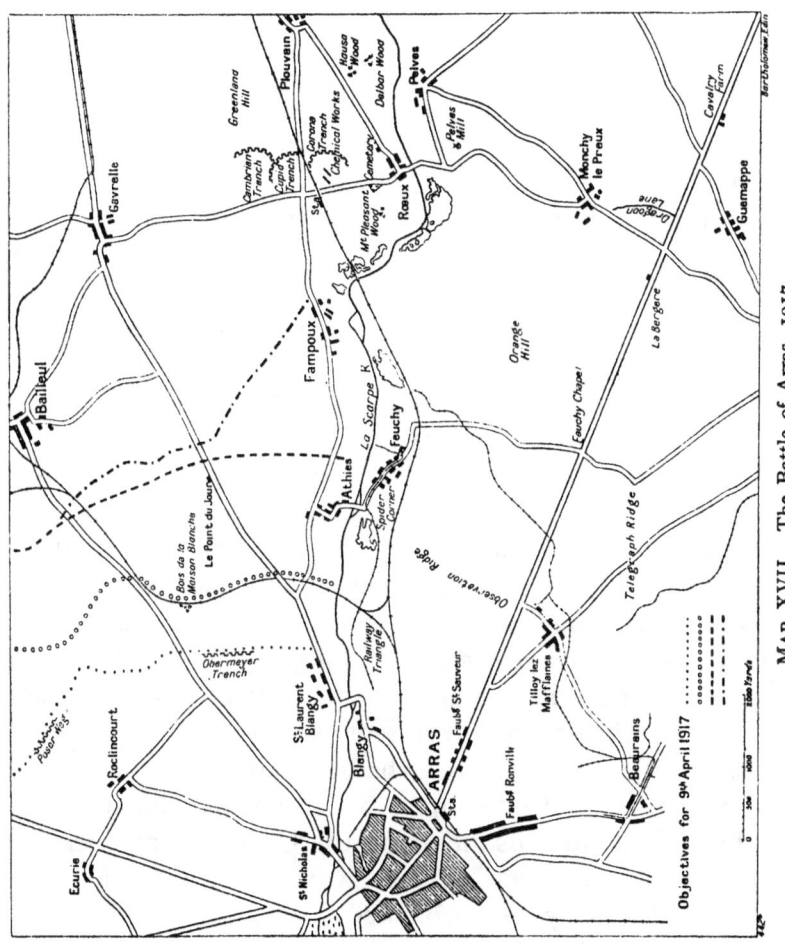

MAP XVII.—The Battle of Arras, 1917.

missed several of the trenches which they had been detailed to clear, but this omission was not attended by any serious consequences, since the Germans who had been overlooked were too demoralised to cause any trouble. The men pressed forward with such ardour that they ran into our barrage, and while still 200 yards from Obermeyer Trench (the first objective) Lieut.-Colonel Thorne of the 12th was killed, probably by one of our own shells. The young veteran Major Hay, formerly of the 2nd Battalion, promptly assumed command, and the 12th Royal Scots with almost incredible ease found themselves securely in possession of the Black Line. While casualties were incurred through our men running into the barrage, their doing so enabled them to tumble on the Germans before the latter were aware that an assault was taking place.

A glance towards Arras showed how extensive was the view commanded from the ridge, but there was no time to admire the scenery, for every minute was required to complete the arrangements for the advance on the Blue Line, which was to begin at 7.36 A.M. Rain was now falling heavily and the men found it difficult to preserve their balance on the treacherous and shell-torn ground. The 12th Royal Scots should at this time have remained in support while the 9th Scottish Rifles passed through, but the latter were late in coming up, so Major Hay led forward his men until the Cameronians overtook them. In the course of this advance Captain J. Murray, who had already been wounded during the attack on the Black Line, had his hand shattered by a machine-gun bullet. Pulling out his revolver he shot away the dangling flesh and bone and marched onwards with his men, till he was brought to the ground by a shell wound in the groin. Even in his pain mindful of his men, he ordered the stretcher-bearers to rescue all wounded before they attended to him. His injuries were so serious that he was not expected to survive, but after hovering between life and death for many days he managed to pull through, and his recovery was regarded by his friends as one of the medical triumphs of the war.

The 11th Royal Scots, scheduled to pass through the 6th K.O.S.B. at the Black Line, were quickly formed up by Lieut.-Colonel Croft for the advance on the Blue Line. From Obermeyer Trench the ground sloped gently to a shallow valley, then rose again to the western edge of the deep cutting of the Arras-Lens Railway. The men dashed off like greyhounds in a marvellously regular line, but as they moved down the slopes of the valley they were fired on by machine-guns stationed at the railway and Maison Blanche Wood. Yet the advance was not even slowed, and the troops, inspired by the fearless leading of their officers, rushed in an irresistible spurt up to the objective, putting out of action the hostile machine-guns in the cutting. They also rendered useful service to their neighbours on the left, the 16th Royal Scots, by silencing two Boche machine-guns which had been firing across the front of the Thirty-fourth Division. Among the fallen of the 11th at this stage was the Adjutant, Captain Loftus, who, quiet and unassuming, was the very embodiment of efficiency, and in the words of his C.O., "always had the detail of the battalion at his finger-tips." The deep railway cutting, honeycombed with dug-outs, must have given the German garrison a safe refuge from our artillery fire, and here, if anywhere, the enemy might have been expected to show fight. The Boches, however, were hopelessly surprised and disorganised, and all were either killed or captured, not a single one escaping from the railway cutting.

For over two hours the whole of the 27th Brigade

had to remain on the Blue Line before the hour came to start the attack on the last objective. Covered by the protective barrage, the 11th Royal Scots with the 9th Scottish Rifles on the right formed up on a position 200 yards east of the railway, while the other units were disposed in depth rearwards up to and including Obermeyer Trench. About 10.30 A.M. a hostile aeroplane flew low over the railway and must have taken back information of our dispositions to the German gunners, for in a short time shells began to fall along the line of the cutting.

The fire fortunately was not heavy enough to cause serious inconvenience, and the final advance started punctually at 12.16 P.M. From the railway the ground rose steadily up to the crest of the ridge marked on the left of the brigade by the Point du Jour. The attack was a procession, and it was well that this was so, for the wire defences of the Brown Line had remained undamaged by our artillery fire. With such an obstacle in front of them, even a few men could have held up a division. But the enemy had been stupefied by the swiftness of our advance and the loss of his strong forward entrenchments, and made no serious attempt to stem the rush of the Royal Scots. While the Jocks were laboriously threading their way through the maze of uncut wire, they could see in the distance scores of Germans bolting in panic-stricken terror to the east. Never since Loos on the Western front had the men such consciousness of having achieved a complete victory. The only anxiety of the 11th Royal Scots was with regard to their left flank, the 101st Brigade being late in starting from the railway, but the 6th K.O.S.B. sent forward a company which protected the northern wing of the 11th and captured the Point du Jour. During the final phase of the battle, Lieut. Ryan won great credit for the signallers of the 12th Royal Scots by managing to run out a wire by means of which touch was maintained between the leading units of the 27th Brigade and Brigade H.Q.

The task of the Ninth Division having been accomplished, the men at once began the necessary work of consolidation, while a protective barrage was laid down on the eastern slope of the ridge. At 3.10 P.M. the leading battalions of the Fourth Division passed through and went on to capture the Green Line without encountering any opposition.

Even the most successful operation reduces the strength of a battalion. The 11th Royal Scots had over one hundred casualties, and besides the Adjutant, Captain Martin, the popular Medical Officer, and 2nd Lieuts. J. M. Grant and C. W. Mason, were killed. The casualties of the 12th were more serious, amounting to nearly two hundred.

The 101st Brigade of the Thirty-fourth Division, on the left of the 27th Brigade, had the 16th Royal Scots on the right, supported by the 15th. The formations for the attack were similar to those of the 27th Brigade except that the assaulting units provided their own "moppers-up." The 16th were disposed with "A" and "B" Companies in front, supported by "C" and "D." The first objective was over 500 yards away, and though the ground was profusely pitted with craters and strewn with loose wire the Royal Scots hugged the barrage closely and captured without difficulty the Black Line. The time allowed here for reorganisation did not prove to be too generous, and the work was not properly completed when the hour arrived for the Royal Scots to advance to the Blue Line, which was expected to be the backbone of the enemy's defence. The prominent obstacles to be encountered were a sunken road, a shallow valley heaped with wire, the railway cutting, and Maison Blanche Wood. Fortunately the opposition was less effective than had been anticipated. The German artillery fire was intermittent and feeble, and although a steady volume of rifle and machine-gun fire from the railway and the wood played havoc with the ranks of the Royal Scots it failed to check the advance. The Jocks had their revenge on reaching the cutting, where they killed a number of the Boches and captured many others from the dug-outs. One group of German machine-gunners fought to the death, and was only put out of action by a gallant charge led by 2nd Lieuts. A. D. Flett and Thurburn, both of whom fell dead just before their men closed with the Boches. While consolidating the new position the 16th were joyfully surprised to discover in a dressing-station Captain Cowan, who had been missing since the raid on the 7th April.

Lieut.-Colonel Lodge had some difficulty in getting his men ready for the final phase of the action. In order to escape the German counter-barrage, the 15th Royal Scots had been instructed to keep on the heels of the 16th, and they followed the leading battalion so closely that many of them were involved in the fighting at the Black and Blue Lines. In consequence the unit was greatly reduced in numbers by the time that the railway was reached, and Lieut.-Colonel Lodge found that he had only four officers and little more than 100 men. This force was inadequate to cover the allotted front of the battalion, so he asked the 10th Lincolns, who were to attack in conjunction with the 15th Royal Scots, to extend their line to the right. But the English battalion could not do this, and the 15th were therefore strung out in one line in order to cover as much of the front as possible.

With a gap of about 100 yards between the two

units, the 101st Brigade advanced towards the Brown Line, the 15th Royal Scots keeping in touch with the 6th K.O.S.B. who had come up on the left of the 11th Royal Scots. The long slope up to the crest of the Point du Jour was thickly protected by uncut wire, but there was no infantry resistance, and the only trouble came from a few Boche field-guns which opened fire at point-blank range, when the Royal Scots were about 600 yards from the objective. A group of about 40 Germans who might, without difficulty, have held back the whole battalion tamely put up a white flag. Just as the Point du Jour line was reached, the Royal Scots detected considerable numbers of the enemy pressing towards them from the east, but these were dispersed by a few shots. It was ascertained later that these Germans had been ordered to make a counter-attack on the railway, and they must have been rudely surprised when they were fired on by British troops at a distance of 1500 yards from their objective. Once the Brown Line was reached, the troops turned their attention to adapting a trench for defence. The 15th had originally intended to go forward some 300 yards down the eastern slope of the ridge, but as 500 Germans were reported to be advancing between Oppy and Gavrelle, and as the projected line was one on which our guns had registered, they decided to remain on the ridge.

Neither the 15th Royal Scots nor the Lincolns were in great strength, so Brig.-General Gore ordered the 16th Royal Scots to move up from the railway and occupy a position in the Brown Line on the left of the English battalion. This was done by 6.30 P.M.

The task which the Fifty-first Division was set to accomplish, the capture of the southern shoulder of the Vimy Ridge, was one of vast difficulty. Success indeed was only possible if the Canadians of the First Army secured a firm hold on the ridge farther north. The attack was carried out by the 152nd and 154th Brigades. The 9th Royal Scots were the right assaulting battalion of the latter, and their task was to capture the Black Line, which at this part was the German trench known as Poser Weg.

The operation in which "D" and "A" Companies led the way was a triumphant success, but the objective was not obtained without a stiff fight. Several clusters of the enemy resisted with conspicuous gallantry, and a series of isolated combats enlivened the front. Major Rowbotham and Captain Lindsay excelled in this type of work, and quickly organised parties of the 9th for assaults on these pockets of Boches. C.S.M. Renwick fought heroically. Along with two signallers he entered a dug-out where he terrified twelve Germans, including three officers, into surrendering, and there he established his Company H.Q. In another *mêlée* Sergeant W. Moncur, who had led his platoon to its objective after his officer was wounded, turned the conflict in our favour by killing four Germans and capturing eight others. Equally decisive was the action of Lance-Corporal T. Palmer, who skilfully used his bombing section to dislodge a machine-gun nest which was interfering with our advance. By a combination of individual dash and sharp-witted leadership the Poser Weg was at last cleared, and the 9th Royal Scots were left to consolidate their gain while the attack was carried on by other units.

On the 9th April all the Royal Scots battalions north of the Scarpe performed what they had been set to accomplish, and the triumph of the whole army was almost as complete. Our chief check occurred at the junction of the Thirty-fourth and Fifty-first Divisions, where at the end of the day the enemy still clung to portions of the Brown Line.

To the south of the Scarpe, where we are concerned with the exploits of the 13th and the 2nd Royal Scots, our progress on the 9th April was almost as marked as it was north of the river. The Fifteenth Division had its left flank on the Scarpe close to the fortified village of Blangy. This had to be cleared in order to protect the left flank of the division, and the task fell to "A" and "C" Companies of the 13th Royal Scots. "A" Company, after seizing a line extending from a ruined house to the river, was to press on to a point beyond the village, from which it could cover the northern wing of the 11th Argylls, while "C" Company was to clear the village and the island lying just north of it, and to assist the attack north of the Scarpe by directing its fire on the high ground beyond the river. These two companies were under the command of Captain J. A. Turner. In passing through Blangy, where the ground was broken by ruins and trees, the companies were to advance in small columns, but when beyond the village were to extend into lines. The other two companies were engaged in carrying for the brigade.

On the night of the 7th April, "A" and "C" Companies moved up from the cellars in the Grande Place by an underground passage into the sewer of the town, which had been boarded over and which ran into the open in some low-lying ground, a few hundred yards behind our front line. On the following night they disembogued into the open and quietly marched to their assembly positions, while the remainder of the battalion sheltered in the sewer, from the exit of which men and officers could clearly observe the progress of the battle.

Even amid the deafening crash with which the barrage opened could be distinguished the peculiar sound caused by the explosion of two mines that had been run under two concrete machine-gun posts in Blangy. The falling debris stunned some of the Royal Scots, and at first caused some confusion, but the men rallied and moved rapidly forward. One of the mines, unfortunately, did not achieve its object and the hostile machine-guns threatened to hold up our attack even before No-Man's-Land was bridged. At this critical juncture Sergeant McMillan of "C" Company dashed gallantly forward, and, discharging his bombs with wonderful accuracy, dislodged the Germans from their emplacement, thus enabling the attack to proceed. "A" Company now swept through the village and reached its objective without a hitch, but "C" Company experienced very stubborn fighting before it succeeded in clearing Blangy. A party of bombers was fired on by a machine-gun supported by riflemen; then a platoon steered a way through the ruins, until it had surrounded the building which housed the machine-gun, and, after plastering it with grenades, attempted to rush it. But these Boches were stout-hearted foemen and beat off the attack. Stokes mortars were then brought up and a vigorous fire fell on the house, from which after a brief interval appeared a wavering white flag, but when some of the Royal Scots went forward to receive the surrender, the Germans suddenly reopened fire. It is unlikely that any wanton act of treachery was intended. The token of submission was probably hung out by the more faint-hearted of the enemy against the will of others who were resolved to fight to the last. The Stokes mortar was again turned on to the house, and with such effect that the Germans were driven from their shelter and forced to yield. After this combat the village was systematically cleared and thirty-three prisoners were taken. All organised resistance was at an end by 8.45 A.M., and at 10 o'clock the island was patrolled and found to be clear of the enemy.

The watchers at the exit of the sewer were cheered by unmistakable evidences of victory. They could see our troops north of the Scarpe swarming up the ridge, followed here and there by tanks looking like huge porpoises, while long strings of German prisoners wended their way towards Arras. After the capture of the first objective "B" and "D" Companies were called on to carry up supplies of ammunition. This work was continued without a break until late in the afternoon and was without incident except that a few Germans, who had been overlooked by the "moppers," were rounded up and taken prisoners by the carrying parties on their return journey. Meantime, "A" and "C" Companies, having satisfactorily discharged their duty of guarding the vital flank of the division, had moved forward beyond Railway Triangle and established themselves in trenches near Spider Corner, in the vicinity of the village of Feuchy. Up to this point the operations had not been very costly. 2nd Lieuts. Buchanan and G. L. Stewart were killed and W. B. Easton and D. S. Fraser were wounded; among other ranks twenty-four were killed, forty-seven wounded, and two missing.

The Third Division was separated from the Fifteenth by the Twelfth Division, and its farthest objective was the Feuchy-Wancourt Line. The 2nd Royal Scots were on the right of the 8th Brigade, which was to pass through the 9th on the Blue Line and attack the final objective. On the 8th April the 2nd Royal Scots were in the Ronville caves near the eastern outskirts of Arras from which, by means of the sewers and other passages, they could move underground close to the front line. At zero, 5.30 A.M., the battalion advanced without loss to its assembly positions in trenches south of the Cambrai Road, about 1500 yards west of Tilloy. The 76th Brigade of the division opened the attack and took its objective, then the 9th Brigade, passing through, also gained its goal up to time. The Brown Line lay some 4 miles east of our front trenches, and as the Blue Line, captured by the 9th Brigade, was only about 1200 yards distant, the 8th Brigade had to advance nearly 3 miles after passing the 9th.

The line of advance was roughly parallel to the Arras-Cambrai Road. Unfortunately Tilloy, which had been taken by the 9th Brigade, had not been thoroughly cleared, and snipers in that village inflicted not a few casualties on the 8th Brigade just as it opened its attack shortly after noon. The 7th King's Shropshire Light Infantry on the left of the Royal Scots were the chief victims of this fire, but by 1.30 P.M. the German snipers had been silenced, and the Royal Scots swept over several trenches, capturing many prisoners. "D" Company on the right came under heavy fire from a machine-gun nest, which temporarily checked its advance. Captain T. Wilson, having located the hostile post, crawled up to it, accompanied by Sergeant Fullarton and three men, and by accurate firing silenced one of the machine-guns. He and his men then dashed into the trench, and after posting a sentry at a dug-out entrance proceeded to attack a second machine-gun. This diversion enabled the whole company to move forward, and the German machine-gunners discreetly surrendered. The company then concentrated on the dug-out, from which was disgorged a large number of prisoners, including one officer.

Our artillery barrage was naturally less sustained and less accurate than it was in the first stages of the battle, and as the 8th Brigade swept on its ranks were raked by fire from a strong-point known as Church

Work near Feuchy Chapel. By the time Chapel Road was reached, this fire was so intense that the left of the brigade could make no more progress. The Royal Scots, veering to the south, managed to push forward some distance and seized another hostile trench, but at this point they were subjected to terrific machine-gun fire from the south as well as from the north. It was suicidal to continue the advance while Feuchy Chapel, which lay in the zone of the Twelfth Division, remained in German possession, and the Royal Scots therefore dug themselves in, some 600 yards short of their objective on Chapel Hill.

The action of the 9th April stands out as one of the greatest British triumphs during the war. Along the entire front practically every objective of value was secured. North of the Scarpe we gained the Vimy Ridge and the Point du Jour, and our line near the river included the village of Fampoux. South of the Scarpe important tactical positions such as Observation Ridge and Telegraph Hill passed into our possession and we had established a footing on the Feuchy Ridge, but our supremacy in this quarter could not be assured without the capture of Monchy le Preux. The victory brought immediate relief to Arras, disengaging it from the enemy's guns, and it soon became possible for us to use the railway between that city and Bapaume.

In some parts of the front the Germans were obviously in a state of demoralisation, and it behoved us to pile on the pressure before they had time to recover from their shock, but a spell of inclement weather sadly hampered our preparations. The intermittent rain during the day developed at night into a blinding blizzard of sleet and snow. Guns and limbers stuck in the mire and our forward troops, being without greatcoats, suffered torments from cold and damp. The plight of the wounded can better be imagined than described. Comparatively happy were the 11th and the 12th Royal Scots, who on the night of the 9th were withdrawn to the Railway Cutting and Obermeyer Trench, where German dug-outs furnished comfortable accommodation. The 13th Royal Scots were also lucky in having dug-outs to shelter them, but other units had no such protection from the rigours of the wintry night. There was no booty more coveted than German greatcoats, but many troops, unable to secure any of these garments, huddled against each other in a vain endeavour to forget their misery in sleep.

Definite tasks remained to be completed on the 10th April. On the front of the Thirty-fourth and Fifty-first Divisions part of the Brown Line had yet to be taken, while south of the Scarpe the Feuchy-Wancourt Line had to be captured and the way prepared for the assault on Monchy. Many were optimistic enough to believe that the enemy would offer less resistance than on the opening day of the battle, but these heedlessly underrated the recuperative capacity of the foe. The amount of uncut wire between the Blue and the Brown Lines conveyed a warning that artillery support would be less effective than on the previous day. Guns had to be taken to new forward positions, and most of these had not yet registered; and since, after weeks of preparation and with the help of aeroplane photographs and air observation, our gunners had made such feeble practice on the thick wire in front of the Brown Line, it could not be expected that they would inflict overwhelming damage on the enemy, whose new positions had in several cases not been definitely located. Moreover, the delay, caused by the unkindly weather, in bringing up our heavy guns and stores gave the enemy time to organise his resistance and to assemble his reserves.

For the next two days the centre of interest lay south of the Scarpe, where we carried on our offensive against Monchy. As soon as it was light, our guns bombarded the Brown Line, and at noon the 8th Brigade, including the 2nd Royal Scots, formed up in two waves and advanced against the Feuchy-Wancourt Line. The attack was completely successful, and the rest of the day was employed in consolidation, the Royal Scots, along with the 7th K.S.L.I., holding the divisional front. Continued sleet and snow ushered in another night of hardship, and while reconnoitring in front of battalion H.Q., established in an old German anti-aircraft gun position, the Adjutant stopped a few limbered wagons, which were proceeding towards the German lines. These turned out to be the battalion's ration party with stores of food and water, which were urgently needed by the men; had it not been for their lucky encounter with the Adjutant, the transport drivers would have passed on unnoticed until they reached the Germans, for our new front line had not yet been connected up across the road.

Farther north, the Thirty-seventh Division, passing through the Fifteenth, had during the night made some progress towards Monchy and occupied the northern slopes of Orange Hill, south-east of the village of Feuchy. The extent of its gains, however, was by no means certain and had been exaggerated, for the 13th Royal Scots, lying near Spider Corner, were in the afternoon ordered to move up and consolidate a line running from Pelves Mill in a north-westerly direction to the Scarpe. On marching up, the battalion discovered that this position was still in hostile possession, and accordingly it took up a line on the railway embankment immediately south of the village of Fampoux. Throughout the day the fighting south of the river was very severe, and an attempt to stampede the Germans by a cavalry charge ended disastrously.

The struggle south of the Scarpe increased in stubbornness on the 11th April. The 76th Brigade of the Third Division made several abortive attacks on the village of Guémappe. The 2nd Royal Scots lay in readiness to support it, and Lieut.-Colonel Lumsden personally led forward "A" Company under Captain Newlands to establish a new outpost line, about 500 yards east of our position facing Guémappe. This line was in full view of the Germans, and not a man dared to expose himself during daylight, but the ground so gained proved later of enormous value as an assembly trench for later operations. It was with this object that Lieut.-Colonel Lumsden carried forward the line, and he was extremely fortunate in being able to do so with no injury to himself and only a few casualties among the company.

To the amazement of the Royal Scots, a brigade of cavalry rode up and waited in mass formation in the snow immediately behind them, forming a target that could not be missed. Salvos of shells crashed into the column of horses and men, but with a stoicism no martyrs could have surpassed, the cavalry endured the storm of projectiles for two hours before they withdrew, the place where they had stood being all too clearly marked by the bodies of men and animals. The Royal Scots sent a message to the cavalry advising them to scatter, but the reply came back that they were merely obeying orders, which must have been founded on the "Do and die" principle, and certainly subjected the men to a barbarous ordeal.

On this day the 13th Royal Scots were engaged in supporting an attack by the 6th Camerons against Lone Copse and a ridge beyond it. The battalion, advancing in artillery formation about 600 yards behind the Highlanders, came under intense machine-gun fire from the north of the Scarpe and suffered more heavily than on the 9th. Seven officers[1] were wounded, and in other ranks there were one hundred and fifty-five casualties. Though no barrage supported the attack the copse and the ridge were captured, and the position taken up by the Royal Scots at the end of the day lay west of Lone Copse.

As a result of our sustained pressure on the 11th April, Monchy le Preux with a number of prisoners came into our hands. Guémappe still defied us, and could not be occupied till the high ground south of the Cojeul had been secured. On the report being received that this had been captured by a division in the south, the 9th Brigade of the Third Division formed up on the 13th April for an attack on the village, and the 2nd Royal Scots watched the assault from their trenches. A very gallant charge was made but failed of its purpose, because the Germans were in fact still in possession of the high ground in question.

While the attack of the 9th Brigade was in progress, and the German counter-barrage was ploughing up the ground in rear of the Royal Scots H.Q., a runner dashed through the smoke and flame, bearing a message from the brigade in a large envelope marked "Urgent." The Adjutant expected to find orders for the battalion to advance in support of the 9th Brigade, but to his astonishment the envelope when opened

[1] Captains J. A. Turner, A. J. Simpson, T. Brydone, 2nd Lieuts. H. F. S. Lowery, Neilson Fyfe, C. M. Coutts and J. C. Howie.

disclosed six sticks of ordinary chewing-gum with a letter demanding that the chewing-gum be tested forthwith, and a report issued within twenty-four hours as to the desirability of issuing it to the troops for thirst-quenching purposes. In a stinging reply the Adjutant remarked that the life of a runner should not be risked on preposterous errands.

A welcome respite was now given to the 13th and the 2nd Battalions. The former was relieved in the small hours of the 12th April and proceeded to Blangy, and later to billets in Arras. The latter, on the night of the 13th/14th, was relieved by troops of the Twenty-ninth Division and went back to Arras, which now seemed far removed from the turmoil of war. During the period from the 9th till the 14th April the 2nd Royal Scots lost seven officers, of whom 2nd Lieuts. J. Sutherland and W. S. B. Wright were killed, the casualties among other ranks numbering thirty-five killed, one hundred and seventy-four wounded, and forty-three missing.

We must turn again to events north of the Scarpe, where there had been a short lull in the fighting. On the front of the 101st Brigade the first thing to do was to get into touch with the enemy, and patrols from the 15th and the 16th Royal Scots pushed forward on the 10th and ascertained that the nearest Germans were disposed in front of the village of Gavrelle. Many damaged guns were discovered, and one patrol, under Lieut. Gavin of the 16th, captured six Germans who were hiding in a gun-pit close to a battery of deserted guns. The enemy, however, did not allow us to enjoy our gains in peace, for about 10 A.M. his guns registered on the Point du Jour line and caused some casualties. During the night and on the following day the line of the Thirty-fourth Division was carried forward to the vicinity of the enemy, the 16th Royal Scots holding an outpost position near the Arras-Gavrelle Road, where they were in touch with the Fourth Division.

On the afternoon of the 12th April, the 15th and the 16th Royal Scots witnessed an abortive and costly attack, in which the 11th and the 12th Royal Scots were involved, against the Chemical Works north of Rœux. These battalions were disposed near the Black Line, when orders arrived for the 27th and South African Brigades to attack Greenland Hill, a gentle rise lying north-east of the village of Rœux. The difficulties attending this operation, which was scheduled to commence at 5 P.M., were enormous. The only possible assembly positions were the old German trenches on the high ground north of Fampoux, about 1000 yards from the Boche position, and before the battle began the battalions had to traverse this extensive intervening space in full view of the enemy and without any artillery support. Under these circumstances the advance was a sacrifice rather than an attack. Yet at one time it seemed as if the Royal Scots would accomplish the impossible. The 11th, led by Major Sir John Campbell, and the 12th under Major MacPherson streamed down the slopes from the Point du Jour Ridge, apparently oblivious of the shrapnel, H.E. shells, and machine-gun fire with which the Germans swept the approach, and advanced with such steadiness that they might have achieved their object had not the hostile front trench been missed by our barrage. The feeling of invincibility, inspired by the triumph of the 9th April, caused the battalions to persevere until each had been reduced to less than one hundred men. Captain E. G. Turner, Lieut. G. P. Smith and 2nd Lieut. J. C. Tredgold, three magnificent officers of the 11th, were slain; eight officers were wounded, and the casualties in other ranks amounted to nearly one hundred and fifty. In the 12th,

2nd Lieuts. J. Macouat and M. B. Scott were killed, and the wounded included Major MacPherson, his Adjutant, Captain Armit, Captain Noble, and Major Hay. The last named received so serious an injury that many doubted if he would ever be able to serve again, but towards the end of the war his friends were amazed to learn that this irrepressible officer was campaigning in Russia. About two hundred and fifty other ranks were killed, wounded, or missing. The survivors returned from the shambles undaunted and with a courage that compelled admiration, but those who watched the battle could only deplore that so many heroic lives had been thrown away to no purpose. The action of the 12th April was the first of many sanguinary fights for the possession of Rœux and the Chemical Works. After this calamitous experience the 11th and the 12th Royal Scots were relieved, and did not return to the line till the beginning of May.

The 15th and the 16th Royal Scots both suffered a few casualties from the counter-barrage put down by the Germans in response to the attack of the Ninth Division, and the men were severely tried by the cold and inclement weather. Relief was necessary to restore the troops to fitness, and on the night of the 14th/15th April, the 15th and the 16th Royal Scots were withdrawn from the front trenches and marched back to Arras. The losses of both battalions between the 9th and 14th April were very high. In the 15th, 2nd Lieut. W. H. Brodie was killed, Captain W. L. Tod and 2nd Lieut J. H. Hislop died from the effects of their wounds, and many more were wounded; in the 16th, 2nd Lieuts. A. D. Flett and E. J. P. Thurburn were killed, and eight other officers [1] were wounded; in

---

[1] Captain J. Macdonald, who died from the effects of his wounds, 2nd Lieuts. W. S. Gavin, J. H. Williamson, H. J. M'Vie, A. Baird, A. Wilson, G. M. Duncan and A. G. Turnbull.

other ranks the 15th lost over two hundred and the 16th over three hundred.

With the 9th Royal Scots matters up to this point had prospered. Nothing occurred on the 10th April to disturb them, but on the 11th they were ordered to attack a small pocket, which the enemy had succeeded in maintaining in the Brown Line. This operation was timed for 2 P.M. The hostile position was violently bombarded, and after the shelling died down, a patrol consisting of officers and N.C.Os. advanced to ascertain if the wire had been adequately cut. Only a few riven strands stood out of the crumpled earth, and the patrol, crawling up to the trench, discovered that the Germans had vanished; a second trench was also found to be vacated. Our artillery fire must have been terribly effective, for numerous mangled corpses lay in and between the two trenches, and it was evident that the survivors, dispirited on finding themselves flanked on both sides by foes, had fled when the fury of the cannonade gave warning of an impending attack. The 9th had nothing to do but consolidate, while patrols went out to ascertain how far off the nearest Germans lay. It was discovered that the Boches were holding the railway line to the north of Bailleul, but the battalion was not called on at this time to take part in further fighting. It was relieved on the night of the 11th/12th April, and proceeded to "Y" huts near Laresset. Its casualties from the 9th to the 12th amounted to twelve officers[1] and two hundred and thirty other ranks.

There was no rest for the 8th Royal Scots. While the other units of the division went back to refit, the pioneers remained in the forward area, where from the

[1] 2nd Lieuts. J. A. W. Adams and W. P. Ferguson were killed; 2nd Lieuts. R. Brown, J. E. Hewison, D. C. M'Ewen, G. Mackie and H. S. Smith died from the effects of their wounds.

9th April they were continuously engaged in cutting new trenches, making new and repairing old roads for the artillery and other vehicular traffic, and constructing strong-points. The roads, especially the Point du Jour Road, were intermittently shelled by the Germans (it is an axiom of war that safety lies in keeping away from the roads), and the strain of working on them was exceptionally severe, but all the labour of the battalion was stamped by the hall-mark of efficiency.

CHAPTER XXII

THE BATTLE OF ARRAS

Actions of the 23rd April, 28th April, 3rd May, and 5th June 1917

Reasons for continuation of Arras Offensive. 9th Royal Scots near Mount Pleasant Wood. 13th and 9th Royal Scots in action of 23rd April. Result of attack on 23rd April. Work of 8th Royal Scots. 15th and 16th Royal Scots at Rœux and Chemical Works, 28th April. Attack of 2nd and 12th Royal Scots, 3rd May. Attack of 11th and 12th Royal Scots, 5th June.

AT the close of the 12th April, it was abundantly apparent that the enemy's resistance had hardened all along the Arras battle front, but by the 14th Sir Douglas Haig had achieved all the objects which he had in view, and if his plans had not been subordinated to those of the French, he would then have broken off the engagement and consolidated his line. He was well aware that "except at excessive cost, our successes could not be developed further without a return to more deliberate methods"[1]; but as the ambitious offensive of General Nivelle was on the point of being launched, he was obliged to maintain a strong pressure against the Germans in order to assist our Allies. A slight lull was inevitable, partly because of the marked increase in the enemy's strength, and partly because our preparations had been retarded by unfavourable weather. The grand French attack opened on the 16th April, by which date the weather on the Arras front was showing welcome signs of improvement, but

[1] Sir Douglas Haig's Despatches, p. 95.

it was not till the 23rd April that we were able to resume our offensive on a big scale.

South of the Scarpe the Monchy le Preux upland was the centre of the most critical fighting. The village had been captured by us on the 11th April, but since then the enemy had continuously menaced it by a series of counter-attacks, and its garrison was harassed day and night by destructive bombardments. To the north of the river we were committed to a costly struggle for the Chemical Works, Rœux, and Greenland Hill.

Between the 12th and the 23rd April the only Royal Scots battalion to come into contact with the Germans was the 9th. After a rest of three days at "Y" huts, it took over trenches near Fampoux on the 15th. The Germans were occupying the woods lying west of Rœux and a trench running in front of Mount Pleasant Wood. On the morning of the 20th, "A" and "B" Companies attempted to rush these positions, but their attack was brought to a summary conclusion by prompt and accurate machine-gun fire. On the following day, after an hour's bombardment of the hostile positions, "A" Company, in the afternoon, succeeded in forcing a passage along the trench in front of Mount Pleasant Wood and, after ejecting the Germans from the corner of a copse in front of the wood, established a post there. This should have been enough, but the company then went on to Rœux Wood, where it was sadly cut up by the Boche riflemen and machine-gunners, and was ultimately forced back to its starting-point. In this unlucky action Captain A. Taylor was killed.

In the general attack, arranged for 4.45 A.M. on the 23rd April, the 13th and the 9th Royal Scots were involved, the former operating south, and the latter north of the Scarpe. Our line at Monchy protruded eastwards in an awkward salient, and it became necessary for us to strengthen our hold on the spur by flattening out the salient, especially to the south. It was to assist in achieving this object that the 13th Royal Scots, commanded in this action by Major J. T. R. Mitchell, were engaged. Forming up astride the Arras-Cambrai Road in front of La Bergère cross-roads, the battalion was to advance on both sides of the highway with the 11th Argylls on its left and a battalion of the 44th Brigade on its right. The attack was led by "B" and "D" Companies. Our barrage was more noisy than effective, and Boche snipers and machine-gunners poured a heavy fire into the leading waves as soon as they left the shelter of their assembly positions. The most destructive sweep of fire, coming from the south, caused the battalion to veer northwards, and Major Mitchell, on observing this, sent his supporting companies to fill the gap thus created on the right. The leading men on approaching the road south of Monchy, known as Dragoon Lane, were met by a murderous fire from the Lane and from a neighbouring Boche trench which completely disorganised the attack. "D" and "C" Companies on the left seem to have sheered off at this point in a north-easterly direction, ultimately gaining touch with the Twenty-ninth Division. The most gallant efforts to expel the enemy from Dragoon Lane were all bloodily repulsed, and within a short time all the officers of the attacking companies were either killed or wounded. The Sergeant-Major of "A" Company, taking over the command of the firing-line, fell dead while leading the men in a last desperate charge against the Lane. Less than 100 of the battalion now remained, and these slowly retired across the open ground, ruthlessly combed by the hostile machine-gun fire, to a series of shell-holes near our front line.

But the sacrifice of the Royal Scots had not been in vain. In stopping the attack the Germans had exhausted their ammunition, and the Royal Scots Fusiliers, who were in support, creeping along the ditch bordering the main Cambrai Road, seized Dragoon Lane and the obnoxious trench which had given such dire trouble to the 13th Royal Scots.

Meantime at H.Q. Major Mitchell was torn with anxiety, because few messages arrived to inform him how the action was developing. The first definite news was brought by the commander of "C" Company, 2nd Lieut. A. Farquharson, who, with a bullet in his chest, called at H.Q. and reported that at the time he was wounded the attack appeared to be going well. Shortly afterwards word was received from the brigade that the assault of the Argylls on the left had failed, and Major Mitchell thereupon issued instructions that the Royal Scots were to hold on to their positions at all costs in order to cover the advance of the troops on their right. Just before 9 A.M. the Battalion Intelligence Officer, 2nd Lieut. Ogilvie, went out to clear up the situation, and half an hour later he sent back a report that he had come across some of the battalion holding a line along Dragoon Lane. At 10.5 A.M. he stated that the Twenty-ninth Division appeared to have captured its objectives, and that some of the 13th Royal Scots, probably men of "D" and "C" Companies, were on its right flank. Major Mitchell then despatched 2nd Lieut. W. A. Henderson with two Lewis gun teams to reorganise the troops at Dragoon Lane and to protect the Twenty-ninth Division with the fire of his Lewis guns. Gloomy tidings were now the order of the day, a communication being received from the Newfoundland Regiment that several Royal Scots were with it in the original front line, and 2nd Lieut. Ogilvie was ordered to collect these men and lead them to Dragoon Lane.

Meantime 2nd Lieut. Henderson had been engaged in consolidating the position, and having assured himself that his garrison was tolerably secure, he succeeded in establishing touch with the Hants Regiment on the left and the Royal Scots Fusiliers on the right. Continuing his explorations, he discovered a few more troops, of whom some were Royal Scots, in a trench near the village of Guémappe, but with the men utterly fatigued and without any other officer to assist him, he dared not commit himself to a further advance and had to content himself with consolidating such ground as had been gained. The repulse seemed decisive, but from an apparent reverse the division was able to pluck a notable victory, for the enemy's resistance had been so severely tried that it totally collapsed when the reserve Brigade, the 46th, attacked at 6 P.M., and secured all the objectives of the division. The 13th Royal Scots kept their positions during the night and were withdrawn on the morning of the 24th to trenches near the old Brown Line. The casualty list was terribly long.[1]

North of the Scarpe the experiences of the 9th Royal Scots on the 23rd April were hardly more fortunate than those of the 13th. There were weighty reasons why our line in front of Fampoux should be carried to Greenland Hill. Near Fampoux the Scarpe took a sharp bend to the south, so that our troops on the right of the line had the river at their backs. Facing the village lay

[1] Lieuts. R. T. Adamson and J. B. Kincaid, 2nd Lieuts. D. R. Cromb, J. F. Scott, and W. K. M. Spence were known to be killed; Lieut. G. V. Davies, 2nd Lieuts. R. Gellatly, K. G. MacLachlan, E. T. Salvesen, R. Mungall, and C. Hoyle Smith (of whom it afterwards transpired that the first four were slain) were missing, and four others were wounded; of the men twenty-one were killed, one hundred and sixty-nine wounded, and seventy-one missing. It was safe to assume that most of the missing were dead.

Rœux, fronted by thick copses, to the north of which were situated the Chemical Works. The Arras-Douai Railway, which ran along a high embankment between Fampoux and Rœux, broke, in a deep cutting, through the summit of the rise known as Greenland Hill, from which the enemy commanded an extensive view over the whole countryside. Our position was distinctly precarious, whether viewed from the point of view of defence or offence; for a sudden hostile attack might easily force our troops into the Scarpe, while the marshy beds that bordered the river limited the area suitable for manœuvre between our front line and the river. Since we were committed to the offensive, advance was necessary, and provided that we could capture Greenland Hill and threaten Plouvain, the Germans between that village and Rœux would find it difficult to extricate themselves from the trap formed by the loop of the Scarpe and the railway.

An ambitious series of objectives was accordingly allotted to the Fifty-first Division. The first was a line west of the Rœux - Gavrelle Road; the second embraced the western half of the village of Rœux, the Chemical Works, and the Rœux - Gavrelle Road; the third was the road running due north from the eastern outskirts of Rœux; the fourth included Greenland Hill, Hansa and Delbar Woods, and Plouvain Station; and the final objective was Plouvain.

The advance of the division was led by the 154th and 153rd Brigades. The 154th Brigade had the 7th Argylls and 4th Gordons in front, with "C" and "D" Companies of the 9th Royal Scots in support of the former and "A" and "B" in support of the latter. The final objective of the brigade was the village of Rœux and a line to the north, at which point the 153rd Brigade on the left was to swing southwards from the railway and carry the remaining objectives. The troops assembled along a sunken road running south from the railway, and under cover of a barrage the attack started punctually. Unfortunately the barrage was not heavy enough to subdue the Boche riflemen and machine-gunners, and the troops soon found themselves involved in what Major F. W. Bewsher has described as "perhaps the most savage infantry battle that the division took part in."[1]

The 9th Royal Scots, being in support, did not move forward till 5.15 A.M., when "C" and "D" Companies, after progressing about 150 yards, came under pitiless rifle and machine-gun fire from the right and front. The Argylls had gained a footing in Rœux Wood, but had been unable to clear it, and it was only by dint of sheer resolution that "C" Company forced an entry into the wood. Bullets sped among the men from apparently every quarter, and the appalling din created by the explosion of shells and the crash of falling trees added indescribably to the awful turbulence of the scene. The trees and the litter of tangled branches rendered it almost impossible for the company to maintain cohesion, and it was compelled by the violence of the hostile fire to draw back its right flank. Yet the Boches were not allowed to have matters all their own way. Private George Fernie with a Lewis gun put out of action a German machine-gun, and also fired with telling effect on clusters of the enemy on the south side of the Scarpe. "D" Company on the left of "C" was fired on savagely by Germans who were occupying a position in rear of Mount Pleasant, but most opportunely a tank came to the rescue, and with its assistance the trench was cleared by a dashing bayonet charge, and the company entered the wood in

[1] *History of the Fifty-first (Highland) Division*, p. 164.

front of Rœux. 2nd Lieut. W. Campbell was one of the foremost in the rush that dislodged the foe. Picking up a Lewis gun he carried it forward, and training it on the Boches inflicted many casualties on them. His shining courage during this tempestuous struggle inspired the whole company, and he treated with indifference a wound which a less resolute leader would not have scrupled to use as an excuse to withdraw from the battle. But the company could not progress beyond the wood, for it had no longer the weight to clear a passage along the sunken road between the wood and the village, which was crammed with Boches.

Advancing behind the Gordons, "A" and "B" Companies, raked by fire from the Chemical Works and from the railway embankment, tried to work forward by section rushes. Some of "B" Company, it is almost certain, pushed past the Chemical Works on the north, but being wholly unsupported, they must have been either captured or killed during one of the numerous counter-thrusts by the enemy. The remainder of the company, along with "A," ultimately dug in on a line facing the road between the Chemical Works and the cemetery. The troops were incessantly harassed by snipers, so skilfully concealed that their lairs could not be located, and by shell fire which increased in virulence as the day wore on. North of the Scarpe, the German resistance was so tenacious that the fact that any ground was gained at all was a signal tribute to the prowess and gallantry of the troops of the Fifty-first Division. And although the barrage put down by our guns was less effective than had been hoped, our artillery rendered great service by smashing several attempts of the Germans to launch a counter-attack from Greenland Hill.

After nightfall, the 26th Northumberland Fusiliers of the Thirty-fourth Division, the 7th Argylls, and the

4th Seaforths held the brigade front, while the 9th Royal Scots moved back to the sunken road in support. Early in the morning of the 24th a counter-attack was repulsed by the division, with heavy losses to the enemy. This ended the fighting of the 9th Royal Scots for the time, as they were relieved on the night of the 24th/25th April and marched back to Arras. In such an action as that of the 23rd April losses were necessarily heavy, and the devotion with which the battalion threw itself into the fight may be measured by the length of its casualty list. Captain P. A. Blair, Lieut. C. Jamieson, and 2nd Lieuts. H. G. Brunsdon, C. H. Smith, and J. M. Sutherland were killed and two other officers were wounded; fifty-four men were killed, one hundred and fifteen wounded, and fifty-five missing.

As a result of the fighting on the 23rd April we improved our position south of the Scarpe by gaining more elbow-room near Monchy le Preux, while north of the river we carried our line close to Rœux and the ill-famed Chemical Works. Our offensive, without doubt, had fulfilled one of its purposes by engaging large forces of the enemy, but though by this time the grand attack of General Nivelle had failed to break the German line, Sir Douglas Haig was still obliged to continue his operations in the vicinity of Arras in order to ease the pressure on the French front. To that end two other general assaults were arranged for the 28th April and the 3rd May.

During this period the 8th Royal Scots had a most unpleasant time. There are certain things—shell fire is pre-eminently one of these—familiarity with which does not breed contempt, and no party of the pioneers ever dug a trench or repaired a road without the accompaniment of gusts of shell fire. Engaged in assisting the Fourth Division, while the remainder of the Fifty-first was enjoying a rest, the 8th Royal Scots had a particularly turbulent experience on the night of the 17th April. A preliminary reconnaissance by Captain J. Tait and Lieut. C. E. Alison for the purpose of inspecting the ground where the battalion was to work was punctuated by deafening crashes, and as the hours sped on the outpour of shells increased. On the way up to the Point du Jour "D" Company was caught in a barrage and Lieut. W. E. Wallace and 2nd Lieut. J. M. Moncur, uncle and nephew, were killed by the same shell. Some time later "A" Company, while repairing the road at this part, also suffered from hostile shelling, three officers being wounded, but the pioneers were no mere fair-weather soldiers, and they performed their tasks with a composure that compelled admiration. During the action of the 23rd April "A" Company cut a trench near Mount Pleasant Wood which proved of vital service in repelling the Boche counter-attack on the morning of the 24th. All the companies did excellent work, but perhaps the most prominent was "A," whose commander, Lieut. Ovens, received a letter from Major-General Harper of the Fifty-first Division complimenting him on the magnificent work done by his men. From the 24th the labour of the entire battalion was devoted to the improvement of communications.

South of the Scarpe, the 2nd Battalion was not engaged in battle again till the 3rd May, but it returned to the line on the 24th April, when "A" and "B" Companies took over part of the defences of Monchy. The unit was under the command of the Earl of Bradford, Lieut.-Colonel Lumsden being temporarily in command of the 8th Brigade. The relief was an unusually tempestuous one, all the companies, especially "B," sustaining several casualties. In the course of two days, hostile shell fire took heavy toll of the battalion, which lost three officers, of whom Lieut. J. S. Morton was killed, and forty-one men.

The 13th Royal Scots, now a skeleton battalion, returned to the line on the 25th April, and on the following day they were in reserve to the 6th Camerons when the Highlanders attacked Cavalry Farm, but they were not required to take an active part in the struggle. After a short spell of front-line duty from the 27th, the battalion was relieved on the night of the 28th/29th and marched to Arras.

In the action of the 28th April, which was limited to the north of the Scarpe, the 15th and the 16th Royal Scots were again engaged. On the morning of the 25th April the Thirty-fourth Division took over from the Fifty-first the line facing Rœux and the Chemical Works. No route being undisturbed by shell fire, the journey up to the front line was a penance, especially since many of the battalions were now composed of men who had never been under fire, and who were now required to soldier under conditions that would have tested veterans, but the raw troops conducted themselves admirably and acted as if showers of shells were a matter of small account.

At zero, 4.25 A.M., the attack of the Thirty-fourth Division was delivered by the 101st and 103rd Brigades, the objective of the former being a line about 100 yards to the east of Rœux. On the extreme right were the 15th Royal Scots, formed up in two waves with "D" and "A" Companies in front, supported by "C" and "B." "A" and "B" Companies of the 16th, who were functioning as "moppers-up," were distributed in six lines, five behind the front and one behind the rear companies of the 15th; similarly "D" and "C" Companies of the 16th were employed as "moppers-up" for the 10th Lincolns and the 11th Suffolks respectively.

While Lieut.-Colonel Lodge's men were responsible for the capture of Rœux, the Lincolns were to operate against the buildings in the vicinity of the cemetery, and the Suffolks were given the formidable task of dealing with the Chemical Works.

From the moment the assault was unleashed cohesion was lost, and no definite information reached the various H.Q. as to how the action was developing. The obscurity continued throughout the engagement, and it was not till the battle ceased that it was possible to ascertain what had happened. In the following account the course of the struggle is traced from left to right.

The 103rd Brigade, on the left of the 101st, was checked by the violence of the hostile machine-gun fire, and made only a few yards beyond the Rœux-Gavrelle Road. Our barrage was too ragged and inaccurate to disorganise the German resistance, and the rapidity with which the enemy brought rifles and machine-guns into action put the whole attack out of gear, the waves being broken up into a series of isolated groups. The Suffolks suffered dreadful losses from a shrivelling fire that came from a trench that had never been touched by our barrage, yet some gallant parties, with one or two groups from "C" Company of the 16th Royal Scots, reached the houses near the Chemical Works. But this devoted remnant had not the strength to maintain its position, and only a few were able to extricate themselves from the encircling foe and make their way back to our trenches.

The operations against the cemetery were in the nature of a forlorn hope as long as the Germans occupied the Chemical Works, and "D" Company of the 16th along with the Lincolns sustained many casualties from the murderous fire of the enemy in these buildings. Nevertheless some of the out-buildings were reached by the Lincolns and the Royal Scots, the latter under 2nd Lieut. Ritchie. But though they had effected a breach in the hostile line, they found that further progress was barred, every approach being swept by hostile machine-guns, while their own position was raked by converging fire, to which they could return but an inadequate reply. In fact annihilation or capture was only avoided by a timely withdrawal, rendered exceedingly difficult by the eager pursuit of the enemy. The pursuit swelled into a determined counter-attack, and when some of our men were seen streaming through Mount Pleasant Wood the situation became very critical. The 20th Northumberland Fusiliers stood firm, however, and during the scuffle Sergeant MacCrae of the 16th Royal Scots assisted by a few men held on to a bombing post in the wood and defied every attack.

Our deepest advance and our worst disaster occurred on the right. Making rapid progress the leading wave of the 15th Royal Scots was soon engulfed in Rœux Wood, but the second wave was met by a shattering blast of fire as soon as it left its assembly positions, and Lieut.-Colonel Lodge, who received this information from 2nd Lieut. Walker of "C" Company, could only conjecture that the battalion had walked into a trap, the Boche machine-gunners having deliberately held their fire until the first wave and the majority of the "moppers-up" had passed into the wood.

From German prisoners we ascertained later that the leading wave, followed by the "moppers-up," penetrated the village, but was then savagely counter-attacked, all the Royal Scots being either captured or killed, and this information was afterwards confirmed by Lieut. Robson of the 15th who was taken prisoner by the enemy.

On the attack being launched, "D" Company, commanded by Captain Pagan, a well-known Edinburgh minister, and "A" Company under Lieut. Dixon pushed into the copses in front of Rœux. The advance was arduous, for all the tracks and paths had been thickly wired by the Boches, who had sited their machine-guns to sweep the clearings. The cloud of dust, whipped up from the dry earth by bullets and shells, formed a veil that the vision could scarcely penetrate, and many of the assailants became helplessly entangled in the wire defences, where they were at the mercy of the Boche riflemen and machine-gunners hidden in the dense bushes. Yet many of the Royal Scots, both 15th and 16th, penetrated the wood in this crazy fighting and went through the ruined streets of Rœux without encountering much opposition in the village. The progress of the advance was under the circumstances astonishingly rapid, for on reaching the village the Royal Scots found that they had outpaced the barrage.

After re-forming along a road between the village and the Scarpe, the assailants, now numbering between 150 and 200, pressed on to their objective, where they commenced to dig in. Captain Pagan, the senior officer, assumed general command, and sent Lieut. Robson to take charge of the left flank. The Royal Scots waited for the Lincolns to appear and continue the line to the north, but the grim truth had soon to be faced that they alone had achieved their goal. Their right flank was fixed on the Scarpe, but their left was open to attack, and little could be done to strengthen the position, for the line lay along the marshy slopes of the river. Sure of their prey, the Germans attacked the isolated group of Royal Scots from the front, from the north, and also from the rear, where Boche snipers and machine-gunners still held positions in the copses and in the village. To the enemy's converging fire it was impossible to make any effective reply, for the ammunition of the Royal Scots was nearly exhausted and had to be carefully husbanded. Men were dropping every minute, and the hearts of the devoted band sank when the heroic Captain Pagan fell stricken to death by a bullet.

Lieut. Robson, now in command, decided to withdraw, and about 9 A.M. the Royal Scots retired to the road leading to the river; it was then that he realised that nothing short of a miracle could save his force. The "moppers-up" who had remained to clear the village must themselves have been mopped up, since the Germans were evidently in undisputed possession of Rœux. A dash was made for the wood, but this was a trap even more deadly than the village, for the copse swarmed with hostile snipers and machine-gunners. But one faint chance remained—to seek safety by swimming up stream—and Lieut. Robson with his followers, now reduced to 30 men, slid into the Scarpe and sought to swim up the river under cover of the bank, but many of the party, including Lieut. Robson, were suffering from wounds, and the attempt proved beyond their strength. The enemy had observed their movements, and the exhausted survivors were hauled from the Scarpe and taken into captivity. Thus ended disastrously one of the most glorious and thrilling exploits in the history of the 15th and the 16th Royal Scots.

Few escaped from the debacle except the rear wave and the last line of "moppers-up," who experienced the full force of the enemy's fire before the wood was reached. Most of these were compelled to throw themselves into shell-holes, where they endeavoured to dig in. Captain Warr, who was with the rear line of the 16th, reported that the position was untenable, and that further advance without the assistance of a smoke barrage was quite impossible, so after remaining some time in the open the survivors gradually returned to our trenches.

The 15th and the 16th Royal Scots entered the battle each only about 400 strong, and their casualties were enormous. The former lost nearly three hundred, among whom, in addition to Captain G. L. Pagan, 2nd Lieuts. D. Munro, L. Croneen, W. S. Mackenzie, F. Westwater, and A. C. Wilson were killed; the latter lost eight officers,[1] of whom 2nd Lieut. A. Brown was killed, and over two hundred men. The mutilated battalions continued to hold the line till the 30th, when they were relieved and proceeded to St Nicholas.

Our territorial gains on the 28th April, a day marked by the vigour of the enemy's counter-attacks, were insignificant, and it was all too obvious that since the characteristics of a wearing-out battle had developed, further operations would certainly entail a heavy sacrifice. But the necessity of helping the French compelled us to persevere with the offensive, and on the 3rd May, at 3.45 A.M., an attack on a wide scale was launched in which the Royal Scots of the Third and Ninth Divisions were involved.

We had been blessed with a belated spell of settled weather, but in the front areas the heat was too intense for comfort. The dead were piled in heaps along the battle front, and only those having no sense of smell could endure, without feeling sick, the reek of decomposing corpses. Near Monchy le Preux where the 2nd Royal Scots were in the line, few could walk through the village without wearing gas masks. A

---

[1] The wounded were Captain A. R. Sturrock and 2nd Lieut. A. M. Gordon; 2nd Lieut. G. H. Dalgety, who was wounded, Captain the Hon. M. Bowes-Lyon, 2nd Lieuts. W. M. Mackenzie, E. H. Henderson and W. D. Howat, were captured by the Germans.

German dug-out on the east side of Monchy, with its entrances open to the east, formed the H.Q. of all the battalions of the 8th Brigade, but it was so small that the Adjutants could not write messages, nor could the signallers work their instruments satisfactorily, while the folding-up process which the inmates had to adopt was not conducive to restful slumber.

For the attack the 2nd Royal Scots had "A" and "B" Companies in front and "C" and "D" in support. As on the 28th April, the irregular and disconnected trenches of the enemy baffled precise location, with the result that our barrage was unable to subdue the hostile machine-gun fire which continued unabated throughout our bombardment. Consequently the onrush of the Royal Scots was shrivelled up at the very start, though the situation was not cleared up till after nightfall. Practically the entire battalion remained the whole day in the open, lying up against the German wire, and impotent to move owing to the enemy's deadly sniping. Darkness gave the men, sorely shaken by their exposure, the chance to crawl back. Captain Tuck of "B" Company, lying about 20 yards from some Boches, with the blazing sunshine beating on his back and feeling as helpless as a manacled prisoner, could plainly hear the Germans talking, and was convinced that they were gloatingly deciding how to deal with him. This was the experience of many of the officers and men, and none who survived the action will ever forget the agony of that prolonged exposure to a scorching sun, when minutes seemed to stretch into hours; many of the men were almost delirious before the friendly cloak of darkness enveloped the battlefield. Among the slain was the gallant commander of "C" Company, Captain G. T. McGill, whose name was never mentioned except in terms of great affection and respect.

During the night instructions arrived at H.Q. that posts were to be established in front of our line as far as possible, and this was done by the survivors of the four companies, each of which manned one post. Misfortune dogged also the transport of the battalion. On the way up it came under very heavy gas-shelling to the south of Monchy, and the Transport Officer, Captain J. Young, telling his men to don their masks, led them through the barrage at the gallop, the C.Q.M.Ss. hanging on to their limbers as they clattered along the road; unfortunately there were several casualties, including two C.Q.M.Ss., and as the carrying parties from the companies had been dispersed by the shelling, most of the men were without water during the night. The battalion was relieved on the night of the 6th/7th May, and was withdrawn to the vicinity of Tilloy, having lost, since the 24th April, twelve[1] officers, and two hundred and fifty-four other ranks.

Disaster also attended the attack north of the Scarpe, where the leading battalions of the 27th Brigade were stricken down by hostile rifle and machine-gun fire, and under the circumstances there was no point in throwing into the battle the 11th and the 12th Royal Scots who were in support. Later in the day, however, the 12th, commanded since the 12th April by Lieut.-Colonel J. A. S. Ritson, came gloriously into the conflict. The left battalion of the brigade, the 6th K.O.S.B., had an experience similar to that of the 15th Royal Scots at Rœux, and broke through the first German defences, but owing to Boche attacks on their flanks and rear the leading companies were cut off. Brig.-General Maxwell, loath to abandon men who had done so well without endeavouring to rescue them, gladly accepted the offer

---

[1] Of these, in addition to Captain McGill, 2nd Lieuts. N. C. Darker, T. T. Halcrow, J. G. Russell, and D. T. Neil were killed.

of the 12th Royal Scots to make an attack that night. Covered on each flank by an artillery and machine-gun barrage, one and a half companies, about 150 men in all, advanced at 8 P.M. and made a valiant charge, and though few of them were able to penetrate the enemy's resistance, their self-sacrificing effort enabled many of the K.O.S.B. to return to our line. Captain R. R. Ritchie, Lieut. Thomson, and 2nd Lieut. W. J. Henderson lost their lives in this attack, the casualties in other ranks amounting to one hundred and twenty-one.

Such gains as were achieved on the 3rd May were wholly out of proportion to the heavy losses sustained, and after this date all fighting on a big scale in front of Arras came to an end for the year. Sir Douglas Haig was anxious to begin his offensive in Flanders, and only such demonstrations took place at Arras as would serve to detain as many as possible of the enemy on this front. Our perseverance at last reaped its reward, and by dint of pounding, we secured many of the places over which the tide of battle had ebbed and flowed: Rœux, the cemetery, and the Chemical Works, all passed into our possession.

As the battle languished, divisions gradually departed from the sector, several, like the 15th, making their way to Flanders. The 2nd Royal Scots were employed on trench duty near Monchy and in furnishing working parties till the 12th June, when they left Arras for a more attractive area in the south. The 9th Royal Scots, after spending three weeks in the hinterland, returned to Arras on the 14th May. A furious counter-attack on the divisional front was valiantly repelled by the 152nd Brigade, and while the fighting was in progress the 9th Royal Scots moved forward to a camp north-east of St Laurent Blangy, but they were not required to take part in the action. The battalion took over the front line on the 24th, and on the night of the 27th/28th a raiding party had a disastrous experience; it left our lines for the purpose of seizing a Boche post, but it was suddenly smitten by machine-gun fire, and the leader, Captain Johnston, was killed. At the end of the month the whole division withdrew and prepared to move northwards.

The 8th Royal Scots, with their customary efficiency, played a notable part in consolidating the area north of the Scarpe, many trenches such as Crete and Corona being constructed by the battalion. Its losses[1] during the spell of duty at Arras were very severe considering that the battalion was never engaged in any attack, and they give some indication of the tremendous strain imposed on men who had to work in the Arras sector during the months of April and May.

The Ninth and Thirty-fourth Divisions remained longest in the Arras district, and in a joint action won a signal success on the 5th June. Both had benefited immensely from the reorganisation and training carried out in the back areas, and returned to the line with restored confidence. The position taken over by the 27th Brigade lay east of Rœux on a line astride the Arras-Douai Railway. The object of the brigade was to advance the front on both sides of the railway as far as Cupid Trench, held by the enemy, on the north side, and a sunken road on the south side. Three companies of the 11th and two of the 12th Royal Scots were detailed to carry out the assault, which was to take place at 8 P.M.

The assembly arrangements presented considerable difficulty, because entry into the front system could be

---

[1] Ten officers—of whom Lieut. W. E. Wallace, 2nd Lieuts. D. H. Barclay, J. C. Bone, J. M. Moncur, and G. W. Snow were killed—and ninety-three other ranks.

effected only under darkness, so that the troops ear-marked for the attack had to proceed to the front trenches during the preceding night and squeeze themselves into their limited accommodation. Since Boche aeroplanes were always prying over our lines throughout the whole of the scorching day, they had to lie packed like sardines in shelters scooped in the sides of the trench and covered with fish-net screens, and it speaks volumes for their discipline that they carried out their instructions to the letter.

The attack was assisted by a *ruse de guerre*, the men waiting for twenty seconds after the fall of the barrage before jumping over the parapets. The Germans were completely deceived. Seeing no men moving forward with the barrage, they concluded that they had nothing more serious to dread than a bombardment, and accordingly drew back into shelter, with the result that our men were able to span No-Man's-Land without a casualty, though subsequently there was brisk fighting. The right company of the 11th Royal Scots encountered in front of the sunken road a strong Boche machine-gun nest, which held it at bay for some time, but, opportunely reinforced by two platoons from the reserve company, it plastered so effectually the hostile emplacement with volleys of rifle grenades that the German resistance was completely subdued. The centre and left companies had no difficulty in capturing their objectives, after which two platoons went forward to establish advanced posts. One of these, moving along the railway, pursued a cluster of Germans and overshot its mark in the excitement of the chase, but returned later to its proper position. The other went forward to clear an organised shell-hole area just east of the road, but it was so slow in moving up that the enemy had time to recover his wits and turn a machine-gun on it; a well-directed volley of rifle grenades, however, silenced the gun and enabled the platoon to fulfil its purpose.

On the north of the railway the two companies of the 12th met practically no opposition except at the junction of Cambrian and Cupid Trenches, from which the enemy was expelled after very stubborn fighting. Two advanced posts were established beyond the objective, one at the railway opposite that held by the 11th Royal Scots. Thus all the objectives of the two battalions were won with ease and at little cost, the casualties[1] in each case being about one hundred in all. It was a welcome success which helped to dispel the gloom that had affected the men since the terrible slaughter on the 12th April.

During the battle Lieut.-Colonel Croft of the 11th Royal Scots passed through a nerve-racking ordeal. The hostile counter-barrage fell accurately on our lines, and a heavy shell blew in the dug-out that formed the H.Q. of the 11th. Most fortunately the dug-out contained a pick and shovel, and the Adjutant, Lieut. Radford, with remarkable calmness bored a hole through to daylight and fresh air. The job was unspeakably grisly, for in clearing the earth Lieut. Radford had to dig through what he afterwards discovered to be the body of one of the signallers who had been killed by the Boche shell.

This was the last of the fighting near Arras as far as the 11th and the 12th Royal Scots were concerned. On the 13th they were relieved with the rest of the division, and went out for a long and well-earned rest. The 15th and the 16th Battalions were not engaged in the fighting on the 5th June and, after a spell of trench duty till about the middle of the month, they too were relieved and marched back to recuperate.

[1] Two officers were killed, 2nd Lieut. J. H. Waddell of the 11th and 2nd Lieut. W. Donaldson of the 12th.

END OF VOLUME I.

ROUTE OF THE 2ND ROYAL SCOTS (20TH AUG. TO 13TH OCT. 1914)   MAP 2

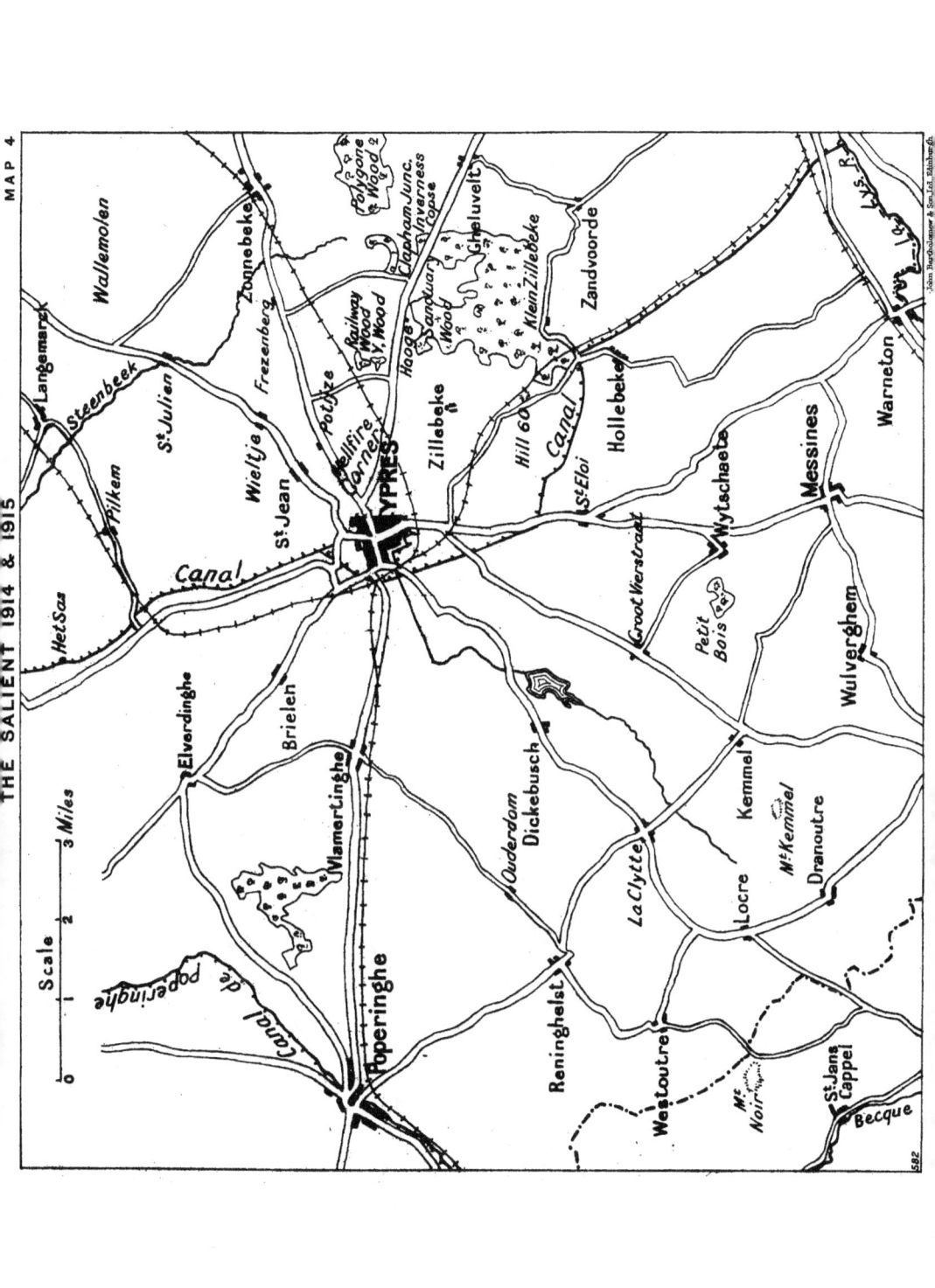

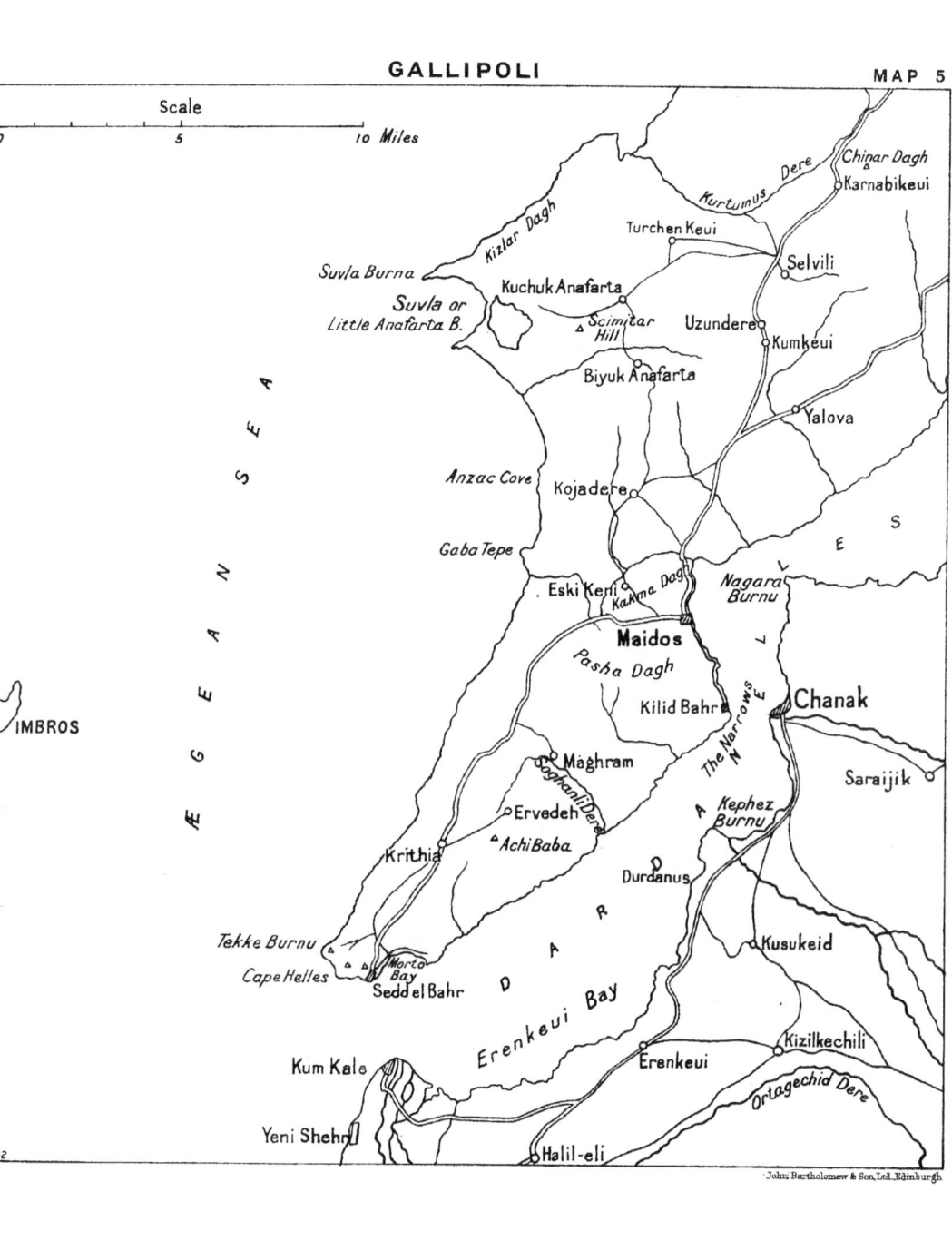

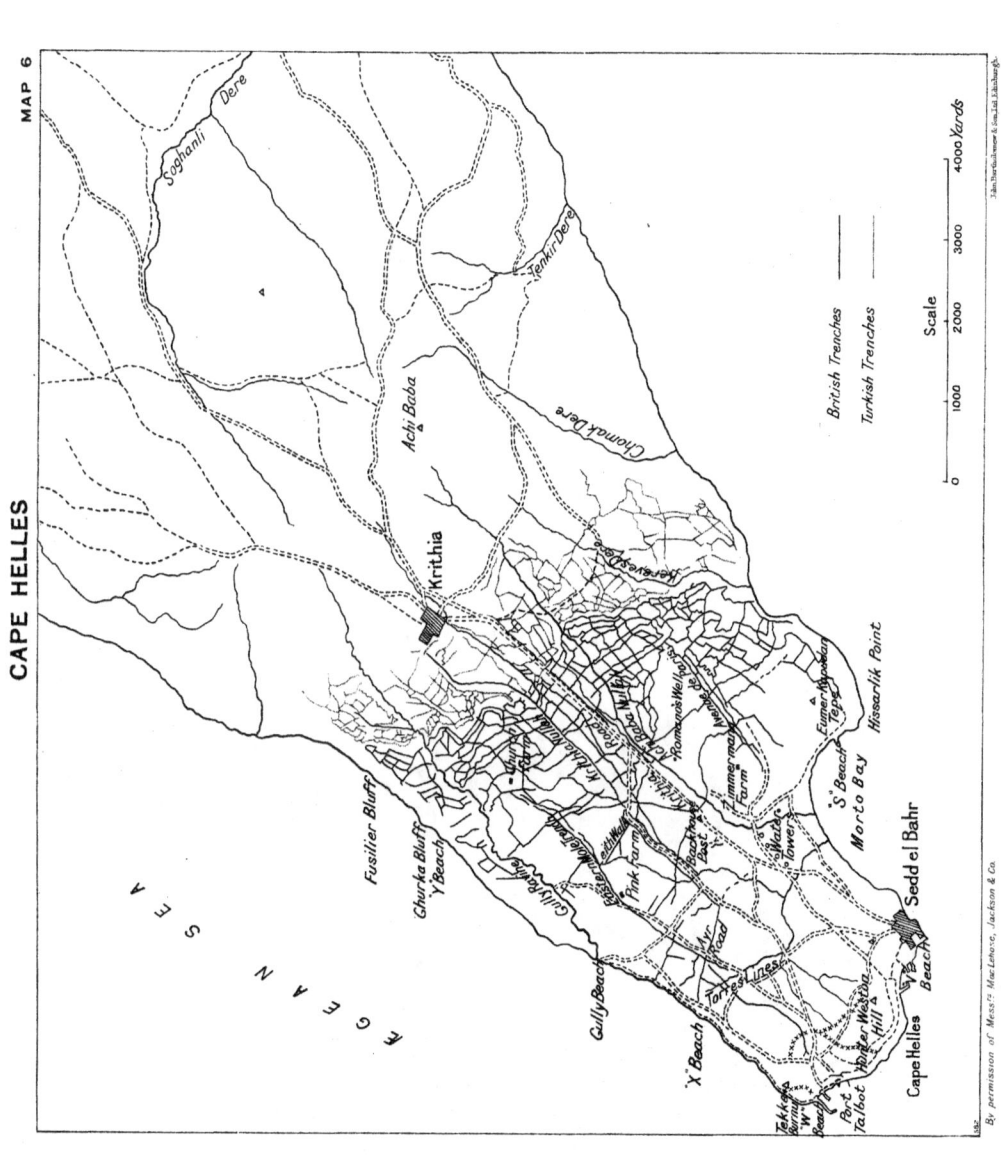

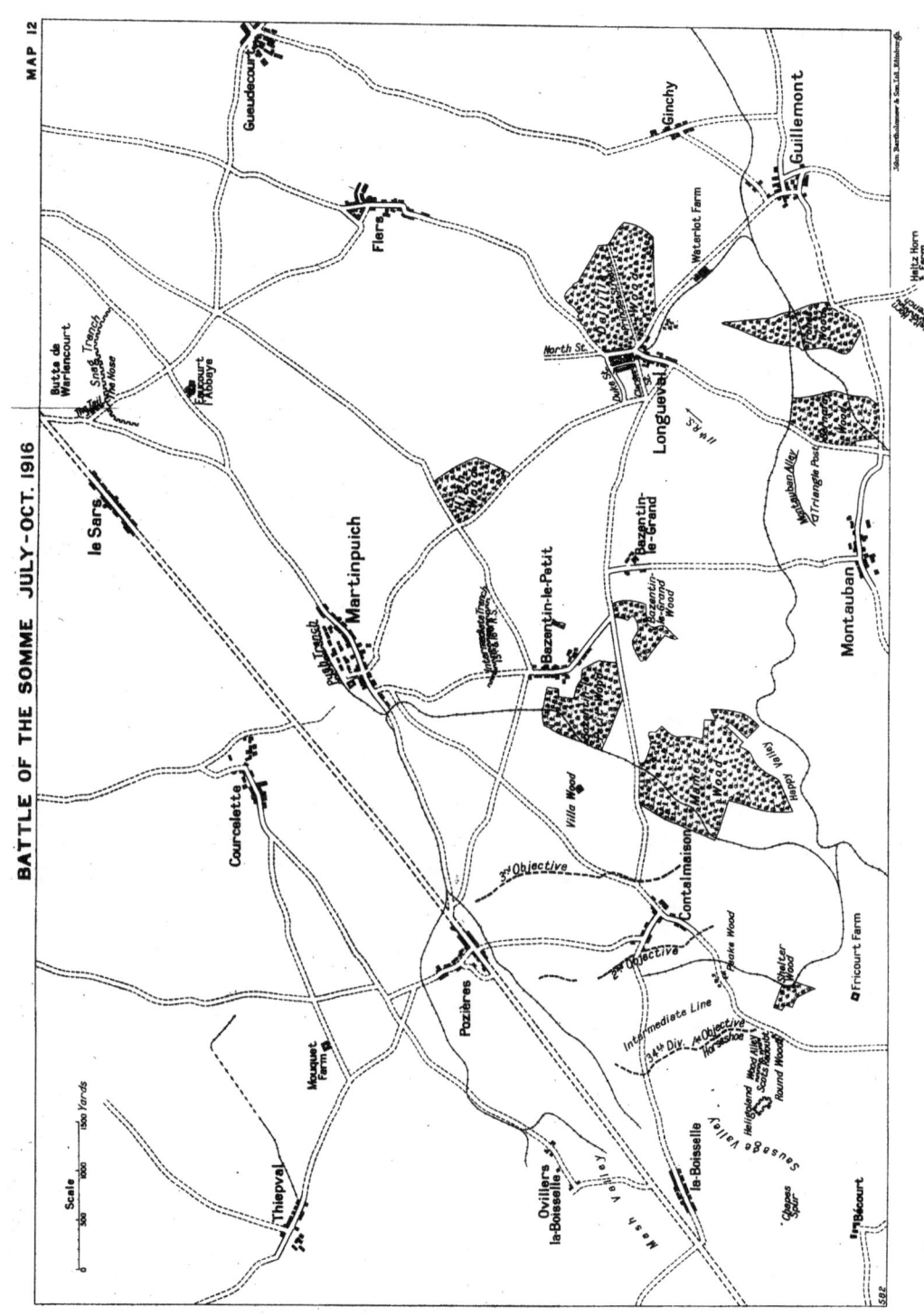

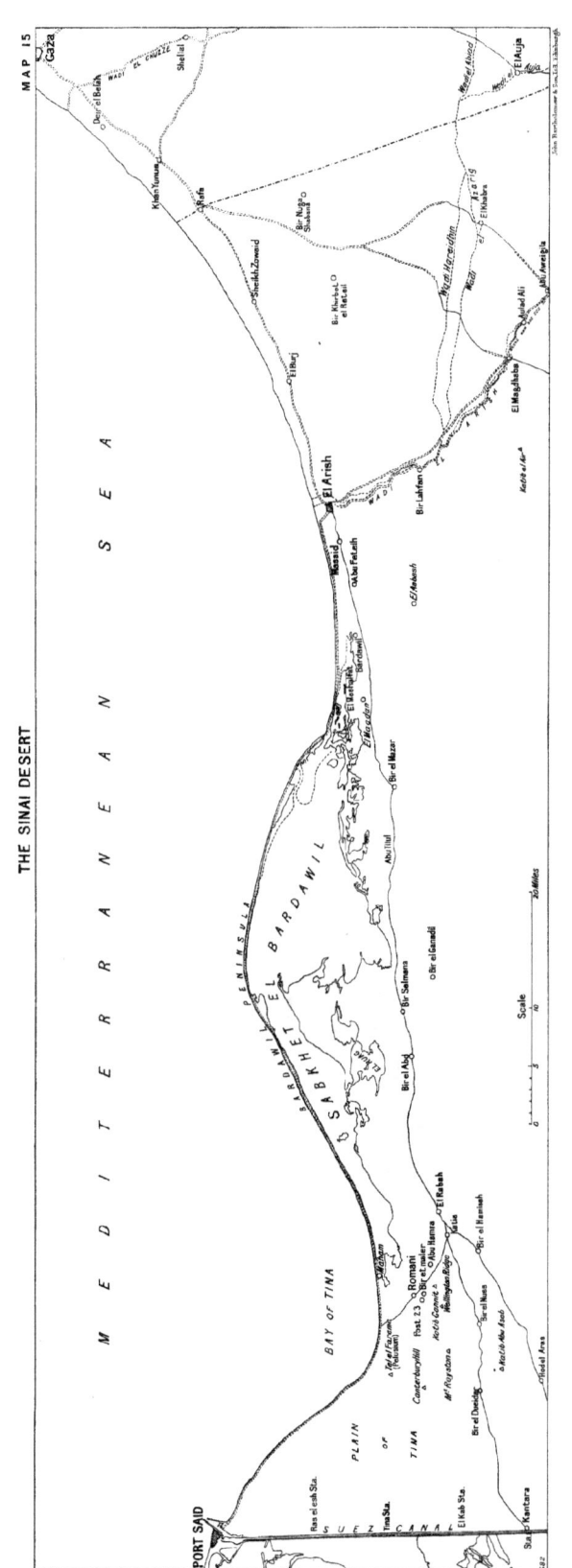

www.ingramcontent.com/pod-product-compliance
Lightning Source LLC
Chambersburg PA
CBHW061923220426
43662CB00012B/1781